More Advance Praise
for *Redeemer*

"It would be hard to imagine a better account of a president's life, faith, and politics. Randall Balmer is an accomplished historian who combines accuracy, insight, and archival diligence with the narrative skills of a novelist. The result is a compelling story of Jimmy and Rosalynn Carter, of conflicting evangelical traditions, and of a great reversal that saw religious conservatives helping to elect one of their own as president and then organizing to bring him down. Randall Balmer gives us an incisive analysis of idealism and realism in the White House, duplicity in unexpected places, and hardball politics in the back rooms of right-wing churches. The book vividly captures the tone and atmosphere of presidential politics in the late 1970s—an era that still resonates in twenty-first-century religious and political battles."

—E. Brooks Holifield, Charles Howard Candler
Professor Emeritus, Emory University

"Randall Balmer's *Redeemer* deftly reveals modern America's most misunderstood president. Randall Balmer melds Carter's famous evangelical sensibilities into a story of cascading successes and failures, the world ultimately indifferent to a man who hoped politics could be religion realized and redeemed more in retirement than in his frustrated presidency—a compelling, wistful tale briskly rendered."

—Jon Bulter, Yale University

"This is religion and politics at its finest. With wit, insight, and narrative freshness, Randall Balmer recalls that dynamic moment in the 1970s before evangelicalism became a handmaiden to political conservatism. Jimmy Carter was the 'born again' president who would redeem the nation from the sins of Watergate and Vietnam. How he tried, how many failed, and the evangelical-conservative knot that rose after his presidency is a tragic and beautiful story, and none explains it better than Randall Balmer. Grab a cup of tea or coffee, for *Redeemer* is one of those books not to skim, but to savor."

—Edward J. Blum, coauthor of *The Color of Christ: The Son of God and the Saga of Race in America*

"Randall Balmer provides an insightful summary and analysis of Jimmy Carter's life and work as farmer, politician, president, humanitarian and born-again Baptist. His study moves beyond biography to place Carter within the larger context of an American evangelicalism that continues to struggle with its role in the political sphere and the impact of personal faith on the lives of elected officials. Randall Balmer knows the issues well and explores them creatively."

—Bill Leonard, James and Marilyn Dunn Professor of Baptist Studies and Professor of Church History, Wake Forest University

REDEEMER

REDEEMER

The LIFE *of*

JIMMY CARTER

RANDALL BALMER

BASIC BOOKS

NEW YORK

Published by Basic Books,
A Member of the Perseus Books Group

Books published by Basic Books are available at special
discounts for bulk purchases in the United States by corporations,
institutions, and other organizations. For more information, please contact
the Special Markets Department at the Perseus Books Group, 2300 Chestnut
Street, Suite 200, Philadelphia, PA 19103, or call (800) 810-4145,
ext. 5000, or e-mail special.markets@perseusbooks.com.

A CIP catalog record for this book
is available from the Library of Congress.

ISBN: 978-0-465-02958-7
ISBN (e-book): 978-0-465-05695-8

10 9 8 7 6 5 4 3 2 1

for Catharine
again, and always

CONTENTS

He came unto his own,
and his own received him not.

John 1:11 (King James Version)

PREFACE

Jimmy Carter and Me

I honestly don't recall when I first heard of Jimmy Carter. But I do remember that by the time I arrived in Washington, D.C., in the summer of 1975 to work as an intern on Capitol Hill, I was more than a little intrigued by the former governor of Georgia. I was a rising senior at an evangelical liberal arts college and for years had been something of a political junkie. I recall watching the 1964 Republican and Democratic national conventions on the new black-and-white television set my father had purchased when we moved from rural southern Minnesota to Bay City, Michigan.

My interest in politics, however, cut against the grain of my white, northern, evangelical world. Cold War anxieties and an enduring fondness for Billy Graham generally predisposed us toward the Republican Party, but we faced other, more pressing matters—like the end of the world. Convinced as we were that Jesus would return imminently, politics rarely entered into our thinking or conversations—infrequently at home and almost never at church. The only exception to the latter that I can recall occurred during a Sunday-evening service in the church basement, where my father's congregation was meeting while the church raised funds to complete construction on the sanctuary overhead. The Sunday-evening services were a tad less formal than those on Sunday morning, and my father casually let it slip before the assembled faithful—not much more than a couple of dozen—that he still hadn't decided how to cast his ballot. The organist blurted out "Goldwater," and my father, clearly embarrassed, quickly changed the subject.

Our belief that Jesus would soon return to gather the faithful effectively absolved us of the task of social amelioration. Why worry, after all, about this world when we were about to be translated to another? Somewhat unusually for evangelicals at the time, my parents voted, but I never had a sense that they thought there was much at stake. This world was doomed and transitory. Better to concentrate on winning souls to Christ than worry about who sat on the city council or in the Oval Office.

Politics, I suppose, represented something of an adolescent rebellion. I remember being fascinated by the pictures of the two "Johns" in the Streleckis' living room next door on South DeWitt Street, John XXIII and John F. Kennedy, along with the yellowed fronds from the previous Palm Sunday. I recall asking my mother about Nelson Rockefeller in the mid-1960s, but she informed me that we could never support him for president because he was divorced. The assassinations of Martin Luther King Jr. and Robert F. Kennedy distressed me deeply. I watched the implosion of the Democratic Party in Chicago during the summer of 1968, the election of Richard Nixon, and the woeful, quixotic candidacy of George McGovern in 1972, the year I started college.

In the ten weeks or so between my arrival on campus and Election Day that fall, I tried over and over to engage fellow students about the impending election, but they evinced little interest. When pressed, many expressed tepid support for Nixon. Billy Graham, the most famous evangelical of the twentieth century, was Nixon's friend, after all, and that was good enough for most of my classmates.

Evangelical colleges can be numbingly insular, but the events of the outside world began to intrude shortly after Richard Nixon's reelection in 1972. Although the Nixon campaign had succeeded in deflecting attention from the Watergate burglary long enough to ensure the president's victory over McGovern, the intrepid reporting of Carl Bernstein and Bob Woodward of the *Washington Post* uncovered a web of deceit and complicity reaching all the way to the Oval Office. In August 1974, I learned of Nixon's decision to resign while I was working at a Bible camp in Minnesota; the camp directors set up a television in the chapel. Many of the campers were sobbing as Nixon, facing impeachment, declared, "I have never been a quitter" but went on to say that the erosion of his support in Congress necessitated his resignation.[1]

While some evangelicals mourned Nixon's demise, others viewed it as yet another cautionary tale about the perils of political engagement and worldly pursuits. Better to focus on evangelism—bring the "lost" to Jesus—

than sully oneself with politics. Still others, however, detected an opportunity to restore a prophetic voice to the political arena, one characterized not by the militarism and callousness of Nixon but one informed by the venerable evangelical tradition of care for those less fortunate.

As I watched Nixon's resignation there along the shores of Lake Shamineau, I considered anew the possibility of politics, and in the ensuing months I sent a letter of inquiry to a member of Congress who had been one of the key voices calling for Nixon's impeachment: John B. Anderson of Illinois, the third-ranking Republican in the House of Representatives. Anderson had recently been appointed to the board of trustees at my college, Trinity College, an evangelical school in Deerfield, Illinois, sponsored by the Evangelical Free Church of America. Anderson (or someone in his office) looked favorably on my application and assigned me to an internship with the House Republican Conference, which he chaired.

ALTHOUGH the label *evangelicalism* has since entered the popular lexicon, the term remained something of a mystery in the mid-1970s, especially for those outside of the movement that in 1976, the year Jimmy Carter won the presidency, encompassed nearly fifty million Americans, a quarter of the population. Some scholars have devised elaborate, technical definitions, but I prefer a simple, three-part (trinitarian!) definition.

First, an evangelical is someone who believes in the Bible as God's revelation to humanity. She or he is therefore disposed to read it seriously and even to interpret it literally, although evangelicals (like other believers) typically engage in selective literalism.[2]

Second, because of their literal reading of the Bible, evangelicals believe in the centrality of conversion, which they derive from the third chapter of St. John in the New Testament. There, Nicodemus, a Jewish leader, approaches Jesus by night and asks how he can gain entrance into the kingdom of heaven. Jesus replies that he must be "born again" or, in some translations, "born from above." Conversion, for evangelicals, is generally understood as a "turning away" from sin to embrace salvation, and the born-again experience is very often (though not always) dramatic and accompanied by considerable emotion. It is also usually a datable experience, and most evangelicals will be able to recount the time and the circumstances of their conversions.

Finally, an evangelical is someone committed to *evangelism*, bringing others into the faith. The biblical warrant for this is what evangelicals recognize as the Great Commission at the end of the Gospel of Mark, where Jesus instructs his followers to "Go into all the world and preach the good news to all creation." Very often, however, rather than do the evangelism themselves, evangelicals hire professionals to do it for them: missionaries, for example, or pastors of outreach or evangelism on the staffs of large churches. Still, most evangelicals will affirm their responsibility to bring others into the faith.[3]

Jimmy Carter differed from most evangelicals, in fact, because he had on several occasions actually engaged in forthrightly evangelistic activities, including knocking on doors to tell others about Jesus. The first time I met Carter, at a small reception prior to an event sponsored by the *Journal of Southern Religion* at Emory University in 1999, the former president wanted to talk about the "unsurpassed joy and privilege" of "sharing Christ" with others. In the opening chapter of his book *Sources of Strength*, Carter details the "Plan of Salvation," a six-part outline, studded with biblical references, to which no evangelical would object.[4]

Before Carter's campaign for the presidency, however, not all evangelicals recognized themselves by the term *evangelical*. Jimmy Carter and Billy Graham in the 1970s, in fact, were far more likely to refer to themselves as "born again" than as "evangelical"; it was Carter and the media coverage of his faith that regularized the term as a generic description of born-again Christians. Some Baptists, especially in the South, still prefer other monikers like "Bible-believing" or "born again" and stumble over the designation "evangelical."[5]

Jimmy Carter not only fit the definition of *evangelical*, he embodied a particular, activist strain of evangelicalism called progressive evangelicalism. Harking back to the Hebrew prophets, progressive evangelicals in the nineteenth century interpreted the prophetic calls for justice as a mandate for racial reconciliation and gender equality. Progressive evangelicalism, at one time the ascendant strain of evangelicalism in America, also took its warrant from the New Testament, especially the words of Jesus. In the Gospel of Matthew, Jesus identified those who will inherit the kingdom of God as the peacemakers and those who cared for the poor and the needy. "I was hungry and you gave me something to eat, I was thirsty and you gave me something to drink, I was a stranger and you invited me in," Jesus said. "I needed clothes and you clothed me, I was sick and you looked after me, I was in prison and you came to visit me." Jesus even said that those who refuse to show compassion "will go away to eternal punishment," whereas the "righteous" will inherit eternal life. Lest anyone miss the point, Jesus instructed his followers to care for "the least of these."[6]

Previous generations of evangelicals, especially in the nineteenth and early twentieth centuries, took an expansive view of their responsibility for "the least of these." A series of evangelical revivals at the turn of the nineteenth century, known collectively as the Second Great Awakening, unleashed moral energies to reform society according to the norms of godliness, especially on behalf of those less fortunate. Evangelical conversion alone was insufficient. Charles Grandison Finney, the most prominent evangelical of the nineteenth century, understood benevolence toward others as a necessary corollary of faith. "I abhor a piety which has no humanity with it and in it," he wrote. "God loves both piety and humanity." A regenerated individual, in obedience to the teachings of Jesus, bore responsibility for the improvement of society and especially the interests of those most vulnerable.[7]

The initial decades of the nineteenth century witnessed an effusion of voluntary associations dedicated to social welfare, and the unmistakable catalyst for such groups was piety. Finney and other antebellum evangelicals envisioned nothing less than a benevolent empire. Evangelicals, especially in the North, sought the abolition of slavery and equal rights for women, including the right to vote. Some evangelicals believed that women should be ordained. They advocated prison reform because, as the editors of the *Virginia Evangelical & Literary Magazine* argued, "It is impossible to bring a man to repentance by fear alone; its legitimate fruit is despair." Evangelicals supported public education, known at the time as "common schools," as a way for children of the less fortunate to improve their lot. "Common Schools are the glory of our land," a writer declared in the *Christian Spectator*, "where even the beggar's child is taught to read, and write, and think, for himself."[8]

These evangelical acts of kindness were considered inseparable from faith. An article in the *Piscataqua Evangelical Magazine*, for instance, argued that a benevolent person "will not say to a brother or sister who is naked and destitute of food, depart in peace, be thou warmed and filled, and, at the same time, give them not those things that are needful to the body." Elias Smith believed that "the middle ranks and the poor, that is, the great majority of mankind, should place a due value in the gospel, not only for its religious, but also for its civil and political advantages." Jesus Christ, Smith believed, "came to put an end to unjust inequality in the world."[9]

Evangelical preferences for the poor and marginalized even led them to criticize usury and to question the morality of capitalism, suggesting that the term "business ethics" was an oxymoron because the pursuit of wealth necessarily elevated avarice above altruism. Finney allowed that "the business aims and practices of business men are almost universally an abomination in the sight of God." Many evangelicals also abhorred violence. The *Western Christian Advocate* inveighed against "the serious and gross impropriety of carrying arms," which it deemed "ungentlemanly, ruffian-like, cowardly and dangerous." Evangelicals organized the New-York Peace Society in 1815 "from the conviction that war is inconsistent with the Christian religion, immoral in its acts, and repugnant to the true interests of mankind."[10]

The reforming impulses of evangelicalism in the North, especially opposition to slavery, finally drove an angry South to secession. By the time Confederate guns blazed against Fort Sumter in the early morning hours of April 12, 1861, evangelical piety in the South had turned inward, while evangelicalism north of the Mason-Dixon line held out for a benevolent empire that encompassed virtually all elements of life, from personal morality to public policy, from individual comportment to economic systems and international relations. The vision of society articulated by Charles Finney and other progressive evangelicals took special notice of those on the margins of society—women, slaves, the victims of war and abuse, prisoners, the poor— those Jesus called "the least of these."

The tradition of progressive evangelicalism faded, however, as evangelicals themselves began to retreat from the broader society in the 1910s and 1920s. Reeling from public ridicule surrounding the Scopes Trial of 1925, evangelicals turned inward and grew suspicious of political engagement. Various evangelical leaders mounted desultory attempts to lure rank-and-file evangelicals into the political arena in the middle decades of the twentieth century, but their campaigns, more often than not some species of anticommunism, bore scant resemblance to the activism of progressive evangelicals from an earlier era. Although some evangelicals responded to the incendiary rhetoric of these leaders, some of them demagogues, most evangelicals were content to remain apolitical—at least until the mid-1970s.[11]

For much of the twentieth century, evangelicals harbored deep skepticism about engaging directly in politics. Because Jesus would return at any moment, why bother trying to make the world a better place? This notion— called premillennialism: Jesus would return *before* the millennium predicted in the book of Revelation—had been the regnant theology among evangelicals for the better part of a century. My Sunday-school teacher, in fact, a man named Donald W. Thompson, produced and directed a remarkable motion picture in the early 1970s, a film called *A Thief in the Night*, which featured my father as the "good" preacher. *A Thief in the Night,* which *Time* magazine once described as a "church-basement classic," depicts the return of Jesus to earth—an event we referred to as the "rapture" or the "second coming"—to collect the true believers and then unleash terrible judgment against those who were "left behind."[12]

Evangelicals' embrace of premillennialism for most of the twentieth century had several consequences, ranging from mundane to profound. At the former end of the spectrum, premillennialism among evangelicals was responsible for some colossally bad architecture: If Jesus is coming soon, the reasoning went, cinderblock will do just fine. But premillennialism also absolved evangelicals of social responsibility. It focused our efforts on individual regeneration rather than social amelioration. This world, after all, was doomed and transitory. Why waste our efforts on making it a better place?

By the early 1970s, however, progressive evangelicalism was mounting a comeback, albeit a modest one. By the time I arrived at college in the fall of 1972, the winds of change were blowing in evangelicalism—or at least breezes of change. A student at the divinity school associated with my college, Jim Wallis, had just left his seminary studies to devote himself to a tabloid he had founded, the *Post-American*, which would become *Sojourners* a few years later. One of the names on the publication's masthead was an evangelical I much admired, Mark O. Hatfield, Republican U.S. senator from Oregon, a longtime opponent of the war in Vietnam and cosponsor with George McGovern, the Democratic senator from South Dakota, of the McGovern-Hatfield Amendment to End the War in Vietnam.

My campus in the sleepy, bedroom suburbs north of Chicago could never be mistaken for Berkeley or Madison or Iowa City. But the dean had assembled a lively cohort of young evangelical professors who challenged, ever so gently, some of the presuppositions of their students, prompting us to think about the morality of the Vietnam War, for example, the misogyny so pervasive in the culture, the yawning disparity between rich and poor, and the scourge of racism. In November 1973, a group of fifty-five evangelicals gathered at the YMCA in Chicago to draft the Chicago Declaration of Evangelical Social Concern, which sounded many of the themes of progressive evangelicalism, including condemnations of militarism, racism, and hunger, together with an affirmation of the rights of women. Many of the signatories had ties with Trinity College and Trinity Evangelical Divinity School.[13]

I majored in history at Trinity College, and although my command of American history was still tenuous, I began to delve into this tradition of progressive evangelicalism and learned that evangelicals of an earlier age had been anything but apathetic. Progressive evangelicalism of the antebellum period had set the social and political agenda for much of the nineteenth century, and I began to see that all of those nineteenth-century evangelical initiatives addressed those on the margins of society: women, the poor and dispossessed, people of color. This seemed to me a noble impulse, one very much aligned with my understanding of the teachings of Jesus, who instructed his followers to love their enemies, turn the other cheek, and care for those less fortunate. This same Jesus had designated the tiniest sparrow as one of God's interests, and it occurred to me in the early 1970s that care for the environment might very well be consistent with that sentiment.[14]

I won't pretend that everyone at Trinity shared these views. Not by any means. But this tiny campus in Deerfield was the locus of intellectual ferment and social concern that maybe, just maybe, as the Chicago Declaration of Evangelical Social Concern indicated, would be spreading to some of the other precincts of evangelicalism.

So when Jimmy Carter, a Southern Baptist Sunday-school teacher, appeared on the national stage during my junior year of college, I took notice, especially because he seemed sympathetic to the rudiments of progressive evangelicalism. And I was not alone. His declaration that he was a born-again Christian was the kind of language that we used to describe ourselves, and one of the expectations among evangelicals was that we would be able, at a moment's notice, to recount all of the circumstances and the details surrounding our own evangelical conversions. What made Carter intriguing was that he didn't seem apologetic or abashed about his faith; he talked about it matter-of-factly. Even though his declaration prompted most journalists in the country to scour their address books in search of someone who might explain what in heaven's name he meant by "born again," we understood perfectly well. Here was a man—a politician, no less, who was running for president—who spoke our language. He was one of us!

Carter embraced the principles of progressive evangelicalism, but he also recognized that, ever since the 1930s, government had a role to play in ameliorating human suffering. Social needs became so acute during the Great Depression that the government had to step in and assume the burdens of charity that religious organizations previously had shouldered. When the economy improved, however, religious groups never reassumed that role, certainly not on a scale that would address social needs in anything close to a comprehensive way. Carter never advocated for an expansive government—

indeed, he spent his entire political career trying to limit the size and the scope of government, to make it more efficient—but he recognized at the same time that government was essential to keeping the peace and meeting human needs. Regrettably, Carter said, "it is usually government officeholders and not religious leaders who are in the forefront of this struggle to alleviate suffering, provide homes for the homeless, eliminate the stigma of poverty or racial discrimination, preserve peace and rehabilitate prisoners."[15]

Some evangelicals, to be sure, were a bit jaded. Billy Graham, even through the dark days of Watergate, kept trying to reassure us about Nixon's moral character and his evangelical sympathies. Nixon had occasionally made feints in the direction of evangelicals, usually in election years, by appearing publicly at one of Graham's crusades. But by the early 1970s, it was pretty clear that Graham had been mistaken about Nixon, if not delusional.

Jimmy Carter, on the other hand, seemed like the real deal. Here was a man who promised never knowingly to lie to the American people, who spoke freely and openly about his faith, and whose policies—concern for the poor and for the rights of women—even approximated the tradition of progressive evangelicalism in the nineteenth century.

JIMMY Carter launched his campaign for the presidency in the mid-1970s at the confluence of two streams, which converged to carry him to the White House. The first, paradoxically enough, given his 1970 campaign for governor, was his visibility as a representative of the so-called New South. Despite the fact that Carter had courted segregationists during his second (and, finally, successful) gubernatorial campaign, the media seized on Carter's inauguration as a transitional moment for the South. When the new governor declared that "the time for racial discrimination is over," his statement seemed to signal that the South was prepared finally, after decades of resistance, to shrug off the pall of racism. Atlanta, the bustling state capital and the venue for Carter's inaugural, quickly became known as the "city too busy to hate." Although these dewy-eyed accounts in the national media bespoke an unwarranted optimism, the Carter campaign was more than willing to play into the New South narrative. The second stream was less visible, especially to nonevangelicals: the brief recrudescence of progressive evangelicalism that bore a striking resemblance to the social ethic of nineteenth-century evangelicals.

Carter's quest for the Democratic nomination was still a long shot when I arrived in Washington for my assignment on Capitol Hill in the summer of

1975, and not all Washingtonians were enthusiastic. One of the people who befriended me that summer, a member of the Capitol Hill police force stationed in the Longworth Office Building, sneeringly referred to the former governor of Georgia as "Hayseed Carter" and wore a PRESIDENT FORD campaign button affixed to the reverse side of his uniform necktie. The conventional wisdom was that any romance with Carter on the part of the electorate would soon dissipate once the field of presidential aspirants began to take shape. By the time I arrived in the nation's capital that summer of 1975, however, I was beginning to believe that Carter might finally lure evangelicals out of their apolitical torpor and revitalize the tradition of nineteenth-century progressive evangelicalism that I had been learning about in my studies.

Turns out I was right on the first count, wrong on the second.

Washington was a dreary place in the summer of 1975. The heat was unusually oppressive, even by Washington's swampy standards. The humidity made even breathing laborious. The Metro was under construction deep below the city, so the streets were torn up. The nation was preparing for its bicentennial, but few people in Washington—or anywhere, for that matter—seemed to be in a celebratory mood. The nation had just endured one of the most serious constitutional crises in its history. A president had been exposed as an inveterate liar, someone who had spun around him a web of deceit and venality. His vice president had resigned for his part in a corruption scandal while he was governor of Maryland. One of the president's two closest aides was convicted of conspiracy and obstruction of justice; the other was convicted of perjury, conspiracy, and obstruction of justice. Even Nixon's attorney general, the man charged with enforcing the law, was brought to justice, the first time in the nation's history that an attorney general had been convicted of criminal activities. Dozens of the president's minions had accepted plea bargains, and many were serving time in prison.

The Watergate scandal, which culminated in Richard Nixon's resignation on August 9, 1974, had tested the durability of the nation's legal and political institutions. The special Senate committee, led by Sam Ervin of North Carolina, had uncovered abuses of power, ranging from campaign "dirty tricks" and White House "enemies lists" to extralegal slush funds and a secret taping system in the Oval Office. The Supreme Court's ruling in July that the transcripts of those tapes must be made public hastened the president's downfall, and the imminent vote on articles of impeachment in the House of Representatives finally forced Nixon to make the valedictory speech I had watched in the chapel along the shores of Lake Shamineau.

That following summer, when I arrived on Capitol Hill, staffers were still buzzing about the Watergate imbroglio. The new president, Gerald R. Ford, was the only president in American history never to have been elected either president or vice president. Most Americans regarded him as a good and genial man, a welcome relief from his predecessor's endless prevarications, but many also questioned whether he was up to the task of dealing with runaway inflation, a depressed economy, and the nation's persistent energy crisis. When we congressional interns crowded into the East Room at 1600 Pennsylvania Avenue for the annual reception at the White House, Ford addressed us in platitudes and bromides. An anonymous voice in the back of the crowd shouted in frustration, "Say something!"

Jimmy Carter, meanwhile, was saying plenty out on the hustings, stumping the small towns of New Hampshire and the precincts of Iowa. He had formally announced his candidacy for the Democratic nomination the previous December, even though a Harris poll a month earlier did not even list Carter among thirty-five potential candidates. Carter's charm, his work ethic, and his evident sincerity began to attract notice and popular favor. His declaration of evangelical faith resonated with voters weary of Nixon's mendacity. Carter scored a huge upset in the Iowa precinct caucuses on January 19, 1976, vanquished a fellow southerner, George C. Wallace of Alabama, in the Florida primary, and secured the Democratic nomination by June 1976, on the eve of the nation's bicentennial. Before leaving that summer on a multiweek canoe trip in the Boundary Waters Wilderness of northern Minnesota, I predicted correctly that Carter would choose Walter Mondale as his running mate.

Not all evangelicals supported Carter over Gerald Ford, the Republican incumbent. Although evangelicals had not participated actively in the political process since the nineteenth century, the Cold War aversion to communism as a godless system had nudged them toward the political right. In addition, the persistence of anti-Catholicism bred suspicion of John F. Kennedy and the Democratic Party, and Billy Graham's clear preference for Republican politicians, especially Dwight Eisenhower and Richard Nixon, reinforced a general sense that, for evangelicals in the North, at least, the Republican Party was the preferred alternative.

Jimmy Carter's appearance on the political scene altered that calculus, albeit briefly. His frequent declarations that he was a born-again Christian proved difficult to ignore, especially because the media had seized on those statements with such glee and incredulity. For evangelicals, however, he was speaking our language, and the fact that he did so openly and without shame or apology made the statements even more striking.

Toward the close of the 1976 campaign, Ford protested that he, too, was a man of faith, seeking to draw evangelical votes back to the Republican ticket. Carter's biggest misstep in the campaign, one of very few, was his granting of an interview to *Playboy* magazine. This provided politically conservative evangelicals the pretext many were seeking to abandon Carter in the general election. Ford, in fact, drew a bare majority of evangelical votes over his avowed born-again challenger in the 1976 election, although Carter's share of that vote was considerably greater than previous Democratic nominees. Carter's unabashed declaration of faith had lured many hitherto apolitical evangelicals into the political arena, and his articulation of the themes of compassion and honesty, women's rights, and racial reconciliation capitalized on the brief efflorescence of progressive evangelicalism in the early 1970s.

In the run-up to Election Day, I handed out Carter campaign literature during rush hour at the Deerfield train station, cast my vote, and celebrated his election on November 2.

CARTER's administration began well enough. He imposed stringent ethical and conflict-of-interest restrictions on himself and on members of his administration. He pardoned nonviolent Vietnam-era draft resisters, a fitting rejoinder to his predecessor's preemptive pardon of Nixon. Concerned about the United States' relations with Latin America, Carter proceeded with a ratification of the revised Panama Canal treaties, something that had been in the works since Lyndon Johnson's administration. Carter proposed measures that would diminish the nation's dependence on foreign oil and installed solar panels on the White House. He called attention to human rights abuses, which angered some of America's allies.

Carter, an outsider in Washington, had been an effective candidate, but he came to be viewed, fairly or not, as a less-than-effective politician. Inflation, which had bedeviled both Nixon and Ford, proved intractable, in large measure because of the lingering effects of the Arab Oil Embargo. The Organization of Petroleum Exporting Countries cartel drove energy prices to levels previously unimaginable, a problem exacerbated by the Iranian Revolution and the Iran-Iraq War—and the combination of these circumstances kept the price of oil high. Events abroad also seemed to conspire against him. Not wanting to escalate the Cold War into a real war, Carter seemed powerless to resist the Soviet invasion of Afghanistan. And when the Islamic revolutionaries in Iran plundered the American embassy in Teheran and took Americans hostage, Carter was unable to secure their release until minutes after his successor was sworn into office. Compounding his political difficulties, Carter's administrative style—he was widely suspected of micromanagement, even to the point of keeping the log for the White House tennis court—added to the impression that the one-term governor of Georgia was in over his head in the Oval Office.[16]

His political adversaries, of course, encouraged that impression. Carter faced a spirited challenge for a second term within his own party from Edward M. Kennedy of Massachusetts. Although Carter had dismissed the senator's candidacy in decidedly unevangelical language—"If Kennedy runs, I'll whip his ass"—Carter's bid for reelection clearly was damaged by Kennedy's challenge. At the 1980 Democratic National Convention, meeting in New York's Madison Square Garden, Kennedy spurned the traditional joined-hands display of party unity.[17]

Once Carter cleared the hurdle for nomination, he faced an unusually contentious general election. Although *Newsweek* magazine had christened 1976 the "Year of the Evangelical," largely on the strength of Carter's bid for the White House, that designation was arguably four years premature. Whereas Carter was the sole candidate who traded on his status as an evangelical in 1976, the 1980 election featured not one, not two, but three candidates who claimed to be evangelicals: Carter, the incumbent; John B. Anderson, running as an independent; and Ronald Reagan, the Republican nominee.

Four years is a lifetime in politics, and during the four years of Jimmy Carter's presidency the political ground shifted seismically beneath him. Media talk about a New South shorn of racism tailed off by 1980; when Reagan opened his fall presidential campaign on August 3, 1980, in Philadelphia, Mississippi, site of the horrific murders of three civil rights activists sixteen years earlier, the New South rhetoric ceased almost entirely. Carter's evangelical base proved equally fickle. In the simplest terms, the brief recrudescence of progressive evangelicalism in the early to mid-1970s gave way to a conservative backlash, a movement known generically as the Religious Right, a loose coalition of politically conservative evangelicals and fundamentalists. The leaders of the Religious Right faulted Carter and his administration for enforcing the antidiscrimination provisions of the Civil Rights Act in evangelical institutions. They criticized his support for human rights abroad and equal rights for women and for gays and lesbians at home. Having joined the ranks of abortion opponents in 1979, the Religious Right castigated Carter for his refusal to outlaw abortion, despite Carter's long-standing opposition to abortion and his efforts to limit its incidence.

By the time of the 1980 presidential election, evangelical voters overwhelmingly abandoned Carter and threw their support to Reagan, the candidate who, with his faltering grasp of the essentials of evangelical theology and his episodic church attendance, had perhaps the most tenuous claim on the label *evangelical*. Reagan, moreover, hailed from Hollywood, not exactly known to evangelicals as an outpost of piety; as governor of California, he had signed into law one of the most liberal abortion bills in the nation. By the time of the 1980 campaign, however, Reagan had come around to a "pro-life" position, which coincided nicely with evangelicals' recent interest in that issue.

The election of 1980, then, represented not only a victory for Reagan over the Democratic incumbent, it also signaled a shift in the direction of evangelical political activism. Not all evangelicals had supported Carter in 1976, but he won many evangelical votes, and, more important, his candidacy had introduced many evangelicals to the political process. It remains one of the great paradoxes of presidential politics over the last half-century that many of the same people who had propelled Carter to the presidency turned so dramatically—and, in some cases, rabidly—against him four years later.

In rejecting Carter in favor of Reagan in 1980, evangelicals set aside the long and noble tradition of progressive evangelicalism. They abandoned the heritage that claims its warrant in the command of Jesus to care for "the least of these" and that found perhaps its fullest expression in nineteenth-century evangelical activism. Carter's inauguration as governor in 1971 had been hailed as a transformative moment for the New South, a region finally shrugging off the taint of racism, but his emergence as a national political figure in the mid-1970s had also built on a revival of these progressive evangelical sympathies, which found expression in the 1973 Chicago Declaration of Evangelical Social Concern. "How we deal with 'the least of these' is a very important and serious issue," Carter declared in one of his Sunday-school lessons. "We *must* remember to serve the poor. It is God's command, and it is our Christian duty." On another occasion, he said, "Since we worship a God of justice, every one of us must speak up for justice in our society. Each of us is responsible."[18]

Carter's defeat in 1980, however, signaled the eclipse of those values of progressive evangelicalism. The leaders of the Religious Right, who worked tirelessly to deny Carter a second term, articulated a dramatically different understanding of the faith, one that celebrated nationalism, individualism, and free-market capitalism over community, human rights, and collective responsibility for those less fortunate. Others have carried on that neglected tradition; names like Jim Wallis, Brian McLaren, John Perkins, Shane Claiborne, Lisa Sharon Harper, Kevin Palau, and Tony Campolo come immediately to mind, among others. But with the defeat of Carter in 1980 and the retirement of Mark O. Hatfield from the U.S. Senate in 1997, no politician of national stature has embodied this tradition of progressive evangelicalism.[19]

Nor was Carter himself always a paragon of those values. He had a strain of self-righteousness, and he could be contemptuous of his political adversaries. Although he advocated at least a measure of racial integration in Sumter County, Georgia, in the 1950s, his 1970 campaign for governor courted segregationists. His inaugural address as governor, however, included a remarkable statement of contrition for that campaign and signaled a redoubled commitment to racial justice and reconciliation, one unprecedented in Georgia history. As governor, Carter also shored up public education, attended to the needs of the poor, reformed prisons, and demonstrated his commitment to environmental protection and the rights of women, all the while seeking to make government more efficient.[20]

If Jimmy Carter was a less-than-perfect oracle for progressive evangelicalism, he nevertheless articulated those ideals, making him the first presidential candidate to do so since William Jennings Bryan, the Democratic nominee in 1896, 1900, and 1908. The interval between Bryan and Carter was a long one, and it coincided with evangelicals' waning interest in the machinations of politics. During those decades of exile, evangelicals had constructed their own subculture of congregations, denominations, publication houses, missionary societies, Bible camps, seminaries, and colleges—including my own—as a refuge from a larger world that they found both corrupt and corrupting. By the 1970s, however, the institutional network that evangelicals had built provided the foundation for their reemergence into the broader world. Jimmy Carter's campaign for the presidency in 1976 both abetted evangelicals' reengagement and, in turn, benefited from it. Within four years, however, that machinery turned against him.

HAVING followed Carter's political career since my years in college, I had some notion of the ways in which Carter's faith had shaped him and his policies, but it wasn't until I listened to recordings of his Sunday-school lessons at Maranatha Baptist Church in his hometown of Plains, Georgia, that

I recognized how profoundly steeped he was in progressive evangelicalism. Here, both in Carter's conversance with the biblical texts and in his asides, the depth of his understanding of evangelicalism became apparent. Identifying oneself as an evangelical, he declared in one of his lessons, entails more than claiming the label *Christian*. Instead, believers should emulate the life of Jesus, especially his example of "love and respect and concern" for others. "Let that be the primary evangelical capability that we exhibit."[21]

Whatever his shortcomings as a person or as president, Carter was a man of faith, and attempts by politically conservative evangelicals since 1980 to write him out of the movement—or even out of the faith itself—suggest a lack of understanding of both Carter himself and the rich tradition of progressive evangelicalism. This biography attempts to take Jimmy Carter's religious commitments seriously as a means for understanding his life and character; it also charts the dramatic shifts in American religious life, especially among evangelicals, that ultimately contributed to his political demise. It is, as nearly as I can determine, the first biography of the thirty-ninth president of the United States to do so.[22]

I have little interest in rehabilitating Carter's political reputation, even though his critics have unfairly besmirched his presidency at least as much as his defenders have embellished his accomplishments since leaving the White House. Carter was dealt a bad hand as president—the reverberations from the Arab Oil Embargo, runaway inflation, the Soviet Union's imperial ambitions, the Iranian Revolution—and it was a hand that, in many ways, he played badly. With the benefit of hindsight, however, many of his policies seem prescient, such as ratification of the Panama Canal treaties and steps toward energy independence (largely reversed by his successor), although the lingering popular memory of the Carter years is not a happy one.

This book may not alter those impressions. But I suspect that readers will come away with a somewhat different understanding of both the religious and political forces surrounding Jimmy Carter's remarkable career. This narrative offers a corrective to standard interpretations of the emergence of the Religious Right, and evangelicals themselves might be chagrined to learn about some of the backroom machinations of preachers like Jerry Falwell and even Billy Graham, actions that probably crossed the line between honest mistakes and outright duplicity. In addition, I happen to believe that one of Carter's most underappreciated contributions to American history was his defeat of George Wallace in the 1976 Democratic primaries, thereby ridding his party—and the nation—of its most notorious segregationist, a battle that Carter waged not merely for his own political benefit but because of convictions informed by his faith. Readers, of course, may not agree with my conclusions, but I hope that this book will prompt a reconsideration of Jimmy Carter, his faith, and the unusually turbulent religious times in which he lived.

The life of Jimmy Carter is the story of how a son of the South, a Baptist schooled in the scriptures from an early age, transcended the prevailing social and racial attitudes of his time and place—not always perfectly or seamlessly, but determinedly. He was catapulted to the highest office in the land by an electorate weary of political corruption, intrigued by the notion of a new, postracial South, and enamored, however briefly, of Carter's evangelical rectitude. He took the principles of progressive evangelicalism with him to Washington, and sought, with mixed success, to govern by those lights. Four years later, betrayed by many of his own faith, he suffered a stinging political loss. From the ashes of defeat, Jimmy Carter returned to the South and rehabilitated himself as a citizen of the world, devoting himself to the causes of peace, justice, and the eradication of suffering.

It is a story that begs to be told in the evangelical parlance of striving, betrayal, defeat, and redemption.

ONE

THE HOUSEHOLD
OF FAITH

VISITORS to the Carter farm in Archery, Georgia, where Jimmy Carter spent most of his childhood, cannot fail to be impressed by his humble origins. Although Carter often emphasized that his family was more successful and prosperous than his neighbors, many of whom were sharecroppers or tenant farmers, young Jimmy Carter was hardly born into the lap of luxury or a life of ease. "We always had enough to eat, no economic hardship, but no money to waste," Carter recalled. "We felt close to nature, close to members of our family, and close to God."[1]

In 1920 and with the thought of pursuing a career in medicine, Bessie Lillian Gordy had moved eighteen miles from her childhood home in Richland, Georgia, to Plains, a town named for the Plains of Dura in the Hebrew Bible, where Shadrach, Meshach, and Abednego endured Nebuchadnezzar's fiery furnace. Lillian Gordy had signed up to be an army nurse during World War I, but her letter of acceptance arrived the day of the armistice that ended the war, November 11, 1918; the army promptly canceled the program. In the course of her nurses' training, Lillian met James Earl Carter, a veteran of World War I, on a double date at Magnolia Springs, a resort near Plains. Earl was her friend's date. Earl and Lillian had one dance together, but Lillian was less than impressed. "After being with him at that Magnolia Springs dance," she recalled, "I couldn't stand him." Earl Carter, however, asked "Miss Gordy" for a date, and Lillian, in a borrowed navy-blue taffeta dress, went driving in Earl's open-topped Model T Ford. When it started raining, Earl pulled out a lap robe, they huddled under a wagon shed, and, as Lillian recounted with a smile, "We were pretty well acquainted by the time we got back to town."[2]

Earl proposed while Lillian was still training as a nurse, and they were married shortly after Lillian's graduation. The new bride was confident that she could break her husband of his Friday-night poker habit, but she was mistaken. If Friday night found Earl Carter at the poker table, however, he just as routinely showed up at Plains Baptist Church on Sunday morning—more regularly than Lillian, in fact, whose embrace of religion was a bit more tepid and whose nursing schedule frequently entailed irregular hours. Still, Earl Carter indulged his wife throughout their marriage, especially her relatively liberal views on race. Earl Carter was more deferential to southern customs on racial matters, but he could hardly be called racist. He was not a member of the Ku Klux Klan. Although he didn't visit the homes of black people, thereby adhering to white southern mores, Earl Carter paid for the medicine and clothes that his wife dispensed to African-American families on her visits.[3]

James Earl Carter Jr. was born at seven o'clock in the morning of October 1, 1924, to Lillian Gordy Carter and the infant's namesake, James Earl Carter. The father was at a fish fry and poker game when the labor pains began. Because Lillian was a nurse, she delivered the baby at the hospital in Plains, making Jimmy Carter the first American president born in a hospital. Lillian Carter recorded in the infant's baby book that he would be known as "Jimmy" while a child; later in life he would be called "Jim," she predicted. "Jim Carter" never made it to the White House. Jimmy Carter did, albeit after traveling a long and winding road that began in Plains and Archery.[4]

The town of Archery, where the young family relocated in 1928 to inhabit a Craftsman-style house built with plans purchased from Sears & Roebuck, was a sparsely settled region—no village green, business district, or town center—of marginally fertile land. Archery has since disappeared from most maps. Jimmy Carter remembered the dust "boiling up from the dirt road that passed fifty feet from our front door" and the Seaboard Air Line Railroad tracks just on the other side of the road, tracks that the young farm boy walked for three miles into Plains, where, as early as five years old, he would sell bags of boiled peanuts for a bit of pocket money.[5]

The Carters were cotton farmers, but declining prices during the Great Depression coupled with the expansion of cotton production in regions to the west led the Carters and other farmers in the area to search for alternative crops, a quest made even more urgent by the fact that the growing of

cotton had seriously depleted the soil. Carter credits George Washington
Carver of the Tuskegee Institute, generally considered the inventor of peanut
butter, with creating a demand for peanuts, and the production of peanuts provided a measure of economic stability for the Carter household. Even so, the
Carters did not have running water or an indoor toilet until 1935; electricity
had to wait until the power lines of Franklin Roosevelt's Rural Electrification
Agency reached Archery in 1938. Jimmy Carter turned fourteen that year.[6]

Tenant farmers and day laborers received a fair shake and a competitive
wage at the Carter farm. Indigent travelers on Highway 61 who knocked on
the back door of the Carter house in search of food or a drink of water were
never turned away. Once, Jimmy's mother, "Miss Lillian," asked one of the
vagrants why so many stopped at the Carter house and not at the houses of
her neighbors. "Ma'am, we have a set of symbols that we use, to show the attitude of each family along the road," he said, after some hesitation. "The post
on your mailbox is marked to say that you don't turn people away or mistreat
us." After the traveler continued down the road, the Carters found the unob-
trusive scratches on the mailbox post. Lillian Carter instructed her children
not to tamper with the markings.[7]

Jimmy Carter grew up in a racially mixed world. His best friend and
playmate was Alonzo Davis, known as A.D., an African American who lived
on the Carter farm with his aunt and uncle. In addition, because of Lillian's
extended absences owing to her job as an itinerant nurse, a young black
woman named Annie Mae Hollis worked full-time in the house, cooking
and caring for the family. "My childhood world was really shaped by black
women," Carter recalled many years later. "I played with their children, often
ate and slept in their homes, and later hunted, fished, plowed, and hoed with
their husbands and children." Another black couple, Jack and Rachel Clark,
lived on the farm, and Jimmy slept in their house many nights; their relationship was so close that Rachel Clark claimed Jimmy as "one of our boys."
Rachel Clark often took young Jimmy on walks, pointing out the flora and
fauna along the way and making the point, as Carter remembered, that "God
expected us to take care of His creation." Carter even credited this woman
with his own moral formation. "Much more than my parents, she talked to
me about the religious and moral values that shaped a person's life, and I
listened to her with acute attention," he recalled. "Without seeming to preach,
she taught me how I should behave."[8]

Young Jimmy Carter never lacked for preaching. "The churches joined
the schoolhouse at the center of our spiritual, educational, and social lives,"

Carter wrote. School opened every day with a chapel service in the auditorium. Students pledged allegiance to the flag and typically sang "Onward Christian Soldiers" or "He Leadeth Me," segued into "America the Beautiful" or "Dixie," and wrapped up with the recitation of some verses from the Bible. The religious menu in town was Methodist, Baptist, and (somewhat unusually for the South) Lutheran. The Carters attended the Baptist church in Plains, although Jimmy's future wife, Rosalynn Smith, hailed from the Methodist church. Earl Carter, Jimmy's father, taught the junior boys Sunday-school class and was also a leader of the Royal Ambassadors, the Baptist equivalent of the Boy Scouts.[9]

Carter started attending school in Plains in September 1930, a month before his sixth birthday. A country boy, Jimmy typically went to school barefoot. Earl Carter finally located a pair of shoes in his store—vintage "witches' shoes" from the 1890s, sharply pointed and buttoned up—and made Jimmy wear them to school. Already acutely conscious of his status as a "country boy," Carter faced the teasing and derision of his classmates; he recalled the humiliation as "one of the worst things Daddy ever did to me." But he endured. Carter loved to read and to learn. He fondly remembered the influence of a particular schoolteacher, Julia Coleman, who frequented the Chautauqua Institution during her summers away from the classroom and who encouraged Carter to read Leo Tolstoy's epic novel, *War and Peace*, at age thirteen. Though nearly blind in one eye, Coleman established a reading club back in Plains, likely modeled on the Chautauqua Literary and Scientific Circle. "Miss Julia" also insisted on the inculcation of Christian values, requiring students to memorize and recite passages from the Bible. Jimmy Carter recited in class both the twenty-third Psalm and the thirteenth chapter of First Corinthians; the famous passage about what subsequent translations rendered as "love" was, in Carter's King James Version, "charity." Coleman also challenged her students to intellectual attainment and to broaden their horizons. "Any boy, even one of ours," she said, "might grow up to be president of the United States." Young Jimmy Carter was listening.[10]

Home provided another font of moral instruction. Earl Carter gave his children a penny every week to be deposited in the Sunday-school collection plate. One Sunday, when Jimmy was four or five years old, he returned from church and placed two pennies on his dresser when he changed out of his church clothes; he had taken a penny out of the offering basket rather than depositing his. Earl Carter noticed the extra penny and administered a whipping. "That was the last money I ever stole," Jimmy recalled. "He was a stern disciplinarian, a tremendous athlete, a good baseball pitcher," Carter said about his father decades later, "a good tennis player, whom I never defeated."[11]

Earl Carter's nickname for Jimmy was "Hot," as in Hot Shot; it was generally a term of endearment, but sometimes he used it as a shot across the bow to check his son's ego. The Carter family added a sister, Gloria, when Jimmy was two, and another sister, Ruth, three years later. William Alton, better known as "Billy," the youngest of the four Carter siblings, was born when Jimmy was thirteen.

Earl Carter's faith—he was a deacon and a Sunday-school teacher at Plains Baptist Church—made a deep impression on his children, especially his oldest son, who memorized Bible verses for Sunday school as well as for school. But young Jimmy Carter also learned that faith was not inherited, that he needed to be "born again" in his own right in order properly to claim the moniker *Christian*.[12]

Like most Southern Baptist congregations, Plains Baptist Church scheduled annual revivals, or "protractive meetings," after crops were planted and before the harvest. These revivals were modeled after those in the nineteenth century, led very often by itinerant evangelists who descended on a community to upbraid sinners and bestir the faithful out of their spiritual lethargy. Like many other congregations in the Southern Baptist Convention, Plains Baptist continued that tradition, inviting guest preachers for a week of renewal. With two meetings a day during revival week, nary a soul could escape the preacher's rhetoric or his importuning to surrender one's life to Jesus and become a born-again Christian. Children, most of them reared in the church and in Sunday school, were especially susceptible. "This was usually the time when children, typically at least eight years old, would accept Christ as Saviour and subsequently be baptized into full church membership," Carter wrote, adding that his father was a tad more conservative about such matters; Jimmy and his sisters waited until they were about eleven years old. "By then we had been carefully instructed in Sunday school and in training union," he added, "and understood the meaning of these decisions, which were considered without question to be the most important of our lives." Jimmy Carter was baptized in the Plains Baptist Church during the summer of 1935, within days of his born-again conversion. "I accepted Christ as Savior and was baptized into the church at eleven," Carter told me years later. "That was kind of a normal evolution for every young person in our church."[13]

Earl Carter also instilled in his son the rudimentary Baptist principles of liberty of conscience, the separation of church and state, and an individual's responsibility before God. According to Jimmy Carter, one of the recurrent lessons in his father's Sunday-school class was that "we should not have a government trying to be involved in religious affairs, and we should not try to get any denomination, even our own, to be interpreted legally as superior to others." Earl Carter also taught the Protestant notion of the priesthood of believers, Martin Luther's conviction that each individual should read and interpret the Bible for himself or herself.[14]

THE specter hanging over Plains and, arguably, over every community in the South, was race. Carter recalled a day at the farm when he was about fourteen years old when his African-American playmates suddenly deferred to him as they approached a gate between the barn and the pasture. "To my surprise, they opened it and stepped back to let me go through first," he wrote. "I was immediately suspicious that they were playing some trick on me, but I passed through without stumbling over a tripwire or having them slam the gate in my face." Thereafter, his playmates treated their white friend with a deference that he sometimes found unnerving. "The constant struggle for leadership among our small group was resolved," Carter recalled, "but a precious sense of equality had gone out of our personal relationship, and things were never again the same between them and me." Carter's childhood experience with African Americans was formative. "I grew up in their culture," he told me, "and I saw the devastating effects of racial discrimination."[15]

Lillian Carter's "liberal" ways—she worked in black households as well as white—sometimes earned her the epithet "nigger lover." But "Miss Lillian," who accepted a two-year Peace Corps assignment to India in her late sixties, was never one to back away from her convictions on racial or political matters. Jimmy Carter recalled his mother watching the entirety of the Joseph McCarthy hearings in 1954, urging Jimmy to watch with her. "She despised McCarthy," Carter wrote. Lillian, a loyal Democrat, headed the 1964 Johnson-Humphrey organization in Sumter County, a forlorn task given Johnson's unpopularity because of the Civil Rights Act, which he had signed into law on July 2 of that year. "People hated Johnson down here because of his stand on civil rights and it got very ugly," Lillian Carter told a reporter in 1976, "but I was never afraid, not even when they threw things at my car and yelled 'Nigger lover, nigger lover' at me." Lillian recalled that her automobile was covered with graffiti nearly every day, the radio antenna broken off or tied in a knot.[16]

Lillian's plucky feminism and indomitable spirit clearly made an impression on her son. Jimmy Carter remembered that when his mother read to the family from the Bible, it was usually from Ruth or Esther, books in the Hebrew Bible that highlighted the agency of women. "Later in life," Carter wrote about his mother, "she never took any notable public positions on the liberation or equality of women but seemed to assume that any secondary or subservient role was the fault of the women involved."[17]

Lillian's feminism shaped her son's attitudes throughout his life. Long after his mother's death, Carter used his Sunday-school class to talk about the relationship between Jesus and women. First-century Palestine consigned women, Carter said, to "a completely subservient position," but the advent of Jesus heralded a new era. Jesus Christ promoted women to a status of equality, he said, noting that it was women who initially spread news of the resurrection. "Jesus showed his care for despised women as he sat at the well with the woman Samaritan and later with the woman who was caught in adultery." The lesson, Carter said, was that women played a central role in the early church. Another Sunday-school lesson centered on St. Paul's letter to the Galatians, which reads: "There is neither Jew nor Greek, slave nor free, male nor female, for you are all one in Christ Jesus." Carter said, "I take this verse, and other places in the Bible, to mean that in God's eyes men and women are the same." He continued: "I believe women have a perfect right, and even a duty, to hold any position in the church." Lillian Carter and legions of progressive evangelicals would have agreed.[18]

During the course of the 1976 presidential campaign, Jimmy Carter elaborated on the origins of his feminist sensibilities. "I come from a part of Georgia where almost every woman worked," he told a group in Clearwater, Florida. "My mother was a nurse. My wife's father died when she was thirteen and her mother became a seamstress, making clothes for the more prosperous women in town. I've seen women working in southern textile mills in a way that shamed and embarrassed me." Those experiences back in Georgia, he said, cemented his commitment to women's rights.[19]

JIMMY Carter encountered a much wider world when he headed off to the U.S. Naval Academy in 1943. Carter had aspired to Annapolis even before he entered the first grade, in part because Lillian's youngest brother, Tom Gordy, had enlisted in the navy, and young Jimmy regarded his uncle as something of a hero. While still in grade school, Jimmy sent an inquiry to the Naval Academy and, without revealing his age, asked for the entrance

requirements; the catalog that arrived by return mail became dog-eared over
the years.

Earl Carter encouraged his son's aspirations in part because an education
at Annapolis would be financed by the U.S. government. Toward that end,
Earl Carter supported the local member of Congress, Stephen Pace, in hopes
of securing the appointment. But when Jimmy graduated from Plains High
School in 1941, the appointment had not yet materialized. He attended college at Georgia Southern in Americus for a year before learning that the appointment was finalized. He then spent a year in the Reserve Officer Training
Corps program at Georgia Institute of Technology in Atlanta.[20]

At Annapolis, Carter endured the ritual hazing dished out to plebes. As a
loyal son of the South, however, he adamantly refused to sing "Marching
through Georgia," even though that refusal cost him several rounds of cor-
poral punishment at the hands of upperclassmen. When he became an up-
perclassman himself, Carter befriended the Academy's only African-American
midshipman at the time, Wesley Brown. Carter defended his friend so vigorously that a classmate called Carter "a God damn nigger lover," but Carter
was unfazed, even though he took a lot of heat from fellow southerners for
standing up for Brown. Another classmate noted that Carter "was treated as
if he was a traitor." Patterns of racial segregation were deeply entrenched,
especially in the South, so Carter was in many ways ahead of his time on racial sensibilities. Decades later, teaching his Sunday-school class in Plains,
Carter recalled that even after his stint in the navy, the churches in Plains
would invite guest preachers who argued for white superiority on the basis of
carefully selected verses from the Bible.[21]

At Annapolis, Carter was known for his probity. "We never swore around
Jimmy," a close friend remembered. "It would have been like cussing in front
of your grandmother or the Lord." Carter attended the Academy's Protestant
chapel during his first year at Annapolis, but he yearned for the familiarity
of Baptist worship and began attending an off-campus Baptist church. In
short order, he followed his father's footsteps and started teaching Sunday
school, a practice he would continue throughout the remainder of his life.
His initial assignment was a class comprised of the daughters, nine to twelve
years old, of those who were stationed permanently at the Naval Academy.[22]

Carter was happy at the Naval Academy, but the one thing he lacked was
a girlfriend. Carter had numerous girlfriends as a teenager but no enduring
relationship. Back in Plains during the summer of 1945, the summer before
his final year at Annapolis, Carter met and began dating Rosalynn Smith,

his sister Ruth's best friend. After their first date, at the Rylander Theatre in nearby Americus, Jimmy announced to his mother that he had met the girl he intended to marry. Although Lillian Carter could hardly be characterized as a doting mother, she worried that the diffident Rosalynn, three years younger than Jimmy, would not be his equal. According to Jimmy, however, one of Rosalynn's attractions, in a small, close-knit community, was that she "was one of the few female residents in Plains who was not related to me, at least within the last 120 years or so."[23]

He proposed marriage while home at Christmas, but Rosalynn demurred; the Plains High School valedictorian was intent on continuing her education. In February 1946, however, she consented, and the couple was married on July 7, 1946, in the Plains Methodist Church. The groom wore his dress white navy uniform, and the bride treated herself to a store-bought, knee-length dress. The union of Rosalynn, a Methodist, and Jimmy, a Baptist, counted as a religiously "mixed marriage" in Plains. Carter later joked in one of his Sunday-school lessons that "in general, Baptists marry Methodists or Lutherans, we don't marry each other." By all accounts, however, theirs was a close and companionate marriage. Rosalynn became her husband's confidante and adviser; contrary to Lillian's fears, Rosalynn, with her iron will and occasional flashes of temper, turned out to be less a shrinking violet than a steel magnolia.[24]

ON June 5, 1946, Jimmy Carter graduated with distinction from Annapolis, was commissioned an ensign, and the Carters embarked on a career in the navy. The life of a navy spouse was not easy; during his posting in Norfolk, Virginia, Jimmy was at sea aboard the USS *Wyoming* four or five days a week. The ambitious and conscientious ensign, however, threw himself into his work, first as electronics and photographic officer on the *Wyoming* and then as aide to the executive gunnery officer on the USS *Mississippi*. During this time, Carter also applied to be a Rhodes scholar, was named a finalist, and was acutely disappointed when he did not win the scholarship.[25]

In April 1948, following the birth of their first son, John William "Jack" Carter, Rosalynn and Jimmy moved to New London, Connecticut, where he reported to the Navy Submarine School. After graduating with distinction, Carter was assigned to Pearl Harbor, Hawai'i, for service aboard the USS *Pomfret*. One night, while he was standing watch on the deck of the surfaced submarine off the coast of China, a huge wave washed Carter into the swirling maw of the dark sea. Somehow, after thrashing about in the water, he landed atop the submarine's gun thirty feet aft. The storm wiped out the submarine's communications, and the navy sent out a message to all ships in the area to look for debris from the *Pomfret*, "believed to have been sunk approximately seven hundred miles south of Midway Island." Rosalynn, back in Plains, learned about the incident only later.[26]

In April 1949, Jack and Rosalynn joined Jimmy in Pearl Harbor, where they enjoyed island life for the ensuing fifteen months. A second son, James Earl "Chip" Carter III, was born in Hawai'i before the *Pomfret* sailed for San Diego, and soon thereafter Carter was assigned once again to New London, Connecticut, where he did engineering work on the new SS *K-1*, later renamed the *Barracuda*. A third son, Donnel Jeffrey "Jeff" Carter, was born in 1952 during the family's stay in New England.

Jimmy Carter continued to earn the respect of his superiors. One described him as "without doubt the most outstanding individual within his age and rank group that I have observed." Carter also showed leadership in other ways. When the *K-1* moored in Jamaica, British officials invited the crew to a shore party—all except for a black sailor. Protesting the exclusion, Carter declined the invitation, and other officers followed his lead.[27]

Ever ambitious, Carter applied to join the navy's highly selective group of engineers under the direction of Hyman Rickover, the demanding and disputatious admiral who was determined to develop nuclear-powered vessels. In the course of his interview, Carter conceded under interrogation that perhaps he had not always given his best in his studies at the Academy, despite his fairly lofty rank as sixtieth out of a class of 820 students. "Why not?" the admiral snapped. Rickover accepted Carter into the program, but he also provided his charge with something to ponder, something to goad him to higher and higher attainment. More than two decades later, Carter used the phrase "Why Not the Best?" as the title for his campaign autobiography, a book that included an acknowledgment that "Admiral Rickover had a profound effect on my life—perhaps more than anyone except my own parents."[28]

Carter found life as a navy man both rewarding and satisfying. Following his acceptance into Rickover's program, the Carters moved to Schenectady, New York, where Jimmy studied nuclear physics and reactor technology at Union College. He visited the reactor in Hanford, Washington, where plutonium was generated, the Idaho site where a *Nautilus* prototype was being made, and interacted with the people at the Atomic Energy Commission in Washington, D.C. "My job was the best and most promising in the navy," Carter later wrote. "The salary was good, and the retirement benefits were liberal and assured." He even managed to win coveted praise from Rickover, who commended Carter's "excellent administrative job," adding that Carter's "leadership of the men assigned and his cooperation have been outstanding."[29]

Why, then, would a young naval officer elect to leave such a fulfilling career, a career that promised a continued trajectory of travel, adventure, and security? Rosalynn Carter asked the same question.

BY 1953, Earl Carter's two-pack-a-day habit had caught up with him. As he lay dying of cancer, Jimmy was given a leave to attend his father at his bedside. For the first time, Jimmy Carter began to learn about his father's quiet acts of charity over the years: buying graduation clothes for families who could not afford such luxury, extending credit for seed and fertilizer, supporting a widow after her husband died. "Hundreds of people came by to speak to Daddy or to bring him a choice morsel of food or some fresh flowers," Carter recalled. "It was obvious that he meant much to them, and it caused me to compare my prospective life with his."[30]

Returning to Schenectady after the funeral, Jimmy informed Rosalynn of his intention to resign from the navy and return to Plains. Rosalynn did not take it well; more than once in their arguments, she raised the specter of divorce. Despite the hardships and the long separations, Rosalynn liked the adventure of navy life and had no interest in returning to what she had come to regard as a restrictive life in Plains.[31]

The husband prevailed, despite what he described as the "almost violent opposition of my wife" and elsewhere characterized as "the first serious argument in our marriage." On their remarkably silent journey from Schenectady to Plains late in 1953, the Carters stopped in Washington to see their representative in Congress, E. L. "Tick" Forrester, who showed the Carters around the Capitol and unburdened himself of the opinion that public-housing complexes were dangerous places. Jimmy and Rosalynn glanced at one another in the knowledge that, because of their modest resources, they had just signed up to live in the new public-housing project in Plains. Jimmy, however, never looked back or regretted the decision. "I resigned my commission in October 1953 to come home, grow seed peanuts, buy and sell farm products to the farmers in the community," Carter wrote later, "and assume some of the responsibilities that had made Daddy's life so admirable." Rosalynn's sentiments about returning to Plains were far more succinct, as she recalled three decades later: "I was miserable."[32]

Although Jimmy's immediate plans were to take charge of the family's farm enterprises, he apparently harbored even then some thoughts about following his father's footsteps in public life as well as agriculture. Earl Carter had served on the Sumter County Board of Education from 1936 until his death, heading a movement that led to the construction of the county's first school for African-American children. Earl was a member of several fraternal organizations, a director of the Rural Electrification Agency, and a member of the Sumter County Commission. In addition, Earl Carter had been elected to the Georgia legislature in 1952, only months before his death. To what extent Jimmy Carter saw himself as responsible for carrying on his father's political legacy remains something of a mystery, but it seems to have informed his decision to leave the navy and return to Plains. "I had only one life to live," Carter explained about that decision in his autobiography, "and I wanted to live it as a civilian, with a potentially fuller opportunity for varied public service."[33]

Even apart from Rosalynn's resistance, Jimmy Carter's return to Plains was not uncomplicated. During his elder son's sojourn in the navy, Earl Carter had groomed his second son, Billy—thirteen years younger than Jimmy—to take over the family business. Billy, an avid reader, had joined the Future Farmers of America in high school and accompanied his father to Atlanta, where he worked as a page during Earl Carter's short stint as a member of the state legislature. Billy was still a teenager when his father was diagnosed with cancer. Earl Carter's death at the age of fifty-nine left a gap in the Carter household, but the return of Jimmy from the navy meant that Billy would be elbowed aside as heir presumptive of the Carter family business.[34]

The early returns on Jimmy Carter's agricultural skills were not auspicious. Owing in part to a drought, the Carter farm turned a profit of less than three hundred dollars in 1954, the first year under Jimmy's stewardship. His request for a small loan from the local bank was denied. But he persisted, talking to and learning from other farmers, taking short courses at the Coastal Plain Experiment Station in nearby Tifton, Georgia. With time, business savvy, improved weather, and Rosalynn keeping the books, the fortunes of the farm began to improve. The Carters moved out of public housing and built an architect-designed house in Plains. By 1960, Carter

Warehouse had grown to be ranked the third-largest business in its tax district, and the farms and warehouse combined into a multimillion-dollar-a-year operation.[35]

THE year 1954, Carter's first as head of the farm, was also the year of the landmark *Brown v. Board of Education of Topeka* decision. When the U.S. Supreme Court handed down that ruling on May 17, 1954, which effectively reversed the 1896 *Plessy v. Ferguson* decision that had legitimized "separate but equal" racial accommodations, no one imagined how that decision would reverberate throughout the nation and especially the South. "That was a strange era in our lives," Carter recalled; by his reckoning, only half a dozen families in Plains were "moderates" on the race issue in 1954, and several of those were "run out of town."[36]

Carter's position on the Sumter County Board of Education forced him to confront his community's handling of race relations. He remembered that he was on the board for months before it registered with him that white children rode buses to their schools while African-American students walked to theirs. As member of the school board, and especially as chair from 1960 through 1962, Carter sought to improve black schools in the district, part of a strategy employed throughout the South to avoid integration by ensuring that facilities were more nearly equal, albeit separate. Carter himself acknowledged that "the 'separate' was the only part honored in the South," however, and that there "was certainly no equality between black and white students."[37]

Carter took a more courageous stand on race in opposition to the White Citizens' Council, a white-supremacist organization begun in Greenwood, Mississippi, less than two months after the *Brown* decision. Local chapters of the Citizens' Councils, sometimes known as the "uptown Klan," worked to resist integration and to intimidate African Americans. In the course of the Montgomery Bus Boycott, for example, a mimeographed flyer distributed at a council gathering read: "When in the course of human events, it becomes necessary to abolish the Negro race, proper methods should be used. Among these are guns, bows and arrows, sling shots and knives."[38]

One day, members of the local chapter of the White Citizens' Council, the chief of police, and the railroad depot agent, who was also a Baptist minister, called on the Carter Warehouse, intent on enlisting another member, someone by then regarded as a leading citizen in the community. Carter refused to join. A couple of days later, they returned, informing Carter that "every white male adult in the community had joined," except Carter. Frustrated a second time, they returned with other members, many of whom were Carter's friends and customers. Carter's standing in the community, not to mention his business, would be imperiled if he refused to become a member, they informed him. They even offered to pay his five-dollar dues if he would consent to join.[39]

Carter was adamant and, by this time, angry. He walked over to the cash register, took out a five-dollar bill, and announced, "I'll take this and flush it down the toilet, but I am not going to join the White Citizens' Council." Carter's refusal prompted a small boycott against his business, but it was short-lived; only a couple of customers stayed away permanently.[40]

Despite Rosalynn's earlier misgivings, the couple's return to their hometown had been successful. Jimmy Carter, with Rosalynn's help, proved himself an astute businessman. More important, he had integrated himself into the community as a Baptist deacon and a member of the school board. Having returned from the navy and established his identity as a citizen of Plains, Jimmy Carter was prepared now to consider broader horizons.

TWO

FROM PEANUTS
TO POLITICS

In the year leading up to the 1962 general election, two developments reconfigured the political landscape in the state of Georgia. In September 1961, leaders of the Student Nonviolent Coordinating Committee (SNCC) chose Albany, Georgia, as the next venue to push their case for civil rights and racial equality. Students from Albany State College marched and picketed, voters were registered, and many protesters were arrested and sent to jail. By December, however, with protests flagging and hundreds languishing in jail, Martin Luther King Jr. was called in to energize what by now was called the Albany Movement. Although the Albany Movement is generally regarded as a setback for the civil rights struggle—Laurie Pritchett, the chief of police, had read King's writings and knew how to counter his nonviolent techniques—the Albany campaign nevertheless served notice that the civil rights movement had arrived in Georgia.

The second development was legal; a series of court decisions revamped Georgia's electoral system and provided Jimmy Carter an opening to seek election to higher office beyond the school board. For decades, Georgia's longstanding hedge against urbanization had been a legal measure called the county unit system. This law, passed by the Georgia legislature in 1917 and known as the Neill Primary Act, allotted representation by counties rather than population. The effect was roughly analogous to the U.S. Senate, where all states, regardless of size, have two senators; Wyoming and Vermont each send two senators to Washington, D.C., the same as California and New York, despite the vast disparities in population. Similarly, under the county unit system in Georgia, Fulton County (Atlanta), with its large population, wielded roughly the same political clout as rural Cusseta County or Quitman County, on the border with Alabama. After the *Brown* decision of 1954, the county unit system became a convenient tool for segregationists to forestall racial integration; rural areas, typically more conservative on racial matters, sent a disproportionately larger number of representatives to the Georgia legislature. As Carter noted, "The county unit system had always been the bastion of the most ardent segregationists in Georgia."[1]

The U.S. Supreme Court's *Baker v. Carr* decision, handed down on March 26, 1962, however, rendered such laws as Georgia's county unit system unconstitutional because they violated the "one man, one vote" principle. Although Georgia and other states tried to delay, or even to subvert, the ruling, federal judges forced its implementation. The effect was to dilute significantly the power of county political bosses; no longer would they be able routinely to monitor the balloting in a central polling place. Georgia senate districts, moreover, now transcended county lines, further eroding the influence of county political organizations.

THOUGH few of his neighbors suspected his intentions, Jimmy Carter was following these developments closely. He much admired his father's civic-mindedness; Earl Carter had been elected to the Georgia legislature a decade earlier, but his untimely death prevented him from serving out a full term. Jimmy Carter's stint in the navy had exposed him to the wider world and also reinforced in him a sense of responsibility for others. Finally, his tenure on the Sumter County School Board had provided a taste of public service. "Over the years, I had been encouraged to run for office by a few of my neighbors and others with whom I had worked on civic affairs," Carter wrote in his account of his first campaign for political office. He had even privately considered a run for Congress, but he had no appetite for a move to Washington, even on a part-time basis.[2]

As he considered the possibility of running for office, however, Carter factored in his relatively liberal views on race, which ran counter to local sentiment. Following the *Brown* decision, Americus, Georgia, the county seat, became a stronghold of the arch-conservative John Birch Society. Koinonia Farm, outside of Americus, an intentionally integrated community headed by Clarence Jordan, was boycotted by local merchants; the Carter Warehouse, however, sold the farm certified seed peanuts and processed the crop in its shelling plant, thereby providing a necessary economic lifeline for the farm. When the young son of Jack Singletary, a white man who had lived at Koinonia, died of leukemia, Rosalynn Carter attended the funeral and brought food for the family, even though the majority of the white community and her fellow congregants at Plains Baptist Church stayed away.[3]

The Carters began to be identified, by people on both sides of the racial divide, as sympathetic to African Americans. Jimmy's refusal to join the White Citizens' Council had not gone unnoticed; he survived a boycott of his business, but the all-white country club in Americus expelled him. When a black friend, a man who had purchased his farm from Earl Carter, was turned away in his attempt to register to vote, Jimmy Carter counseled him on the process and offered to accompany him on his second, successful attempt.[4]

Carter's opposition to segregation made him unpopular among some in the community. As chair of the Sumter County Board of Education, Carter had championed a proposal to consolidate the Americus and Sumter County schools, an initiative that, he argued, would be economical and also provide for better education. Opponents, however, led by Hugh Carter, Jimmy's first cousin, countered that such consolidation would entail longer bus rides for students and would also pave the way for desegregated education. In a close referendum, consolidation failed. The next morning, when Carter arrived at the warehouse, he found a sign nailed across the door: COONS AND CARTERS GO TOGETHER.[5]

Despite the prospect of repercussions over the race issue, Carter decided to forge ahead. On the morning of his thirty-eighth birthday, October 1, 1962, he pulled on his Sunday trousers rather than his work clothes and announced to Rosalynn that he was headed to Americus to file as a candidate for state senate. "The force driving me was a somewhat naïve concept of public service," Carter wrote. "Neither did I ever have any thought that the state Senate might be a stepping-stone to higher office; this ambition alone was stretching my imagination."[6]

Carter was remarkably unreflective, at least publicly, about his initial decision to run for public office, but his claim of innocence about ambitions for higher office should probably not be accepted as the final word. Perhaps even then, although Carter never acknowledged as much, Julia Coleman's remark that one of her students might someday be president was reverberating in his head. One thing, however, is certain: Beginning with this initial run for public office and throughout his political career, Carter was utterly convinced of two things. First, he was the superior candidate; second, sheer hard work, grit, and determination would persuade voters of the previous point. His naïveté lay in the conviction that elections provided confirmation that America was indeed a meritocracy. All Carter needed to prevail was to present his case, and his superior qualifications, before the voters.

Carter proceeded to do just that. With only fifteen days before the Democratic primary (due to the protracted uncertainty over legal challenges to the county unit system), Jimmy and Rosalynn went to work. Rosalynn placed hundreds of phone calls and helped design campaign posters and calling cards. "Whenever I could leave the warehouse, a few hours each day," Carter recalled, "I moved around the district trying to visit friends, peanut and cotton customers, my relatives and Rosalynn's, fellow Lions Club members, city and county officials, and other community leaders who might be willing and able to help me garner a few votes." His opponent, Homer Moore, hailed from Quitman County and had already won an earlier primary—before the redistricting mandated by the courts. "By the time I realized how doubtful my victory would be," Carter wrote, "I was already committed to the race and never considered turning back."[7]

Although the energy of the Carter campaign, together with pride in a local boy running for office, seemed to allay concerns about the candidate's views on race, not everyone was enamored of Carter's foray into politics. In the course of dinner at Lillian's house, a visiting Baptist preacher challenged Carter's notion that public service was a worthy vocation for a believer. For decades, evangelicals had been chary about political involvement, and the visiting minister shared those mid-twentieth-century suspicions. "If you want to be of service to other people," he asked, "why don't you go into the ministry or some honorable social service work?" The preacher's clear inference was that serving in political office was not an "honorable" calling for a believer. Carter, a Baptist deacon, shot back: "How would you like to be the pastor of a church with eighty thousand members?"[8]

On the day of the Democratic primary, October 16, Carter voted and then set out to visit key precincts in the fourteenth district. Soon, he began to hear about voting irregularities in Georgetown, the Quitman County seat. Joe Hurst, the political boss of Quitman County, had decided that Moore would win the senate seat. Voters coming to cast their ballots in Georgetown were ushered into a small room, handed a ballot together with a Herman Moore campaign card, and informed that Hurst wanted them to scratch out Carter's name and vote for Moore—in full view of Hurst or one of his surrogates. According to court documents, when one couple apparently cast their votes for Carter, Hurst retrieved the ballots, tore them up, and vowed to teach them how to vote. He took six fresh ballots, scratched out Carter's name on each one, and stuffed them into the box. "That's the way you are supposed to vote," he announced. "If I ever catch you all voting wrong again, your house might burn down!"[9]

When the tally came in, Carter had lost Quitman County 360 to 136, even though there were only 333 stubs in the ballot book. Although Carter had carried Sumter and Chattahoochee counties, his losing margin in Quitman County cost him the primary-election victory.[10]

Carter's account of that election, *Turning Point: A Candidate, a State, and a Nation Come of Age*, bristles with indignation. "I could still see the grin on Joe Hurst's face, and it burned me up," Carter said. "I had been betrayed by a political system in which I had confidence, and I was mad as hell!"[11]

Carter refused to accept the results. He rallied friends and legal help. He goaded reluctant local newspapers to expose the fraud and finally caught a break when he persuaded John Pennington, a reporter with the *Atlanta Journal*, to investigate. Pennington minced no words in reporting the story. "The statewide Democratic primaries held in this Southwest Georgia town," he wrote, "were conducted with no apparent regard for the law." Pennington went on to report that several of the county's deceased had shown up at the polls on Election Day and that "a hundred and seventeen people, out of a total vote of 733, are listed as having lined up and cast their ballots in alphabetical order, even down to the second and third letters of the last name."[12]

Carter pursued the case through the courts, several hearings, intense politicking, and a write-in general election. It wasn't until the lieutenant governor called his name to take the oath of office on Monday, January 14, 1963, that Jimmy Carter was finally assured of victory in his first run for public office.[13]

BECAUSE Carter's seat hadn't been secured until the last minute, he missed out on the plum committee assignments. Undeterred, he accepted mundane, time-consuming jobs that no one else wanted. As with every other endeavor, Carter threw himself into his work. He arrived early to the state capitol and resolved to read every bill under consideration by the Georgia state senate. In time, his attention to detail became so legendary that fellow senators would vet their bills with Carter before submitting them to the legislative process. Carter also advocated openness in government, noting that politicians "who deliberately hide their actions from the people rarely do so with benevolent motives."[14]

It was during his tenure as state senator that Carter began to appreciate Reinhold Niebuhr's maxim: "The sad duty of politics is to establish justice in a sinful world." During his time in Atlanta, Carter began to read widely in theology—Paul Tillich, Søren Kierkegaard, Dietrich Bonhoeffer, and Karl Barth—but he later described Niebuhr as his favorite theologian. It was Niebuhr who helped Carter understand how a believer deals with public affairs and political adversaries, how to apply Christian principles to the vocation of public life. The highest possible aspiration of any given community, Carter said, paraphrasing Niebuhr, was to establish justice and fairness. In Carter's understanding, "that means guaranteeing human rights, it means treating everybody fairly, it means not having prejudice in the laws, it means not having special favors for your friends; it means not taking bribes." This pursuit of justice in a sinful world, according to Carter's reading of Niebuhr, represented a political leader's most solemn duty. The Christian community, Carter went on, must aspire to an even higher standard: love, even "love for someone who doesn't love you back." Indeed, paradox lay at the center of Niebuhr's thought. Jesus enjoined his followers to be peacemakers and to turn the other cheek, Niebuhr wrote, but sometimes a believer must take up arms to restrain evil. Similarly, Carter carefully distinguished between a believer's individual responsibility and a public servant's official responsibility to his constituents. As a public official, it would be inappropriate to confuse the two; altruism may be a noble aspiration for an individual, but that same individual must remain vigilant in protecting the interests of those for whom he is responsible. Carter recognized, for example, "I could not sacrifice the well being of my nation for the well being of other nations."[15]

Even in his limited role as a Georgia state senator, Carter was beginning to consider the place of the believer in public life. He recognized that legislation could function as a tool in the pursuit of justice. Such laws may be imperfect, Carter acknowledged, but they nevertheless "represent a striving for justice and fairness."[16]

THE legislative session in Georgia lasted only forty days, during months of the year that, typically, were slow ones for the Carter Warehouse. Carter would spend his weeks in Atlanta, where he stayed at the Piedmont Hotel, and then drive home to Plains for the weekends. The Carter business interests rested in the capable hands of Rosalynn Carter, who began to recognize not only her talent for business but also her interest in politics. Although Rosalynn cringed to hear criticisms of her husband, especially from acquaintances, she began to think of herself, in her own words, as "more a political partner than a political wife."[17]

Despite his growing appreciation for the comportment of a believer in public life, Jimmy Carter could be ruthless toward political adversaries. In the spring of 1964, he managed to exact revenge against his old nemesis in Quitman County, Joe Hurst. In the run-up to the 1964 election, the county's executive committee refused to certify Ralph Balkcom, Rosalynn's cousin, to run against Hurst for state representative. Carter intervened, won a place for Balkcom on the ballot, and for good measure furnished the Federal Bureau of Investigation with evidence of Hurst's various criminal activities—his moonshine business, his rigging of previous elections, and his pilfering of land from unsuspecting citizens. Hurst went to prison, and Balkcom won election to the Georgia legislature, narrowly defeating Hurst's wife, who had replaced him on the ballot.[18]

Most of Carter's efforts as a first-term state senator, however, were directed toward improving the lot of his constituents. As state senator, Carter focused on conservation and on access to education and health care, all the while remaining faithful to Baptist principles, including liberty of conscience and the separation of church and state. Roger Williams, founder of the Baptist tradition in America, had warned that the "wilderness of the world" would contaminate the "garden of the church" if not for a "wall of separation" between the two. Although Thomas Jefferson later used that same imagery to prevent religious factions from impeding the functions of government, Carter, a Baptist and now an elected official, shared both concerns. When a bill passed the Georgia senate requiring the worship of God, Carter voted against it, a vote that was later used against him as "proof" that he was an atheist.[19]

Carter's careful attention to local matters won favor among his constituents. He supported measures that would provide free textbooks and free transportation to public schools, and he introduced legislation to aid poor school districts. His effort to transform Georgia Southwestern into a four-year college made him so popular that no one opposed him for reelection in 1964.[20]

That same election, however, provided evidence that the civil rights movement was beginning to alter Georgia politics. John F. Kennedy's embrace of civil rights had aroused the suspicions of many white southerners. When news of Kennedy's assassination on November 22, 1963, was announced to students at Plains High School, Chip Carter's classmates applauded. If white southerners expected Lyndon Johnson of Texas to be more sympathetic to segregation, they were disappointed. When the new president addressed Congress following the assassination, he declared that "no memorial oration or eulogy could more eloquently honor President Kennedy's memory than the earliest possible passage of the civil rights bill for which he fought so long." Johnson, in fact, proved far more effective in pushing civil rights legislation through Congress, much to the chagrin of southern segregationists, including Georgia's senior U.S. senator, Richard B. Russell Jr., an implacable foe of integration. Johnson's signature on the Civil Rights Act of 1964 marked the beginning of a long decline of Democratic Party dominance in Georgia politics. That November, as Jimmy Carter cruised to reelection to the Georgia senate, a Republican, Howard "Bo" Callaway, was elected to Congress from the district that included Plains, the first time the state of Georgia had sent a Republican to Congress since Reconstruction. Georgia was one of six states that Barry Goldwater, the Republican nominee, carried in the 1964 presidential election.[21]

Embarking on his second term in the Georgia senate, Carter continued to advocate for education reform, articulating the aspiration that Georgia public schools should be able to compete with any in the nation. He also declared that the state should provide a low-cost college education to anyone who wanted it. Arguing for greater efficiency in state government, Carter continued to oppose additional taxes. He won praise from the governor, Carl Sanders, and Carter's colleagues voted him one of Georgia's five most influential legislators. An article in the *Atlanta Constitution*, noting Carter's physical resemblance to the late John F. Kennedy, described him as "one of the most outstanding members of the Senate."[22]

By now, the peanut farmer from Plains harbored ambitions beyond the Georgia state legislature. The most obvious step would be a run for Congress, if for no other reason than to deny Bo Callaway a second term. Although Callaway was popular, Carter thought he could defeat him; Carter announced his bid for Congress on March 4, 1965. Callaway, however, switched course and decided to run for governor, and soon Carter was fielding requests to challenge him. Carter weighed the choice carefully. He concluded that, with Callaway out of the congressional race, he would win the seat easily. Still, Carter's competitive streak prompted him to reconsider the bid for Congress. Carter acknowledged that Callaway was "a staunch enemy of mine in every way," and he was loath to see Callaway cruise into the governor's office. The two men had clashed earlier over Georgia Southwestern College; as a member of the board of regents, Callaway had tried unsuccessfully to block Carter's proposal to make Georgia Southwestern a four-year college. In many ways, aside from differences in party affiliation, the two men were alike: Carter and Callaway were about the same age; both were businessmen, although Callaway was scion of a textile family, while Carter was essentially a self-made man. Even their military affiliations were competitive: Calloway had graduated from West Point, Carter from Annapolis.[23]

Once again, as Carter considered his political options, the issue of race emerged. Late in the summer of 1965, Plains Baptist Church was confronted with the prospect of racially integrated worship. With the advent of the civil rights movement, some African Americans were staging what became known as church visitations; a black person would show up for Sunday-morning worship service, during what Martin Luther King Jr. called the most segregated hour in America, and seek to be seated. Most were turned away. Carter, a deacon at Plains Baptist Church, was out of town when the matter came before the board of deacons, and the deacons decided that any blacks trying to worship would be blocked. When Carter found out about this, he was disturbed, and at the subsequent meeting of the congregation's church conference he argued forcefully that any blacks seeking to worship be admitted, "as long as their motives seemed peaceful."[24]

Out of approximately two hundred people in attendance, the resolution received only six votes—Lillian Carter, Jimmy and Rosalynn Carter, their two sons, and one other congregant. When the Carters returned home, their phone was ringing; some congregants called to express their support, even though they had lacked the courage to take a public stand. Others criticized. "It was tough," Rosalynn later said. "People wouldn't speak to us in church." In a community like Plains, churches very often serve as the nexus of social relations, so the Carters' principled stand for racial equality, as Rosalynn indicated, exacted a cost.[25]

As the 1966 election approached, Carter tried to persuade other Democrats to enter the race for governor against Callaway. Daunted by the challenge, no one took the bait, and so, encouraged by others, Carter reconsidered his course. In the end, he found that the prospect of vanquishing a popular up-and-coming Republican, Callaway, proved too tempting. He abandoned his campaign for Congress and announced his candidacy for governor on June 12, 1966.[26]

This would be the first time that race would figure explicitly into a Carter campaign. Callaway appealed unabashedly to segregationists; Carter equivocated. He distanced himself from Lyndon Johnson, who had shepherded the Civil Rights Act through Congress, and sought to wrap himself in the mantle of Richard Russell, the Georgia senator who had led the opposition to civil rights legislation since his arrival in the Senate in 1933. "My name won't be under Lyndon Johnson on the ballot," Carter declared. "I consider myself a conservative. I'm a Dick Russell Democrat."[27]

Although Carter had anticipated a head-to-head contest with Callaway, the Republican nominee, his real challenge lay in the Democratic primary, where his reputation as a "racial moderate" hurt him. Carter, in fact, was caught in the middle among the Democratic candidates. On his left stood Ellis Arnall, a former governor whose tenure in the statehouse was remembered for its progressive stance on racial issues, including his proposal to allow African Americans a vote in party primaries. Carter was far outflanked on the right by Lester G. Maddox, owner of the Pickrick restaurant in Atlanta who brandished an axe handle to keep African Americans out of his restaurant. Maddox had won notoriety in July 1964 when three black students from Georgia Tech tried to buy fried chicken at his restaurant. Maddox waved a pistol at them and shouted, "You no good dirty devils! You dirty Communists!" Some of the patrons joined in the resistance, taking up the axe handles, known as "Pickrick drumsticks," that Maddox sold for two dollars apiece. The incident made Maddox a celebrity, a symbol of resistance to integration. Before 1966, he had run unsuccessfully for mayor of Atlanta and for lieutenant governor of Georgia. He carried his axe handle throughout his campaign for governor.[28]

Although Carter ran an energetic campaign, he finished third in the Democratic primary, behind Arnall and Maddox. Stunned by his loss, Carter refused to endorse either candidate in the runoff for the Democratic nomination. Due in part to Republican crossover votes from those who thought Maddox would be a less formidable opponent for Callaway, Maddox won the runoff, and in the general election Callaway won a plurality of votes, but not a majority. Under Georgia law (subsequently changed), in such a circumstance the state legislature chose the new governor. Lester Maddox, the segregationist, was sworn in as governor of Georgia on January 10, 1967.[29]

JIMMY Carter was stung and embittered by his loss. Decades later, when talking about disappointment during a Sunday-school class, he reflected on his defeat in the race for governor in 1966. "In many ways I was alienated from politics and even from God," he said. "I blamed everybody except myself for my defeat. I was taken aback because the man who defeated me was a racist." Elsewhere, he acknowledged that some of his anger was directed toward God. Maddox's racism, in Carter's reckoning, rendered him utterly unworthy of political office: "I could not believe that God, or the Georgia voters, would let this person beat me and become governor of our state."[30]

Carter returned to Plains disappointed and deeply in debt. He had lost more than twenty-two pounds in his campaign exertions. Lillian said that her son "cried like a baby," and a cousin found him walking alone in a peanut field, utterly dejected. Peter Bourne, a psychiatrist and an early supporter, diagnosed Carter as having "an acute reactive depression."[31]

In his campaign autobiography, Carter characterized himself as bouncing back almost immediately from defeat, with the resolve: "I did not intend to lose again." But as he conceded elsewhere, the healing process was in fact considerably more protracted. The unsuccessful campaign had dealt a blow to his confidence, and he began a period of intense introspection. About this time, the pastor at Plains Baptist Church preached a sermon entitled "If You Were Arrested for Being a Christian, Would There Be Enough Evidence to Convict You?" The sermon hit home. "I'd never done much for other people," Carter concluded. "I was always thinking about myself."[32]

Carter's sister, Ruth Carter Stapleton, moved Jimmy farther along the road toward religious renewal. By the mid-1960s, Ruth had married a veterinarian, moved to North Carolina, and reared a family. After her own bout with depression, she decided to attend college and study theology, emerging as a successful pentecostal evangelist and author of popular books. Her brother described Ruth's ministry as traveling around the world and addressing large audiences about cultivating a fuller life "based on an intimate relationship with Jesus Christ."[33]

In the wake of the 1966 campaign, Ruth Carter Stapleton took on one of her most formidable projects: her older brother. "I talked about my awareness of Christ," Ruth remembered, "and I shared with Jimmy how it was to come to a place of total commitment, the peace and joy and the power it brings." She remembered her brother becoming emotional, moved to tears. Jimmy Carter recalled the episode in much the same way, although he denied coming to tears. "Ruth drove down to see me," Carter remembered, and urged him to learn from his disappointment, to understand his loss as a summons to spiritual maturity. Ruth suggested to her brother that he was ready for a transcendent religious experience similar to ones she described in her lectures. Jimmy initially rejected that notion, but he eventually embraced it.

Decades later, Carter summarized his understanding of the experience: "I put my faith completely in God."[34]

Some pentecostals would have interpreted this renewal as a "second blessing" of the Holy Spirit, the moment when the Holy Spirit enters into an individual as it did with the disciples after Christ's ascension, prompting them to speak in tongues. Despite his exposure to pentecostalism through the conduit of his sister, Carter's religious experience in 1967 did not take the form of speaking in tongues. What he shared in common with the "second blessing" experience of pentecostals, however, was the conviction that his religious commitments demanded expression in concrete acts of charity toward others.

This transcendent moment occurred the year following Carter's election loss. "I recognized for the first time that I had lacked something very precious—a complete commitment to Christ, a presence of the Holy Spirit in my life in a more profound and personal way," Carter declared. "And since then I've had an inner peace and inner conviction and assurance that transformed my life for the better." If his religious experience and subsequent baptism at age eleven constituted his "born again" moment, Carter, in evangelical parlance, "rededicated" his life to Jesus following his gubernatorial loss. That moment in 1967, Carter said, was "a deeply profound religious experience that changed my life dramatically."[35]

Once Carter emerged onto the national scene, Ruth was frequently asked about that interaction; she repeatedly corrected the impression that she was responsible for Jimmy's "born again" conversion. "No, I think Jimmy was a born-again Christian from early, early years," she told U.S. News & World Report in 1978. "He's always been very devout." Elsewhere, Ruth explained that "Jimmy was having a series of awarenesses of some lacks in his life, maybe motivation, a sense of direction." Her brother wondered, she said, "whether he was doing enough, caring enough for mankind." His religious experience signaled a "deeper commitment" and "a new phase of life that he was moving into. It was to serve Christ in his work."[36]

Jimmy Carter had his own understanding. "In 1967, I realized my own relationship with God was a very superficial one," he said. "I began to realize that my Christian life, which I had always professed to be preeminent, had really been a secondary interest in my life, and I formed a very close, personal intimate relationship with God through Christ."[37]

Church, thereafter, became far more meaningful, Carter said. He took a new interest in lay missionary work, serving a week-long mission in Loch

Haven, Pennsylvania, during May 1968, and another in Springfield, Massachusetts, in November of the same year. "The whole week was almost a miracle to me," Carter said about his time in Pennsylvania. "I felt the sense of the presence of God's influence in my life." Carter remembered knocking on doors. "We approached each family with sincere prayers, and learned to rely on the presence of the Holy Spirit to overcome our timidity and uncertainties," he wrote. "I was fairly successful," Carter remembered, "with the help of my associates and with the presence of the Holy Spirit."[38]

The assignment in Springfield, Massachusetts, was even more formative. There, Carter met Eloy Cruz, a Cuban-American pastor of a small church in Brooklyn. Cruz was Carter's companion on the mission to Springfield, and Carter later referred to him as "a hero of mine." Their task, according to Carter, was to evangelize Puerto Ricans who had settled in Springfield. With his rudimentary command of Spanish, Carter would read the Bible, and Cruz would preach. "I was amazed at how their attitude was transformed; he didn't seem to me that he was all that eloquent," Carter told his Sunday-school class. "But there was something about him, obviously the presence of the Holy Spirit that amazed me." At the conclusion of their week together, Carter asked Cruz for the secret of his success. "He was very embarrassed; he thought I was much superior to him," Carter said. "He finally said that he didn't know much about theology," Carter recounted, but he said, "Señor Jimmy, we only need to have two loves in our lives: for God, and for the person who happens to be in front of us at any time."[39]

Carter paused in his recounting of that moment. "I don't know of a more profound and practical philosophy than that, or theology," he said. "It's easy to say, 'I love God, and I love those poor people in Haiti or Togo or Mozambique, or I love those poor folks over on the other side of town.'" Loving God and the person in front of you, however, requires diligence and persistence. Jesus did this, Carter continued. Jesus, in fact, went out of his way to encounter those on the margins, Carter said, "tax collectors, lepers, adulterers, prostitutes, Samaritans, Gentiles."[40]

Out of the crucible of defeat in his quest for governor in 1966, Jimmy Carter's conversations with his sister led to a transformative religious experience. His embrace of evangelical Christianity, more fervent than before, reordered his priorities and impelled him to do evangelistic work on a scale and with a passion that exceeds that of most evangelicals. But Carter's redoubled faith in no way diminished his political ambitions. Even in the midst of his own religious renewal, he never took his eyes off of the Georgia statehouse.

"There was never the slightest hesitancy on my part about what to do," he recalled. "I thought I could run and win, and I never worried at all about who else might be in the race against me."[41]

Carter's understanding of Reinhold Niebuhr provided an appreciation for paradox. The burden of politics, as Carter said many times, quoting Niebuhr, was to "establish justice in a sinful world." Carter was eager to play that role—to establish justice—but he wanted a political office from which to do so. As it unfolded, his second campaign for governor would be mired in paradox—a newly devout evangelical engaged in tawdry politicking, albeit with the goal of doing good once in office.

In 1958 in neighboring Alabama, a circuit court judge named George C. Wallace had run against John Patterson in the Democratic primary for governor. Patterson enjoyed the support of the Ku Klux Klan, and Wallace was endorsed by the National Association for the Advancement of Colored People. After Wallace lost the primary, he famously vowed that no one would "ever out-nigger me again." Although Carter was never explicit about it, and he would never be guilty of such offensive language, his 1970 campaign for governor suggests a similar resolve.[42]

As he prepared for his second gubernatorial campaign, Carter traveled and lectured across the state to various civic groups. He filled in for vacationing preachers. He chaired the state chapter of the March of Dimes as well as a Billy Graham evangelistic initiative, featuring a motion picture called *The Restless Ones*, in nearby Americus, a project that Carter declared had yielded over five hundred "decisions for Christ." After each screening of the movie, Carter stepped to the front of the theater and, in classic evangelical style, invited viewers to walk forward and give their lives to Jesus. "Everyone was startled," Carter said, because they witnessed "black and white people walking down the aisles, together, in front of the theater, to place their faith in Christ."[43]

Polls in 1968, two years ahead of the next gubernatorial election, indicated that Carter, who had yet to announce his candidacy, was favored over both Callaway and Carl Sanders, a popular former governor. (Under Georgia law at the time, Maddox could not run for a second consecutive term, although he would eventually run for lieutenant governor.) During one of his many public appearances, this time in Athens, Georgia, Carter playfully admitted that his peregrinations throughout the state were motivated by something other than "strictly to sell seed peanuts." In 1967, back in Plains,

Rosalynn had given birth to Amy Lynn Carter. On April 3, 1970, Jimmy Carter announced his candidacy for governor in the Georgia statehouse, holding Amy in his arms.[44]

Carter's road to the governor's mansion, however, was by no means assured, especially if he positioned himself as a racial moderate. White resentment over the Civil Rights Act of 1964, the Voting Rights Act of 1965, and desegregation in general had congealed into rage. George Wallace, the segregationist governor of Alabama, had won Georgia's electoral votes in the presidential election of 1968 with his rallying cry of "states' rights," thinly coded language for the South's resistance to federal mandates for racial integration.

Toward the other end of the political spectrum sat Carl Sanders, who would emerge as Carter's principal opponent in the Democratic primary. Sanders had been considered a moderate during his term as governor, from 1963 until 1967. Ineligible for a second consecutive term because of Georgia law at the time, Sanders was trying to return as governor after the interval of Lester Maddox's term. In his second run for governor in 1970, Sanders quickly harvested the endorsements of many groups—sheriffs, bankers, lawyers, and the like—as well the state's major newspapers. A poll commissioned by the Carter campaign in the fall of 1969 found that Sanders enjoyed a favorable rating among 84 percent of Georgia voters; 20 percent graded him "excellent."[45]

An analysis of that poll, written by W. Van Loan for the Carter campaign, put the matter starkly: "In reviewing the opinion research study conducted last September, there is no question that Jimmy Carter has an uphill fight to gain the democratic [*sic*] nomination." Van Loan suggested that the candidate "position himself as the champion of the average guy, while at the same time *not* pander to racial bigotry." Such a campaign was tricky, but possible. "I don't think it is a question of how far right Jimmy has to go," the analysis concluded. "I firmly believe that the common man can be won by appealing to his aspirations and his basic humanity."[46]

Carter decided that the path to victory lay in conducting an aggressive, negative campaign. He portrayed Sanders as brash and ambitious. The Carter campaign suggested that Sanders had profited from his political connections, not necessarily while governor but after he left office. "Cuff Links Carl," as the Carter campaign branded its opponent, was too liberal and too citified for most Georgians, too beholden to the power élite and to the Washington establishment. Repeatedly, Carter declared that "Georgians never again want a governor who will use the tremendous power and prestige of office for his own personal wealth." Carter, meanwhile, characterized himself as an outsider, a peanut farmer, someone who understood the average working people of Georgia.[47]

Carter's campaign as a populist, however, sometimes verged into race-baiting. Although Carter sought the votes of African Americans, he also courted Wallace voters, even to the point of appropriating Wallace's campaign slogan, "our kind of man," generally recognized as shorthand for a working person who opposed integration. The Carter campaign circulated a photograph, which originally ran in the *Atlanta Constitution*, showing Sanders, part owner of the Atlanta Hawks basketball team, being doused with champagne by black members of the team in the course of a victory celebration. The photograph accomplished several purposes for the Carter campaign—associating Sanders with wealth (as an owner), alcohol, and African Americans. Campaign operatives, who referred to themselves as the "stink tank," also made sure voters knew that Sanders had attended the funeral of Martin Luther King Jr.[48]

Toward the close of the campaign, the *Macon Telegraph* captured the paradox of Carter the man and Carter the candidate. The newspaper called Carter "a good man whose high standards have been undermined by political ambition." Carter sought the endorsement of Roy V. Harris, an influential figure among white Georgians who had served as president of the Citizens' Councils of America from 1958 until 1966, the umbrella organization for local chapters of the White Citizens' Council. Harris edited the *Augusta Courier*, a segregationist tabloid, and served on George Wallace's campaign committee for the state in 1968. As member of the state board of regents, Harris opposed the racial integration of the University of Georgia and other schools in the state system; he applauded the rioting of white students at the University of Georgia on January 11, 1961, in opposition to the enrollment of two black students. In the course of the 1970 campaign, Carter met with Harris behind closed doors, and despite Carter's principled refusal to join the White Citizens' Council back in Plains, he emerged from the meeting with Harris's endorsement.[49]

Carter's avid courting of disgruntled white segregationists paid off. In the Democratic primary against Sanders, he captured 48.6 of the total vote, just shy of the 50 percent needed to avoid a runoff. The *Washington Post* credited Carter's victory to his "ear to the ground"; though once considered the most liberal candidate in the race, Carter had changed course and, similar to George Wallace, appealed to the base instincts of white Georgia voters.

As the *Post* noted, Carter "spoke the voters' frustrations aloud for them." Sanders, the second-place finisher, vowed to "take his coat off" and plunge into the fray of the runoff. Although Sanders took to the offensive, calling Carter a liar, a "smiling hypocrite," and an "unprincipled grinning chameleon," Carter dismissed the attacks as the rantings of a "sore loser." In the runoff against Sanders for the Democratic nomination, Carter won 60 percent of the vote. "Carter ran as a George Wallace segregationist," Sanders recalled decades later. "He put me in the position of being a liberal integrationist."[50]

Having dispatched Sanders in the Democratic primary, Carter faced the Republican nominee, Hal Suit, a political novice, in the general election. Although Carter softened some of his segregationist rhetoric, he continued the line of attack he had used so effectively against Sanders, calling Suit a liberal and suggesting that he was more interested in the favor of political allies in Washington than the people of Georgia.

At the conclusion of Carter's four-year quest for the statehouse, he left nothing to chance. He was willing even to swallow hard and endorse his political nemesis, Lester Maddox, the Democratic candidate for lieutenant governor. On the final day of the general-election campaign, Carter announced that he intended to vote for Maddox, the axe-handle-wielding outgoing governor. "Lester Maddox," Carter said, "is the embodiment of the Democratic Party." Carter prevailed handily in the general election, winning 59.3 percent of the vote.[51]

Despite its unsavory moments, the campaign also provided Carter with his trademark as a populist. By his own reckoning, he delivered more than eighteen hundred speeches in the four years between 1966 and 1970, and he and Rosalynn shook more than 600,000 hands. He crisscrossed the state tirelessly, often arriving back in Plains long past midnight to grab a few hours of sleep before heading off in the early morning for another round of country stores, Lions clubs, street corners, or shift changes at factories. When he couldn't return to Plains, Carter stayed in the homes of local citizens rather than hotels; it allowed him to save campaign resources and also to connect with the concerns of ordinary people. No one outworked Jimmy Carter. That was part of his appeal. It was one of the characteristics that set him apart from "Cuff Links Carl" Sanders and other politicians who sometimes gave the impression that they were entitled to election.

Carter finally had attained his goal, but doing so had exacted a fearsome cost. Although few people questioned the sincerity of Carter's religious renewal following the 1966 campaign, his 1970 campaign for governor, with its unabashed courting of segregationists, could hardly be characterized as godly or charitable. Taking a page out of George Wallace's playbook, Carter had won the election, but he also suffered from a bad conscience. On election night, Carter's aide Hamilton Jordan remembered, "I said, 'Well, Jimmy, I guess it's about time to start calling you governor,' and he just shrugged and said, 'Well, whatever you want.' He didn't seem the least bit excited about it." Carter's only prospect for redemption lay in his conduct as governor, the office for which he had prostituted his integrity. "You won't like my campaign," Carter had warned Vernon Jordan, president of the National Urban League, during the course of his quest for the statehouse, "but you will like my administration."[52]

THREE

NEW SOUTH
GOVERNOR

On January 12, 1971, in the face of a biting wind and with Atlanta temperatures in the mid-fifties, Jimmy Carter took the oath of office as the seventy-sixth governor of Georgia. The Naval Academy band played "Anchors Aweigh," and the choir from Morris Brown College, a historically black school, sang "The Battle Hymn of the Republic." Shortly after Carter stepped to the podium to deliver his address, the sun poked through the clouds. The new governor was prepared immediately to make amends for the campaign just past, the campaign that had propelled him to this time and place. "At the end of a long campaign, I believe I know the people of this state as well as anyone," he said. "Based on this knowledge of Georgians north and south, rural and urban, liberal and conservative, I say to you quite frankly that the time for racial discrimination is over." The new governor's declaration met with tepid applause from whites in the audience; racial reconciliation was still a long way off, both in Georgia and in the nation. Six hundred miles northeast of Atlanta, in Washington, D.C., African-American members of the House of Representatives met that same day to form the Black Congressional Caucus.[1]

In the course of the campaign just past, Reinhold Niebuhr's "sad duty of politics" had taken on a valence beyond the lofty task of establishing justice in a sinful world. For the new governor, winning political office had been a tawdry affair. Carter might have mounted an end-justifies-the-means defense of his campaign—do whatever necessary to win the office and then act on your nobler impulses as governor—but all of those Sunday-school lessons and all of his reading in theology left little doubt about the moral bankruptcy of that argument. The campaign left a bitter taste in his mouth, especially the racist overtones. Carter, according to some accounts, promised Rosalynn that he would "never go through such a campaign again." An associate of Carl Sanders reported that a distraught Carter called his defeated opponent to apologize for the personal attacks. But clearly all was not forgiven: On the dais at Carter's inauguration, the seat assigned to Carl Sanders was vacant. The former governor had elected not to attend.[2]

During his inaugural address, Carter appeared eager to revisit the campaign, almost in an effort to telegraph his regrets. "I realize that the test of a leader is not how well he campaigned," Carter said, "but how effectively he meets the challenges and responsibilities of the office." The new governor was ready to reclaim his better self. "Our inherent human charity and our religious beliefs will be taxed to the limit," he told his fellow Georgians. "No poor, rural, weak, or black person should ever have to bear the additional burden of being deprived of the opportunity of an education, a job, or simple justice."[3]

The national press paid little notice to Carter's apparent apology and focused instead on his remarkable declaration calling for an end to racial discrimination. An article on the front page of the *New York Times* the following morning opened with Carter's inauguration, pointing out that the new governor "delighted blacks in his inaugural audience by making an unqualified call for an end to racial discrimination in Georgia." Noting Carter's physical resemblance to John F. Kennedy, the article hailed the new governor, along with Dale Bumpers of Arkansas and Reuben Askew of Florida, as part of "a new generation of moderates taking office this month in the South." The *Times* characterized these new governors as "basically liberal, but in the election campaign they all struck moderate to conservative positions."[4]

Carter embodied these contradictions—a left-of-center politician who, during the heat of the campaign, hedged to the right, even to the point of race-baiting. The media, however, were more interested in heralding him as a representative of the New South, an embodiment of a region prepared to move finally beyond racial animosities. Carter's visage appeared on the cover of the May 31, 1971, issue of *Time* magazine, with a banner that read, "Dixie Whistles a Different Tune." The cover story opened with Carter's inaugural quote that "the time for racial discrimination is over" and limned the story of the peanut farmer's improbable, yet determined rise to the statehouse. Again invoking Carter's resemblance to John Kennedy, the article quoted the governor at length. "I know my people, and I am saying what they are thinking," Carter said. "Our black and white citizens have decided there will be no more restraint on their search to work together. Our problems and our opportunities are completely mutual." Carter's rhetoric was clearly aspirational, and it belied his comportment during the campaign. The article concluded that "Carter is a man as contradictory as Georgia itself, but determined to resolve some of the paradoxes."[5]

IN order for Carter to claim his mantle as representative of the New South, however, his first task was to resolve the paradoxes within himself, specifically the disjunction between his campaign and his convictions. Although he would insist in later years that, "I was the same person before and after I became governor," Carter recognized that he needed to chart a different course as governor from what he had suggested as candidate. Carter's inaugural address had declared that the "major and difficult decisions" surrounding racial relations had already been decided, albeit by forces outside the state, a reference to federal laws outlawing segregation. Now, the governor continued, Georgians faced the challenge of "hundreds of minor decisions" related to the implementation of those larger changes. To exercise the requisite leadership, Carter sought to reclaim his evangelical convictions.[6]

In the New Testament, for instance, Jesus characterized his followers as those who fed the hungry, clothed the naked, healed the sick, and visited those in prison. Carter believed that "improving the criminal justice system in my state could be my greatest contribution as governor." He reformed Georgia's prisons, adding education and treatment programs, increasing dramatically the number of professional counselors in the corrections system.

Carter especially made his mark in race relations. He appointed dozens of African Americans to policy positions in corrections, pardon and parole boards, law enforcement, professional examination boards, and the university system. He called for the peaceful integration of public schools. The governor's intervention defused volatile racial tensions in Macon and Sparta, Georgia. Carter developed a friendship with Andrew Young, an associate of Martin Luther King Jr. who in 1972 would become the first African American elected to Congress from Georgia since Reconstruction. LeRoy Johnson, a black state senator, called Carter the best governor for African Americans in "the history of the state." The redoubtable Benjamin E. Mays, president of Morehouse College and mentor to King, assured Carter that, among all of the governors in the state's colorful history, "your name stands among those at the top in the leadership for justice and fair play for all of the citizens of Georgia."[7]

Carter's support for African Americans, moreover, was symbolic as well as substantive. In October 1973, he announced that he had appointed a committee to honor three black Georgians with portraits to be hung in the state capitol. On a Sunday afternoon, February 17, 1974, Martin Luther King's portrait was unveiled. Carter hailed the martyred civil rights leader and insisted that the honor reflected "a change that has already taken place in the minds and hearts of the people I represent." A small contingent of the Ku Klux Klan, estimated by the *Atlanta Constitution* at fifteen, protested nearby. Coretta Scott King, present at the event, compared the occasion to her husband's Nobel Peace Prize a decade earlier, suggesting that the statehouse honor was "even in some ways more meaningful because it's here." Later, she thanked Carter for the gesture, adding that it "marked a significant step in the journey toward human dignity." Maynard Jackson, Atlanta's first African-American mayor, praised the "extraordinary strength and courage of our governor, Jimmy Carter." Six months later, Carter unveiled two additional portraits: Henry McNeal Turner, bishop of the African Methodist Episcopal Church, and Lucy Craft Laney, a school teacher from Augusta, Georgia.[8]

Carter addressed matters other than race. A disciplined and frugal man in his personal life, Carter believed that government should abide by those standards, so he pushed a bill through the legislature that authorized him to reorganize state government and thereby save taxpayers' money. But Carter never shared the reflexive distaste for government itself that other politicians professed. He believed that government could play—indeed, *must* play—an ameliorative role in society, that governing wisely would, in Niebuhr's words, advance "justice in a sinful world." Carter's agenda as governor, in fact, hewed closely to the principles of progressive evangelicalism. His Adequate Program for Education in Georgia plan provided money for vocational education, reduced class size, and equalized funding among school districts. Carter called attention to the disparity between rich and poor, arguing in a speech before the Lions Club convention for "a mandatory relationship between the powerful and the influential and the socially prominent and wealthy on the one hand, and the weak, the insecure and the poor on the other." Although many state agencies faced spending cuts, Carter increased the budget of the Department of Natural Resources and successfully thwarted plans by the Army Corps of Engineers to dam the Flint River, which flows from the upper Piedmont region south of Atlanta down into Carter's native southwest Georgia.

Looking beyond Georgia (and with an eye already on higher office), Carter expressed concern about world hunger and declared his support for the proposed Equal Rights Amendment to the United States Constitution. He called for an end to the war in Vietnam, careful at the same time to express support for American troops.[9]

Carter found other ways to distance himself from the stench of segregation and regain his footing as a liberal, at least by the standards of Georgia politics. When Richard Russell, Georgia's U.S. senator and implacable foe of integration, died only days into Carter's term, the governor passed over more conservative and conventional choices, including a former governor who had supported Carter's run for the statehouse, in favor of a liberal attorney, David Gambrell, to serve out Russell's term.

The chasm between Carter the candidate and Carter the governor grew so large that Lester Maddox, the lieutenant governor, accused Carter of acting as Edward M. Kennedy's surrogate in pursuing a liberal political agenda in Georgia. Carter replied drily that he had never met the senator from Massachusetts.[10]

ON racial matters, Carter's successful campaign for governor in 1970 had shown the candidate in less than flattering light, but it also reflected the pragmatic bent of both Carter himself and his aides. The core of advisers Carter assembled around him in 1970—and who would remain with him throughout the balance of his political career—were known more for loyalty than for ideological rigidity.

Charles Kirbo, a partner at the Atlanta law firm King and Spaulding, had signed on to help Carter with the legal challenges surrounding the contested 1962 election that eventually propelled Carter to the state senate. Although Kirbo's junior associate David Gambrell did most of the heavy lifting, Kirbo was intrigued with the earnest, young peanut farmer from southwest Georgia. Carter came to rely on Kirbo for advice, legal and otherwise, and Kirbo became Carter's chief of staff in the governor's office.[11]

Carter and Thomas Bertram "Bert" Lance shared a number of interests, including business, religion, and politics. Lance, grandson of a Methodist circuit rider, had married into wealth and risen from clerk to president of First National Bank in Calhoun, Georgia. Lance advised the 1966 campaign and remained with Carter, in one capacity or another, for more than two decades. During Carter's term in Atlanta, Lance served as state highway director and ran unsuccessfully to succeed Carter as governor in 1974.[12]

Hamilton Jordan, nephew of Clarence Jordan of Koinonia Farm in Americus, often referred to himself as a "political animal." Ineligible for military service because of flat feet and a bad knee, Jordan went to Vietnam instead with a humanitarian organization, International Voluntary Services, and returned an opponent of the war. After Jordan heard Carter address the Elks Club in Albany during the course of the 1966 campaign, he volunteered as youth coordinator. Four years later, Carter hired him to manage his second gubernatorial campaign.[13]

Joseph Lester Powell Jr., known as Jody, grew up in Vienna, Georgia, about forty miles from Plains. After he was caught cheating on a history examination, Powell was dismissed from the U.S. Air Force Academy for violating the honor code. He bounced around for several years, completed his degree at Georgia State University, married, and began a doctoral program at Emory University. In the course of his studies, Powell analyzed the results of the 1966 gubernatorial primary and noticed this dark-horse candidate from his own corner of Georgia who ran a liberal campaign and very nearly qualified for the runoff. Powell contacted Carter, who invited him to Plains where discussions were already under way about the 1970 campaign. Powell signed on as Carter's personal assistant.[14]

Other aides—Gerald Rafshoon, Stuart Eizenstat, Jack Watson, and others—would later join Carter's inner circle, but the 1970 campaign apparatus, under Jordan's direction, had proven both effective and efficient. It would be this same group of advisers, led by Jordan, who both recognized and stoked Carter's ambitions for higher office.

CARTER never spoke publicly about when he began contemplating a run for the presidency, but a cryptic line from Rosalynn's autobiography suggests that the new governor and first lady of Georgia discussed the matter between themselves as early as their move into the governor's mansion in January 1971. "We had been thinking privately that Jimmy might run for President in 1976," Rosalynn wrote, reflecting on the stream of Democratic politicians who headed to Atlanta to pitch their candidacies for the 1972 Democratic presidential nomination. Carter received them—Henry M. "Scoop" Jackson of Washington, George S. McGovern of South Dakota, Hubert Humphrey of Minnesota, Edmund Muskie of Maine, George C. Wallace of Alabama—and listened to their appeals. The contenders for the 1972 Democratic nomination left him underwhelmed. If they could be considered presidential timber, why couldn't he? "I lost my feeling of awe about presidents," he wrote. Besides, Carter was constitutionally limited to one term as Georgia governor, and the U.S. Senate held little interest for him; if Carter wanted to continue his political ascent, he needed to transfer his ambitions into a larger arena. The parade of candidates coming through Atlanta served merely to build Carter's confidence in his own prospects.[15]

In laying the groundwork for his presidential run, Carter began to court like-minded believers. On Wednesday, April 26, 1972, he strode to the podium at the Civic Center in Atlanta to address the delegates gathered for the General Conference of the United Methodist Church. Carter opened with a homey anecdote about selling bags of peanuts in the nearby town of Plains. "I very quickly was able to judge," he said, who were the good people and who were not: "The good people were the ones who bought boiled peanuts from me, and the bad ones were the ones that didn't."[16]

In what evangelicals would readily recognize as a "testimony," a public declaration of faith, the governor quickly segued into an unabashed statement of conviction. "I am a peanut farmer and a Christian," he declared. "I am a father, and I am a Christian. I am a business man and a Christian. I am a politician and a Christian." Then, lest anyone miss his point, Carter continued. "The single most important factor in my own life is Jesus Christ," he said, "and I have a very deep feeling of inadequacy as Governor responsible for the vision and inspiration, the problems, the hopes, the dreams, the doubts, the fears, the prejudices of 4.5 million people." He spoke of the difficult decisions he faced and said that he had found guidance for his task in the writings of Reinhold Niebuhr, especially his declaration that "the purpose of politics is to establish justice in a sinful world."[17]

Carter invoked the New Testament injunction to visit the prisoners when he told of meeting incarcerated men in Georgia and observing that almost invariably they were poor and lacking in political influence. This forced the governor to reconsider his views of the penal system. Carter believed that it was his responsibility to persuade the people of Georgia "that a man who has sinned against the law is worthy of love and compassion and understanding and retraining, that he deserves a chance for rehabilitation, that he hungers, as we do, for an amount of human dignity."[18]

Carter acknowledged that people in the South still struggled with the issue of race, but he said that changes were coming. He recalled that after his defeat in the race for governor in 1966 he reluctantly agreed to head a mission program in his home county. He characterized the enterprise as "the first interracial religious effort in the history of our county." Carter then recounted his time as a missionary in Springfield, Massachusetts, with Eloy Cruz, and he repeated Cruz's advice about the importance of having "two loves in your heart, one for Jesus Christ and the other one for whatever person happens to be in front of you at any particular time."[19]

The governor was not averse to dropping a few names in front of the assembled Methodists. He noted that he had hosted Billy Graham at a recent governor's prayer breakfast and concluded his remarks by invoking another Protestant religious leader, Paul Tillich. In typical evangelical fashion, the governor asked for prayers and invoked "our common commitment to a love for Christ and a love for the man who happens to be in front of us at any given time."[20]

The Methodists responded with a standing ovation.[21]

Carter clearly recognized the political advantages of his religious commitment, and he spoke the argot of evangelicalism both fluently and unabashedly. For example, he told an international gathering of the Christian and Missionary Alliance that, "My family, my business customers, the people of Georgia know that the most important thing in my life is Jesus Christ" and that "the most important pursuit for us in this present life and for eternity is to let others know about the grace of God in our own lives and what it can mean to them." The head of the denomination responded enthusiastically. "I'm sure none of us wants to mix politics with this occasion," he said, "but regardless of our party affiliation, Governor, I hope if the Lord tarries, that all of us will have opportunity to vote for you for some national office sometime in the future."[22]

Billy Graham was also impressed. He admired Carter's "genuine and unashamed Christian commitment." Graham asked the Georgia governor to serve as honorary chair of the evangelist's 1973 Atlanta revival campaign, held over a series of evenings at Atlanta Stadium. "Almost every night," Graham recalled, "he sat on the platform with us to indicate his support."[23]

In positioning himself for a presidential campaign, Carter frequently invoked the vocabulary of evangelicalism. "I'm a born-again Christian," he told a reporter for the *National Courier* early in his term as governor, "and I don't want anything that's not God's will for my life." When pressed about whether his faith was compatible with politics, Carter acknowledged the possibility of tension, but he refused to back down. "I think every one of us in our own lives has inherent conflicts built in as we equate our Christian beliefs with our worldly responsibilities," he said. "I've found when I reassert my relationship with God, conflicts disappear." Still, Carter was careful to portray his religious life as nothing out of the ordinary. "I wouldn't want it connoted as a mystical set of events," he said of his spiritual experience following his conversation with his sister Ruth. "It's a typical experience among Christians."[24]

CARTER was also looking beyond the religious vote. Although it was premature to mount his own run for the Democratic nomination, Carter, with the 1976 campaign already in mind, was eager to step onto the national political stage. George Wallace, who was badly injured by a gunman at a Maryland shopping center on May 15, 1972, leaving the governor paralyzed from the waist down, avidly sought Carter's support. Carter held him at bay, even though some of his advisers believed that if Carter nominated Wallace at the Democratic National Convention it would propel the Georgia governor into the national spotlight. Carter rejected that idea, convinced that Wallace, because of his racial views, was not "fit to lead the American people." The Georgia governor instead threw his support behind Henry Jackson, the senator from Washington, a move that placed him at odds with the front-runner going into the Democratic National Convention, George McGovern. Carter, fearing that McGovern was too liberal and that his candidacy would fizzle in the South, led a forlorn, last-minute effort to deny McGovern the nomination.[25]

At the convention itself, held in Miami Beach, the Jackson camp invited Carter to place Jackson's name in nomination. Carter readily agreed, although the speech did not harvest the publicity that Carter had sought. Changes to party rules between 1968 and 1972 had produced the desired effect of making the Democratic National Convention more open and participatory, one more accommodating to women and minorities and less pliable at the hands of political bosses. But the business of the convention was bogged down by endless parliamentary delays and roll-call votes. Carter delivered his speech well past prime time, and it made little impression on the distracted McGovern delegates eager to nominate their candidate.

The following day, with McGovern's nomination assured, Carter waited by the phone in hopes that McGovern might tap the Georgia governor as his running mate. McGovern, however, had no inclination to run on the same ticket with the man who had sought to derail his nomination; the candidate chose his Senate colleague instead, Thomas Eagleton of Missouri. Carter received twenty-seven votes for the vice-presidential nomination, all from members of the Georgia delegation.[26]

JIMMY and Rosalynn Carter returned from the Democratic National Convention disappointed, but determined. Weeks later, on October 17, 1972, Hamilton Jordan, Carter's executive secretary, convened a meeting with Carter and several top aides. "Governor," Jordan began, "we've come to tell you what you're going to do about your future." On November 4, 1972, the day before George McGovern suffered a landslide loss to the incumbent president, Richard Nixon, Jordan presented Carter with a seventy-page memorandum that outlined how Carter could win both the Democratic nomination and the presidency of the United States in 1976. "It is my hope that this memorandum will stimulate your own thinking and will serve as a starting point for the formulation of your plans," Jordan wrote. For too long, Jordan argued, the Democratic Party had looked to the Senate for its presidential candidates; a governor, on the other hand, could position himself both as an outsider to Washington and someone with executive experience. Although Edward M. Kennedy of Massachusetts was generally considered the favorite for the nomination four years hence, Jordan had doubts that Kennedy would run, due both to family obligations and to the lingering memory of Chappaquiddick, the 1969 incident when a car the senator was driving plunged off a bridge on Martha's Vineyard, killing his female companion. Jordan also believed that George Wallace, because of his physical limitations, would not run, and Jordan also foresaw that Wallace might even lose his bid for reelection as Alabama governor in 1974.[27]

At the time Jordan drafted his memorandum, the extent of Nixon's corruption, epitomized in the Watergate scandal, was not yet fully known; the break-in at the Democratic headquarters at the Watergate complex had occurred on June 17, 1972, and the Nixon White House cover-up had held through Election Day, thereby assuring Nixon's reelection. Nevertheless, Jordan discerned a hankering for moral leadership in the nation, especially after the debacle of Vietnam. "Perhaps the strongest feeling in this country today is the general distrust and disallusionment [sic] of government and politicians at all levels," Jordan wrote. "The desire and thirst for strong moral leadership in this nation was not satisfied with the election of Richard Nixon," he added. "It is my contention that this desire will grow in four more years of the Nixon Administration." Carter, the outsider, the Southern Baptist Sunday-school teacher, had a real shot at both the nomination and the presidency.[28]

Jordan counseled Carter to shore up his foreign-policy credentials by reading, travel, and forming councils of advisers. Carter should read the *New York Times* every day, despite "its liberal orientation and bias." He suggested that Carter "continue to take a very active part in the affairs of the National Democratic Party," adding that "it is not too early to be thinking now about the primaries." Jordan pointed especially to New Hampshire, with its retail politics; he thought that Carter's "farmer-businessman-military-religious-conservative background would be well received there."[29]

As Carter and his aides began plotting the Georgia governor's ascent to the presidency, a remarkable movement was gathering force among evangelicals in the North in the early 1970s. After decades of relative apathy on the part of evangelicals, a small cohort sought to reclaim the mantle of progressive evangelicalism. Several catalysts prompted the movement: growing questions about the morality of the war in Vietnam, sensitivity toward issues of poverty and economic justice, and impatience with the progress toward equality for women and minorities. Add to that a disillusionment with Nixon, whom many evangelicals had supported, and this new generation of progressive evangelicals began to receive a hearing.

Ronald J. Sider, professor at Messiah College in Grantham, Pennsylvania, had led the way for more explicit involvement in the political process. In September 1972, Sider organized a small group called Evangelicals for McGovern, in support of the Democratic nominee, who was the son of a Methodist minister and himself a former seminary student. Jim Wallis, editor of the *Post-American* and a recent student at Trinity Evangelical Divinity School, hailed McGovern as "a first ray of hope in the midst of widespread despair." McGovern, who had fashioned his candidacy around opposition to the war in Vietnam and who had devoted his entire career to the alleviation of poverty and hunger, articulated positions consistent with progressive evangelicalism throughout the campaign. Robert Webber, a professor at Wheaton College and another member of Sider's new group, praised McGovern for his concern about "hunger, war, poverty and ecology."[30]

The signal achievement of Evangelicals for McGovern was an appearance at Edman Chapel on the leafy, suburban campus of Wheaton College, at that time a bastion of conservative, white evangelicalism. (The student government issued invitations to both Nixon and McGovern, but Nixon declined.) On a Wednesday morning, October 11, 1972, McGovern stepped to the podium following an introduction by Tom Skinner, an African-American evangelist.

Although the Democratic nominee invoked his own evangelical past and credentials, Wheaton students responded with jeers, booing, and catcalls. Bands of students paraded around the perimeter of the chapel with huge Nixon campaign banners before, during, and after McGovern's address.[31]

Sider and other members of Evangelicals for McGovern, however, refused to abandon hope for a resurgence of progressive evangelicalism. Despite its failure to win the White House, McGovern's campaign had articulated the concerns of progressive evangelicals, and Sider wanted to amplify that message more broadly among evangelicals. "There is a new movement of major proportions within evangelical circles," Sider wrote. "It is still a minority movement, but it is widespread and growing."[32]

Over Thanksgiving weekend, 1973, a year and several weeks after McGovern's loss to Nixon, Sider convened a gathering of fifty-five evangelicals at the Chicago YMCA. Those in attendance included a veritable who's who of progressive evangelicalism: David O. Moberg, a sociologist at Marquette University; John F. Alexander, editor of *The Other Side*; John Perkins, founder of Voice of Calvary Ministries; Richard V. Pierard, historian at Indiana State University; Nancy A. Hardesty, who taught English at Trinity College in nearby Deerfield, Illinois; and Samuel Escobar, a theologian from Latin America. Jim Wallis, at that time head of the People's Christian Coalition and editor of the *Post-American*, which would later become *Sojourners*, remembers a diverse group, from places like Wheaton College, Calvin College, and Trinity College and Trinity Evangelical Divinity School. Also present were several prominent Southern Baptists, including Foy Valentine and James Dunn; Carl F. H. Henry, the founding editor of *Christianity Today* magazine, and his son, Paul Henry, who would later win a seat in Congress.

The conferees set about the task of crafting a document that would affirm the principles of progressive evangelicalism. Tom Skinner, the black evangelist who had introduced McGovern at Wheaton College, called on evangelicals to "emphasize social sins and institutionalized evils as vigorously as personal sins." Carl Henry, according to Wallis, was probably the most politically conservative voice in the room, someone reluctant to accede to some of the more radical sentiments expressed by the younger generation. Eventually, little by little, according to Wallis, Henry came around.[33]

The Chicago Declaration of Evangelical Social Concern won approval on November 25, 1973, and the tenets of the Chicago Declaration bore a striking similarity to the concerns of nineteenth- and early twentieth-century evangelicals. "We acknowledge that God requires justice," the Declaration read.

"But we have not proclaimed or demonstrated his justice to an unjust American society. Although the Lord calls us to defend the social and economic rights of the poor and oppressed, we have mostly remained silent." The Declaration condemned evangelical complicity in racism and strongly denounced the nation's reliance on militarism. It called attention to the problem of hunger and attacked the "materialism of our culture and the maldistribution of the nation's wealth and services."[34]

At the urging of Nancy Hardesty, the conferees also adopted language that challenged the prevailing evangelical ethic of male domination. "We acknowledge that we have encouraged men to prideful domination and women to irresponsible passivity," the statement read. "So we call both men and women to mutual submission and active discipleship."[35]

The Chicago Declaration was merely the most visible manifestation of this resurgence of progressive evangelicalism, which in its twentieth-century iteration emphasized equality for women and minorities, economic justice, and a repudiation of militarism. Several organizations emerged out of the Chicago Declaration to act on these impulses, including Evangelicals for Social Action, Evangelicals Concerned, and the Evangelical Women's Caucus. Others already in place, such as the National Black Evangelical Association, the People's Christian Coalition (Sojourners), and Voice of Calvary Ministries, tapped into the renewed energies of a resurgent progressive evangelicalism.[36]

Despite the absence of a national profile, some evangelicals had participated in politics at the local level in the middle decades of the twentieth century, even though most had avoided specific affiliation with political parties. After decades of fretting over how to be politically active (or whether they should be), a number of evangelicals by the mid-1970s were awakening to the possibility of organized politicking; some even ventured that it was good and godly to engage in such enterprises. The Chicago gathering suggests that evangelicals were beginning to talk, however tentatively, about organizing at the national level. The text of the Chicago Declaration itself demonstrated that at least a few of those evangelicals sought to reclaim the tradition of progressive evangelicalism, with its emphasis on nonviolence and peace, racial and sexual equality, economic justice, and care for those Jesus called "the least of these." Even the venue of the meeting, the Chicago YMCA, just down Wabash Street from the historic Pacific Garden Mission, symbolized a rededication on the part of evangelicals to their nineteenth-century concern for the urban poor.[37]

In the ensuing years, Wallis would expand the readership of the *Post-American*, move his operations from Chicago to Washington, D.C., and rename the magazine *Sojourners*. Other publications—*The Other Side, Eternity, Right On*, and others—propagated these themes of progressive evangelicalism and called for a new evangelical political activism, one that tilted toward the left of the political spectrum and advocated for those on the margins. In 1977, Sider himself published *Rich Christians in an Age of Hunger*, one of the most successful evangelical books of the decade, which challenged evangelicals to rethink their own complicity in a culture of consumerism that left so many of the world's people hungry and impoverished. By the end of the decade, even the reliably conservative *Christianity Today*, rarely in the vanguard of evangelical sentiment, was publishing articles with titles like "Human Rights: A Concern of the Righteous," "Our Response to the Poor," "Challenging Christians to the Simple Life," and "Finding the Energy to Continue."[38]

The writers of the Chicago Declaration had been careful to close their document by saying "we endorse no political ideology or party, but call our nation's leaders and people to that righteousness which exalts a nation." Not all of the signatories to the Chicago Declaration would come to see Jimmy Carter as an oracle for their sentiments; a few even opposed him vociferously, both from the right and from the left. Nor was Carter entirely sympathetic with every tenet of progressive evangelicalism, especially the suspicion of militarism. But the reassertion of progressive evangelicalism together with the prospective Carter campaign represented a confluence of interests that would alter the political and religious landscape of the 1970s.[39]

ALREADY on the campaign hustings in his improbable quest for the presidency, Jimmy Carter was sounding many of the same themes as the Chicago Declaration, especially racial reconciliation, women's equality, and calling attention to disparities of opportunity between rich and poor. Only months after the Chicago gathering, Carter seized the opportunity to broadcast those themes as an undercard speaker at Law Day in Athens, Georgia. The annual event at the University of Georgia Law School serves as an occasion to honor student achievements as well as to invite distinguished lecturers, and the roster of speakers for Law Day is impressive, ranging from Supreme Court justices and U.S. senators to ambassadors, secretaries of state, and attorneys general. The lecturer invited to give the annual Law Day Address in 1974 was Edward M. Kennedy, the senior senator from Massachusetts. Jimmy and Rosalynn Carter had hosted Kennedy in the governor's mansion before the Law Day event, a gesture of hospitality to be sure, but also an occasion to size up Carter's most formidable opposition for the 1976 Democratic nomination.

Kennedy, in his keynote address at the law school, spoke about the impeachment process then gearing up in the House of Representatives. The real challenge in the wake of Nixon's Watergate scandal, Kennedy said, was "whether America can still muster the strength and skill to carry on the work of rebuilding the people's shattered confidence in the integrity of their government."[40]

Two hours after Kennedy's speech, the next event on the Law Day calendar was the Law School Association luncheon. The featured speaker for this lesser event was the governor of Georgia. Carter opened by acknowledging his second-tier status as well as the fact that he was not a lawyer. "My own interest in the criminal justice system is very deep and heartfelt," he said, adding that his own sense of justice derived from two sources. The first was Reinhold Niebuhr and his mandate to establish justice in a sinful world; Niebuhr recognized the importance of law in establishing justice, Carter said. But the second source for Carter's sense of justice took everyone by surprise: Bob Dylan. It wasn't until he heard Dylan's "I Ain't Gonna Work on Maggie's Farm No More," Carter said, that he began to appreciate the plight of the poor, especially tenant farmers.[41]

Carter talked briefly about his accomplishments as governor, including the infusion of "hope and compassion" into the state's penal system. The thrust of the new program, he said, was "to try to discern in the soul of each convicted and sentenced person redeeming features that can be enhanced."[42]

Carter then unleashed a blistering extemporaneous critique, speaking to lawyers and prospective lawyers as a governor "who is still deeply concerned about the inadequacies of a system of which it is obvious that you're so patently proud." Kennedy, seated at the head table, looked quizzically at the Georgia governor. "I'm a Sunday-school teacher," Carter continued, "and I've always known that the structure of law is founded on the Christian ethic, that you shall love the Lord your God and your neighbor as yourself—a very high and perfect standard." Perfection, as Niebuhr reminds us, eludes humanity, but we must continue to strive for equality, Carter added. That task, however, is more difficult because the powerful and well connected wield an outsized influence on the legislative process, bending it to their advantage. The status quo, Carter argued, serves their interest: "This creates a reluctance to change because the powerful and the influential have carved out for themselves or have inherited a privileged position in society, of wealth or social prominence or higher education or opportunity for the future."[43]

Carter, seizing on one of the issues that had occupied progressive evangelicals in the nineteenth century, lamented the fact that Georgia's prison population consisted overwhelmingly of poor people; they are the only ones, he said, who serve time. Part of the problem, he suggested, is that "we assign punishment to fit the criminal and not the crime." Carter lit into lobbyists and noted that his attempt to pass an ethics bill was thwarted by lawyers. A similar situation obtained with regulatory agencies, whose regulations too often were written by industries themselves. "Is that fair and equitable?" Carter asked. "I don't think so." The audience fell utterly silent as Carter concluded his remarks by reciting the populist theme that he was already honing for his presidential bid. Any hope for the future, Carter said, lay in "the combined wisdom and courage and commitment and discernment of the common ordinary people."[44]

Carter's sentiments on prison reform and the abuse of power among the élite would have drawn favorable reviews from progressive evangelicals like Charles Grandison Finney or William Jennings Bryan. But Carter's Law Day address also captured the imagination of a journalist in the audience, Hunter S. Thompson. During the course of his speech, Carter noticed that Thompson had briefly left the room; he surmised that the self-proclaimed "gonzo journalist" had simply exited to refresh whatever adult beverage he was drinking that day. Thompson, however, scurried to the parking lot to retrieve a tape recorder so he could record what he believed was an extraordinary moment: a politician who dared to speak the truth.

"I have heard hundreds of speeches by all sorts of candidates and politicians," Thompson wrote later, "but I have never heard a sustained piece of political oratory that impressed me any more than the speech Jimmy Carter made at Law Day at the University of Georgia on that Saturday afternoon in May 1974." Thompson described it as a "bastard of a speech," and by the time it was over, "it had rung every bell in the room." Thompson had no idea that Carter had already decided to run for president, and if Carter had mentioned anything of the sort at the time, Thompson wrote, "I'm not sure I'd have taken him seriously." But if he had, Thompson continued, "I would probably have said he could have my vote, for no other reason except the speech I'd just heard."[45]

If Kennedy was offended by Carter's blunt remarks or astonished by the improbable affinity between Jimmy Carter, the Sunday-school teacher, and Hunter Thompson, the ruffian journalist, the senator didn't let on. His thank-you note to the Carters for his stay at the governor's mansion brimmed with patrician politeness. "The people of Georgia are fortunate to have the Carters as their first family," Kennedy wrote in appreciation, "and it was a delight for me to feel so welcome in your home."[46]

CARTER'S speech at Law Day was an unalloyed success. His articulation of progressive evangelical and populist themes won plaudits from those in the audience, including Thompson, and he upstaged his most formidable prospective rival for the 1976 Democratic nomination.

The Carters had barely settled into the governor's mansion when Jimmy Carter began laying the groundwork for a national campaign. He initially reached out to his most natural constituency, people of faith, and did so in language they understood. The modest surge of progressive evangelicalism in the early 1970s abetted his efforts by reinforcing the themes of equality and economic justice. On the political stage, the 1972 Democratic National Convention had introduced Carter to his fellow Democrats and, to a lesser degree, the nation. McGovern's overwhelming loss in the November election, though disastrous for the Democratic Party, paved the way for consideration of a less conventional candidate, someone outside of Washington. Indeed, leaders of the Democratic Party had already taken notice of the New South governor of Georgia. Late in 1973, Robert Strauss, chair of the Democratic National Committee, invited Carter to head the 1974 Democratic Congressional Campaign Committee, a post that would entail travel around the country and an opportunity to introduce himself to voters and office-holders.

Midway through his term as governor, Carter was already running, galloping, toward the White House, though at the time only a small cohort of family and his closest advisers knew it. Americans would soon become familiar with the peanut farmer and Sunday-school teacher from Plains.

FOUR

HE CAME UNTO
HIS OWN

IF evangelicals in the mid-1970s had knocked on the door of central casting in search of a political candidate they could support, they'd probably have asked for someone with political experience but who was not part of the Washington culture that had been so tainted by Richard Nixon and the Watergate scandal. Someone with a military record would be attractive. Although some evangelicals in the North, reflecting their admiration for Billy Graham, would probably have preferred a Republican, Nixon had so tarnished the brand that a Democrat from the South would probably be a good choice. If he were a Baptist—someone who understood the importance of the First Amendment and the separation of church and state—that would solidify the candidate's credentials as someone who understood that the Christian faith had flourished in the United States precisely because the government had stayed out of the religion business. And if central casting offered a candidate who was also openly pious and who regularly taught Sunday school, evangelicals might have pinched themselves.

Carter, the one-term governor of Georgia, fit all of those criteria. His positions and policies, moreover, were consistent with those of nineteenth-century evangelicalism—his concern about poverty and human rights, his support for public education, his quest for a less imperial foreign policy. Carter's positions, in fact, were remarkably similar to those articulated in the Chicago Declaration of Evangelical Social Concern, which called for an end to racism and the war in Vietnam, expressed support for feminism, and focused attention on the plight of the poor. While no one, least of all the organizers or the signatories, would claim that the sentiments expressed in the Declaration spoke for a *majority* of evangelicals in the middle of the twentieth century, the very existence of such a document attested to the persistence of such values within evangelicalism.

Even when Carter addressed nonreligious groups, he rehearsed the more generic themes of responsibility and integrity, drawing a clear contrast with the moral bankruptcy of the Nixon White House. Appearing before the American Bar Association in August 1973, Carter quoted scripture to criticize the embattled president, suggesting that Nixon's mendacity was undermining the nation. "If the trumpet give an uncertain sound," Carter said, quoting St. Paul's first letter to the Corinthians, "then who shall prepare himself for the battle?"[1]

Such principles also applied to policy. "A nation's domestic and foreign policy actions should be derived from the same standards of ethics, honesty, and morality which are characteristic of the individual citizens of the nation," Carter wrote in his campaign autobiography. To a populace still battered by the ignominious end to the war in Vietnam and stung by Nixon's deceit, Carter was ready with bromides to assure Americans of their innate goodness. "The people of this country are inherently unselfish, open, honest, decent, competent, and compassionate," he wrote. "Our government should be the same, in all its actions and attitudes."[2]

ON December 12, 1974, Jimmy Carter stood before the National Press Club in Washington to declare his candidacy for the Democratic nomination for president of the United States of America. "We Americans are a great and diverse people," Carter began, but our commitment to the American dream "has been sapped by debilitating compromise, acceptance of mediocrity, subservience to special interests, and an absence of executive vision and direction." Carter offered himself as someone who could heal the wounds of the nation and summon Americans to their better selves. "With the shame of Watergate still with us and our 200th birthday just ahead, it is time for us to reaffirm and to strengthen our ethical and spiritual and political beliefs," he said. Carter called for tax reform and universal access to health care, for a simplified and compassionate welfare program, nuclear disarmament, environmental protection, and an end to cronyism in diplomatic appointments. "Our people are hungry for integrity and competence in government," he said. Carter called attention to the line from his inaugural address as governor, when he declared that "the time for racial discrimination is over," and promised to champion racial equality.[3]

Still, Carter had a long road to travel to make it to the White House as president, far longer that the few short blocks that separated the National Press Club from 1600 Pennsylvania Avenue. He remained almost completely unknown to American voters. A year before he announced his candidacy, Carter had stumped the panelists on the television program *What's My Line?* Even after a round of intense questioning, none of the three celebrities could identify the governor of Georgia. A month before his announcement, a Harris poll sampled public opinion on thirty-five possible candidates for president; Jimmy Carter's name was not among them.

Following his appearance at the National Press Club, Carter flew to Atlanta for a second announcement in front of his fellow Georgians at the Atlanta Civic Center. He walked to the podium and said, "Hello! My name is Jimmy Carter, and I am running for president." The crowd of several thousand roared its approval. Throughout the campaign, Carter would use his faith and his reputation as a New South governor comfortable with racial diversity to appeal to voters, and he had already garnered a crucial ally, Andrew Young, an African-American minister and former associate of Martin Luther King Jr., to help him make his case. "Jimmy Carter is a good man," Young told a reporter for the *Washington Post*, "and I'll help him wherever he asks me to." Years later, Young recounted his attraction to Carter. "All of the liberals that I had worked with got nervous in a room full of black people, and Jimmy Carter didn't," Young said. "He was very comfortable, very relaxed. When I talked with him, I realized that he read more, he was more disciplined, more organized, his personal life was more meaningful. His religion was really way down deep in the marrow of his bones. And I said, that's the kind of guy that ought to be running this country."[4]

CARTER's road to the White House began in Iowa and New Hampshire. In March 1975, the still-obscure southern governor, on his way from Manchester, New Hampshire, to Concord, instructed his driver to pull off Route 3A in Hooksett, hard by the Merrimack River. At Robie's Country Store, the visitor ordered coffee and a doughnut, thrust his hand across the counter, and flashed a toothy grin. "Hi, I'm Jimmy Carter," he said, "and I'm running for president of the United States." Dorothy Robie, the woman behind the counter, called to her husband in the back office to come and meet the visitor. Lloyd Robie's response was later immortalized as the candidate's political fortunes began to rise. "Jimmy *who*?" he asked.[5]

Only two years after the drubbing George McGovern absorbed at the hands of Richard Nixon and the Committee to Re-Elect the President (universally known as CREEP), the Democratic nomination for president suddenly looked like a prize, one coveted by a growing number of Democratic politicians. Nixon and the Watergate scandal had so tarnished the Republican Party that Democrats believed the White House was theirs for the taking in 1976; the Democratic nominee, whoever it might be, seemed likely to become president. The early field of contenders was large and included senators and former senators: Birch Bayh of Indiana, Lloyd Bentsen of Texas, Robert Byrd of West Virginia, Fred Harris of Oklahoma, and Henry M. "Scoop" Jackson of Washington, the man Carter had nominated at the 1972 Democratic National Convention. Morris K. Udall, member of Congress from Arizona, was an early favorite among liberals. Several governors and former governors, who recognized, as Carter did, the appetite for someone outside of Washington, campaigned for the nomination: Terry Sanford of North Carolina, Milton Schapp of Pennsylvania, and George C. Wallace of Alabama. Ellen McCormack of New York, someone with no previous political experience, ran on a pro-life platform, and Sargent Shriver, McGovern's running mate four years earlier, also mounted a campaign for the nomination. Later in the primaries, too late to capture enough delegates, Frank Church, U.S. senator from Idaho, and Edmund G. "Jerry" Brown, governor of California, would enter the primaries.

Carter, however, understood what the other contenders seem not to have grasped, namely that, in the wake of the Nixon scandals, the path to the Democratic nomination coursed through the grass roots, not through party bosses or political operatives. The candidate best able to make connections with ordinary voters would prevail, and Iowa and New Hampshire provided the perfect venues to vindicate that strategy. The Iowa precinct caucuses in particular, where neighbors gathered with neighbors on a cold night in January to discuss their preferences for president, rewarded grassroots organizing. Carter brought to the campaign the same energy and determination he had mustered during his runs for governor. Before any other candidate had announced for the presidency, Carter had already traveled more than 50,000 miles and visited thirty-seven states. He believed that he could win the nomination—and the presidency—simply by outworking everyone else. "Seems like everywhere I've been lately, they tell me Jimmy Carter was just through there a week or so ago," Morris Udall, one of Carter's rivals for the Democratic nomination, complained. "The sonofabitch is as ubiquitous as the sunshine."[6]

Freed from his duties as governor with the inauguration of his successor on January 14, 1975, Carter plunged into the rigors of a grassroots candidacy for national office. A memorandum from Tim Kraft to Hamilton Jordan, dated August 28, 1975, reinforced the importance of Iowa. "Bear in mind that Iowa is first, a priority state," Kraft reminded Jordan. "Money can't buy the kind of press we'll get if JC finishes first in the precinct caucuses." By his own account, Carter visited 110 towns in Iowa, and Rosalynn visited 150; his sister Ruth's list of 6,000 Iowans who followed her ministry proved valuable. Carter's Iowa campaign, under Kraft's direction, asked supporters to show up and participate in the straw poll at the state Democratic Party's Jefferson-Jackson Day dinner at Iowa State University on October 26, 1975, nearly three months before the precinct caucuses. Carter received the largest share of votes, a showing that prompted the national press to pay more attention to the peanut farmer from Plains. "Jimmy Carter of Georgia appears to have taken a surprising but solid lead in the contest for Iowa's 47 delegates to the Democratic National Convention next year," an article on the front page of the October 27, 1975, *New York Times* read. "Iowans like courtesy and the personal touch," the story continued, and they found Carter's low-key style winsome. According to a county chairman, "He doesn't yell at them, and he answers questions."[7]

On January 19, 1976, Carter won a plurality in the Iowa precinct caucuses with 29.1 percent of the vote. The *New York Times* credited his "assiduous personal campaigning and rural style," which gave Carter a two-to-one margin over the second-place finisher, Birch Bayh of Indiana. "My husband and I wanted a fresh face and a new approach," a woman in Davenport, Iowa, said. "We wanted someone who could clean up the mess in Washington because he wasn't part of it." Carter, anticipating a victory, had traveled home to Georgia on the night of the caucuses but was back on the campaign trail the following morning.[8]

Carter's down-home, aw-shucks demeanor masked a fierce competitiveness. He may have marketed himself as an antipolitician, but he never lacked a politician's confidence in the effects of his charm. "I don't really believe this, of course," he said on the campaign trail in New Hampshire, "but I like to think that if I could shake the hand of every voter and just sit down and talk with them a little bit, I'd get every damned vote—every single one of them." A large part of Carter's appeal, however, lay in his apparent modesty and his provenance outside of Washington. When asked at a luncheon in Manchester, New Hampshire, what he thought might hamper his bid for the nomination, Carter coyly replied that he might be handicapped by the fact that he was not a lawyer or a member of Congress. "That's good," a voice rang out from the front table.[9]

Carter persisted in his grassroots populist campaign. Assisted once again by the "Peanut Brigade," supporters from Georgia who had ventured north to campaign for their former governor, Carter won the New Hampshire primary with 29.4 percent of the vote on February 24, 1976; his nearest rival, Udall, tallied 22.7 percent, with Bayh in third place at 15.1 percent. More important, Carter, a southerner, had proven that he could win in the North.

Carter's next primary victory was arguably his most important, both for himself as a representative of the New South and for the Democratic Party. On March 9, Carter defeated a fellow southern governor, George C. Wallace of Alabama, in the Florida primary. Andrew Young campaigned vigorously for his fellow Georgian, and Carter garnered 75 percent of the African-American vote. With that victory, not only did Carter claim for himself an entire region, he distanced the Democratic Party from its legacy of racism. Riffing on Wallace's 1972 campaign slogan, "Send Them a Message," Carter had invited Florida voters to "Send Them a President."[10]

The North Carolina primary was nearly as momentous. At a campaign event in Winston-Salem, just a few days before the March 23 primary, someone in the crowd asked Carter if he was a born-again Christian. Carter said yes, recalling later, "This has been a natural answer for me since I was a young adult." Although some of his advisers had urged the candidate to avoid using the overt language of evangelicalism, Carter disagreed, insisting that, "It will help me—even in California." Carter told the backyard gathering in North Carolina that he relied on his faith to help him navigate the rigors of political life. "I spent more time on my knees the four years I was Governor," he said, "in the seclusion of a little private room in the governor's office, than I did in all the rest of my life put together."[11]

Carter's declaration represented a departure from the norm in presidential politics. Ever since John F. Kennedy's speech before the Greater Houston Ministerial Association on September 12, 1960, in which he declared his absolute fidelity to the First Amendment and foreswore any influence from "outside religious pressure or dictates," a candidate's religious views simply did not figure into presidential politics. Few Americans knew, for instance, that Lyndon Johnson was affiliated with the Disciples of Christ or that Nixon was nominally a Quaker. Nixon's mendacity changed that equation, and Carter astutely recognized the desire on the part of voters to know that their president possessed a moral compass. Carter, the Sunday-school teacher, came by it honestly, and he spoke the language of born-again evangelicalism fluently.[12]

There was nothing new about Carter's declaration in Winston-Salem; he had made similar statements many times before. But it was made in full view of the national media and offered, once again, without shame or apology. By now, the press was paying attention. Carter weighed carefully how to handle the sudden media interest in his faith, and he decided not to back away. "If there are those who don't want to vote for me because I'm a deeply committed Christian," he declared, "I believe they should vote for someone else." Still, Carter did not want to be misunderstood. The morning following his "born again" comment, he held a news conference to explain further and, once again, to demystify evangelicalism for the general public. "It wasn't a voice of God from heaven," he said of the religious experience following his 1966 defeat for governor. "It might have been the same kind of experience as millions of people have who do become Christians in a deeply personal way."[13]

Carter's declaration of faith paid off in the Bible Belt. On March 23, the Democratic voters of North Carolina affirmed their southern neighbor with 54 percent of the vote, the first primary in which Carter won a majority. Wallace, who had hoped to keep his faltering campaign alive after his defeat in Florida, received 35 percent, effectively ending his decade-long quest for the presidency. "I told my people I wanted to beat you in North Carolina worse'n I ever wanted anything in my life," Wallace later told Carter. With Wallace's defeat in North Carolina, the Democratic Party was now, finally, rid of its most pugnacious segregationist, and Jimmy Carter had delivered the knockout punch.[14]

Having vanquished Wallace, Carter was free to offer forthright statements of support for racial equality. "The best thing that ever happened to the South in my lifetime," he told a rally in Englewood, New Jersey, "was the passage of the civil rights act, granting to black people the chance to vote, to hold a job, to buy a house, to go to school, to participate in public affairs on an equal basis with whites."[15]

Carter did not win all of the Democratic primaries—he lost Massachusetts to Henry Jackson and several later primaries to Frank Church of Idaho and Jerry Brown of California—but momentum was on his side. Carter's victories in Illinois, Ohio, and Pennsylvania proved that he could win northern industrial states, and by early June it was clear that the former governor of Georgia would be the Democratic nominee for president.

As more and more voters sized up the presumptive nominee, Carter's faith figured prominently in their assessments of him. Carter, for his part, provided plenty of information to attest to his faith and probity. "I feel that I have one life to live. I feel that God wants me to do the best I can with it," Carter told Bill Moyers in a PBS interview. "And that's quite often my major prayer." The candidate went on to say that he harbored no doubts about his faith and that he prayed frequently. Carter reaffirmed his commitment to honesty and noted a president's responsibility to provide a standard of ethics and morality for the entire nation. "I see no reason for the President to lie," he said, promising that if members of his cabinet lied they would lose their jobs. When Moyers asked about the influence of Reinhold Niebuhr, Carter replied that "one of the major responsibilities I have as a leader and as a potential leader is to try to establish justice." That task, he said, "applies to a broad gamut of things—international affairs, peace, equality, elimination of injustice in racial discrimination, elimination of injustice in tax programs, elimination of injustice in our criminal justice system and so forth."[16]

Despite—and, to some degree because of—Carter's many declarations of faith, some voters were wary. Liberals in particular wanted some clarification about Carter's religion. An article in the June 5, 1976, issue of the *New Republic*, written by E. Brooks Holifield of Emory University, sketched the contours of Carter's faith. Late in the primary season, Holifield had received a phone call from Martin Peretz, the magazine's publisher, asking him to explain Carter's religion. Holifield agreed; he embarked on an exhaustive analysis of Carter's speeches and writings, and he conducted interviews with the candidate's associates, including William Gunter, an associate justice on the Georgia Supreme Court who had introduced Carter to the writings of Reinhold Niebuhr. "The Three Strands of Jimmy Carter's Religion" confirmed the influence of Niebuhr's "Christian Realism" and also traced the candidate's religious pedigree back to the Puritans of the seventeenth century by way of southern evangelicalism. Carter's spiritual rebirth in 1967, Holifield argued, "followed a time-honored pattern: a sense of unworthiness, a moment of resignation, an experience of release," a textbook example of what evangelicals describe as a born-again conversion. Holifield, who initially preferred Morris Udall in the Democratic primaries, acknowledged Carter's affinities with some elements of fundamentalism, but he insisted that Carter was not a biblical literalist; he refused, for example, to accept the notion that women were subordinate to men. Jewish leaders in Georgia, Holifield pointed out, were entirely comfortable with Carter and his piety, in part because of his commitment to the Baptist principle of liberty of conscience and the separation of church and state. Without question, Holifield's article helped allay readers' fears that, in the author's words, Carter was "a red-neck Baptist with a hot line to God."[17]

For his part, the candidate was seldom loath to trade on his faith or his connections with Southern Baptists. Although he had already prevailed in Iowa, New Hampshire, and Florida, Carter remembers arriving in Texas as a "forlorn, woeful, forgotten, hopeless candidate for president." He credited Jimmy Allen, pastor of First Baptist Church in San Antonio, with giving his campaign credibility among Texas Baptists. Though initially reluctant to tender an endorsement, Allen wanted to validate someone who was willing to run for the presidency as an acknowledged born-again Christian. Carter, who later described Allen as "the personification of what a Christian should be," finished first in the Texas Democratic primary.[18]

Although he lost the California Democratic primary to Brown, the state's governor, on June 8, Carter won both Ohio and New Jersey the same day, thereby securing enough delegates to win the nomination. By mid-June, with his nomination assured, Carter began to turn his attentions to the Democratic ticket. Mindful of George McGovern's disastrous choice of Thomas Eagleton as his vice-presidential running mate four years earlier, Carter approached his selection with a methodical care and thoroughness unprecedented in presidential history. "I had made only one early decision about the Vice President," Carter wrote, "that it was important for me to choose a member of Congress as my running mate in order to provide some balance of experience to our ticket." Three of the finalists—Edmund Muskie of Maine, Walter Mondale of Minnesota, and John Glenn of Ohio—all of them U.S. senators, were carefully vetted and invited to Plains for interviews with the presumptive nominee. Carter chose Mondale, a preacher's son, who was prepared with specific ways that he could help Carter both as a candidate and as vice president; in Carter's words, Mondale "had excellent ideas about how to make the Vice Presidency a full-time and productive job." Not only did the senator from Minnesota provide geographical balance to the Democratic ticket, his dry wit also addressed what the traveling press long recognized as a humor deficit in the Carter campaign. "The first thing I did was read the most remarkable book ever written, called *Why Not the Best?*," Mondale said impishly about his summons to Plains. "I found every word absolutely brilliant."[19]

Like any nominee, Carter set about to broaden his appeal in advance of the general election. He called for full employment and reiterated his plans for a comprehensive health-care program, including coverage for mental illness. Carter lamented high inflation and economic inequality; the United States should raise the minimum wage, he said, so that it would be a living wage, and he affirmed the rights of workers to organize. Carter called for investment in renewable sources of energy, both for environmental reasons and as a way of heading off the disastrous consequences of another oil embargo. Carter advocated honesty in the government's dealings both with its own citizens and with other nations. He affirmed his commitment to human rights and his intention to seek the release of political prisoners.

Carter very often rehearsed the themes of progressive evangelicalism. He reaffirmed his commitment to the proposed Equal Rights Amendment to the Constitution, and he invited Barbara Jordan, member of Congress from Texas and an African American, to deliver the keynote address at the Democratic National Convention. Carter declared his unequivocal support for civil rights and voting rights. "I stand before you a candidate for President, a man whose life has been lifted, as yours have been, by the dream of Martin Luther King," Carter declared at the dedication of a new wing of a hospital named for King in Los Angeles. "He was the man, more than any other of his generation, who gazed upon the great wall of segregation and saw that it could be destroyed by the power of love." Carter praised the Voting Rights Act of 1965 as "the best thing that happened to the South in my lifetime" because it paved the way for the South to discard the past and enter the mainstream of American society. Still, Carter continued, there was much to do to redeem King's promise. "We still have poverty in the midst of plenty," the candidate said. "The few who are rich and powerful still make the decisions, and the many who are poor and weak must suffer the consequences."[20]

Evangelicals remained a key component of his base. "When Jimmy Carter speaks," Michael Novak had written during the primaries, "millions of Protestant Americans experience a sudden smack of recognition." It was not merely that he spoke the language of evangelicalism; in many ways, Carter represented their own better selves. How many evangelicals, despite the regular incantation of the "Great Commission"—"go ye into all the world and preach the gospel"—in their churches, had ever devoted an entire week to knocking on doors and inviting strangers to accept Jesus into their lives? Carter had done that—not once, but twice. How many evangelicals spoke openly and unabashedly about their faith in the workplace or among acquaintances at youth-league soccer games? Carter did so in front of the national media. As Novak, a Catholic theologian, said about the Democratic candidate, "He's for real. He's them in their idealized selves." Jim Wallis of *Sojourners* concurred from the other end of the political spectrum. In Carter, he told *Time* magazine, evangelicals "see they've got a real, live one all of their own."[21]

For some evangelicals, Carter's candidacy assumed almost messianic dimensions. At the annual gathering of the Southern Baptist Convention, Carter's own denomination, which convened shortly after Carter had secured the Democratic nomination in June, Bailey Smith told the messengers (delegates) that America "needs a born-again man in the White House"; his initials, Smith continued, "are the same as our Lord's." More than a few fundamentalists even jumped on the Carter bandwagon. "No candidate for the presidency of the United States has excited so many evangelical Christians as has Jimmy Carter of Plains, Georgia," Billy James Hargis, the notorious anticommunist preacher, enthused. "It is refreshing to see an obviously clean, moral man seeking the high office of the presidency."[22]

By June 1976, evangelicals were beginning to acknowledge talk about the "evangelical voting bloc" and the role they might play in the election. "Carter's public expression of down-home religious commitment," an article in *Christianity Today* noted, "has unquestionably gained him evangelical support." The piece noted that Carter's professions of faith had helped him win a plurality of votes in the Iowa precinct caucuses and victories in North Carolina, Illinois, and Indiana, all states with significant evangelical populations. The article concluded with a prediction: "Carter should win the Presidency with ease." Writing in the *Reformed Journal*, Nicholas Wolterstorff of Calvin College acknowledged the "standard mix" of evangelicalism with conservative politics. With Carter, however, the mix was different: "Evangelical Protestantism with rather progressive politics." Wolterstoff hadn't yet seen enough of Carter to know whether or not the two traditions were intimately connected or merely juxtaposed, but the initial indications suggested that Carter's progressive politics were in fact interwoven with his faith.[23]

ON July 14, 1976, delegates to the Democratic National Convention, meeting in New York City, overwhelmingly nominated Jimmy Carter for president, the first time since Zachary Taylor in 1848 that a major party had chosen someone from the Deep South. "With honest talk and plain truth, Jimmy Carter has appealed to the American people," Peter Rodino of New Jersey declared in his nomination speech. "His heart is honest, and the people will believe him."[24]

Carter opened his acceptance speech the following night with the same words he had used so often on the campaign trail: "My name is Jimmy Carter, and I'm running for president." Madison Square Garden erupted in cheers and applause. Carter lamented a moral drift in the nation and the failure of leadership. "Our country has lived through a time of torment," he said. "It is now a time for healing." He noted that he had spoken a lot about love on the campaign trail, but he added that "love must be translated into simple justice." A Gallup poll released the day of Carter's acceptance speech showed him favored over Gerald R. Ford by a margin of 53 to 36 percent.[25]

Three days after accepting the Democratic nomination, Carter was back in Plains teaching Sunday school. He told members of the class (and the covey of journalists) that the first Bible verse he had memorized was "God is love," and then he quizzed the class about his speech before the Democratic convention. "As I put it in my acceptance speech the other night, out of love must come one more thing," he said. "Does anyone remember?" Someone answered "obedience," but Carter corrected him: "Simple justice." The candidate went on to point out that Jesus spent his time with "prostitutes, cheaters, tax collectors, the common people, the dark-skinned people." By inference at least, Carter criticized his own church, which he tried and failed to integrate years earlier, rehearsing once again the themes of progressive evangelicalism. "Quite often, if we go into a Baptist church in the South, there's a social and economic élite," Carter said. "We're the prominent people in town. There's a tendency to think that because I've been accepted by God, I'm better than other people." Carter, referring once again to the Democratic convention several days earlier, repeated what Martin Luther King Sr. had told the delegates, "If you have got any hatred left in your heart, get down on your knees." This Carter characterized as "simple faith."[26]

Carter reiterated the themes of progressive evangelicalism throughout his campaign against Ford. Public servants "have a responsibility to bypass the big shots," he told an audience in Los Angeles, "and to make a concerted effort to understand people who are poor, black, speak a foreign language, who are not well educated, who are inarticulate, who are timid, who have some monumental problem."[27]

Carter's candidacy, however, did not always meet with unalloyed evangelical enthusiasm. Wes Michaelson, managing editor of *Sojourners* magazine, framed the Carter candidacy against the background of evangelicals' long-standing alienation from the larger culture. "Jimmy Carter can give to millions of evangelicals that sense of respectability in America for which they have deeply longed and believe they deserved," he wrote. Michaelson recognized Carter as a fellow evangelical, but he also discerned a "consummate" politician. Michaelson criticized Carter's failure to condemn the Vietnam War until 1975, long after the bombing had stopped, and he worried that the candidate too often separated his faith from his policies. Still, in the wake of the Nixon administration, Carter's appeal was undeniable, and Michaelson invoked Gerald Ford's preemptive pardon of Nixon. "Carter's response to Vietnam and Watergate is not to call Americans to repentance; rather, he offers us a cheap pardon," Michaelson wrote. "And millions of Americans—especially evangelicals—are likely to feel as grateful to him as Nixon did to Ford."[28]

Carter, however, did not have evangelical voters to himself. "In 1976 both candidates count themselves as born-again Christians," *Christianity Today* noted in an editorial, "although they differ significantly in their expression of their faith." Ford, an active Episcopal layman, was clearly a person of faith; his son Michael, moreover, was a student at an evangelical divinity school, Gordon-Conwell Theological Seminary, in South Hamilton, Massachusetts. Ford also enjoyed a good relationship with Billy Graham, who repeatedly throughout the campaign sought to bolster Ford's standing among evangelicals. Graham had agitated behind the scenes for a presidential pardon, and perhaps he felt some responsibility that Ford's pardon of Nixon, arguably the defining act of his presidency, was weighing so heavily on Ford's prospects for election.[29]

Despite an earlier pledge to remain "a million miles away from politics" in 1976, Graham could not resist inserting himself into the political conversation; early in 1976, he asked Ford to call him "if there is anything that I can do to help in the months ahead." Just before the Republican National Convention, while Ford was still locked in competition with Ronald Reagan for the nomination, Graham remarked that "I would rather have a man in office who is highly qualified to be President who didn't make much of his religious profession than to have a man who had no qualifications but who made a religious profession." Graham went on to suggest that there wasn't "a hair's difference between what Jimmy Carter, Gerald Ford and Reagan believe religiously."

Because the Carter campaign had defined itself so relentlessly around the issues of morality and integrity, emphasizing the candidate's evangelical credentials, Graham's remarks were widely interpreted as an attempt to boost whichever Republican candidate emerged with the nomination.[30]

By September, Ford's staff recommended that the president redeem the offer that Graham had made earlier that year and enlist the evangelist's support. "Privately, Bill, his wife Ruth and most of his staff are going to vote for President Ford," an aide wrote. Ford then reported on his phone call with Graham to Dick Cheney, the White House chief of staff. "Excellent conversation," Ford wrote. "Will help in many ways & has." Graham followed up by inviting the Fords to attend his revival crusade in Pontiac, Michigan, in October, just weeks before the general election. "Because it would be so close to the election, it would be impossible to ask you to speak," Graham wrote. "However, if you came and sat in whatever area the Secret Service would decide is best, and were recognized from the platform, I am sure you would get a rousing reception."[31]

Despite Graham's best efforts to steer evangelical voters toward Ford, however, Carter's ability to secure evangelical support derived from his unabashed statements of faith and the sheer novelty for evangelical voters of being able to vote for someone who shared their religious views. But Carter's cause was also abetted by the ham-handedness of the Ford campaign. A Ford campaign briefing book identified Carter as an "evangelic," and a section on "Ethnic and Religious Groups" contained a series of sophomoric analyses: "Protestants have a tendency to be moralistic in their political attitudes—they like to believe they support a cause because it is 'right.' This is particularly true of rural fundamentalists, but also of Methodists and Presbyterians."[32]

As the campaign entered its final weeks, evangelicals grew even more confident of their political importance, if somewhat puzzled by their popularity. "For the first time in the memory of anyone that I've talked to," Jim Wallis of *Sojourners* wrote, "*Time* now analyses the 'evangelical bloc' along with the farm bloc, the black bloc, the blue collar bloc, etc." Evangelicals basked in the movement's sudden popularity. "Evangelicals suddenly find themselves number one on the North American religious scene," David Kucharsky of *Christianity Today* wrote. "After being ignored by much of the rest of society for decades, they are now coming into prominence." Kucharsky cited the recent popularity of the book *Born Again*, a best-selling spiritual autobiography by Charles Colson, one of Richard Nixon's most ruthless surrogates, as well as the evangelical conversion of Eldridge Cleaver, former leader of the Black Panthers. "Evangelical recovery has taken fifty years," Kucharsky wrote. "During the fundamentalist-modernist controversy, biblical orthodoxy retreated to the cultural periphery," he continued. "But it has again come to the center as theological alternatives have fallen on hard times." In the midst of the presidential campaign, Kucharsky suggested that "1976 seems to be the year of the evangelical." As if on cue, the cover story of the October 25 issue of *Newsweek* declared 1976 the "Year of the Evangelical."[33]

LATE in the summer of 1976, abortion suddenly surfaced as a campaign issue. As early as the Iowa precinct caucuses in 1972, Roman Catholic bishops had urged their communicants to support candidates who favored making abortion illegal, but evangelicals generally regarded it as a Catholic issue. In 1968, for example, the Christian Medical Society and the evangelical magazine *Christianity Today* convened a symposium on abortion and birth control. "The question for our generation," one of the participants said, "is whether we do not throw overboard the mother and those dependent upon her if we refuse to sacrifice the fetus." Twenty-six contributors wrestled with the issue, but these evangelicals stopped far short of condemning abortion. "As to whether or not the performance of an induced abortion is sinful we are not agreed," the statement coming out of the gathering declared, "but about the necessity of it and permissibility for it under certain circumstances we are in accord." The statement cited "individual health, family welfare, and social responsibility" as possible justifications for abortion and acknowledged that there may be instances when fetal life "may have to be abandoned to maintain full and secure family life."[34]

Although even such conservative evangelical theologians as Bruce Watke and Norman Geisler argued that the fetus was emphatically not the moral equivalent of a developed person, a few evangelicals began to register their concerns about abortion in the early 1970s. In February 1971, Carl F. H. Henry, editor of *Christianity Today* and, later, one of the signatories to the Chicago Declaration of Evangelical Social Concern, published an article about the rising acceptance of abortion, but he sought to frame it in the language of progressive evangelicalism. He affirmed that a "woman's body is not the domain and property of others," but he argued that a woman yields control when she enters into a sexual relationship with "a second party, and through conception to a third party, and indeed to human society as a whole." Harold Lindsell, Henry's successor as editor of *Christianity Today*, declared that for an unbeliever, abortion posed no moral problem. For an evangelical, however, "a viable fetus must be delivered alive if possible," although he allowed that, "if there are compelling psychiatric reasons from a Christian point of view, mercy and prudence may favor a therapeutic abortion." By any reckoning, Lindsell occupied the far-right flank of evangelicalism.[35]

Evangelicals in the late 1960s and throughout most of the 1970s by and large refused to see abortion as a defining issue, much less a matter that would summon them to the front lines of political activism. Abortion simply failed to gain traction among evangelicals, and some groups with historic ties to evangelicalism even pushed for legalization. In 1970, for example, the United Methodist Church General Conference called on state legislatures to repeal laws restricting abortion, and in 1972, at the same gathering that Carter addressed as governor, the Methodists acknowledged "the sanctity of unborn human life" but also declared that "we are equally bound to respect the sacredness of the life and well-being of the mother, for whom devastating damage may result from unacceptable pregnancy." Meeting in St. Louis, Missouri, during the summer of 1971, the messengers (delegates) to the Southern Baptist Convention passed a resolution that stated, "we call upon Southern Baptists to work for legislation that will allow the possibility of abortion under such conditions as rape, incest, clear evidence of severe fetal deformity, and carefully ascertained evidence of the likelihood of damage to the emotional, mental, and physical health of the mother." The Southern Baptist Convention, hardly a redoubt of liberalism, reaffirmed that position in 1974, the year after the *Roe* decision, and again in 1976.[36]

When the *Roe* decision was handed down on January 22, 1973, W. A. Criswell, former president of the Southern Baptist Convention and pastor of First Baptist Church in Dallas, Texas, expressed his satisfaction with the ruling. "I have always felt that it was only after a child was born and had a life separate from its mother that it became an individual person," one of the most famous fundamentalists of the twentieth century declared, "and it has always, therefore, seemed to me that what is best for the mother and for the future should be allowed."[37]

While a few evangelical voices, including *Christianity Today* magazine, mildly criticized the ruling, the overwhelming response on the part of evangelicals was silence, even approval; Baptists, in particular, applauded the decision as an appropriate articulation of the line of division between church and state, between personal morality and state regulation of individual behavior. "Religious liberty, human equality and justice are advanced by the

Supreme Court abortion decision," W. Barry Garrett of *Baptist Press* wrote. Floyd Robertson of the National Association of Evangelicals disagreed with the *Roe* decision, but he believed that legal redress should not be a priority for evangelicals. "The abortion issue should also remind evangelicals that the church must never rely on the state to support its mission or enforce its moral standards," he wrote in the summer 1973 issue of the organization's newsletter, *United Evangelical Action*. "The church and state must be separate. The actions and conduct of Christians transcend the secular community for which the state is responsible."[38]

Carter's dealing with the abortion issue in the 1976 campaign, then, was principally a matter of placating the Catholic bishops, who sought to press him on the issue, seeking his support for a constitutional amendment prohibiting abortion. Carter refused, insisting that although he was "personally opposed" to abortion, because the Supreme Court had declared it legal, he would be obliged as president to observe the law. Carter, in fact, had been remarkably consistent throughout the campaign, in part because he had faced the issue as governor. "Georgia had a very strict law (I favored it) which was stricken down by the Supreme Court," Carter explained to a concerned voter from Massachusetts in October 1975, adding that he signed a bill as governor that restricted abortion as much as possible within the parameters of the Supreme Court decision. "I do not believe it is feasible nor advisable to pass a special constitutional amendment regarding abortion," Carter wrote, although he also opposed further liberalization of existing laws.[39]

For the general election, the Carter-Mondale campaign had a form letter it sent to those inquiring about Carter's stand on abortion. "While I am personally opposed to abortion, I cannot in good conscience support a Constitutional amendment that would force all Americans into the same value judgment as mine," the letter read. "I believe this issue provides room for a difference between one's personal conviction and a public policy that is binding on all."[40]

Carter's position on abortion differed little from Ford's; he too opposed abortion on demand, although Ford favored an amendment that would let states decide the matter. Because polls indicated that Carter enjoyed a lead among Roman Catholic voters, however, the Catholic bishops continued to press Carter on the issue. By September, Birch Bayh, Democratic senator from Indiana and one of the people Carter had defeated to win the Democratic nomination, chimed in with advice for the nominee on abortion. "Perhaps it is a bit presumptuous of me to say so," Bayh wrote, "but I've been picketed longer and been called more dirty names on this issue than anyone else in America, so I have a bit of understanding of what you are going through right now." Bayh warned that there was no way to win on the issue; he advised Carter not to bring it up in his speeches. "At this stage of the campaign, strategy has to be devised on how to minimize those votes lost," and the best way to do that was simply to emphasize the need for "family planning, counseling, and other programs you have already stressed."[41]

Carter himself detected a divide between the Catholic bishops and the Catholic laity. "Among the leaders within the Catholic Church there is an open, expressed concern about the abortion issue, about my Baptist beliefs that is not mirrored among the average citizens in the country who happen to be Catholic," Carter told *U.S. News & World Report* in September. Carter also repeated his conviction that "abortion is wrong" and cited the need for measures that would limit the incidence of abortion, including sex education, family planning, and laws more congenial to adoption.[42]

In its September issue, *Christianity Today* raised the abortion issue in an editorial, casting it principally as a challenge for Carter with the Catholic hierarchy, especially after Joseph L. Bernardin, archbishop of Cincinnati, declared that the bishops "continue to be disappointed with the governor's position." Although the editorial noted the efforts of the Christian Action Council, an evangelical pro-life organization, the magazine expressed sympathy for the beleaguered candidate forced to negotiate among competing constituencies within his own party: "Democratic nominee Jimmy Carter has been working since his party's convention to try to undo the damage his platform writers did when they inserted a plank opposing an anti-abortion constitutional amendment."[43]

OF far greater consequence to his election prospects was Carter's interview in *Playboy* magazine, which hit the newsstands on September 20—just weeks before the general election. Jody Powell had prevailed on Carter to submit to the series of interviews, arguing that both Jerry Brown and the venerable Walter Cronkite had appeared in *Playboy* interviews. Carter finally agreed, eager to dispel somewhat the lingering impression that, because of his straight-laced Baptist ways, he was smug and self-righteous. At the final interview session, Carter joked that Robert Scheer and Barry Golson, from *Playboy*, "must have some kind of blackmail leverage on Jody. I've spent more time with you than with *Time, Newsweek*, and all the others combined."[44]

The interview itself ranged over many issues, including his relationship with Rosalynn. "I was by far the dominant person in the marriage at the beginning, but not anymore," Carter said. "She's just as strong, if not stronger than I am. She's fully equal to me in every way in our relationship, in making business decisions, and she makes most of the decisions about family affairs." When asked the secret to his successful marriage, Carter cited love and the couple's children, but he also talked about religious compatibility. "We also share a religious faith," Carter said, "and the two or three times in our married life when we've had a serious crisis, I think that's what sustained our marriage and helped us overcome our difficulty."[45]

Carter spoke extensively about his Baptist faith. "I'm not unique," Carter said. "There are a lot of people who have the same religious faith." One of the hallmarks of the Baptist tradition, Carter added, was liberty of conscience. "I don't accept any domination of my life by the Baptist Church, none," Carter emphasized. "The reason the Baptist Church was formed in this country was because of our belief in absolute and total separation of church and state."[46]

On a more personal level, Carter said he didn't worry about assassination because "I have an assurance of eternal life." Carter acknowledged that he prayed frequently throughout any given day, usually for the needs of others but sometimes merely for strength or assurance when facing an uncertain situation. "I'll pray then, but it's not something that's conscious or formal," he said. "It's just a part of my life." Carter took pains, however, to say that he did not consider himself morally superior to others. "The main thing is that we don't think we're better than anyone else," he said. "We are taught not to judge other people."[47]

According to the interviewers, Carter's most candid comments—and the ones that would generate the most attention—came at the last moment, following the final interview. Carter seemed eager to talk, unusually expansive for a highly scripted candidate. Carter elaborated on his earlier point about refraining from passing judgment on others. 'The thing that's drummed into us all the time is not to be proud, not to be better than anyone else, not to look down on people but to make ourselves acceptable in God's eyes through our own actions and recognize the simple truth that we're saved by grace," the candidate said. "I try not to commit a deliberate sin," Carter continued. "I recognize that I'm going to do it anyhow, because I'm human and I'm tempted." Then, the most quoted passage of the interview. "I've looked on a lot of women with lust," Carter said. "I've committed adultery in my heart many times." Carter's aides signaled to the candidate that the tape recorder was still

on. Carter nodded and continued: "Christ says, Don't consider yourself better than someone else because one guy screws a whole bunch of women while
the other guy is loyal to his wife. The guy who's loyal to his wife ought not to
be condescending or proud because of the relative degree of sinfulness."[48]

For evangelicals, the sentiments themselves were unremarkable. Jesus
himself said that "anyone who looks at a woman lustfully has already committed adultery with her in his heart." For evangelicals, sin was inherent not
merely in action but also in disposition, so no one was sinless, which was
precisely the point Jesus was making in the Sermon on the Mount—and the
point Carter echoed in the interview. Carter's evangelical theology may have
been simple, but it was also unassailable: the doctrine of sin and redemption,
of temptation and salvation by grace. When the interviewers asked Carter if
he had any problems appearing in *Playboy*, he replied that he did not. "I don't
believe I'll be criticized," he said.[49]

He was mistaken. For a campaign so carefully calibrated and scripted,
the *Playboy* interview represented a serious stumble. Pundits had a field day
with the "adultery in my heart" comment, but most evangelicals confined
their objections to the use of the colloquial verb *screw* as well as to the venue
of his remarks. "It was a devastating blow to our campaign," Carter acknowledged many years later. "In ten days I dropped fifteen percentage points because of that *Playboy* interview."[50]

W. A. Criswell of First Baptist Church, Dallas, Texas, climbed into his
pulpit on October 10 to question Carter's judgment for granting an interview
to a "salacious, pornographic magazine." A smiling Gerald Ford sat in the
congregation on that Sunday morning. Bailey Smith, the preacher who in
June had played on Jimmy Carter's initials to endorse him before the meeting
of the Southern Baptist Convention, told the press that, "well, 'screw' is just
not a good Baptist word." Glen Thompson, pastor of Evergreen Hills Baptist
Church in Anderson, South Carolina, characterized Carter as "a wolf in
sheep's clothing," and Bob Jones Jr., the former president of Bob Jones University, also weighed in. "Carter is a foul-mouthed, double-crossing hypocrite, a
complete phony," he said. "It's blatant in Carter's speech that he's perverting
Christianity, that he's at variance with a man thinking pure thoughts." Jones
described Ford as the "lesser of two evils." (The famous fundamentalist had
nothing kind to say about the first lady, however. "Betty is a plain slut," Jones
said. "If he didn't have her, he'd be a much better man in my opinion.")[51]

More than a few evangelicals, habituated over the years to Republican
candidates, seized on the *Playboy* interview as a pretext for abandoning

Carter. The *New York Times* quoted unnamed evangelicals to the effect that, "Jimmy Carter wears his religion on his sleeve but Jerry Ford wears it in his heart," and the Ford campaign let it be known that the president and his wife read the Bible every night. By the end of September, the *Washington Post* ran an article entitled "Evangelicals Seen Cooling on Carter." The catalyst was the *Playboy* interview. "It was not lost on evangelicals that a few days after the *Playboy* article, Graham—burned by Nixon and vowing to remain out of this election—visited President Ford," the article pointed out. "Like many, I am quite disillusioned," Jerry Falwell said. "Four months ago the majority of the people I knew were pro-Carter. Today, that has totally reversed." Some evangelicals, like the pastor of Grace Brethren Church, in Johnstown, Pennsylvania, used the interview as an opening to criticize Carter for other perceived lapses. "I do feel that he has been 'born again' but it's a watered down version," Cliff Weeks told the *Post* reporter. "He approves of social drinking."[52]

Patrick Anderson, Carter's speechwriter during the campaign, remarked that "it is difficult to overstate" the significance of the *Playboy* interview. "It destroyed his lead, soured his press relations, threw him on the defensive and his campaign into chaos, and probably cost him the big electoral victory he had expected." But the long-term effects were even greater. "Carter's remarks first raised the possibility to millions of voters that he might be a bit too different, too strange for them to be comfortable with for four or eight years," Anderson said. "The honeymoon was over."[53]

Carter, however, was not without his defenders. Stephen Charles Mott, a United Methodist minister and professor at Gordon-Conwell Theological Seminary (the school where Michael Ford studied), drafted a letter to the mailing list of Evangelicals for McGovern, the organization that gave rise to the Chicago Declaration, to shore up support among progressive evangelicals. The editorial pages of the *Omaha World-Herald* also came to Carter's defense. "If there are people who think Jimmy Carter shouldn't be president because he uttered a commonplace vulgarity for the public prints, they shouldn't be allowed to vote," the editorial read. Nonetheless, they acknowledged the gaffe. "Carter needn't worry about looking like a rakehell sinner, but after this he ought to worry about looking faintly ridiculous."[54]

ALTHOUGH the *Playboy* interview represented a miscalculation—the candidate himself conceded as much on the final day of the campaign—the Carter camp once again benefited from even more grievous missteps by Ford and Robert Dole, U.S. senator from Kansas and Ford's running mate. In the course of the second debate, held in San Francisco on October 6, the president said, "There is no Soviet domination of Eastern Europe and there never will be under a Ford administration." The astonished questioner, Max Frankel of the *New York Times*, gave Ford an opportunity to retract the statement, to acknowledge the iron rule of the Soviet Union in the throes of the Cold War. Instead, Ford doubled down, insisting that Soviet bloc nations were independent and autonomous. In the vice-presidential debate, on October 15, Dole asserted that both of the world wars, Korea, and Vietnam were all Democratic wars—begun and fought during Democratic administrations—an unreasonable claim that Mondale easily refuted. Mondale said many years later, "I think they blew the election right there."[55]

On November 2, 1976, following an election-eve rally in Flint, Michigan, Jimmy Carter, the one-term former governor of Georgia, peanut farmer, and Southern Baptist Sunday-school teacher, was elected president of the United States with 50.1 percent of the popular vote, winning 297 electoral votes to Ford's 240. Likely owing to the *Playboy* interview, Ford garnered 3.2 million more evangelical votes than Carter, but even so, Carter's evangelical support in fifty crucial evangelical counties represented a significant 20 percent increase over George McGovern's tally four years earlier. Given the stain of Watergate and the unpopularity of Ford's preemptive pardon of Nixon, the Republican ticket came much closer to victory than anyone had expected when the campaign began.[56]

After the votes were counted, evangelicals lined up for the spoils of a victory they helped to secure. "As you know the 50 million evangelicals in the United States of America are highly supportive of you as their future President," Pat Robertson wrote to the president-elect. "We want to support you and to marshall [*sic*] this enormous reservoir of prayer and good will in your behalf." Robertson outlined his specific concerns, including "the education of our young and the compassionate assistance to the poor, the elderly, the needy, the mentally retarded," but mentioned nothing about abortion. "Again let me assure you that the evangelicals of America will stand behind you when difficult times arise for your administration," Robertson concluded, although he added that continued evangelical support would come at a price: the appointment of evangelicals to positions of influence in the Carter administration. Robertson, at Carter's invitation, agreed to supply a list of names.[57]

Christianity Today weighed in on the outcome. The magazine's editorial following the election characterized Gerald Ford as a "good man" and expressed "great admiration for his service." Turning to Carter, the editors recounted his campaign promises, including cutting bureaucracy and the defense budget, advocating for religious liberty, and discouraging "abortion on demand at public expense." *Christianity Today* applauded those stands, but it was also clear about what it deemed most important. "We agree with these objectives," the editorial stated, "and especially with his desire to restructure the vast federal bureaucracy so as to lower costs and improve performance." The editorial also noted that Carter's "frequent public affirmations of personal faith in Christ provide him with a singular opportunity and also expose him to many pitfalls."[58]

In the run-up to Carter's inauguration, evangelicals began to assess the significance of one of their own in the White House. Reflecting on the culture of corruption that surrounded the Nixon administration, Stephen V. Monsma, formerly a professor of political science at Calvin College and now a member of the Michigan House of Representatives, saw in Carter someone who "recognizes Christianity as being relevant to his personal moral life." Monsma, writing in the pages of *Christianity Today*, anticipated a "presidency more fully permeated with high moral standards" than those in previous years. "After the lies of Watergate, congressional sex scandals, and the gifts of foreign influence-peddlers," Monsma suggested, "Washington could stand more Christian morality."[59]

Still, Monsma continued, evangelicals should temper their expectations. "An evangelical president will go through the same struggles and agonies of decision-making as does any president," he wrote, but evangelicals could expect that the new president would bring "a sharpened moral imperative" to the task. "There are two dangers that the evangelical church should seek to avoid," Monsma concluded. The first is that evangelicals "will disown Carter and fail to provide him with the love, support, encouragement, and prayers he needs." The opposite danger, he said, was too close an identification: "The evangelical church should maintain enough independence from Carter that it does not lose its ability to criticize and correct."[60]

As the ensuing four years unfolded, a growing number of evangelicals both disowned and criticized.

JIMMY Carter's long and arduous run for the White House had been built on popular disgust with Richard Nixon and general dissatisfaction with Washington. Carter's outsider status, together with his evident probity, provided a welcome contrast, even though his opponent, Nixon's successor, was untainted by scandal. The 1976 campaign also represented a turning point in presidential politics. Whereas John Kennedy had instructed voters effectively to bracket out a candidate's faith, Carter unabashedly offered his faith to voters as corroboration of his morality.

Evangelicals were initially intrigued by the opportunity to support one of their own for president; not since William Jennings Bryan's final campaign in 1908 had an evangelical mounted a serious bid for the White House. As the 1976 campaign wore on, however, some evangelicals, following Billy Graham's lead, found Ford more attractive, and Carter's misbegotten interview in *Playboy* supplied a pretext for their return to the Republican Party. Carter, the Southern Baptist, had been able to forestall the Catholic bishops with his declaration that he was "personally opposed" to abortion, but his continuing refusal to seek a constitutional amendment allowed the issue to fester. The evangelical discovery of abortion as a political issue in 1979, as Carter was gearing up for reelection, would thrust politically conservative evangelicals, willingly or not, into a coalition with conservative Catholics, a coalition that would contribute to the termination of Jimmy Carter's political career.

For the moment, however, as Carter prepared for his presidency, he was blissfully unaware of the challenges to come. His margin of victory was not as wide as polls and pundits had predicted it would be, not as great as might have been expected following the Watergate scandal. But it was a victory nonetheless, and the Carters prepared, for the second time in their married life, to leave Plains, Georgia—this time for 1600 Pennsylvania Avenue.

FIVE

REDEEMER
PRESIDENT

JANUARY 20, 1977, in Washington, D.C., dawned sunny and cold. Early in the morning, about five thousand people gathered in twenty-degree temperatures at the Lincoln Memorial for a People's Prayer Service. Martin Luther King Sr. was there, together with Bruce E. Edwards, Jimmy Carter's pastor from Plains, Georgia, and Ruth Carter Stapleton, the president-elect's sister. Leontyne Price, soprano from the Metropolitan Opera, sang "He's Got the Whole World in His Hands."[1]

Carter watched the proceedings on television and then headed to First Baptist Church for a Pre-Inaugural Service of Prayer. The congregation, which included Walter Mondale, the vice president–elect, and his family, sang "O God, Our Help in Ages Past." Nelson L. Price, pastor of Roswell Street Baptist Church in Marietta, Georgia, and Carter's "prayer partner" over the previous eight years, preached the sermon.[2]

By noon, the temperature had risen to twenty-eight degrees. On the east portico of the U.S. Capitol, Carter placed his hand on both the Bible that George Washington had used for his inauguration in 1789 and a King James Version of the Bible given to him by his mother, opened to Micah 6:8: "He hath showed thee, O man, what is good; and what doth the Lord require of thee, but to do justly, and to love mercy, and to walk humbly with thy God."

After taking the oath of office, the new president addressed the nation. In an extraordinary gesture, he thanked his predecessor and erstwhile political adversary, Gerald R. Ford, for "all he has done to heal our land." Carter then invoked the promise of the United States. "Ours was the first society openly

75

to define itself in terms of both spirituality and of human liberty," he said, and that unique combination conferred moral duties on Americans, including a commitment to human rights, fairness in laws, and preservation of natural resources. In this society, he continued, "the powerful must not persecute the weak, and human dignity must be enhanced."[3]

John F. Kennedy's inaugural in 1961—"Ask not what your country can do for you"—had set the twentieth-century standard for inaugural addresses, and Carter's address did not approach the soaring rhetoric of his predecessor. Instead, as befit Carter himself, his speech was earnest and workmanlike with a dash of Baptist piety, the same combination that had propelled him to the presidency.

Carter sought to heal and to reconcile. At the conclusion of his time in office, the new president said, he hoped that people might say "that we had torn down the barriers that separated those of different race and region and religion, and where there had been mistrust, built unity, with a respect for diversity" and that "we had remembered the words of Micah and renewed our search for humility, mercy, and justice."[4]

Jimmy and Rosalynn Carter, to the chagrin of the Secret Service, then walked down Pennsylvania Avenue from the Capitol to the White House. "I thought it would be a good demonstration of confidence by the president in the people of our country," Carter wrote about the decision to walk, "and also would be a tangible indication of some reduction in the imperial status of the president and his family." Many people along the way, expecting a motorcade, began to weep when they saw the new president and first lady walking hand in hand down Pennsylvania Avenue.[5]

IT is impossible to imagine Jimmy Carter taking the oath of office on January 20, 1977, had it not been for Richard Nixon. John F. Kennedy's address to the Greater Houston Ministerial Association at the Rice Hotel on September 12, 1960, had effectively removed religion from presidential campaign rhetoric. Kennedy, seeking to neutralize his Roman Catholicism as a political issue, argued, effectively, that voters should disregard a candidate's religion when they entered the voting booth. Presidential campaigns for more than a decade thereafter, until 1976, were remarkably free of all but the most anodyne references to faith or spirituality.[6]

Nixon changed that. The culture of corruption surrounding the Nixon administration made Americans receptive to a candidate willing to talk about his faith. After what many Americans regarded as the treachery of the

Nixon presidency, voters sought some reading on a candidate's moral compass. Carter obliged, and although by the end of the campaign many voters knew more about Carter's church, his Sunday-school teaching, and his understanding of theology than they cared to know, many other voters found his probity reassuring. "He loves the Lord and wants to bring the country back to what it was," one of Carter's neighbors in Plains told a reporter during the 1976 campaign. Carter's promise never knowingly to lie to the American people resonated with an electorate wearied of Nixon's endless prevarications.

Carter represented a clean break with the recent past, an opportunity to redeem the nation. The Carter campaign had played to that sentiment; pulling the lever for Carter, they suggested, would lay the sordid Nixon presidency to rest. "The damage that has been done to people's attitudes toward Government has been severe in the last few years," Carter had said during the campaign, promising to "restore respect for and trust of the Government within the consciousness of the American people." The electorate, after all, had been complicit in Nixon's transgressions because voters had elected him to the presidency not once, but twice—despite the fact that "Tricky Dick's" long history of dirty dealings was hardly a secret. Casting a ballot for Carter, the redeemer president, would expunge the voters' sins and absolve them of complicity. Carter recognized that his piety grated on some of the voters, but his evident probity is what had catapulted him to the White House. "People wanted someone who wasn't going to tell another lie, who was not going to mislead the public and who was going to try to reestablish, in my judgment, ethics and morality in international affairs," he said. Even Billy Graham, Nixon's friend, agreed about Carter's appeal: "After the disillusionment of Watergate, the American people were attracted by Carter's summons to a moral revival." While some Americans found Carter's evangelical piety cloying and even, in light of the *Playboy* interview, insincere, many others were willing to take their chances on the Sunday-school teacher from Plains. "One of the reasons I was elected president," Carter told his Sunday-school class in 2002, "was because people were looking for a leader to tell the truth."[7]

Once the Carters settled into the executive mansion, a quintessentially evangelical task awaited them: finding a church. Here again, Carter meant to break with the recent past, specifically Nixon's practice of hosting worship services in the White House, gatherings that rather quickly had devolved into political theater.

On Sunday morning, January 23, just three days after the inauguration, Fred M. Gregg noticed a scrum of photographers and reporters as he arrived at First Baptist Church in Washington, just eight blocks north of the White House. Gregg, who had recently moved to Washington from Nashville, had agreed to teach the church's Couples Class. "I felt as though my Adam's apple dropped to my shoes," he recalled when he noticed the president and his family standing outside. "Is there any chance you would care to teach today?" Gregg asked Carter. "No," the president replied, "but I will sometime." Within a month, Carter had made good on his promise.[8]

A few days after his appearance at First Baptist Church, Carter attended the National Prayer Breakfast. Following an address by the majority leader of the House of Representatives, Carter, according to press accounts, "launched into a seventeen-minute sermon without notes on Second Chronicles 7:14 and its call for national humility." Later the same day, Billy Graham noted that it was the first Prayer Breakfast where the president spoke about Jesus Christ in a personal way.[9]

Only five days after the inauguration, Graham sent a letter to Rosalynn Carter. "I would like you to know privately that you and your family are daily in my prayers," Graham wrote. "I don't think Ruth and I ever pray together or have family devotions that your names are not called in prayer. We thank God for your Christian witness." Evangelicals on the other side of the Atlantic even took notice of the new president and his faith. "For the first time in the history of the United States the authentic voice of evangelical Christianity is heard," Malcolm Muggeridge wrote, "not just at Moody and Sankey revivalist conventions and Billy Graham crusades, but in the very citadel of American power, Washington DC."[10]

CARTER plunged into his presidency with the same work ethic he had employed many times before, from the navy and the Carter Warehouse to the Georgia statehouse and his various political campaigns. He resolved to be an active president. At 8:10 the morning following his inauguration, Carter signed an executive order, his first official act as president, pardoning those who had evaded the Vietnam draft. In the course of the campaign, Carter had been careful to make a distinction between *pardon* and *amnesty*. "To me amnesty means that what you did was right and you are to be congratulated for it," the candidate said. "Pardon means that what you did, whether it was right or wrong, is forgiven." Although some veterans' groups had opposed pardon for draft resisters, and the Ford-Dole campaign had sought to make it an issue during the campaign, many Americans viewed the new president's gesture as an appropriate response to Ford's pardon of Richard Nixon.[11]

After issuing the pardon, Carter moved on to policy. He sent a flurry of legislation to Capitol Hill, so much that Edward M. Kennedy remarked four months into the Carter administration that the new president's "reforms are already lined up bumper to bumper." John B. Anderson, Republican member of Congress from Illinois, complained that despite the candidate's "fuzziness on the issues, it turns out Carter had a huge agenda tucked away in his coat pocket," an agenda that included national health insurance, welfare reform, tax reform, and streamlining of the executive branch and the Pentagon.[12]

Carter called the nation's attention, early and often, to the energy crisis, which he characterized as "the moral equivalent of war." In an address to the nation on April 18, the president warned about America's excessive dependence on foreign oil and pressed the importance of energy conservation. Carter subsequently authorized the installation of solar panels on the White House in the hopes that Americans would begin seriously to consider alternate sources of energy. Not all Americans wanted to hear Carter's call for conservation, but at least some pundits understood the straight talk as a step toward restoring credibility to the presidency. "Carter's problem is that trust in Presidents has been in understandably short supply recently," columnist George F. Will remarked. "With his energy program, Carter has drawn his sword of leadership." Martin F. Nolan of the *Boston Globe* wrote that Carter was "preaching from the 'bully pulpit' of a Presidency eroded by 12 years of Vietnam, Watergate and increasing public cynicism."[13]

Carter also sought to chart a different course on foreign policy, one dictated less by the Cold War and by more attention to human rights. The new president sent an early signal of his resolve when he embraced Soviet dissidents shortly after his inauguration. "Human rights is the central concern of my administration," Carter wrote to Andrei Sakharov, the Soviet dissident, on February 5, just a couple of weeks into his administration. "You may rest assured that the American people and our government will continue our firm commitment to promote respect for human rights not only in our country, but also abroad." The president instructed all U.S. ambassadors to provide information about human rights abuses.[14]

In foreign policy, Carter sought to nudge the United States away from the reactive anticommunism of the Cold War and toward a policy that was more collaborative, less interventionist, and sensitive above all to human rights. The recent past, especially the ignominy of Vietnam and the scandal of Watergate, made such a move possible, he thought, even essential. In addition, the Senate Select Committee on Intelligence (known as the Church Committee for its chair, Frank Church of Idaho) had brought to light some of the unsavory activities of the Central Intelligence Agency, including covert attempts to overthrow governments in Indonesia, Iran, Cuba, Guatemala, and Chile. Just as Carter had emphasized his own morality in his campaign for the White House, he believed that the foreign policy of the United States should be guided by moral principles as well.[15]

Carter laid out these principles in the course of his commencement address at the University of Notre Dame on May 22, four months into his presidency. He called for a foreign policy consistent with America's fundamental values, which entailed the exercise of power for humane purposes. He declared that Americans were finally confident enough in their own future that "we are now free of that inordinate fear of Communism which once led us to embrace any dictator who joined us in our fear." Carter invoked Vietnam, where the United States had supported a series of corrupt rulers simply because they were anticommunists, as a tragic example of the "intellectual and moral poverty" of American foreign policy. "For too many years," he said, "we have been willing to adopt the flawed principles and tactics of our adversaries, sometimes abandoning our values for theirs." Central to the nation's new direction, Carter said, was a policy that reflected Americans' commitment to human rights and a foreign policy that sought to alleviate suffering and narrow the gap between rich and poor. A peaceful world cannot exist, the president said, "one-third rich and two-thirds hungry."[16]

Carter later explained that his passion for human rights derived from both his understanding of the Bible and his experience as a southerner. Those who came of age in the South during the civil rights struggle, he said, "were confronted with one of the most tortuous, self-inflicted wounds that a society could suffer." That experience was transformative. "To watch the slow evolution into racial harmony—to see the elimination at least of legal discrimination—was something that was both emotional as well as memorable."[17]

Carter also insisted that his understanding of human rights was informed by his reading of the Hebrew prophets. "I have been steeped in the Bible since childhood," he told a reporter several months into his presidency, "and I believe that anyone who reads the ancient words of the Old Testament with both sensitivity and care will find there the idea of government as something based on a voluntary covenant rather than force—the idea of equality before the law and the supremacy of law over the whims of any ruler; the idea of dignity of the individual human being and also of the individual conscience; the idea of service to the poor and to the oppressed." Addressing the World Jewish Congress on November 2, 1977, the president declared that contemporary understandings of human rights can be traced to the Jewish prophetic tradition. In the contemporary context, Carter believed that human rights also included the right to good health, a job, a place to live, and an education. "If I am my brother's keeper, it's not enough for me to learn about or even pray about his troubles," Carter wrote after he left office. "I'm called upon to act on his behalf, even when that requires fighting injustice and tyranny." Zbigniew Brzezinski, Carter's national security adviser, clearly understood that the president's "commitment to human rights reflected Carter's own religious beliefs."[18]

Taking the United Nations' 1948 Universal Declaration of Human Rights as his standard, Carter pressed Congress for a requirement that the State Department produce a "full and complete report" on human rights around the world. The first such report, covering eighty-two countries, was released in 1977. On the basis of those findings, Carter denounced human rights violations in the Soviet Union and its Eastern bloc allies. Carter's administration voted against World Bank loans to nations with poor records on human rights. Although Carter preferred positive inducements to sanctions, the president was not averse to the latter. He suspended military and economic aid to some of the worst offenders, including El Salvador, Nicaragua, Chile, and Uganda. In Nicaragua, Carter pressured Anastasio Somoza to loosen restrictions on the press and to curb the abuses of his national guard; when forced by Somoza's intransigence to choose between the dictator and the insurgent Sandinistas, Carter abided by his commitment to human rights, even though his abandonment of Somoza effectively propelled the Marxist Sandinistas to power. When the Sandinistas assumed control of Nicaragua in July 1979, the Carter administration communicated its willingness to be "generous in its assistance and supportive of the democratic aims of the Sandinista revolution."[19]

If the situation in Nicaragua epitomized the shift from Cold War dualism to an emphasis on morality and human rights, it also illustrated the vexations of foreign policy in a complex world. Carter and his administration recognized that, in the words of Cyrus Vance, secretary of state, ensuring human rights would be "a long journey" and that the United States would not win immediate concessions from authoritarian regimes. The administration also acknowledged that, in the interests of national security, the United

States could not press the issue relentlessly or uniformly, that strategic considerations might at times trump the call for human rights.[20]

For Carter, however, the push for human rights was inseparable from the quest for a more peaceful world. "There's no doubt in my mind that the greatest violator of human rights that we know is armed conflict," he said. Governments are adept at waging war, he added, but the international community had few mechanisms for the propagation of peace. These concerns prompted the president to address what he characterized as festering international problems, including estrangement from China, continuing conflict between Israel and Egypt, the lack of progress with the Soviet Union on disarmament, and the failure to conclude and ratify the Panama Canal treaties. For Carter, progress on those fronts would also diminish the chance of war and therefore advance the cause of human rights.[21]

Although Billy Graham called the White House to express his support for Carter's stand, many on the political right criticized the president's emphasis on human rights. His speech at Notre Dame, they charged, betrayed a simplistic view of the world and underplayed the Soviet challenge. The editorial page of the *Wall Street Journal* worried that Carter's emphasis on human rights would alienate trading partners, lamenting that Carter pursued "a human rights policy that seemed designed to hurt our allies more than our adversaries." Carter's relentless rhetoric about human rights drew criticism from the left as well. John B. Anderson, a fellow evangelical who would challenge Carter for reelection in 1980, criticized the president's "lecturing on human rights," which "turned out to have been conducted in such a public and sanctimonious way as to provoke the pride of the offenders, cause hardening of positions, and in the end proved counterproductive." Anderson wondered why, in light of the president's declared position on human rights, American foreign policy still supported dictatorships in places like South Korea, Nicaragua, Haiti, and Zaire. In the June 1977 issue of *Sojourners*, Wes Michaelson also criticized Carter's inconsistency on human rights.[22]

Carter himself saw things differently. When asked near the conclusion of his first year in office about his successes and failures, the president listed his attention to human rights in the former column. "If I have achieved anything, it has been to restore a tone to our Nation's life and attitude that most accurately exemplifies what we stand for," he said. "I use the human rights issue as one example. It gratifies me to know that the Nations in Africa now look to us with friendship and with trust, whereas, just a short time ago, they wouldn't permit our Secretary of State to come in their country."[23]

The beneficiaries of Carter's emphasis on human rights concurred. Argentinian dissident Jacobo Timerman, who was incarcerated and tortured for thirty months and finally released in the fall of 1979, credited Carter with his freedom as well as saving the life of Alfredo Bravo, another political prisoner. "There is absolutely no doubt that Carter's policy saved thousands of lives," Robert Cox, editor of the *Buenos Aires Herald*, wrote. Suharto, Indonesia's strongman and president, responded to the Carter administration's diplomatic and economic pressures by releasing 30,000 political prisoners during Carter's time in office, and over 118,000 Soviet Jews were allowed to emigrate. "It was the first time—and I fear the last—in this violent and criminal century," Timerman said about Carter's human rights policy, "that a major power has defended human rights all over the world."[24]

NOWHERE was Carter's insistence on a moral foreign policy more evident than in his push to revise the Panama Canal treaty. The canal had been constructed early in the twentieth century under the terms of the Hay-Bunau-Varilla Treaty of 1903, which established the Panama Canal Zone in the isthmus of Central America as United States territory. The forty-eight miles of the canal, completed in 1914, provided a shortcut between the Atlantic and Pacific oceans, allowing vessels to avoid both the time and the perils of navigating south around the hazardous Cape Horn, the southernmost tip of South America. Although crucial both to trade and to military maneuvers, the canal also symbolized American imperialism, and successive presidents as far back as Lyndon Johnson had been working to revise the treaty in order to improve relations with Latin America and move away from colonialism. Carter chose to expend a good deal of political capital early in his presidency to negotiate a new agreement and then to secure its ratification in the U.S. Senate. As president-elect, Carter had told *Time* magazine that "the Panama treaty ought to be resolved quite rapidly."[25]

The new treaties, signed on September 7, 1977, and known as the Torrijos-Carter treaties, effectively abrogated the 1903 treaty and transferred both the ownership of the canal and responsibility for its defense to Panama in 1999. "In the peaceful process of negotiating the treaties," Carter declared at the signing in Panama City, "we have shown the world a spirit which recognizes and respects the rights of others and seeks to help all people to fulfill their legitimate aspirations with confidence and dignity." Omar Torrijos Herrera responded by referring to the U.S. president as "a man of great morality fully dedicated to the cause of the weak."[26]

The Senate's ratification of the treaties, however, was by no means assured. Many leftists in Latin America opposed the treaties as too generous to the United States, especially because they allowed for American military action in defense of the canal. Many American conservatives, including politically conservative evangelicals, opposed what they characterized as a "giveaway," one that would only encourage, and potentially empower, suspected leftist groups in Panama. But evangelical opinion on the treaties was divided. A guest editorial in *Christianity Today* argued in favor of the treaties, pointing out that ratification would remove a potent symbol of American imperialism and deprive leftists of an issue. "That North American conservative evangelicals and Panamanian Marxists would unite to oppose the treaty," the editorial noted, "proves that politics does indeed make strange bedfellows."[27]

One of the treaties' loudest critics was the former governor of California, Ronald Reagan, who called it a "retreat by the United States" and wrote a letter to his political supporters criticizing Carter and the treaties. In the course of the 1976 Republican primaries, Reagan had frequently attacked Ford for his willingness to renegotiate the treaties, saying about the canal, "We bought it, we paid for it, and it's ours."[28]

Although the *Wall Street Journal* dismissed the treaties as a "strategic sideshow" of little consequence, other editorial pages offered support for ratification. "To a great majority of Panamanians, the terms of the 1903 treaty are an unsatisfactory holdover from a colonialist era," the *Los Angeles Times* wrote. "This country's relations with Latin America as a whole would be freed of a serious impediment" if the treaties were approved. The *Hartford Courant* encouraged senators to vote to ratify "because it is the right thing to do for a mature, self-confident nation." Foreign newspapers also chimed in. *The Economist* noted that the treaties had at last settled "the United States' longest running argument with the region," and the *Vancouver Sun* warned that failure to ratify the treaties would damage "the credibility of American morality in international affairs."[29]

When the treaties first came before the Senate, Carter could count on only forty of the sixty-seven votes needed for ratification. "I put my whole life on the line on the Panama Canal treaty," Carter recalled after leaving office. "And it was by far the most severe political challenge I've ever faced in my life, much more difficult to get the Panama Canal Treaties ratified by two-thirds vote in the Senate than it was to get elected president." Carter made his case with a televised address to the nation. In ratifying the treaties, he said, the United States would demonstrate to the world its resolve to deal fairly with all nations. With the help of Gerald Ford and Henry Kissinger, and on the strength of his own lobbying, Carter was able to secure ratification of the treaties by a single vote. "This is a day of which Americans can always feel proud, for now we have reminded the world and ourselves of the things we stand for as a nation," the president said. In the flush of victory, some of the president's allies succumbed to hyperbole. "This vote marks the end of American colonialism in the world," Alan Cranston, Democratic senator from California, declared.[30]

The *Christian Science Monitor* praised ratification as the dawn of a new era and "a turning point in U.S. relations with Latin America." Wallace Nutting, who commanded U.S. forces in Latin America from 1979 to 1983, characterized the new treaties as "one of the most magnanimous acts in history by a great power." Hispanics, in particular, appreciated the significance of the new treaties. "President Carter set the standard for U.S. presidents in treating Latin Americans with an equality of respect," Maury Maverick, an attorney and columnist, wrote in the *San Antonio Express-News* after the transfer of ownership. "Unfortunately, no president since has chosen to emulate him."[31]

Carter's stands on human rights and the Panama Canal set an unmistakably moral tone for American foreign policy, one that not all Americans approved. Conservatives saw no reason to cede the Panama Canal, especially to a government that many regarded as unstable and perhaps even hostile to American interests. Many Americans also believed it was premature to abandon Cold War dualism and a foreign policy centered around containment of Soviet ambitions; they found vindication for their objections when the Sandinistas came to power in Nicaragua and when the Soviet Union invaded Afghanistan.

CARTER also sought to bring a moral vision to the thorny situation in the Middle East. In 1947, the United Nations had voted to partition the British mandate in Palestine into a Jewish state, an Arab state, and an independent Jerusalem governed by the United Nations as a trustee. Arabs opposed the partition, and when Israel proclaimed its independence on May 14, 1948, the action precipitated the Arab-Israeli War, in the course of which Egypt claimed the Gaza Strip and Jordan the West Bank of the Jordan River. Israel captured most of that territory as well as the Golan Heights and the Sinai Peninsula in the Six-Day War of June 1967. In November of that year, the United Nations passed Resolution 242, which called for Israeli withdrawal from the occupied territories, Arab recognition of Israel, and a resettlement of Palestinian refugees from both the 1967 war and the formation of the State of Israel.

Carter staked out Resolution 242 as the framework for his peace efforts. He met with Anwar el-Sadat, the Egyptian president, and found him congenial and eager for stronger ties with the United States. Carter met with Israel's Menachem Begin as well, who had been elected as prime minister because of his reputation as a hard-liner in defense of Israel's interests. Carter saw in both men something that no one else had discerned: Each of them wanted peace for his people, and both were willing to make serious concessions to attain it.

In November 1977, Sadat made a dramatic visit to Jerusalem and addressed the Israeli Knesset. Begin's reciprocal visit to Egypt was less successful, but Rosalynn Carter suggested to her husband that he invite both leaders to the presidential retreat at Camp David, Maryland, to continue their negotiations.

The summit began on September 5, 1978, and lasted thirteen days. Begin and Sadat were cordial toward one another, albeit wary. Carter tried to bracket out aides as much as possible and confine the conversations to the two principals. When negotiations broke down, as they did frequently, Carter shuttled between the cabins of the two men, trying to broker an agreement. At one point, when an impasse threatened to derail the talks, Carter appealed to both men, Begin especially, to think about their grandchildren and the world they would inherit.

On the final day of the Camp David summit, Begin agreed to allow the Knesset to determine the fate of the Israeli settlements on the Sinai Peninsula. The final "Framework for Peace in the Middle East," negotiated at Camp David, provided for Palestinian self-rule in the West Bank and Gaza, a peace treaty between Egypt and Israel that returned control of the Sinai to Egypt, and a template for peace between Israel and other Arab neighbors. In announcing the historic agreement, the product of thirteen days of negotiations, Carter recalled that "the first thing upon which we agreed was to ask the people of the world to pray that our negotiations would be successful." Begin and Sadat nodded in agreement. "Those prayers have been answered," Carter added, "beyond any expectations."[32]

Indeed, *Christianity Today* noted that the negotiations had opened with a prayer that Carter formulated, one that was acceptable both to Anwar el-Sadat, a Muslim, and Menachem Begin, a Jew, as well as to Carter himself, a Christian. Such a prayer had been suggested to Rosalynn Carter by Harold E.

Hughes, the Democratic former senator from Iowa and an evangelical. Another evangelical weighed in with his support for the Camp David negotiations. "The problem with Israel and the Arab nations and the Middle East is a particularly knotty and complex one, I know, and I'm sure you pray much about it," Pat Boone wrote to the president. The entertainer expressed concern about what he perceived as "hostility in Israel toward Christian evangelicals—after all, you and I are in that number!" The Southern Baptist Convention encouraged its thirteen million members to pray, the Greek Orthodox patriarch telegrammed his support, and the Roman Catholic pontiff, John Paul I, prayed for the talks before forty thousand in St. Peter's Square.[33]

Carter generally enjoyed evangelical support for his overtures for peace in the Middle East. Because of both the Hebrew Bible and the apocalyptic prophecies in the New Testament, especially in the book of Revelation, evangelicals have long favored Israel. "God has an interest in all peoples," an editorial in *Christianity Today* declared, "yet he has a distinguishable interest in the people of Israel." Evangelicals had celebrated the formation of the State of Israel in 1948 as a fulfillment of biblical prophecies, and some saw Israel's success in the Six-Day War of 1967 as a harbinger of the second coming of Jesus. Carter shared many of those evangelical sentiments. "I have a feeling of being at home when I go to Israel," Carter had told the New York Board of Rabbis during the 1976 campaign. He also affirmed his belief that the formation of the nation of Israel in 1948 represented a fulfillment of biblical prophecies.[34]

"The leaders of Egypt and Israel have overcome major substantive obstacles, and they are now daring to break the pattern of thirty years of bitterness and war," Carter said on his return to Washington from negotiating the final agreement. "They are following the advice of the biblical proverb, 'When a man's ways please the Lord, he maketh even his enemies to be at peace with him.'" When reporting on the agreement to Congress, Carter added an extemporaneous sentence to his prepared speech: "And I would like to say, as a Christian, to these two friends of mine, the words of Jesus, 'Blessed are the peacemakers, for they shall be the children of God.'" The treaty that Begin and Sadat signed on the White House lawn on March 26, 1979, officially ended the state of war between the two nations.[35]

Billy Graham sent Carter a congratulatory telegram, and *Christianity Today* praised the agreement and the president's efforts. "We take satisfaction from the manner in which the treaty was achieved," the magazine wrote. "In contrast to the Kissinger practice of realpolitik, avoiding moral judgments, and calculating how to exert power, President Carter has served as a true reconciler, willing to take risks in pursuit of a settlement based on principle."[36]

For Carter, the Camp David accords represented a triumph of moral vision, a repudiation of violence, and an end—potentially at least, if not yet realized—to enmities that had festered for decades, even centuries and millennia. The painstaking quest for peace that culminated at Camp David, he suggested, also represented the best of America. In his address before the Israeli Knesset on March 12, 1979, Carter spoke of the enduring relationship between the United States and Israel "because it is rooted in the consciousness and the morals and the religion of the American people themselves."[37]

For Carter, morality in foreign policy also demanded a reduction in nuclear weapons. Carter enlisted an unlikely ally to generate support for the treaty, Billy Graham, the inveterate Cold Warrior going back to the days of Harry Truman. "I'm in favor of disarmament and I'm in favor of trust," Graham declared on the *CBS Evening News* on March 29, 1979. "I'm in favor of having agreements not only to reduce but to eliminate. Why should any nation have atomic bombs?" Graham continued his advocacy in the pages of *Sojourners*, the magazine of progressive evangelicalism. "I cannot see any way in which nuclear war could be branded as God's will," he said. "I've come to the conviction that this is the teaching of the Bible." Graham even waxed historical. "There was a time when evangelicals were in the vanguard of some of the great social movements," he said, citing the fight against the slave trade. "Then, in some respects, we lost sight of our responsibility to fight social evils." The battle against nuclear weapons was, Graham believed, a worthy one.[38]

The first round of Strategic Arms Limitation Talks, known as SALT I, between the United States and the Soviet Union, concluded in a treaty that reduced the number of intercontinental missiles armed with nuclear weapons. The U.S. Senate ratified the treaty on August 3, 1972. A second round of negotiations, SALT II, began in November 1972 and continued for seven years; the goal was to curtail the manufacture of nuclear weapons. In Vienna, Austria, on June 18, 1979, Carter and Leonid Brezhnev, the Soviet leader, signed SALT II. In the final negotiations, Brezhnev had laid his hand on Carter's shoulder and said, "If we do not succeed, God will not forgive us!"[39]

Despite the fact that the treaty limited Soviet intermediate-range missiles and allowed the United States to retain its Trident and cruise missiles, conservatives complained that Carter had been too placatory, that SALT II had conceded too much to the Soviets. Carter had also extended full diplomatic recognition to the People's Republic of China the previous January, thereby completing the process that Richard Nixon had set in motion. But he began to face criticism that he was soft on communism, both because of SALT II and because he recognized "Red" China.

Fundamentalists in particular castigated the president for what they perceived as a betrayal of Taiwan in favor of Beijing. Ever since the Maoist takeover of China had sent Chiang Kai-shek and his Chinese Nationalists (Kuomintang) into exile on Taiwan in 1949, fundamentalists in particular had railed against the "godless communism" of Mao Zedong's government. The task of restoring Chiang to China emerged as a kind of crusade that would restore godliness—and missionaries—to the mainland. Even though Nixon had begun the process of establishing diplomatic relations with the People's Republic of China, the Carter administration finally consummated those efforts, and for that Carter faced the obloquy of fundamentalists.

Fundamentalism, a militant form of evangelicalism that took its name from a series of pamphlets called *The Fundamentals* in the second decade of the twentieth century, differed from evangelicalism not so much in theology as in temperament. As Jerry Falwell once noted, a fundamentalist is an evangelical who's mad about something. When fundamentalists waded into politics, they generally did so on the right of the political spectrum, and nothing energized them more than resisting the specter of "godless communism." The ranks of twentieth-century fundamentalist leaders were filled with colorful characters, from Robert "Fighting Bob" Shuler and Carl McIntire to Jack Wyrtzen and Falwell himself.

None were more colorful or pugnacious than the Joneses: Bob Jones, Bob Jones Jr., and Bob Jones III. The senior Bob Jones was an itinerant preacher and revivalist who founded Bob Jones College in the Florida panhandle in 1927. The school moved to Cleveland, Tennessee, in 1933 and then to its current location in Greenville, South Carolina, in 1947, where it is now known as Bob Jones University. All three generations of Joneses, each of whom served as president of their eponymous school, were ardent segregationists and fervent anticommunists, so when Jimmy Carter extended diplomatic recognition to the People's Republic of China, he was bound to hear from Greenville. "I question Mr. Carter's Christianity now more than ever," Bob Jones III, president of Bob Jones University, said. "I can't see how a Christian would do this to the 17 million souls in Taiwan. It's an immoral action." Jones promised to spend the ensuing two years working with religious leaders, "stirring up

Christian Americans" to unseat Carter during the 1980 presidential election. "This is not a political thing for me," he said, "it's a religious thing."[40]

The charges that Carter was soft on communism, however, do not square with the facts. Despite his successor's attempts to portray American defenses as diminished during the Carter presidency, Carter had pressed NATO to re-arm early in his term, and when the Soviet Union deployed SS-20 missiles, Carter provided Pershing and cruise missiles for Western Europe. He also dispatched an additional 35,000 soldiers to boost U.S. forces in Europe, which more than restored the cuts made under his Republican predecessors.[41]

The Soviet Union's invasion of Afghanistan a scant six months after the signing of SALT II, however, rendered the treaty moot, and Carter withdrew it from Senate consideration on January 3, 1980. Although both sides agreed to abide by the terms of the treaty, it would never win ratification in the Senate so long as the Soviets remained in Afghanistan.

Carter had been willing—eager, in fact—to move beyond the Cold War and its relentless, potentially deadly faceoff between two ideological adversaries. Nixon, with his overtures to China and his policy of détente, an easing of relations between the United States and the Soviet Union, had already been heading in that direction. Carter sought to continue down that road. He wanted a reduction of nuclear weapons and a policy that emphasized human rights over confrontation, but the invasion of Afghanistan made it clear that the Soviet Union refused to reciprocate, that it was not yet prepared to forsake its imperial ambitions.

Carter's political adversaries, including many conservative evangelicals, seized on his foreign policy as a sign of weakness. They much preferred the trusty dualisms of the post–World War II era—freedom *versus* communism, godly *versus* godless—to Carter's vision of a world where human rights prevailed and where no superpower could exert its will unilaterally or hold the planet hostage with its nuclear arsenal. Carter's willingness to criticize putative allies for human rights abuses upset those dualisms, and events in places like Nicaragua and Afghanistan allowed conservatives to settle into the familiar orthodoxy of Cold War dualism.

No president survives even a day in office without criticism, and the Soviet invasion of Afghanistan represented a serious setback for Carter's vision of a new foreign policy. But Carter also tallied a number of victories. He pardoned Vietnam-era draft resisters and hoped, in so doing, to close a festering wound in America's recent past. Although Carter's resolve that human rights would trump Cold War confrontation in American foreign policy came to be seen as naïve once the Soviets invaded Afghanistan, the new emphasis succeeded both in calling attention to the issue and also in ameliorating the plight of many political prisoners. Carter embarked determinedly on his mission to bring peace to the Middle East, and the ratification of the Panama Canal treaties represented a major political triumph, one that Carter thought was essential to any improvement in relations with Latin America. Carter also insisted that America's dependence on foreign sources of oil had parlous consequences for American foreign policy and urged bold steps toward energy independence.

The expenditure of so much political capital early in his presidency, however, would exact a fearsome cost. Carter's political adversaries were amassing against him, and they were preparing a pincer action. Edward Kennedy from Carter's own political party deemed the president insufficiently liberal on domestic issues, while a host of conservatives characterized him as weak, ineffectual, and too liberal. The Watergate scandal had thrown conservative activists off balance during the 1976 election, but they were quickly regaining their footing during Carter's presidency. What no one could have predicted was that these activists, capitalizing on discontent over domestic issues, would enlist Carter's fellow evangelicals in their mission to topple his presidency.

SIX

ENDANGERED EVANGELICAL

JIMMY Carter's shift in foreign policy away from Cold War dualism and toward emphasis on human rights had provoked charges that he underestimated the continuing threat of communism, a criticism that gained currency with the Sandinistas' rise to power in Nicaragua and the Soviet invasion of Afghanistan. Many of Carter's fellow evangelicals, hewing to the familiar post–World War II polarities of godliness and communism, joined that chorus.

Despite several notable achievements in foreign affairs, especially the Panama Canal treaties and the Camp David accords, Carter's domestic policies represented more of a minefield, one that would contribute mightily to his political undoing. Carter was essentially a social conservative on matters of family and sexuality; he had spoken frequently on the campaign trail about the importance of family, and although he stopped short of calling for a constitutional amendment on the matter, he emphasized again and again that he was "personally opposed" to abortion.

During the course of Carter's presidency, however, politically conservative evangelicals would find reason to abandon him, and the pretext they used was domestic policy, especially social issues. Although homosexuality and, eventually, abortion, would figure into their critique, the real catalyst for their disaffection was race, especially the issue of desegregation. The fact that evangelicals seized on the issue of race to abandon Carter was freighted with irony. Carter's ascent to the presidency was possible in large measure because he had repented of the aberrational racial politics he used to win election as governor in 1970; his fresh image as a New South governor, his defeat of George Wallace in the Democratic primaries, and his support from African Americans had pushed him toward the White House.

Some conservative evangelicals, however, did not share Carter's progressive views on race, although they struggled mightily—and with remarkable success—to frame their opposition in more acceptable terms like freedom of religious expression. They protested moves on the part of the Internal Revenue Service to revoke the tax exemption of racially discriminatory schools and then blamed Carter, unfairly and inaccurately, for the action. Once mobilized in opposition to Carter, these leaders constructed an equally implausible case against Carter around social issues.

JIMMY Carter himself, who celebrated his thirtieth wedding anniversary during the 1976 campaign, was a paragon of "family values," and his personal views, like his own life, were traditional and conservative. Carter had spoken often during the 1976 campaign about threats to the family, including divorce and out-of-wedlock births. "I intend to construct an administration that will reverse trends we have seen toward a breakdown of the family in our country," he told an audience in Manchester, New Hampshire. Early in his presidency, Carter addressed employees of the Department of Housing and Urban Development. "It's very important that all of us in government not forget that no matter how dedicated we might be and how eager we are to perform well, we need a stable family life to make us better servants of the people," the president said. "So those of you who are living in sin, I hope you'll get married. Those of you who have left your spouses, go back home. And those of you who don't remember your children's names, get reacquainted." Several of Carter's close aides took his advice and solemnized their long-term relationships.[1]

Indeed, few people, even his political foes, could find fault with Carter's personal life. "I believe that one of Carter's biggest contributions as president has been the morality and model of his private life," Wesley Pippert, an evangelical who covered the Carter campaign, wrote almost two years into his presidency. Carter, following in the wake of Richard Nixon's corruption, provided a welcome contrast. "It is just as important that a nation have a leader to whom it can look as a model of private morality," Pippert added. "Recent presidents have failed utterly here and we have been embarrassed as a result."[2]

Although Carter's views on marriage and the family would generally be construed as conservative, he stood solidly within the tradition of progressive evangelicalism on women's rights. Indeed, Carter was a strong supporter of equal rights for women, both as governor and as president. While governor, Carter casually remarked that although he supported the proposed Equal Rights Amendment to the Constitution, Rosalynn opposed it. On seeing the news story, Rosalynn, who had once walked out of a Bible study when the male teacher declared that wives should be subservient to their husbands, marched into the governor's office with two of her feminist allies and, in no uncertain terms, upbraided the governor. Carter later said that he was glad no one recorded the conversation lest anyone "hear what she said to me." While campaigning for president, Carter told a gathering called the Women's Agenda Conference of his appreciation for feminism. "There have been few political developments in America in recent years that have impressed me more than the movement of women toward equal rights," he said.[3]

Until Carter's presidency, the proposed Equal Rights Amendment to the Constitution had been relatively uncontroversial. The idea for such an amendment was first proposed in 1923 by Alice Paul, a suffragist leader, on the heels of the Nineteenth Amendment, which granted women the right to vote. The Republican Party began incorporating support for an Equal Rights Amendment into its platform in 1940; the Democrats did so as well, beginning in 1944. Dwight D. Eisenhower renewed the appeal for such an amendment before a joint session of Congress in 1958, but it was not until 1972, on the heels of second-wave feminism, which began in the 1960s, that Congress finally—and overwhelmingly—approved the Equal Rights Amendment and passed it along to the states for ratification.

Thirty states ratified the amendment by the end of 1973 and three more the following year, leaving the amendment just five states shy of inclusion in the U.S. Constitution. Both political parties in 1976, Republican and Democratic, unequivocally endorsed ratification of the Equal Rights Amendment. The momentum for ratification began to slow, however, in the mid-1970s, due in large measure to the efforts of Phyllis Schlafly, a Roman Catholic and conservative Republican lawyer from Alton, Illinois. Schlafly, who often opened her speeches by thanking her husband for allowing her to appear, launched a Stop ERA campaign in 1972. She claimed that the proposed Equal Rights Amendment would subject women to the military draft and unisex bathrooms. She characterized her organization, Eagle Forum, as a "pro-family" group, and by the time of the Carter presidency, Schlafly had begun to enlist some evangelical leaders in her campaign to defend "traditional" values.

Among evangelicals themselves, the tradition of progressive evangelicalism on women's rights had thinned out in the postwar era, and many white evangelicals, including evangelical women themselves, increasingly suburban, professed to prefer "traditional" gender roles. Moreover, as women's equality became increasingly identified with flamboyant personalities and radical politics in the 1960s and 1970s, Carter's continuing support for women's issues began to emerge as a dividing line between the president and conservative evangelicals.

While in office, however, Carter appointed more women to his administration than any previous president. He signed an extension of the proposed Equal Rights Amendment to the Constitution, allowing more time for states to ratify, and lobbied state legislatures for its passage. The failure to win the approval of thirty-eight states, Carter said, represented a huge setback for both the president and first lady; Rosalynn Carter characterized it as the "greatest disappointment in all the projects I worked on during the White House years." Jimmy Carter was especially miffed that many religious figures had led the charge against women's equality. "The discrimination by male religious authorities, who claim it is the will of God," Carter said, "is one of the root causes of the worldwide abuse of women and girls."[4]

The issue of abortion also became increasingly fraught during Carter's term in office. The U.S. Supreme Court's *Roe v. Wade* ruling on January 22, 1973, effectively struck down laws restricting abortion before "viability," when a fetus could survive outside of the womb. Although evangelical response was muted, Roman Catholic bishops condemned the ruling, and many Catholic politicians in the Democratic Party—among them Edward M. Kennedy and Sargent Shriver—numbered themselves among the opponents of abortion. George McGovern, the party's nominee in 1972, was uneasy about legalized abortion, and the surge in legal abortions in the months following the *Roe* decision unsettled many Americans.

As the 1976 election approached, however, feminists insisted that the Democratic Party adopt a "pro-choice" position, arguing that women's reproductive decisions should not be a matter of public policy. The 1976 Democratic Party platform reflected those sentiments. "We fully recognize the religious and ethical nature of the concerns which many Americans have on the subject of abortion," the platform read. "We feel, however, that it is undesirable to attempt to amend the U.S. Constitution to overturn the Supreme Court decision in this area." The Republican Party sought to straddle the issue without taking a clear position. "There are those in our Party who favor complete support for the Supreme Court decision which permits abortion on demand," the 1976 Republican platform read. "There are others who share sincere convictions that the Supreme Court's decision must be changed by a constitutional amendment prohibiting all abortions."[5]

The Democratic Party plank roughly tracked Carter's position on abortion: uneasy about abortion itself but opposed to a constitutional amendment. Carter himself, as he reiterated many times throughout the campaign, opposed abortion. In choosing a secretary for the Department of Health, Education and Welfare, the president wanted a "good Catholic" who reflected his own views and who would restrict the use of public funds to pay for abortions. Joseph A. Califano Jr., an ardently pro-life Roman Catholic who had served in the Lyndon Johnson White House, fit the bill. "Carter never asked my views on the subject and I never expressed them," Califano recalled, adding that the two men "simply assumed complete agreement."[6]

Many of Carter's staff members, however, took a different position on abortion, including Margaret "Midge" Costanza, Carter's assistant for public liaison. When Congress renewed the Hyde Amendment in July 1977, which prohibited federal funding for abortion, Carter stated publicly that he had no problem with the restriction. When pressed on how this might affect poor women, the president replied that "there are many things in life that are not fair, that wealthy people can afford and poor people can't."[7]

In response, Costanza drafted a memorandum to the president, which, she said, reflected the sentiments of many staff members. Costanza wrote that "those who have called me hope that you will reconsider your position and support the use of Federal funds for abortions when 'medically necessary,' " to which Carter wrote in the margin, "No." Costanza continued: "On the second point, there are those who feel that in expressing your personal view on the role of the States in the question of funding for abortions, you have provided negative guidance to legislators and governors and interfered in a State process in an unfair way." Carter's gloss: "If I had this much influence on state legis[latures] ERA would have passed." At the bottom of the memorandum, Carter wrote: "My opinion was well defined to U.S. during campaign. My statement is actually more liberal than I feel personally."[8]

Rosalynn Carter claimed that her husband was more conservative on abortion than she was. "I oppose it for myself," she wrote, "but I have a hard time with deciding for other women what is right or wrong or best for them." Jimmy Carter felt caught between his own views—"Because of my religious beliefs I have never supported abortions, except to protect the life and health of the mother or in cases where pregnancies resulted from rape or incest"—and his responsibility, as president, to uphold the law. His middle ground on the issue, which he had articulated during his presidential campaign, was to honor the law while simultaneously seeking to minimize the incidence of abortion by means of sex education, support for pregnant women, and laws that encouraged and facilitated adoption.[9]

MIDWAY through his first year in office, another ominous social issue—homosexuality—suddenly roiled to the surface; once again, Carter's own relatively conservative views would conflict with policies he felt obligated to pursue as president. Carter refused to characterize homosexuality as a "normal relationship," but he was steadfast in his insistence that gays and lesbians were entitled to full rights as citizens. "I don't see homosexuality as a threat to the family," he told a reporter for *Christianity Today*. "I don't feel that society, through its laws, ought to abuse or harass the individual."[10]

In 1977, Dade County, Florida, passed an ordinance that prohibited discrimination on the basis of sexual orientation. Anita Bryant, a former Miss Oklahoma and runner-up Miss America, was livid, arguing, she claimed, on the basis of her evangelical convictions, that homosexuality was wrong and that gays and lesbians were out to recruit children to their sinful lifestyle. Bryant, spokeswoman for the Florida Citrus Commission, led a political coalition, Save Our Children, that rallied public support to overturn the ordinance. At Bryant's invitation, Jerry Falwell, pastor of Thomas Road Baptist Church in Lynchburg, Virginia, came to Miami to speak against homosexuality; he later recalled that it was his first taste of political advocacy.

On June 7, 1977, voters repealed the ordinance by a margin of 69 to 31 percent. More important, Bryant's campaign marked the beginning of conservative evangelical activity on a national level. "I am going to speak out against all the evil forces that threaten our children and the security of our families and individuals," Bryant promised in a letter to supporters. In addition to "radical, militant homosexuals," Bryant pilloried television, pornography, and "liberal newspapers." Gays and lesbians, she warned, "want to recruit your children and teach them the virtues of becoming a homosexual."[11]

Many evangelicals, including Billy Graham, expressed support for Bryant's efforts. "She is a very brave woman," Graham said. "Homosexuality is a sin," although he acknowledged that he would have taken a somewhat different approach: "Some of the things she and her associates said I would not have said in the same way." The evangelist demurred that he understood his calling as a preacher and not an activist, and he expressed his apprehensions that Bryant would energize gay and lesbian activists.[12]

Bryant's crusade did indeed trigger a counter-campaign among gays and lesbians. They mobilized to boycott orange juice, prompting the Florida Citrus Commission to allow Bryant's endorsement contract to lapse in 1979. By then, however, Falwell and others had taken up the cudgels of antigay rhetoric, casting it as a struggle against a secularized culture. "Animals like Johnny Carson get on television and make jokes about everything that is sacred and holy," Falwell lamented in a sermon. "And when somebody like Anita Bryant stands up against homosexuality and stands up for right, your actors and actresses and screen personalities, organize a battalion to ridicule her and laugh her to scorn." Falwell continued preaching against the "growing cancer of homosexuality" in 1978. He reiterated Bryant's claims about gay recruitment and compared homosexuality to an infectious disease. "Because God will judge the nation given over to homosexuality," he said, "I believe the United States will be destroyed if we permit homosexuality as an alternative lifestyle."[13]

Carter, for his part, failed to see the gathering storm. He regarded abortion and homosexuality as a distraction, and he worried that they diverted attention of his staff from his legislative and policy agenda. "I've been concerned about her involvement in the abortion and gay rights business," Carter recorded in his diary about Midge Costanza, his aide, "but she takes a tremendous burden off me from nut groups that would insist on seeing me if they couldn't see her."[14]

As politically conservative evangelicals began to consider their response to abortion and homosexuality, the president continued to nurture his faith. Aside from teaching Sunday school at First Baptist Church when his schedule permitted, Carter maintained a relationship with Harold E. Hughes, the liberal Democrat from Iowa who had suggested organized prayer in advance of the Camp David peace talks. In November 1978, the president found time to attend what he characterized as "a Christian fellowship meeting" at a retreat in Cedar Point, Maryland, with Hughes, several senators, a general, and Doug Coe, the evangelical leader of Fellowship Foundation. Later, in a handwritten postscript at the bottom of a letter to Hughes, the president wrote: "Within the next week or two I would like to join the Senate prayer group." Before signing the postscript "J," the president instructed: "No publicity." Carter did in fact join the prayer group, whose membership included Mark O. Hatfield, Republican of Oregon, a Baptist and a progressive evangelical who enjoyed wide respect. Carter participated in the prayer group on several occasions. "Mark Hatfield was a kind of hero of mine," Carter said. "I was filled with admiration for him."[15]

Carter, in classic evangelical fashion, understood his presidential work as ministry. Writing to a Baptist pastor, Carter promised that, "I will continue to make my personal witness." He added: "With your prayers, and with the prayers of the American people, I know that we will accomplish much by example as well as by precept." The chief executive affirmed that prayer was very much part of his life. "I do pray often and seek His guidance before I make any major decision," the president told a Sunday-school class in Calhoun, Georgia, on Easter Sunday 1977. When Rosalynn inadvertently disclosed to a reporter that her husband repeated a Bible verse to himself on his way to the Oval Office each morning, the president revealed that it was a verse from the Psalms: "Let the words of my mouth and the meditations of my heart be acceptable in thy sight, O Lord, my strength and my redeemer." Carter explained that it was a verse he had memorized as a child, "and I think as President I need to be cautious about what I say and what I think so that it will be compatible with my own faith and the principles of our country." The president also kept a Bible on his desk in the Oval Office.[16]

The president's piety, however, did nothing to forestall his political adversaries. The 1978 elections, a barometer of public sentiment, did not go well for Carter and the Democratic Party. Although Carter himself, midway through his term, was not on the ballot, Democrats suffered a net loss of three seats in the Senate and fifteen seats in the House of Representatives. Though not unexpected for the party in power—Republicans suffered far greater losses in the previous bi-election year of 1974, the year of Nixon's resignation—those reading the election returns could see that abortion was beginning to emerge as a political issue.

In Iowa, for example, polls and pundits expected that the incumbent Democratic senator, Richard C. "Dick" Clark, would coast easily to reelection; no poll heading into the November balloting indicated that Clark held a lead of fewer than 10 percentage points. Six years earlier, Clark had walked across the state to call attention to his grassroots, upstart challenge to Jack Miller, the two-term Republican incumbent, and Clark prevailed with 55 percent of the vote. He remained a popular figure in the state. Pro-life activists, however, had targeted Clark, and on the final weekend of Clark's reelection campaign representatives of Iowans for Life (predominantly Roman Catholics) distributed approximately 300,000 pamphlets in church parking lots. Two days later, in an election with very low turnout, Roger Jepsen, the Republican pro-life challenger, defeated Clark. An Election Day survey by the *Des Moines Register* indicated that about 25,000 Iowans voted for Jepsen because of his stand on abortion. "I personally believe that the abortion issue was the central issue," Clark told Bruce Morton of CBS News. The senator's campaign manager agreed. "It comes right down to those leaflets they put out," he said.[17]

Christianity Today noted Clark's unexpected defeat, and the magazine also credited pro-lifers for the Republican trifecta in Minnesota, where Republican candidates who opposed abortion captured both Senate seats (one for the unexpired term of Hubert Humphrey) and the office of governor. "Anti-abortionists figured in the collapse of Minnesota's liberal Democratic-Farmer-Labor Party," the magazine reported, adding that the campaign of Albert Quie, the governor-elect and ally of Charles Colson, "distributed 250,000 leaflets to churchgoers throughout the state on the Sunday before election day."[18]

None of this was lost on Paul Weyrich, the conservative strategist who would become the principal architect of the Religious Right. Earlier that year, Weyrich, one of the founders of the Heritage Foundation and head of the Committee for the Survival of a Free Congress, had received a check in the amount of twenty-five dollars from Georgia G. Glassman, of Gravity, Iowa. "Please make Good use of the proceeds," she wrote, "as soon as we hear that a good Republican, a Lawyer I hope, has announced his candidacy for the U.S. Senate, we Republicans will try to 'Hang Sen. Dick Clark on a telephone pole!'"[19]

WEYRICH's discovery of abortion as an issue that could energize conservative evangelicals was a long time coming. Ever since Barry Goldwater's campaign for the presidency in 1964, Weyrich had been trying to organize evangelicals politically. Their numbers alone, he reasoned, would constitute a formidable voting bloc, and he aspired to marshal them behind conservative causes.

Weyrich had the blueprint in place. "The new political philosophy must be defined by us in moral terms, packaged in non-religious language, and propagated throughout the country by our new coalition," Weyrich wrote in spelling out his vision. "When political power is achieved, the moral majority will have the opportunity to re-create this great nation." Weyrich believed that the political possibilities of such a coalition were unlimited. "The leadership, moral philosophy, and workable vehicle are at hand just waiting to be blended and activated," he wrote. "If the moral majority acts, results could well exceed our wildest dreams."[20]

But Weyrich's dreams, still a hypothetical coalition, which he already referred to as the "moral majority" (lower-case letters), lacked a catalyst. He needed not simply an event or issue that would ignite all the indignation that had been accumulating, but also a standard around which to rally. For nearly two decades, Weyrich, by his own account, had tried various issues to pique evangelical interest in his scheme, including abortion, pornography, school prayer, and the proposed Equal Rights Amendment to the Constitution.

Snubbed on these issues, Weyrich recognized by the mid-1970s the necessity of a multipronged approach to mobilize evangelical voters. First, he needed to enlist evangelical and fundamentalist leaders in his political crusade; once the leaders were onboard, grassroots evangelicals would follow. Opposition to abortion, as it turned out, would be the secondary, populist issue, the issue that would energize grassroots evangelicals in the late 1970s. Evangelical leaders, however, had shown little interest in abortion as a political matter, and so Weyrich needed a different, antecedent issue that would rally evangelical leaders. After searching for the better part of a decade, Weyrich finally found his issue, a federal court ruling that would rouse evangelical leaders out of their apolitical stupor.[21]

In May 1969, a group of African-American parents in Holmes County, Mississippi, had filed suit to prevent three new whites-only academies from securing tax exemption from the Internal Revenue Service (IRS); each of the schools had been founded to evade desegregation of the public schools. In Holmes County, the number of white students enrolled in the public schools had dropped from 771 to 28 during the first year of desegregation; the following year, that number fell to zero. Elsewhere in the South, nearly two hundred private schools opened in Mississippi, Louisiana, Alabama, Florida, North Carolina, and South Carolina between 1964 and 1967, just as officials were beginning to implement the provisions of the *Brown v. Board of Education* ruling, the landmark decision of the Supreme Court on May 17, 1954, which mandated the desegregation of public schools. Most of these schools opened in the 1960s were avowedly segregationist. White Citizens' Councils operated more than 150 such "segregation academies."[22]

The court case out of Mississippi was known as *Green v. Kennedy*—Green, the African-American plaintiffs, against David M. Kennedy, secretary of the treasury, the cabinet department responsible for the Internal Revenue Service. The plantiffs won a temporary injunction against granting tax exemption to "segregation academies" in January 1970, and later that year, Richard

Nixon ordered the IRS to enact a new policy that would deny tax exemptions to segregated schools. In July 1970, the Internal Revenue Service announced that, in accordance with the provisions of Title VI of the Civil Rights Act of 1964, which forbade racial segregation and discrimination, it would no longer grant tax-exempt status to private schools with racially discriminatory policies. Such institutions were not—by definition—charitable organizations, and therefore they had no claims to tax-exempt status; similarly, donations to such organizations would no longer qualify as tax-deductible contributions.[23]

The IRS, charged with enforcing the regulations, cast a wide net. On November 30, 1970, the IRS sent letters of inquiry to schools in an effort to ascertain whether or not they discriminated on the basis of race. Bob Jones University, the fundamentalist school in Greenville, South Carolina, responded defiantly that it did not admit African Americans to its student body, a response that virtually guaranteed that the agency would pursue the matter and challenge the school's tax-exempt status.

Meanwhile, the *Green v. Kennedy* suit was joined with a similar suit to become *Green v. Connally* (John Connally had succeeded David Kennedy as secretary of the treasury in February 1971). On June 30, 1971, the U.S. District Court for the District of Columbia issued its ruling in the *Green v. Connally* case: "Under the Internal Revenue Code, properly construed, racially discriminatory private schools are not entitled to the Federal tax exemption provided for charitable, educational institutions, and persons making gifts to such schools are not entitled to the deductions provided in case of gifts to charitable, educational institutions."[24]

Weyrich saw his opening. Because the *Green v. Connally* ruling was "applicable to all private schools in the United States at all levels of education," Bob Jones University and, by extension, other evangelical schools stood directly in the IRS crosshairs. Weyrich was astute enough to recognize that evangelical institutions, discriminatory or not, would not take kindly to this sort of governmental intrusion into their affairs. Evangelicals had largely stayed out of politics during the middle decades of the twentieth century precisely because their institutions—the evangelical subculture—allowed them a measure of autonomy from an outside world that they regarded with both detachment and suspicion. Indeed, a point of pride for these institutions, articulated frequently and with great passion, was that they accepted no money from the federal government and therefore the government could not tell them how to run their affairs—who to accept or reject, who to hire or fire.[25]

When the Internal Revenue Service began "snooping" into the policies of these evangelical institutions, therefore, the reaction was fierce and immediate. Ignoring the fact that tax exemption itself represents public subsidy—taxpayers fund the tax exemptions for these institutions—evangelical leaders decried the IRS actions as an impingement of their religious freedom, which for some included the "right" to discriminate.

No institution howled louder or longer at the IRS than Bob Jones University. In response to *Green v. Connally*, Bob Jones University had admitted a married black man, a worker in the school's radio station, as a part-time student. He dropped out a month later. Out of fears of racial mixing, the school maintained its restrictions against admitting *unmarried* African Americans until 1975. Even then, however, the school stipulated that interracial dating would be grounds for expulsion, and the school also promised that any students who "espouse, promote, or encourage others to violate the University's dating rules and regulations will be expelled."[26]

The Internal Revenue Service pursued its case against Bob Jones University and on April 16, 1975, notified the school of the proposed revocation of its tax exemption. The university refused to alter its discriminatory policies. On January 19, 1976, the IRS officially revoked Bob Jones University's tax-exempt status, effective retroactively to 1971, when the school had first been formally notified of the IRS policy. As Bob Jones University sued to retain its tax exemption, Weyrich pressed his case, framing it as an issue of religious freedom rather than racial discrimination. Following Weyrich's lead, evangelical leaders, especially those whose schools were affected by the ruling, construed the decision as government intrusion into religious matters. Weyrich used the *Green v. Connally* case to rally evangelicals against the government. When "the Internal Revenue Service tried to deny tax exemption to private schools," Weyrich recalled later in an interview with *Conservative Digest*, that "more than any single act brought the fundamentalists and evangelicals into the political process."[27]

Although Jimmy Carter had nothing to do with this policy—he was running for the Democratic nomination when Bob Jones University lost its tax exemption—the Internal Revenue Service during Carter's time in office poured fuel on the embers of evangelical resentment. Although there is no evidence to suggest that the Carter White House participated in drafting the regulations, Jerome Kurtz, the IRS commissioner, proposed on August 22, 1978, that schools founded or expanded at the time of desegregation of public schools in their locality meet a quota of minority students or certify that they operated "in good faith on a racially non-discriminatory basis." The regulations, in effect, shifted the burden of proof from the Internal Revenue Service to the schools. The American Conservative Union wasted no time providing an interpretation: IRS SAYS: GUILTY UNTIL PROVEN INNOCENT. Evangelicals picked up the cue. "Our schools are not racially discriminatory," a couple from Ithaca, New York, wrote, "and we strongly dislike being placed in a position of being considered guilty until proven innocent."[28]

Evangelical leaders interpreted the IRS proposals as an unwarranted abrogation of their religious freedom. *Christianity Today* characterized "the interference of the federal government in the Christian school movement" as the "Stamp Act of the Religious Right," a reference to one of the provocations that triggered the American Revolution. Evangelicals flooded the IRS with letters of protest, more than 125,000 in all. The proposed regulations "kicked a sleeping dog," Richard Viguerie, one of the founders of the New Right, said. "It was the episode that ignited the religious right's involvement in real politics." When *Conservative Digest* catalogued evangelical discontent with Carter in August 1979, the Internal Revenue Service regulations headed the list. Abortion was not mentioned.[29]

Although the Internal Revenue Service backed away from many of the proposals, the fires of resentment flared. "To impose student and faculty quotas on private schools is a treacherous intervention into a Constitutionally protected activity," John Ashbrook, Republican member of Congress from Ohio, wrote to Carter. "Its arbitrary formula for student and staff recruitment will place Federal bureaucrats at the helm of policy formation for private schools." Ashbrook's House colleague, Robert Dornan of California, warned that Americans "are sick and tired of unelected bureaucrats engaging in social engineering at the expense of our cherished liberties." Weyrich encouraged Robert J. Billings, an evangelical, to form an organization called Christian School Action as a vehicle for building on evangelical discontent, an organization Weyrich came to regard as a "tremendous asset" to his hopes for politicizing conservative evangelicals. Billings, who had earlier founded the National Christian Action Coalition to thwart what he characterized as "an attempt by the IRS to control private schools," quickly mobilized evangelical ministers. Billings later declared, "Jerome Kurtz has done more to bring Christians together than any man since the Apostle Paul." Even Anita Bryant, who had been goaded into activism by gay rights, recognized the centrality of the school issue. "I believe the day of the comfortable Christian is over," Bryant declared. "Maybe it hasn't reached everybody in the rural areas, but it's a battle in the cities to keep them from taking over and reaching private and religious schools."[30]

Aside from Bob Jones Jr. and Bob Jones III, his successor as president of their eponymous university, no one was more agitated than Jerry Falwell, who complained, "In some states it is easier to open a massage parlor than to open the doors of a Christian school." Falwell, a southerner, was an acknowledged segregationist for much of his life. He had loudly protested *Brown v. Board of Education.* In a sermon entitled "Segregation or Integration: Which?" Falwell declared: "If Chief Justice [Earl] Warren and his associates had known God's word and had desired to do the Lord's will, I am quite confident that the 1954 decision would never have been made." Falwell stated his conviction that school "facilities should be separate. When God has drawn a line of distinction, we should not attempt to cross that line." He referred to the Civil Rights Act of 1964 as "civil wrongs," and in 1966 he started his own school to circumvent the *Brown* ruling; the local newspaper, the *Lynchburg News*, described Lynchburg Christian Academy as "a private school for white students." (Falwell himself later expressed contrition for his racist attitudes. "It took me several years to get segregation flushed out of my soul," he told an interviewer in 1983.)[31]

In ramping up for political activism, evangelicals portrayed themselves as victims, forced to defend what they considered the sanctity of the evangelical subculture from outside interference. Weyrich encouraged those sentiments. "What caused the movement to surface was the federal government's moves against Christian schools," Weyrich reiterated in 1990. "This absolutely shattered the Christian community's notions that Christians could isolate themselves inside their own institutions and teach what they pleased." For agitated evangelicals, Weyrich's conservative gospel of less government suddenly struck a responsive chord. "It wasn't the abortion issue; that wasn't sufficient," Weyrich recalled. "It was the recognition that isolation simply would no longer work in this society."[32]

Although Weyrich was ostensibly defending evangelicals' right to isolation, he was actually seeking to terminate their insularity, to push evangelicals into political activism. Paradoxically, that evangelical isolationist impulse was the same sentiment that Jimmy Carter had encountered when he ran for the Georgia state senate in 1962—when the itinerant Baptist preacher challenged Carter to pursue an "honorable" vocation rather than run for political office. Carter defied that prevailing evangelical wisdom by embarking on a political career, and his open declarations of faith over the course of that career brought other evangelicals into the political arena, as voters at least, if not necessarily as candidates. In so doing, Carter, together with other evangelical politicians like Mark Hatfield and Harold Hughes, revived many of the nobler impulses of progressive evangelicalism: an aversion to armed conflict, care for the poor and hungry, prison reform, and equal rights for women and minorities.

Although Carter's political ascent had lured many evangelicals into politics, Weyrich's machinations in the 1970s revealed that not all evangelicals were yet persuaded of the legitimacy of political activism. Weyrich and others labored to change that, but the irony is that they did so by pitching their appeals from an ideological perspective that bore scant resemblance to evangelical activism in the nineteenth and early twentieth centuries. Whereas Carter advocated for women's equality, the Religious Right opposed the Equal Rights Amendment to the Constitution. Whereas Carter as member of the Sumter County School Board and as governor and president worked for racial reconciliation—the courting of segregationists during his 1970 campaign for governor remains an anomaly—Weyrich, Falwell, and others organized effectively, if not avowedly, to defend racial segregation at Bob Jones University and similar institutions.

Although leaders of the Religious Right in later years would seek to portray their politicization as a direct response to the *Roe v. Wade* ruling of 1973, Weyrich and other organizers of the Religious Right have emphatically dismissed this abortion myth. *Green v. Connally* served as the catalyst, not *Roe v. Wade*. Although many evangelicals certainly felt troubled by abortion and viewed it as symptom of promiscuity in American society, most of them regarded it as a Catholic issue in the realm of politics until the late 1970s. (Falwell acknowledged as much when he preached against abortion on February 26, 1978, from his pulpit at Thomas Road Baptist Church.) Evangelical leaders, prodded by Weyrich, chose to interpret the IRS ruling against segregationist schools as an assault on the integrity and the sanctity of the evangelical subculture, ignoring the fact that exemption from taxes is itself a form of public subsidy. That is what prompted them to action and to organize into a political movement.

Despite the persistence of the abortion myth, other early leaders of the Religious Right have corroborated Weyrich's account that defense of Bob Jones University and other institutions galvanized evangelical leaders into a political force. "The Religious New Right did not start because of a concern about abortion," Ed Dobson, formerly Falwell's assistant at Moral Majority,

said in 1990. "I sat in the non-smoke-filled back room with the Moral Majority, and I frankly do not remember abortion being mentioned as a reason
why we ought to do something." More recently, another conservative activist, Grover Norquist, confirmed that the *Roe v. Wade* decision did not factor
into the rise of the Religious Right. "The religious right did not get started in
1962 with prayer in school," Norquist told Dan Gilgoff, of *U.S. News & World
Report*, in June 2009. "And it didn't get started in '73 with *Roe v. Wade*. It
started in '77 or '78 with the Carter administration's attack on Christian
schools and radio stations. That's where all of the organization flowed out of.
It was complete self-defense."[33]

The actions of the Internal Revenue Service especially affected Bob Jones
University, goading those associated with the school into political activism.
Elmer L. Rumminger, longtime administrator at the university who became
politically active in 1980, remembered that the IRS case "alerted the Christian
school community about what could happen with government interference" in
the affairs of evangelical institutions. "That was really the major issue that got
us all involved to begin with—at least it was for me." What about abortion? "No,
no, that wasn't the issue," he said emphatically. "This wasn't an anti-abortion
movement per se. That was one of the issues we were interested in. I'm sure
some people pointed to *Roe v. Wade*, but that's not what got us going. For me it
was government intrusion into private education."[34]

WITH evangelical leaders now prepared for political battle, Weyrich still
needed an issue that would energize politically conservative evangelicals at
the grass roots, something that would not only lure them to the polls but also
motivate them to engage in the kinds of activities that win elections. In 1977,
Weyrich had appealed to the head of the Republican National Committee to
court evangelical and fundamentalist voters, but his appeal fell on deaf ears;
the chair of the committee "didn't understand what I was talking about," Weyrich said, "it was so foreign to him that it didn't make any sense." Undeterred,
Weyrich resolved to "go out and elect some improbable people in the '78 elections." The defeat of Dick Clark at the hands of a pro-life Republican in Iowa
and the triple win for pro-life Republicans in Minnesota suggested that abortion might very well be the issue that would galvanize grassroots evangelicals
and fundamentalists into a cohesive political movement.[35]

Weyrich could barely contain his delight with the 1978 returns, especially the Senate elections in Iowa and in New Hampshire, where Gordon
Humphrey, another pro-life candidate, had ousted Thomas J. McIntyre, a

three-term Democratic incumbent. "The election of Roger Jepsen and Gordon Humphrey to the U.S. Senate is true cause for celebration, especially in view of the fact that two of the most liberal senators went down to defeat," Weyrich wrote. Even more notable, however, was how it happened: with the support of politically conservative evangelicals. Weyrich immediately set about to fortify the nascent coalition. On December 5, just a month after the election, Weyrich brought Humphrey, the senator-elect from New Hampshire, and his wife to a gathering of evangelical activists. The following day, Robert Billings penned an exultant letter to Weyrich, praising him for his "wise remarks" and congratulating him on the "smashing success" of an evening. "Paul, we did something that no-one has done in years," Billings wrote, a reference to the mobilizing of conservative evangelical voters. "I believe something was started last night that will pull together many of our 'fringe' Christian friends." Billings concluded his handwritten letter: "Thank you for your important part. God bless you!"[36]

Weyrich, a member of the Melkite Greek Catholic Church, continued his assiduous courting of politically conservative evangelical leaders, demonstrating his fluency in the vocabulary of evangelicalism. "Tears came to my eyes when the sun came out at the proper moment," Weyrich wrote to Falwell after attending the televangelist's patriotic "I Love America" rally at the Capitol. "I believe we are on the right track and that together we may work for the Lord's glory and to preserve our great nation." Three days later, Weyrich wrote to James Robison. "It is obvious that we share fundamental values," Weyrich wrote. "I look forward to a long and productive relationship. I am confident that the Lord has seen to it that we can work together for His purposes."[37]

FOR Weyrich and for other conservative leaders, the Lord was working in mysterious ways in the political world of the 1970s. Conservative attempts early in the decade to use abortion to entice evangelical leaders into political activism had failed to elicit a response; for most evangelicals, abortion was a Catholic issue, and they wanted no part of it. The debacle of the Nixon presidency and the discrediting of the Republican Party had contributed to the election of a progressive evangelical, a Democrat, to the White House. Carter's ascendance had momentarily disrupted the general postwar preference on the part of white evangelicals for Republican politicians. Weyrich sought not merely to restore politically conservative evangelicals to the ranks of Republican voters, he wanted also to organize them as a conservative political force.

With the abortion issue having failed as an inducement, Weyrich seized on the Internal Revenue Service's pursuit of racially segregated schools. The fact that this action began during the Nixon administration, and that Nixon himself authorized the policy of denying tax exemption to schools that discriminated on the basis of race, did nothing to dampen the outrage of evangelical leaders. Contrary to all logic, they directed blame for this action against Carter, their fellow evangelical. By the early months of the Carter presidency, Weyrich finally had discovered the issue that would persuade evangelical leaders of the importance of political activism: defense of racial segregation, albeit framed as a defense of religious expression.

Having finally enlisted evangelical leaders in his crusade, however, Weyrich recognized that the political mobilization of those leaders represented only half of the equation. The IRS pursuit of Bob Jones University and other schools may have captured the attention and ignited the ire of evangelical leaders, but summoning rank-and-file evangelicals to the front lines in defense of racial segregation was a tough sell. Unless these leaders could enlist grassroots evangelicals, Weyrich's dream of a politically conservative coalition of evangelicals would remain unfulfilled.

Upsets in the 1978 bi-elections suggested that grassroots evangelicals would respond politically to an agenda that centered around opposition to abortion. Not only was there a growing restiveness in the general population about the increase in legal abortions since the *Roe* decision, but evangelicals themselves were beginning to express concern.

None was more persuasive than Francis A. Schaeffer, a goateed, knickers-wearing philosopher and Presbyterian minister. Schaeffer, together with his wife, Edith, ran a community and study center in Switzerland, which became a destination for both disaffected and intellectually curious evangelicals. Beginning in the mid-1970s, Schaeffer, considered by many the intellectual godfather of the Religious Right, excoriated the pervasiveness of what he called "secular humanism" in American society. He lamented the loss of a Christian consensus and asserted in 1979 that, "we now live in a secularized society."[38]

By the late 1970s, Schaeffer had begun to cite abortion as one consequence of a troubling cultural shift away from the mores of evangelical Christianity and toward the reviled "secular humanism." Schaeffer viewed abortion as the inevitable prelude to infanticide and euthanasia, and he wanted to sound the alarm. When Schaeffer visited Fulton J. Sheen, the famous Roman Catholic bishop, in the late 1970s, Sheen applauded Schaeffer for his attempts to engage Protestants on the abortion issue. "The problem is," Sheen said, "that abortion is perceived as a Catholic issue. I want you to help me change that."[39]

Schaeffer did so through his writings and lectures, but he also teamed with C. Everett Koop, a pediatric surgeon, to produce a series of five films, collectively titled *Whatever Happened to the Human Race?*, directed by Schaeffer's son, Frank Schaeffer. In the first episode, Koop stood on a rock in the Dead Sea, the lowest place on earth, with hundreds of plastic doll babies strewn across the saline shores, representing the untold number of aborted fetuses since the *Roe v. Wade* ruling. Koop, looking earnestly into the camera, decried abortion as an abomination, the "slaughter of the innocents." Schaeffer corroborated this critique, suggesting that any society that countenanced abortion had stepped onto the slippery slope of moral decline.[40]

These films found a wide audience among evangelicals when they appeared in 1979, and their impact was amplified by the fact that most of the screenings took place not in church basements but in movie theaters, a relatively unfamiliar, and somewhat exotic, venue for many evangelicals at the time. Protestants, especially evangelicals, Schaeffer reported in March 1979, "have been so sluggish on this issue of human life, and *Whatever Happened to the Human Race?* is causing real waves, among church people and governmental people too." *Whatever Happened to the Human Race?*, together with a companion book by the same title, served to reinforce among evangelicals their nascent sense that abortion was a moral concern. The films also legitimated evangelical political action as a way to redress the depredations of "secular humanism," the most glaring of which, according to Schaeffer, was legalized abortion. "By the end of the *Whatever Happened to the Human Race?* tour," Frank Schaeffer recalled, "we were calling for civil disobedience, the takeover of the Republican Party, and even hinting at overthrowing our 'unjust pro-abortion government.'"[41]

Francis Schaeffer's jeremiad against abortion built upon the emergence of abortion as a political issue in the 1978 elections. Paul Weyrich's dream of an evangelical political coalition was beginning to materialize. He had found a standard—the mounting evangelical outrage over legalized abortion—that would unite politically conservative evangelicals. It built in turn on the simmering resentment on the part of evangelical leaders toward the federal government over the *Green v. Connally* ruling, but it also tapped into evangelical anger over the gay rights initiative that Anita Bryant had opposed in Miami.

The issue of homosexuality continued to fester, as gays increasingly pressed for their rights. In 1979, James Robison, a television evangelist in Dallas, lost his slot on WFAA television because he preached against homosexuality. In response, he organized a "Freedom Rally" at Reunion Arena to protest the action, which he characterized as an assault on religious freedom. Not surprisingly, Robison turned to Weyrich for support. "You are very familiar with the battle that I find myself now engaged," Robison wrote. "I am convinced that we will be of much help to one another, as we join forces and strength together in the battle for the conservation of a free America." Robison believed that an alliance with Weyrich could make for a formidable coalition. He concluded his letter by saying, "I anticipate a very profitable relationship with you, as we work together for a great cause."[42]

Robison told the *Fort Worth Morning Star–Telegram* that the purpose of the Reunion Arena gathering was to "rally people around the word of God and the Constitution. We want to let people hear from the Christians—the moral majority." Jerry Falwell also registered his support for Robison. "I think this is the first time a television station has blatantly attempted to tell a gospel broadcaster what he can't say," Falwell said. "All gospel broadcasters want to make sure it doesn't stick."[43]

In the wake of the 1978 election, Weyrich and other conservative activists were beginning to feel confident about their efforts to organize politically conservative evangelicals into a voting bloc. "In the next few years, you are going to see the fundamentalist Protestants, the religious charismatics and their organizations playing more of an active role in the political process," Richard Viguerie predicted early in 1979. "I think they are going to come down strongly for the conservative cause."[44]

As the 1980 presidential election loomed on the horizon, the target of this evangelical activism became increasingly clear: Jimmy Carter himself, the evangelical Sunday-school teacher turned president. His attempts to govern in harmony with the venerable principles of progressive evangelicalism—an emphasis on the importance of family, on human rights, on nuclear disarmament and a less imperial foreign policy, his push for women's equality and for conservation of natural resources—all of those initiatives were imperiled, paradoxically enough, by a coalition of fellow evangelicals.[45]

By no means was this nascent Religious Right the only impediment to Carter's reelection, however. His tenure in office was not going well, and the Bert Lance affair in particular struck at the heart of Carter's appeal: his reputation for integrity.

Thomas Bertram "Bert" Lance, a small-town banker in Georgia, had forged a strong friendship with Carter during the 1966 gubernatorial campaign. The two shared evangelical convictions and became prayer partners. Following his election as governor in 1970, Carter appointed Lance as state highway director, where he reduced the department's staff by 26 percent while tripling the number of contracts for highway construction and repair. Lance sought to succeed Carter as governor, but he lost in the Democratic primary. He became president of National Bank of Georgia until Carter tapped him to be head of the Office of Management and Budget in his administration.

Shortly after Lance's confirmation, however, questions began to surface about some of his bank dealings back in Georgia. Critics alleged that he had used his position to obtain a sweetheart loan, that bank officers and their families had received preferential treatment, and that Lance had used a corporate plane to attend University of Georgia football games.[46]

Washington was already grumbling about the heedless "Georgia mafia" running the White House—Hamilton Jordan, Jody Powell, and others—so the whole Lance affair reflected badly on Carter, who, amid the investigation, had declared, "Bert, I'm proud of you." Despite the fact that these banking lapses had occurred before Lance's arrival in Washington—and Lance was eventually acquitted of all charges—the incident represented an embarrassment to Carter, who had campaigned so assiduously on ethics and restoring faith in government. Carter's approval rating stood at 70 percent before the Lance affair; by the time Lance finally resigned on September 21, 1977, that number had dropped twenty-five points. James M. Wall, editor of the *Christian Century* who headed Carter's Illinois campaign in 1976, remarked that the Lance episode dealt a "rather serious blow" to the administration's image of probity. "He who lives by the steeple may die by the steeple," Wall said. As *Time* magazine noted about the president, "when he likes and instinctively trusts someone, he readily overlooks his weaknesses."[47]

Some of the most searing criticisms of Carter came from inside the White House. The cover of the May 1979 issue of the *Atlantic* magazine featured a sepia-toned photograph of Carter and the words, "The Passionless Presidency." The author of the cover article, James Fallows, had been Carter's chief speechwriter for more than two years before his resignation in November 1978. Fallows lauded Carter's intellect, his sanity, and his essential goodness: "If I had to choose one politician to sit at the Pearly Gates and pass judgment on my soul, Jimmy Carter would be the one." But those encomiums set up a devastating critique. Carter, Fallows argued, had failed to translate his personal qualities into an effective style of governing. Fallows resurrected the story about Carter keeping the appointments for the White House tennis court, insisting it was true. He criticized Carter's emphasis on foreign affairs

at the expense of domestic policy and the insularity of the Georgians running the White House. Most distressing to Fallows, Carter lacked passion or
an overall vision for what he wanted to do as president. "I came to think,"
Fallows wrote, "that Carter believes fifty things, but no one thing." The president thinks in lists, not arguments, Fallows said, "but he fails to project a
vision larger than the problem he is tackling at the moment."[48]

Although Carter himself evenly referred to Fallows as "a fine young man,"
at least one of the Georgians in the White House was furious. Jody Powell, the
press secretary, complained that Fallows was disloyal, that his criticisms were
appropriate for a letter perhaps, but not for publication. Fallows stood by his
critique; for many, the article's portrayal of the president captured their growing sense of unease about Carter's administration.[49]

Indeed, Carter faced a list of vexing challenges, much more immediate
and more ominous than the nascent Religious Right. The nation's perilous
dependence on foreign sources for energy made the continuing effects of the
Arab Oil Embargo all the more painful, which in turn hobbled the economy.
Exorbitant interest rates crippled the construction industry and the real-
estate market. Many Americans continued to resent the recognition of "Red"
China and the "giveaway" of the Panama Canal. Other developments, though
well beyond Carter's control, seemed ominous and contributed to a sense of
anomie. In March 1979, the core of the nuclear power plant at Three Mile Island, outside of Harrisburg, Pennsylvania, nearly melted down. Two months
later, a DC-10 airliner bound for Los Angeles crashed while taking off from
Chicago's O'Hare airport, killing 271 people, the worst plane crash in the nation's history. If Jimmy Carter needed a barometer of public sentiment and
simmering rage, he could have found it on July 12, 1979, on the south side of
Chicago. At Comiskey Park, the White Sox staged "Disco Demolition Night"
in the midst of another lackluster season; anyone coming to the park with a
disco record was admitted for ninety-eight cents. When the records were
detonated between games of the doubleheader against the Detroit Tigers,
fans stormed the field and a riot broke out, forcing the White Sox to forfeit
the second game.

The president bore no responsibility for these incidents, of course, but
Carter appeared powerless and his administration stymied in the face of
myriad developments, unwilling or unable to seize the initiative and reassert
America's superiority in a chaotic world. By the middle of 1979, his approval
rating stood at an anemic 33 percent. When the president appeared before
the nation to deliver his "Crisis of Confidence" speech on July 15, 1979, an

apparent attempt to revive his listless presidency, Americans looked to him for bold leadership. Carter had spent several days at Camp David consulting with a wide variety of Americans, including, by Carter's account, fifteen clergy, on the economic and spiritual condition of the nation.

Carter's advisers were divided about the wisdom of such a speech, especially as it proposed to look deep into America's soul. The draft went through several iterations, and one speechwriter, Hendrik Hertzberg, recalled delivering a version to Carter early one morning in the company of several presidential aides, including Gerald Rafshoon, Carter's media adviser. Referring to a particular passage in the speech, Rafshoon warned, "Mr. President, the press is gonna kill you for this." Carter, according to Hertzberg, nodded thoughtfully and then, expressing his own frustrations and doubtless channeling his days as a sailor, smiled and declared in his soft Georgia drawl, "Fuck the press."[50]

On Sunday, the Carters, back from Camp David, attended First Baptist Church in Washington the morning of the speech, where Cal Thomas, the Sunday-school teacher that morning, said, "I feel now more than ever our brother Jimmy Carter and his wife Rosalynn need our prayers if three-quarters of the things people are saying about him are true." Thomas prayed that the president would have "the wisdom of Solomon, the patience of Job, the leadership of Moses and the mind of Jesus Christ."[51]

That evening, the president addressed the nation from the Oval Office, three years to the day after he accepted the Democratic Party's nomination for president. He opened by identifying "a moral and a spiritual crisis" in the United States. Americans, he said, had become complacent and must mend their ways by reclaiming traditional values. "In a nation that was proud of hard work, strong families, close-knit communities, and our faith in God, too many of us now tend to worship self-indulgence and consumption," Carter said. "Human identity is no longer defined by what one does, but by what one owns." The president summoned the nation to "the path of common purpose and the restoration of American values."[52]

The address then turned specifically to energy. Carter outlined once again the need for a comprehensive energy policy, which included a windfall-profits tax on the oil companies to finance alternative sources of energy, including solar energy. He asked Congress for authority to impose mandatory conservation and, if necessary, gasoline rationing. He also asked for increased appropriations to aid "the poorest among us" to deal with rising energy prices. "With God's help and for the sake of our nation, it is time for us to join hands in America," Carter concluded. "Let us commit ourselves together to a re-birth of the American spirit."[53]

Although initial public reaction to the speech was positive, pundits de-rided Carter's address as his "malaise" speech (even though the word *malaise* appears nowhere in it). "Carter deplored the prevailing lack of confidence in government, but did little to restore it," an editorial in the *Chicago Tribune* said. Conservatives were especially critical of Carter's energy proposals, which they regarded as unnecessarily draconian and punitive toward the oil companies. "The first part of the President's speech was theology," Michael Novak wrote, "which he shamefully tried to bend to his own partisan pur-poses." The crisis of confidence, Novak insisted, was created by Carter him-self, adding, "As a political leader, he lacks knowledge and confidence, and so does his staff." The *Wall Street Journal*, citing the president's "sermonic and confusing rhetoric," declared that the "real Jimmy Carter has finally stood up, on the far left of the Democratic Party."[54]

Those who inhabited the left-leaning precincts of the Democratic Party, however, were among Carter's least dependable allies. Many liberal Demo-crats had criticized Carter during the 1976 primaries for his belated oppo-sition to the Vietnam War, and their criticisms continued during his administration. Liberals were suspicious of some of Carter's appointments: Griffin Bell as attorney general, Harold Brown as secretary of defense, and Joseph Califano as secretary of health, education and welfare. Although Cyrus R. Vance, Carter's secretary of state, was known and respected for his gentle demeanor and his preference for negotiation over confrontation, some liberals remained suspicious of Zbigniew Brzezinski, Carter's national secu-rity adviser, whom they regarded as a pugilistic Cold Warrior. Carter's auster-ity budgets for social services coupled with increases in defense spending to counter the Soviet threat further riled the liberals in his own party.[55]

Liberals also criticized Carter's support for the Hyde Amendment, which prohibited taxpayer funding of abortions. Edward Kennedy, who had shifted to pro-choice on abortion by the mid-1970s, disagreed with Carter's propos-als for comprehensive health-care reform as too modest and sought to push his own initiative. Carter believed that Kennedy's proposed legislation would never pass Congress and that it was far too costly, especially in a time of bud-get stringency. The two men had conferred at the White House in July 1978, and Carter came away from that meeting with the impression that Kennedy would cooperate in a more incremental approach to health-care reform. Within a few hours, however, Kennedy called a press conference to condemn

Carter's plan and press ahead with his own. As he faced reelection, the president would be forced to parry a challenge from Kennedy for the Democratic nomination.[56]

The most tangible threat to Carter's presidency, however, came from afar. In a misguided humanitarian gesture urged on him by David Rockefeller, Howard Baker, and Henry Kissinger, Carter allowed the embattled shah of Iran, Mohammad Reza Pahlavi, to come to the United States for medical treatment. Iranian students responded in anger, and on November 4, 1979, they stormed the U.S. embassy in Teheran and took sixty-six Americans hostage (fourteen were soon released). "This crisis is a crisis in every sense," Hamilton Jordan warned his boss. "It is a crisis for your Presidency, for the hostages, and for our country's image around the world."[57]

By the time Carter formally announced his candidacy for reelection on December 4, 1979, a month to the day after the embassy invasion, it was clear that his religious support was eroding, even among leaders of the Southern Baptist Convention, his own denomination. At its meeting in Houston the previous June, theological and political conservatives, led by Paul Pressler and Paige Patterson and abetted by busloads of fellow conservatives, had elected Adrian Rogers as president of the denomination. Rogers, pastor of Bellevue Baptist Church in Memphis, assumed the office with a mandate to use his appointive powers to transform the Southern Baptist Convention into a more conservative body. Earlier in the decade, the denomination had supported the legalization of abortion, and several of its leaders—James Dunn, Jimmy Allen, Foy Valentine, and others—advocated the teachings of progressive evangelicalism; both Dunn and Valentine had signed the Chicago Declaration of Evangelical Social Concern. At the same Houston gathering that elected Adrian Rogers, the Southern Baptists approved a resolution "to oppose specifically the Internal Revenue Service's proposed intrusions into church owned and operated schools."[58]

Just a month before the Southern Baptists chose Rogers as their president, another meeting took place in Lynchburg, Virginia, a gathering of leaders of both the New Right and the nascent Religious Right: Paul Weyrich, Howard Phillips, Richard Viguerie, Robert Billings, Ed McAteer, and Jerry Falwell. While waiting for Phillips to arrive, McAteer asked Weyrich to comment on political matters and lay out his vision for a movement of politically conservative evangelicals and fundamentalists. Weyrich allowed that "out there is what you might term a 'moral majority,' but that group has been fractured by history, by politics, by denominational differences, and what we have to do is to try, and if we do we can elect anybody." Falwell seized on Weyrich's term "moral majority" and declared, "That's the name of our organization." Moral Majority was incorporated on June 6, 1979; Falwell tapped Billings as the organization's first executive director.[59]

"Because of this rapid degradation of our free society, I have been greatly burdened by God to lead the 'Moral Majority' in America and to stand up and be counted," Falwell told his followers in 1979. "I am absolutely convinced that the vast majority of all Americans believe in decency, the family, the home, Bible morality, and all that we have long considered holy and sacred. However, this great 'Moral Majority' has been silent all too long."[60]

Just as Falwell sought a different political trajectory for evangelicals from the progressive evangelicalism of Jimmy Carter, so too Adrian Rogers and the new leadership of the Southern Baptist Convention sought to move the denomination in a different direction from the past. "I see myself more as a prophet than a politician," Rogers said many years later. "I'm not a political creature." Perhaps not, but as Jimmy Carter faced reelection in 1980, Rogers and other Baptists, including Billy Graham and Jerry Falwell, rallied in opposition.[61]

Nine days after Carter's "Crisis of Confidence" address, Cal Thomas, the Sunday-school teacher who had prayed publicly for Carter at First Baptist Church the morning of the speech, sent a letter to the White House seeking a job on the president's staff. "It was my joy to teach his Sunday School class the day of his television speech and he was very complimentary afterward," Thomas wrote, professing his "great love for and faith in the President."[62]

Within months, Thomas signed on as one of Jerry Falwell's associates in his new venture called Moral Majority, the purpose of which was to thwart Jimmy Carter's reelection.[63]

SEVEN

HIS OWN RECEIVED HIM NOT

As the 1980 presidential campaign reached its climax, an interested citizen, a preacher, picked up the telephone. Although the race was still fluid, his preferred candidate was trailing in the polls, and yet inserting himself explicitly into the race was dicey. His knack for swaying voters, especially religious voters, was undisputed, but that influence derived precisely from his ability to appear above the fray. Over the course of a long and distinguished career, he had perfected the art of the discreet political gesture—a strategic handshake, a brief touch on the shoulder, a whispered aside in front of the cameras—to telegraph his preferences.

But this election was especially fraught for Billy Graham. One candidate, the incumbent running for reelection, was known as a family man who shared the preacher's evangelical theological convictions almost verbatim. The other major candidate, divorced and remarried, had spent much of his career in Hollywood, a province not known to evangelicals as an outpost of piety. Still another candidate, John B. Anderson, who was mounting a third-party challenge, was a member of the Evangelical Free Church, an evangelical denomination with deep roots in Scandinavian pietism.

Receiver in hand, the preacher considered his options one last time and punched the numbers. At the other end of the line was Paul Laxalt, U.S. senator from Nevada and national chairman of Ronald Reagan's campaign for president. A memorandum in the Reagan Library tells the remainder of the story. "Billy Graham called," the senator wrote. "Wants to help short of public endorsement." Then, Laxalt added: "His presence, in my view, would be exceedingly helpful in some of our key states."[1]

Eleven days after offering to help the Reagan campaign, Graham sent a letter to Robert L. Maddox, Jimmy Carter's religious liaison, asking to discuss the campaign. "As you know, with the Lord's help I am staying out of it," Graham wrote, adding that his refusal to be involved had cost him the support of some followers. Graham sought to distinguish himself from "the extreme right-wingers who are getting a great deal of exposure right now," but he provided no indication to Maddox, a fellow Baptist minister, that he had already pledged to help defeat Carter. Graham's letter, in fact, stated the opposite—that he was "staying out of" the campaign.[2]

Graham's statement of neutrality in the 1980 presidential campaign was, to say the least, disingenuous. Nor was this the first political campaign where Graham pushed the boundaries of credibility. Twenty years earlier, on August 10, 1960, Graham had sent a letter to John F. Kennedy, the Democratic nominee, pledging that he would not raise the "religious issue" in the fall campaign. Eight days later, Graham convened a group of American Protestant ministers in Montreux, Switzerland, to strategize about how they might prevent Kennedy's election that November. Later in the same campaign, Graham visited Henry Luce at the Time & Life Building and, according to Graham's autobiography, said, "I want to help Nixon without blatantly endorsing him." Graham drafted an article praising Nixon that stopped just short of a full endorsement. Luce was prepared to run it in *Life* magazine but pulled it at the last minute.[3]

In 1960, eight days had elapsed between Graham's letter of assurance to Kennedy and the Montreux gathering. During the 1980 campaign, eleven days separated Graham's phone call offering help to the Republican nominee and his pledge of neutrality to a staff member of the Democratic nominee.

Although Carter was never personally close to Graham, the Carters had invited Graham and his wife, Ruth, to dinner at the White House the previous November. "For several hours, we reminisced about our southern backgrounds and talked about national affairs," Graham remembered. "We shared our mutual faith in Jesus Christ and discussed some of the issues that sometimes divide sincere Christians." The Grahams stayed overnight in the Lincoln Bedroom. "Ruth and I came away with a new insight into the dedication of both of you to the cause not only of peace and justice in the world, but evangelistic urgency," Graham wrote to the Carters in appreciation.[4]

What Carter didn't know was that Graham was already working—even then, at an earlier date—to undermine the Democratic president. Just a couple of weeks prior to Graham's overnight stay at the White House, a year before the 1980 election, Graham and Bill Bright, head of Campus Crusade for Christ, had convened a dozen fellow preachers in Dallas for what Graham called "a special time of prayer" and talk about the upcoming presidential campaign. Carter's liaison for religious affairs had only recently returned from a visit to the evangelist's home in Montreat, North Carolina, with a report that Graham "supports the President wholeheartedly." But that support was apparently less than robust; Graham had already begun his machinations aimed at denying Carter a second term as president.[5]

In addition to Bright, the Dallas guest list, formulated by Graham himself, included his brother-in-law, Clayton Bell; Rex Humbard and James Robison, both of them televangelists; and a roster of well-known Southern Baptists: Charles Stanley, Jimmy Draper, and Adrian Rogers, the new president of the Southern Baptist Convention, who had recently visited Carter at the White House and pronounced it "one of the highlights of my life." The ministers, gathered at Graham's behest, occupied nearly an entire floor of the Airport Marina Hotel at the Dallas–Fort Worth airport. "It really was Billy's meeting," Robison recalled. "What he wanted us to do was pray together for a couple of days and to understand something very significant had to happen." The unmistakable subtext of the gathering was the need to rally behind someone who could mount a challenge to Carter. "No one was talking about Jimmy Carter's faith," Robison said. "It was his ability to lead."[6]

Just as he had done at the Montreux gathering of Protestant ministers in 1960, Graham made it clear to the participants in Dallas that he could not be the point person for such a crusade in opposition to Carter; the evangelist was still too damaged from his associations with Richard Nixon, and he wanted—publicly, at least—to remain above the fray of politics. According to Robison, a consensus emerged "that if former California governor Ronald Reagan had the conviction that he appeared to have," he would be a good choice to displace Carter. Robison was chosen to approach the Reagan camp to ascertain how serious he was about another run for the presidency. In the course of their meeting at a hotel in Atlanta, Reagan told Robison that Jesus was more real to him than his own mother.[7]

Reagan, however, was not the only contender for evangelical sympathies; his divorce and his Hollywood pedigree made many evangelicals uneasy.

Some evangelicals preferred Philip M. Crane, member of Congress from Illinois, and others were enamored of John Connally, the former Democratic governor of Texas who had served as Richard Nixon's secretary of the treasury and who had changed his party affiliation to Republican in 1973. In December 1979, William Brock, chair of the Republican National Committee, summoned Religious Right leaders to discuss the merits of various candidates, and a delegation of conservative evangelical leaders visited Connally at his ranch in Texas. The meeting was going smoothly until one of the preachers asked Connally's views on secular humanism. No one, apparently, had briefed the former governor that the term *secular humanism* was Religious Right code language for everything amiss in America. "Well, I don't know much about it," Connally declared, "but it sounds good to me!"[8]

The leaders of the Religious Right settled on Reagan.

GRAHAM was not the only evangelical guilty of duplicity during the 1980 campaign. After a meeting at the White House on January 22, 1980, Jerry Falwell began spreading the word that Carter had told the assembled group of evangelical preachers that he supported gay rights. In the course of a Moral Majority rally in Alaska, Falwell claimed he had asked the president why "practicing homosexuals" served on the White House staff. Carter, according to Falwell, replied, "I am the president of all the American people and I believe I should represent everyone." Falwell said that he responded, "Why don't you have some murderers and bank robbers and so forth to represent?" A tape recording of the gathering, however, proved that the president made no such comment, that Falwell had fabricated the entire exchange. "That simply was not said," Jimmy Allen, who was also present, confirmed. "Anecdotes that do not tell the truth certainly ought to be avoided in any pulpit I know of," he added. When the White House exposed Falwell's deception, the preacher dismissed the whole incident as an attempt by the president to discredit any evangelical minister who disagreed with him. As a letter to the editor of the *Washington Star* noted, Falwell's "use of such an 'anecdote' seems a strangely loose use of language coming from a man who demands a literal interpreatation [sic] of the Bible." Carter himself, decades later, said simply and without rancor, "He just lied about it."[9]

The idea for the January gathering at the White House had originated with Robert Maddox, who joined Carter's staff as religious liaison in October 1979. Maddox, a Southern Baptist minister from Georgia, had already served as a kind of informal adviser and had drafted several speeches for both

Rosalynn and Jimmy Carter, including Carter's remarks at the signing of the Mideast peace treaty. Maddox wanted to help repair ties with religious leaders, especially evangelicals, in advance of the 1980 election. As early as 1978, "I began to know that the President was in pretty bad trouble with a lot of religious people," Maddox said. Rosalynn Carter had also begun to sound the alarm about the defection of evangelical voters, and the first lady pushed for the hiring of Maddox to improve relations and massage the egos of evangelical preachers. "I was the preacher at the White House," Maddox recalled. As soon as he arrived, he said, he was inundated with preachers and religious leaders eager to secure a hearing with the president.[10]

Maddox had been in Houston in June 1979 for the Southern Baptist Convention gathering that elected Adrian Rogers as its president, but he detected in Houston a "broad-based, very strong, unswerving support for the President." His soundings among fellow Southern Baptists returned generally positive readings. "On several occasions platform speakers spontaneously commended the President and prayed for him," Maddox reported. Just a few weeks after the Southern Baptist gathering, however, Maddox confessed that the "super-conservative religious groups" made him anxious. Carter's standing with conservative evangelical leaders was deteriorating rapidly, so much so, Maddox recalled, that "by the time I got here, he was in such deep trouble with the more conservative groups that I spent most of my time trying to put out the fires—unsuccessfully most of the time—put out the fires among the conservatives who were, by then, really deeply set against Jimmy Carter."[11]

When Bailey Smith, the newly elected president of the Southern Baptist Convention, paid a courtesy visit to the Oval Office on August 7, 1980, he informed the dumbfounded president, a fellow Southern Baptist, "We are praying, Mr. President, that you will abandon secular humanism as your religion." Carter, recounting the conversation to his wife later that day, asked Rosalynn, "What is a secular humanist?" She didn't know either.[12]

As the president's reelection campaign unfolded in the fall of 1979, Maddox became the canary in the coal mine, warning campaign operatives about the political machinations of the Religious Right. He cautioned that their "politics tend to be very conservative, even rightist," and urged the campaign to approach carefully. These conservative evangelicals, Maddox warned, harbored "serious reservations about the President—SALT, Prayer in Public Schools, Panama Canal, etc.," but he still saw an opening if Carter made overtures in their direction. "Understated contact with some of them could

soften their political rhetoric and tap their strengths to help realize some of
President Carter's transcendent goals for the country," Maddox wrote.[13]

Maddox busily began organizing meetings between evangelical leaders and the president, both to mend fences and to shore up defenses against
the Religious Right, arguing that it was "a matter of urgency that the President meet with selected conservative ministers as soon as possible." Maddox
urged the president to address the Washington for Jesus rally that evangelicals were planning for April 1980, "not as a candidate, but as God's leader to
the nation," noting that the organizers were willing to weather criticism for
inviting Carter and no other candidates. The president elected not to address the Washington for Jesus rally, which drew 200,000 to the Mall on April
29, 1980. Many of the participants waved placards that read THE BIBLE—
IT's TRUE and AMERICA, YOU NEED JESUS. Bill Bright, one of the co-chairs
of the event, waxed hyperbolic, calling the day of the rally "the most important day in the history of our nation since the signing of the Declaration of
Independence."[14]

Despite his optimism that the president could retain evangelical support,
Maddox also recognized that Falwell himself had already charted his course,
so all Maddox could do was try to placate his anger and mitigate his activism. "As you increasingly speak for and to a large segment of evangelicals in
this country, I make a commitment to you to keep you informed of President
Carter's policies and programs," Maddox wrote to Falwell after the two had
met. "While it may not be possible to have you in President Carter's camp on
every issue, we can at least let you know what he says and thinks."[15]

Maddox was increasingly aware that a larger gesture of accommodation
on the president's part was necessary; he viewed the "coalescing of conservative, evangelical, religious groups for political action" as an ominous development. When an invitation arrived for Carter to address the gathering of
National Religious Broadcasters, Maddox urged the president to accept. And,
with so many of the televangelists in town for the event, Maddox argued, the
president should invite several evangelical leaders to the White House.[16]

Carter hosted the preachers for breakfast at the White House the day
after he addressed the National Religious Broadcasters at the Washington Hil-
ton. "I serve Christ. I also serve America," Carter told the broadcasters. "And
I have never found any incompatibility between these two responsibilities for
service." Carter, aware of the restiveness among many of the evangelical
leaders, was nervous in advance of the gathering at the White House the following morning. In his opening remarks over breakfast, the president spoke

of his attempts to encourage China to admit missionaries and allow the distribution of Bibles.[17]

The meeting at the White House, however, was a disaster. If Carter thought he could placate the preachers with bromides about faith or missionary initiatives, he was mistaken. The guests had their own agenda. They grilled the president on military preparedness, prayer in public schools, the family, his failure to appoint evangelicals to high-ranking positions, and federal funding for abortion. Carter patiently responded to their queries, although he made it clear that, as a Baptist committed to the First Amendment and the separation of church and state, he opposed mandating prayer in public schools. The relentless line of questioning on domestic social issues revealed that these conservative evangelical leaders had already abandoned Carter—although the preachers could claim, with some justice, that Carter had neglected them. "I had breakfast with evangelical leaders," the president recorded in his diary. "They're really right-wing: against ERA, for requiring prayer in school, against abortion (so am I), want publicly committed evangelicals in my cabinet, against the White House Conference on Families."[18]

The Religious Right leaders, all of them "media savvy," knew how to derive maximum benefit from their star turn at the White House. Within half an hour of leaving their breakfast meeting with the president, according to Maddox, the preachers began inflecting what had just transpired for the benefit of the press. Because the National Religious Broadcasters convention was in town, the media were interested, and the preachers obliged. "Many in the delegation were disappointed by his answers," Robert Dugan of the National Association of Evangelicals declared.[19]

Whatever hopes Maddox harbored about a rapprochement between evangelical leaders and the evangelical president were disappointed. In front of reporters just outside of the White House, Maddox said, "they were just kind of shading the meeting, distorting it, not lying about it, but distorting it." Falwell's fabricated exchange with the president about homosexuality, according to Maddox, was merely the most egregious example of the distortions.[20]

As these leaders of the Religious Right prepared to oppose Carter's reelection, they deployed a powerful weapon: their media empires. By the late 1970s, television preachers like Jimmy Swaggart, Oral Roberts, Jerry Falwell, Pat Robertson, James Robison, and Jim and Tammy Faye Bakker were ubiquitous. Not all of the televangelists used their programs for political ends, but several did, either directly or by speaking in politically coded language about

America's moral crisis or the need for righteous leadership. "Conservatives had taken over religious radio, and they had taken over religious television," Maddox noted. Falwell openly declared his intention to mobilize conservative voters, educate them about issues, and get them to the polls. "We are the largest minority bloc in the United States," Falwell told a group of two hundred evangelical and fundamentalist ministers in January 1980. "Fifteen years ago I opposed what I'm doing today, but now I'm convinced that this country is morally sick, and will not correct itself unless we get involved."[21]

Falwell's declaration spoke volumes about shifting evangelical attitudes toward political engagement. As late as 1965, consistent with evangelical sentiment at the time, Falwell had criticized fellow clergy for their political activism. By 1980, however, Falwell and other televangelists were prepared to use their media presence to mold evangelical opinion to their political ends. Although the precise tally of viewers remains a matter of dispute—at the beginning of 1980, the *New York Times* pegged the estimate at forty-seven million every week—millions of Americans tuned into the televangelists, and millions of dollars flowed into their coffers, which many of the televangelists used, in part, to register and energize voters. The money was copious. According to the *Los Angeles Times*, for example, Oral Roberts took in approximately $60 million in 1978, with Robertson, Bakker, and Falwell not far behind.[22]

Although Bakker remained loyal to Carter, other televangelists, some at the urging of Weyrich, used their media empires to undermine the president. "I believe that you would benefit greatly in all aspects of what you are doing by establishing a Washington bureau of some kind," Weyrich wrote to Robertson after appearing on his *700 Club* television program in September 1979. "I would be delighted to work with you on this matter if you so desire." In addition to television, the crusade to unseat the president and the promotion of various associated Religious Right causes benefited from the largesse of deep-pocketed donors. Businessmen had long supported Graham's evangelistic efforts, but the names of stalwart political conservatives like H. L. Hunt, Joseph and Holly Coors, Richard DeVos, and Howard Ahmanson began to show up on the donor lists for politically oriented organizations like Christian Crusade, Church League of America, Christian Freedom Foundation, and Moral Majority.[23]

Not all evangelicals, however, cooperated in the effort to deny Carter a second term, even though they opposed him. "I myself do not belong to the Moral Majority," Jack Hyles, fundamentalist minister from Hammond, Indiana, declared. "I'm just too much a separatist, I guess, to cooperate in any kind of venture with liberals, Catholics, or Mormons." Bob Jones III harbored similar misgivings, a sentiment fairly common among fundamentalists, who distrusted any alliance with those whose theological orthodoxy they regarded as suspect. But they were not politically inactive; Jones in particular had sworn to oppose Carter because he had extended diplomatic recognition to "Red" China. Fundamentalists like Jones were notoriously reluctant to cooperate with anyone, and more than occasionally, Jones's criticisms turned personal. "Everybody knows that Falwell has no spiritual discernment when it comes to his associations and that he will go along with anything or anybody who will get him a crowd," he wrote to a fellow fundamentalist.[24]

As the 1980 presidential campaign unfolded, Jerry Falwell emerged as a central figure in opposition to Carter's reelection. Falwell, whose father had sold bootleg whiskey during Prohibition, converted to evangelical Christianity, attended Baptist Bible College in Springfield, Missouri, and returned to his childhood home in Lynchburg, Virginia, to found Thomas Road Baptist Church in 1956 at the age of twenty-two.

Like many other evangelicals in the middle decades of the twentieth century, Falwell's relationship to politics had been anything but clear and consistent. Ever since the Scopes Trial of 1925, evangelicals had often expressed concerns about being too heavily involved in politics, which many regarded as a species of "worldliness" and was therefore suspect. On Sunday evening, March 21, 1965, for example, Falwell delivered perhaps the most frequently quoted sermon of his career, "Of Ministers and Marches." The occasion was Martin Luther King's march from Selma to Montgomery, Alabama, on that very day. Falwell openly questioned the sincerity of King and other civil rights leaders and declared: "Believing the Bible as I do, I would find it impossible to stop preaching the pure saving gospel of Jesus Christ, and begin doing anything else—including fighting communism, or participating in civil rights reforms." Falwell's sentiments in 1965 were fairly typical of most evangelicals, many of whom, convinced of their larger mandate to seek conversions, had not bothered to register to vote. "If as much effort could be put into winning people to Jesus Christ across the land as is being exerted in the present civil rights movement," Falwell continued, "America would be turned upside down for God."[25]

Precisely two weeks earlier, in one of the most famous confrontations of the civil rights era, King, John Lewis, and other civil rights leaders had been attacked by Alabama state troopers wielding tear gas and truncheons when they crossed the Edmund Pettus Bridge on their way to Montgomery to protest racism and the police brutality that had led to the death of Jimmie Lee Jackson in nearby Marion. As Falwell held forth from the pulpit at Thomas Road Baptist Church, King had resumed the abortive march from Selma to Montgomery, fortified this time with a court order and marching arm in arm with religious leaders from around the country. "Preachers are not called to be politicians but to be soul winners," Falwell thundered back in Lynchburg. "I feel that we need to get off the streets and back into the pulpits and into the prayer rooms."[26]

Falwell's turnaround on political engagement was dramatic. In a 1976 sermon, for example, delivered more than a decade after his pledge to remain apolitical, Falwell was singing a different tune. "The idea that religion and politics don't mix was invented by the Devil," he declared, "to keep Christians from running their own country." On the face of it, Falwell, an avowed segregationist in the 1960s, was saying that if the political issue of the day was civil rights, clergy should remain quiet. By the late 1970s, however, when the defense of "Christian" schools and "family values" was at stake, that state of affairs demanded that preachers become politically active.[27]

Falwell was unrepentant about his turn to politics, although as late as 1979 he recognized that such a foray would have consequences. "I can honestly say I do not relish the idea of taking such a ministry," he wrote to his followers. "I am well aware that I will make many enemies."[28]

Paradoxically, the same preacher who had earlier forsworn politics chose to unleash his rhetoric and resources to unseat a fellow born-again Christian, Jimmy Carter, in the 1980 presidential election. Gone were the scruples about politics from the pulpit; the moral crises facing the nation, he reasoned, mandated his entry into the political fray. "I'm not afraid to endorse candidates," Falwell declared in 1980. "I'm not saying Jerry Ford was the perfect candidate in 1976 but he was better than the other guy."[29]

THE emergence of the Religious Right was not the only threat to Carter's political future. Without question, the hostage situation in Iran hobbled Carter's campaign for reelection, both because it represented a failure on the part of his administration, or at least unfinished business, and because it hampered the president's ability to campaign. After leaving office, Carter compared the hostage situation to a lingering personal debt, one that cast a pall over everything. "No matter what else happened, it was always there," he recalled. "It was always painful because I was failing to accomplish what seemed to be a simple task to get those hostages home, and the personal responsibility I felt for them was there."[30]

Like many Americans, leaders of the Religious Right interpreted the Iranian hostage situation as yet another sign of Carter's weakness, the consequence of a naïve foreign policy. Other religious leaders took a different view and applauded Carter's diplomatic efforts. Early in the hostage crisis, several United Methodist bishops urged Carter to exercise restraint and resist "the temptation to return evil for evil"; the denomination's conference in May 1980 congratulated the president for his patience and his "tireless efforts" to negotiate freedom for the hostages. On July 30, 1980, Mark O. Hatfield, Republican senator from Oregon and a progressive evangelical, called the president to assure him of the senator's prayers in the midst of the hostage crisis.[31]

Carter, eager to avoid military conflict, sided with those who counseled restraint. Although some of his advisers, not to mention many politicians and pundits, urged Carter to direct a military strike against Iran, even at the considerable risk of harming or killing the hostages, the president refused. "I have always tried to use America's strength with great caution and care and tolerance and thoughtfulness and prayer," he explained during the campaign. Unleashing a massive military attack on Teheran might have paid political dividends, he acknowledged, but such wholesale and indiscriminant action would have been reckless and irresponsible. Ultimately, Carter was constrained by just-war criteria. "I could have destroyed Tehran with one F15 strike," Carter recalled years later. "It might have been a popular political thing to do," but it would have violated the just-war principles of proportionality and protecting civilians from collateral damage. "I would have killed tens of thousands of Iranians who were not guilty," Carter said, "and we would also have lost the American hostages."[32]

In part out of frustration at the impasse, however, Carter authorized a daring rescue attempt, one he undertook against the advice of his secretary of state, Cyrus Vance. On April 24, 1980, six C-130 transport planes carrying ninety commandoes landed in the Dasht-e Kavir desert of Iran, and eight helicopters were dispatched for an assault on the embassy. Only six made it to the rendezvous point, and one of them was damaged. The mission's commander determined that the mission could not proceed, and the president reluctantly concurred. Tragically, however, in the course of retreat one of the helicopters struck a transport plane that was refueling on the ground. Eight soldiers died, and two were badly burned, the only casualties attributable to a military operation during Jimmy Carter's presidency.

THE aborted mission in Iran, audacious as it was, failed to enhance Carter's standing in the eyes of voters, including politically conservative evangelicals. But other shortcomings, perceived or real, also contributed to the president's ebbing popularity. One of Carter's campaign promises in 1976 had been to convene a conference to discuss challenges to family life. "One of the reasons that we have begun to rely much more heavily on the government to provide our needs," Carter had told Pat Robertson on the *700 Club* television program, "is because of the destruction of relationships within the family or within the church." In the press of other issues, however, the initiative on families had been postponed several times. On January 30, 1978, Carter announced his intention to convene the conference by the end of the year, and he did so by reiterating many of the concerns he had articulated during the campaign: high divorce rates, children born out of wedlock, and runaway teenagers. Still, Carter expressed his confidence in the strength and resilience of American families.[33]

An initiative that should have been anodyne and uncontroversial—and might even have redounded to Carter's political benefit—became highly contested instead. Even the nomenclature was charged. When conservatives learned that what they thought would be a conference "on the family" would actually be a conference "on families," they feared—correctly, it turned out—that some of the organizers took a capacious view of families, one that included single-parent households or same-sex parents. The naming of Patsy Fleming, a divorced, African-American mother of three teenagers, as chair in 1978 sparked controversy among Roman Catholics, especially Andrew Greeley, a priest and syndicated columnist, who objected to a divorced woman heading the conference. When Joseph Califano, secretary of health, education and welfare, informed Fleming that she would have to work with a co-chair, she resigned.[34]

By late 1979, the planning for the conference had also been disrupted by the hostage crisis, leading to some uncertainty about its fate. Jim Guy Tucker of Arkansas, the new chair of the conference and a Southern Presbyterian layman, felt obliged to announce that the events had been postponed, not canceled. Amid the uncertainty, however, the Religious Right seized the opportunity to press its agenda and preemptively to define the event. Robert Maddox remembers his first meeting with Weyrich, who was already in high dudgeon about the grave moral dangers posed by the upcoming conference. Incredulous, Maddox asked, "What in the world are you talking about?" At the White House breakfast with evangelical leaders in January 1980, Tim LaHaye had also expressed his reservations. "Our immediate concern is the White House Conference on the Family," LaHaye told the president. "There are reports that the conference seems to be leaning toward a weak, liberal interpretation of the family."[35]

Jerry Falwell joined the chorus of protest. "Unable to define the family, President Carter and his White House Conference on Families (WHCF) are going to the grassroots of America to find the answer," Falwell's "Clean Up America Hotline Report" announced in January 1980. "Between now and March 31, 1980, each state will be holding meetings to draw resolutions and elect delegates to go to one of three Regional WHCF to be held in Los Angeles, Minneapolis, and Baltimore." The report warned of the prevalence of "liberals and humanists" and predicted the agenda: "Critical issues in defining the family revolve around homosexuals and heterosexual couples living together." As the conferences drew closer, Falwell ramped up his warnings. "One of the most dangerous proposals mentioned to date are [*sic*] the right of homosexuals to adopt children and mandatory government control of children," he declared. "Some leaders in the WHCF are suggesting a definition of the word 'family' could be any two persons living together." Unwittingly or not, conference organizers played into those fears. "Families are changing and adapting," a spokeswoman said, "and there's nothing that's going to change that process."[36]

While some evangelicals, such as James Dobson, participated constructively in the White House Conference on Families, other leaders of the Religious Right were spoiling for a confrontation. A group called the National Pro-Family Coalition succeeded in electing a majority of "pro-family" delegates from several states; Connaught "Connie" Marshner, chair of the group and an associate of Paul Weyrich, proposed in a workshop on family violence that "any society which professes to be concerned with the abuse of children should prohibit the ultimate form of abuse: abortion."[37]

At the Baltimore conference, about fifty conservative delegates staged a walkout in protest of the delegate selection process as well as the issues slated for discussion. Delegates in Baltimore included 25 percent racial minorities, 10 percent low income, 8 percent over sixty years old, 4 percent handicapped, and 11 percent single parents. The Baltimore conference debated the issues of divorce, domestic violence, inflation, and unemployment, and delegates approved resolutions to fight alcohol and drug abuse, to encourage care for the elderly at home, and support business, labor, and government in their efforts to provide parental leave and flexible scheduling. An omnibus resolution combining support for the Equal Rights Amendment, the right of access to abortion and family planning services, and the elimination of sexual discrimination passed by a single vote, 292 to 291. Conservatives fared better at the Minneapolis conference, where a resolution defined family as individuals related by blood, heterosexual marriage, adoption, or extended family ties. The final conference, in Los Angeles, passed resolutions calling for greater partnerships between parents and teachers, help for the handicapped, and tax policies that would help families. A resolution supporting the Equal Rights Amendment also won approval, albeit by a lesser margin. During the vote on a resolution in favor of family planning, including "safe, legal abortion," about fifty of the delegates tore up their ballots and threw them at the foot of an American flag to protest abortion.[38]

For the Religious Right, the White House Conference on Families fit into a larger pattern of rapidly eroding "family values." Early in 1979, the U.S. Supreme Court had declared unconstitutional a Pennsylvania statute that required doctors performing abortions to choose the method most likely to save the life of a fetus if it stood any chance of surviving outside of the womb. In July of that same year, the court struck down a Massachusetts law mandating that an unmarried, minor woman secure the approval of her parents or a judge before having an abortion. Throughout his presidency, Carter tried to limit the incidence of abortion by simplifying adoption procedures, advocating sex education, and reducing the stigma of unwed pregnancies. With opposition to abortion now firmly ensconced as a cornerstone of the Religious Right, however, Carter's efforts to reduce abortions were deemed insufficient. Whatever the other arguments for or against his reelection, his refusal to seek a constitutional amendment rendered him, in the eyes of some activists, unworthy of support.[39]

The contestations over the White House Conference on Families played into the dualistic narrative that Paul Weyrich was laboring to construct. In the May–June 1980 issue of *Conservative Digest*, Weyrich predicted that issues surrounding the family, which he characterized as "the age-old conflict between good and evil, between the forces of God and the forces against God," would help to galvanize politically conservative voters: "a number of evangelical, fundamentalist and even conservative Catholic and other religious groups will participate in the political process who were reluctant to do so before." The 1980 campaign was unfolding according to Weyrich's script. "Thank Jimmy Carter for WHCF," Weyrich wrote in a memorandum. "It mobilized the pro-fam mvmt."[40]

THE reaction of conservative evangelicals to the White House Conference on Families demonstrates how dramatically the political ground had shifted beneath Jimmy Carter's feet. Even though *Christianity Today* had endorsed the proposed Equal Rights Amendment to the Constitution in 1974 and its survey of evangelicals showed three-to-one support for the measure, Phyllis Schlafly's crusade against the ERA had gained traction among conservative evangelicals. Schlafly warned that the ERA would create a "unisex society" and "drive the wife out of the home." Feminists, she said, "are making our laws" and were in league with pornographers. Even more ominous, "They are taking over our educational system and the media and they are going to get all the male jobs, too."[41]

Many evangelicals, despite the legacy of feminism that had shaped evangelicalism itself, paid attention to Schlafly's warnings. Writing to the Carter White House about the president's appointment of women in his administration, Curtis T. Porter, pastor of Amherst Baptist Church in Tonawanda, New York, allowed that "I would have preferred to see more of a feminine woman rather than a feminist." Porter insisted that his objection was not to women, but to feminists. "In a day when the home is breaking down more and more, it behooves us as pastors and ministers and political leaders to do all we can to go back to the Biblical patterns to discover how to build Christian homes." A pastor of another Baptist congregation, Immanuel Baptist in Berwyn, Illinois, wrote to report that even the women in his church were opposed to the proposed Equal Rights Amendment. Many conservatives conflated women's rights with gay rights. Carl W. Garrett, a Baptist minister in Carthage, Missouri, reported that the president was "increasingly under fire in our area," especially on the issue of gay rights. "I would very much like to continue to be supportive of the President," Garrett wrote. "I have been a staunch defender, but, I find, my defence [sic] weakening." Dallas E. Pulliam of Greenbelt, Maryland, addressed the president directly. "In light of your increasing stand for gays and the stand of the Democratic Party platform for E. R. A., Gay Rights, and Pro Abortion, I cannot support you or in good conscience ask others to," he wrote. "As a Southern Baptist pastor I voted for you in 1976 but this will not be the case this year." That sentiment was far from unique. "There were a lot of people in our camp who voted for him and then regretted it later," Elmer L. Rumminger of Bob Jones University remembered.[42]

Although John B. Anderson, Republican member of Congress who mounted a third-party challenge, won the support of some progressive evangelicals, Ronald Reagan's campaign would harvest far more of the evangelical defections from Carter. Ralph C. Bearden and his wife, from Plantation, Florida, for example, praised Reagan for his "moral courage for coming out against ERA and abortion." Patricia A. Fitzgerald of Covina, California, who described herself as "a satisfied housewife," sent a mailgram of support to the Reagan campaign: "I'M A BORN AGAIN SPIRIT FILLED ON FIRE FOR JESUS CHRISTIAN AND I'M VOTING FOR YOU IN NOVEMBER DON'T BE INFLUENCED BY A FEW HUNDRED PROTESTERS I'M ALSO AGAINST ABORTION AND THE ERA I LOVE YOU IN JESUS' NAME."[43]

Weyrich and the Religious Right relentlessly pressed the abortion issue. Maddox recalled that when he visited leaders of the Religious Right in Virginia Beach, "they tore into me about abortion." Although mainline Protestants and even a lot of Catholic clergy, according to Maddox, understood the president's position, conservative clergy "were really set against Jimmy Carter." Leaders of the Religious Right excoriated the president for refusing to seek a constitutional amendment outlawing abortion. They also criticized his appointments, especially when Sarah Weddington, a Methodist minister's daughter and lead attorney for "Jane Roe" in the Roe v. Wade case, was appointed to replace Midge Costanza. The rhetoric soon turned nasty, Maddox recalled, "an out-and-out hatchet job," especially from the television and radio preachers. Convinced that Carter favored abortion, despite his clear denunciations and his attempts to limit abortions, leaders of the Religious Right hammered away at an issue that was beginning to capture the passions of rank-and-file evangelicals. "There was no dealing with them," Maddox recalled. "They were gonna get him on abortion."[44]

Maddox thought that Carter had been blindsided by the growing evangelical outrage over abortion. "It was just not an issue in Georgia," he said, and Maddox retained the impression many years later that it was "ginned up by some cabal" to damage the president. By the summer of 1980, Maddox concluded that the campaign would not end well for the president. "It was bad," he said. As James Dunn, a Southern Baptist, ally of Carter, and signer of the Chicago Declaration, wrote to Maddox, "the abortion issue plagues us all."[45]

Maddox was not the only Carter operative sounding warnings about conservative evangelicals. "In the last four years, the fundamentalist right-wing elements of the church in America have become more organized, more vocal and much more solvent," Phil Strickland warned in a memorandum to Hamilton Jordan and Robert Strauss, chair of Carter's campaign committee. "The number of dedicated extremists is small, but their appeals to fear and uncertainty are increasingly effective. The religious community will clearly play a more significant role in this election than in the last one."[46]

Strickland was correct that religion would play a significant role in the 1980 election. Midway through the election year, however, Reagan and leaders of the Religious Right still had not closed the deal with evangelical voters; Carter's support among many evangelicals remained surprisingly sturdy. But it was not for a lack of effort on the part of Falwell and other televangelists. Their media presence alone ensured that their message about the perils of secular humanism and what they characterized as Carter's lassitude on the family and moral issues would continue to reach many evangelical voters. For his part, preoccupied as he was with economic matters and the Iranian hostages, Carter would find it increasingly difficult to mount an effective defense—especially against a confident and charismatic opponent.

EIGHT

ELECTION YEAR
OF THE EVANGELICAL

In October 1976, just prior to Jimmy Carter's election as president, *Newsweek* had christened 1976 the "Year of the Evangelical." Carter's candidacy had introduced many Americans to the term *evangelical*, and his articulation of the themes of progressive evangelicalism—care for the poor, concern for human rights, and an aversion to military conflict—brought many evangelicals into the arena of politics, some of them for the first time. Nearly half of evangelical voters in 1976 favored Carter, which represented a significant increase from the showing of Democratic candidates in years past; white evangelicals, following the lead of Billy Graham and others, had generally tilted Republican in the postwar era. In 1980, four years after Carter's victory, however, the evangelical vote was very much in play. Three candidates were competing for the presidency, and all three claimed to be evangelical Christians: Carter, the Democratic incumbent; Ronald Reagan, the Republican nominee; and John B. Anderson, Republican member of Congress from Illinois, running as an independent.

The political winds had shifted dramatically during Carter's term in office. High inflation and soaring energy prices at home coupled with Soviet aggression and the taking of American hostages abroad had eroded his support among the general population. But Carter himself was astonished to learn that some of his fellow evangelicals were mobilizing against him. Initially distressed by the Internal Revenue Service's rescission of tax exemptions for racially discriminatory schools, these evangelical leaders directed their anger toward Carter, even though the policy was formulated at the behest of

Richard Nixon and enforced during Gerald Ford's administration, long before Carter became president. Once Paul Weyrich and other conservative leaders had enlisted these evangelical leaders in the fight against Carter, they found that a growing evangelical uneasiness over abortion could bring grassroots evangelicals to the front lines of what was increasingly characterized as a moral crusade. By early 1980, Carter, the Southern Baptist Sunday-school teacher and husband for more than three decades, was being pilloried as an enemy of the family and "traditional" values.

Such was the general discontent with Carter and his presidency that few people, and not many evangelicals, rose to his defense. The Carter-Mondale campaign took it upon itself to counter the attacks from the Religious Right. "I think I know President Carter better than anyone outside his immediate family," Walter Mondale told the congregation of North Christian Church in Chicago. "I am with him sometimes four, five, and six hours a day. And I can tell you there is no man who is more deeply moral."[1]

Despite attacks from the Religious Right, however, Carter was not entirely bereft of evangelical support. R. Douglas Wead, who would later serve as an adviser to both George H. W. Bush and George W. Bush, applauded the Carter campaign's "sensitivity" to the evangelical voter. "Though she may be fickle and ungrateful at times," Wead wrote, "she is coming into her own as a political force and may be your best friend in a crisis." Some observers attuned to the evangelical community expressed confidence that evangelical voters would never succumb to the rhetoric of the Religious Right, that the agenda was so blatantly at odds with progressive evangelicalism. "It's all scare," Tom Getman, an aide to Mark O. Hatfield, said about the Religious Right. "It's all playing on people's dark side. They say nothing about social justice. Nothing about the nuclear arms race. Nothing about our militarism or materialism."[2]

Carter, however, was losing support among some progressive evangelicals as well as the Religious Right. Wes Michaelson at *Sojourners* never forgave Carter for what he considered Carter's tardy condemnation of the Vietnam War. Progressive evangelicals tacked on other complaints during the course of Carter's presidency. He was timid about addressing the economic roots of racial inequality and inconsistent in his demands for human rights. Carter, they believed, was too cozy with business and corporate interests. He did not press hard enough for education funding or lobby sufficiently for ratification of the Equal Rights Amendment. Even Ronald Sider, who convened the gathering that approved the Chicago Declaration in 1973 but was tacking toward the right by the end of the decade, criticized Carter for failing to govern according to the biblical mandates of justice.[3]

In a blistering editorial in the January 1978 issue of *Sojourners*, Jim Wallis castigated the president for failure to attend adequately to the needs of the poor. "The biblical demands for justice and compassion bring the harshest kind of judgment to the system of wealth and power upon which Jimmy Carter has built his presidency," Wallis wrote. "It is these standards of social righteousness that our evangelical president has set aside during his first year in office." John F. Alexander of *The Other Side*, another signatory to the Chicago Declaration in 1973, was almost flippant about the 1980 election. Although he acknowledged the moral rectitude of Carter's policy on human rights—"we can be reasonably sure that fewer people are being tortured now than if Ford had been elected"—Alexander expressed doubts that an evangelical in the White House made any difference whatsoever. While he applauded Carter's cancellation of the B-1 bomber, Alexander criticized the president's approval of the MX missile. "Personally I see little point in not voting," he concluded, although he suggested that his readers cast their ballots for Donald Duck.[4]

If evangelical publications like *Sojourners* and *The Other Side* were defecting to the left (or to indifference), *Christianity Today*, which had generally looked favorably on Carter's candidacy in 1976, began hewing the Religious Right party line. By the time of the Washington for Jesus rally on April 29, 1980—the mass demonstration on the Mall organized by leaders of the Religious Right—the magazine was singing the praises of Falwell, Robertson, and the thousands of evangelicals who showed up in the nation's capital to rally against moral drift in America. At the event, James Robison and others lamented what they characterized as attacks on Christian values. "I'm sick and tired of hearing about all the radicals and the liberals and the leftists and the Communists coming out of the closet," Robison shouted. "It's time for God's people to come out of the closets, out of the churches, and change America." *Christianity Today* concurred. "These Christians believe the country would be a better place to live and have a much stronger and more respected voice in the world if in fact the legislators, jurists, and members of the executive branch from President Carter on down to every bureaucrat were somehow captured by a commitment to honesty, integrity, self-sacrifice, and courage," the magazine said. The editorial failed to specify how Carter himself, although mentioned by name, had fallen short of those standards—honesty, integrity, self-sacrifice, courage—but it concluded by saying that if the rally "starts the process of confession, repentance, and restitution, we shall have much for which to be thankful."[5]

By early summer, according to Robert Maddox, the White House liaison to the religious community, "all kinds of anti–Jimmy Carter/pro-Reagan pieces of literature were being cranked out and mailed all over the country, supposedly bipartisan but always painting Reagan as the paragon of Christian virtue and Jimmy Carter as kind of the antichrist." The Reagan campaign took a brief hit when George H. W. Bush, a pro-choice Republican, was chosen for vice president. After an extended flirtation with Gerald R. Ford, Reagan selected Bush, former director of the Central Intelligence Agency and Reagan's rival for the Republican presidential nomination, as his running mate. Bush immediately repented of his pro-choice views and pledged fidelity to the Republican platform, which, in a departure from 1976—and one that signaled shifting political sentiments—condemned both abortion and the Equal Rights Amendment.[6]

PRESIDENTIAL campaigns are exercises in political theater, rife with symbolism, and no politician of recent memory understood that better than Ronald Reagan. After winning the Republican presidential nomination at his party's convention in Detroit, Reagan took the customary few days off for vacation and then launched into the general-election campaign. He might have opened his campaign in any number of places, including his home state of California or his native state of Illinois, both considered strategic battlegrounds in the November election. He might have visited a steel mill or an automobile plant in the so-called rust belt, a region reeling at the time from economic recession. Or he might have sought a loftier venue to emphasize a theme for his candidacy—the Statue of Liberty, perhaps, or the Gettysburg battlefield, where the nation played out its defining moral crisis.

The Reagan campaign, however, chose the Neshoba County Fair for its opening event, in the remote town of Philadelphia, in central Mississippi. Only sixteen summers earlier, one of the most horrific chapters of the civil rights movement had unfolded in Philadelphia, Mississippi. Three civil rights workers were arrested and beaten and then, with the collusion of the sheriff's office, abducted by members of the Ku Klux Klan and murdered. Their mangled bodies were discovered weeks later, buried in an earthen dam outside of Philadelphia.

Reagan, the master of symbolism, might have used the macabre setting to put to rest any lingering suspicions that his campaign would appeal to racism in any form. Instead, invoking the battle cry of George Wallace and dozens of other segregationist politicians, the candidate declared, "I believe in states' rights."[7]

From a purely tactical perspective, the Reagan campaign was signaling that it had no intention of ceding the South to Carter, a Georgian; two months before the Nashoba event, William J. Casey had suggested to Reagan that he kick off the campaign with a rally in Atlanta, "to keep Jimmy nervous and concerned about his home base." But the Philadelphia, Mississippi, venue and the candidate's remarks went well beyond the mere staking out of political territory; the Reagan campaign could have conveyed that message from New Orleans or Knoxville or Mobile, Alabama—or Atlanta—all of them southern locations with a less fraught attachment to civil rights and a less visceral connection to racism and racist violence.[8]

Andrew Young, formerly Carter's ambassador to the United Nations who had marched alongside Martin Luther King Jr. in the civil rights struggle, questioned Reagan's motives for visiting a place that, Young said, "always sends chills up my spine." Writing in the *Washington Post*, Young recalled his own visits to Neshoba County, the first time in the wake of the Klan murders of James Chaney, Andrew Goodman, and Michael "Mickey" Schwerner during that fateful Freedom Summer of 1964. Young had visited a second time on the heels of the shooting of James Meredith, the first African American admitted to the University of Mississippi, during the March against Fear in 1966, encouraging voter registration. On that occasion, Young recalled, King stood on the steps of the Neshoba County courthouse, described the still unsolved killings two years earlier, and remarked that, "The murderers of Goodman, Chaney and Schwerner are no doubt within the range of my voice." From the white mob guarding the courthouse door, Young recalled, a voice rang out, "Ya damn right. We're right here behind you." Young pointed out what everyone in Reagan's Nashoba County Fair audience already knew, that the candidate's invocation of "states' rights" was intended to conjure the days of southern resistance to desegregation. "Traditionally, these code words have been the electoral language of Wallace, Goldwater and the Nixon southern strategy," Young wrote, noting that one leader of the Ku Klux Klan had already endorsed Reagan and had commented that the Republican Party platform "reads as if it were written by a Klansman."[9]

The Reagan campaign tried to turn the tables by portraying Carter as the true friend of the Klan. When Jimmy Carter held a rally in Tuscumbia, Alabama, Reagan accused the president of "opening his campaign down in the

city that gave birth to and is the parent body of the Ku Klux Klan." The remark
backfired. Although the Klan had a presence in Tuscumbia, just as it did in
many other places, Carter had used the occasion to issue a stinging attack on
racism in general and the Ku Klux Klan in particular; the Klan had demonstrated against the president prior to the event. Reagan's comment, moreover,
was inaccurate; the Klan had originated in Pulaski, Tennessee, in 1865, and the
second iteration of the Klan began at Stone Mountain, Georgia, in 1915. Seven
southern governors, all of them Democrats, demanded an apology, citing "Mr.
Reagan's callous and opportunistic slap at the South." Reagan-Bush campaign
headquarters was besieged with calls, prompting one staffer to note, "we're in a
hell of a lot of trouble." The candidate finally apologized, protesting that he had
not intended to disparage the city of Tuscumbia or the state of Alabama.[10]

IN addition to its efforts in the South, the Reagan campaign avidly courted
the evangelical vote, even if the candidate himself didn't fully understand the
appeal. In February 1980, he had insisted to a television interviewer that
he too was born again, although he seemed a tad uneasy about the label.
When briefed about the particulars of that designation, Reagan concluded,
"I suppose I would qualify." Even as the candidate struggled to master the
vocabulary of evangelicalism, however, his campaign operatives attained
perfect fluency, adeptly using evangelical code language just as they had employed racially coded language in Mississippi.[11]

By August, Moral Majority was boasting that it had registered three million new evangelical voters; the organization claimed a membership of 400,000,
including 72,000 ministers. Abortion now topped Falwell's listing of the five
"sins of America," followed by homosexuality, pornography, humanism, and
the fractured family. "There can be no doubt that the sin of America is severe,"
Falwell wrote in his manifesto, Listen, America! "We are literally approaching
the brink of national disaster."[12]

Tim LaHaye, Falwell's co-belligerent on moral issues, reiterated the same
concerns in his book, Battle for the Mind, also published in 1980. LaHaye
listed opposition to homosexuality as an essential initiative for those who
would "stop our descent into amorality" and arrest the nation's moral decline. "Our laws are already too weak in this area," he wrote. "This will include opposition to ERA, for it opens the door to homosexuality." The
previous year, LaHaye's wife, Beverly, had formed an organization called
Concerned Women for America to counter the National Organization for
Women and to oppose passage of the Equal Rights Amendment.[13]

"We are in a battle—and it takes armies to win wars," Tim LaHaye wrote. "We need an army of moral activists, led by their Bible-believing ministers, who will provide America with the moral leadership for which this country hungers." The message was already trickling down to grassroots evangelicals, and the foot soldiers of the Religious Right were beginning to gather confidence. When Christian Voice, another Religious Right organization, determined that Donald W. Stewart, Democratic senator from Alabama, scored only a 23 out of 100 on its "morality rating," activists confronted the senator and beckoned him to fall on his knees and repent. Stewart demurred, whereupon conservative evangelicals targeted him for defeat.[14]

The Reagan-Bush campaign determinedly courted politically conservative evangelicals. The Religious Roundtable, a kind of clearinghouse of Religious Right groups, organized a National Affairs Briefing, which took place on August 21–22 at Reunion Arena in Dallas, Texas. The letter of invitation, signed by Edward McAteer, James Robison, and Tom Landry, head coach of the Dallas Cowboys, promised insight into "the domestic crisis which is morally enslaving our country" and strategies "to inform and mobilize your church and community in this non-partisan effort to do something that can determine the moral character of America." The organizers invited both major presidential candidates, although Carter declined. In his letter of invitation to Reagan, Robison had assured the candidate that the National Affairs Briefing would be "the largest, most significant, political and spiritual gathering" in the South. "I am thrilled with the progress you are making toward the Presidency of the United States," Robison wrote. "As one seeking to know and do the will of God, I stand firmly convinced that you are the best candidate to lead us during these crisis days in American history. I will do everything possible within the limits of my ministry to be of help to you."[15]

The event in Dallas was carefully scripted to appeal to conservative evangelical voters, invoking dualistic categories and conjuring the specter of apocalyptic doom. "We see everything in black and white perspectives because scripture sees things in black and white perspectives," Weyrich told the assembled evangelicals. Adrian Rogers, president of the Southern Baptist Convention, played on nostalgia for a simpler time, expressing his aspiration "to get America back like it was when I was a boy." D. James Kennedy, pastor of Coral Ridge Presbyterian Church in Fort Lauderdale, Florida, warned darkly that "1980 could be America's last free election."[16]

The evening rally opened with a prayer by Pat Robertson, followed by remarks from Bill Armstrong and Jesse Helms, both U.S. senators. After a succession of stem-winding preachers who decried moral decay in America, Reagan famously opened his remarks by telling his audience, "I know this group can't endorse me, but I endorse you and what you are doing." The line brought down the house and arguably sealed the evangelical vote. "Today, you and I are meeting at a time when traditional Judeo-Christian values, based on the moral teachings of religion, are undergoing what is perhaps their most serious challenge in our nation's history," the candidate warned. "As our schools have tried to educate without ethics, we have seen the mounting evidence in crime rates, drug abuse, child abuse, and human suffering." Reagan went on to extol "traditional moral values," to register his doubts about evolution, and to excoriate "the unconstitutional regulatory agenda launched by Mr. Carter's IRS Commissioner against independent schools." He concluded with the declaration that if he were shipwrecked on an island, he would want to have the Bible for his reading material. At the conclusion of Reagan's address, Falwell, with a wink toward the supposedly nonpartisan nature of the gathering, instructed those in attendance to vote for the "Reagan of their choice."[17]

The entire event had been planned meticulously. In transmitting a draft of Reagan's speech in advance of the National Affairs Briefing, a speechwriter for the campaign wrote: "Please note: there are *an awful lot* of code words, religious allusions, and whatnot built into this, which might be missed if one is not close to evangelical religion. It is not important, however, for the speaker to understand each and every one of them. His audience will. Boy, will they ever!"[18]

Reagan's speech before fifteen thousand cheering evangelicals, however, included no mention of abortion; the candidate's strategists understood, as subsequent polling would confirm, that not all evangelicals had bought into the abortion issue as a litmus test for their loyalties. The campaign also recognized that courting politically conservative evangelicals too assiduously could backfire with independent, or even with traditional Republican, voters. Weyrich acknowledged some uneasiness in the Reagan camp about the candidate's appearance before a crowd of evangelical conservatives, "because aides feared a backlash if Reagan were too closely identified with the so-called Christian Right." The campaign, however, had decided to take the gamble, ensuring that the candidate's remarks were carefully scripted. "Reagan aides constructed a speech for the candidate which had just enough emotional appeal for the audience," Weyrich wrote just days after the event, "but which carefully avoided the issues of abortion, the Equal Rights Amendment, Gay Rights and Prayer in the Schools, each of which is a bottom line issue with the Evangelical/Fundamentalist community represented at the gathering."[19]

If the rally in Dallas gave Reagan a boost, it didn't show up immediately in the polling. Despite the president's battering at the hands of preachers and pundits, Carter's evangelical support was remarkably resilient. A Gallup poll released in early September, a couple of weeks after the Dallas gathering, showed that "66 percent of nonevangelicals favor the Equal Rights Amendment, but so do 53 percent of evangelicals," and 41 percent of evangelicals supported a legal ban on abortion. The poll findings track with other, anecdotal evidence that a majority of evangelicals had not yet fully connected with abortion or with the Equal Rights Amendment as moral concerns. Reagan's avoidance of both issues suggested that the Reagan-Bush campaign understood that. Another indication that abortion was not yet a central concern was a chain letter targeting "Church Voter Groups" late in the campaign; the letter made no mention of abortion among its five objections to Carter, although it did call for a "halt on the unconstitutional regulatory vendetta launched by Jimmy Carter's Internal Revenue Service against independent schools."[20]

The Gallup poll caught the attention of the Reagan campaign. "While President Carter and Ronald Reagan are in close contention nationally," the poll found, "Carter is the overwhelming choice of evangelicals." The poll's release prompted a frantic memorandum from Alex Ray at the Republican National Committee, clipped to the newspaper article. "This coalition was supposed to be one of our strongest support groups and we're getting our butts handed to us," he wrote. "Someone had better address this problem immediately."[21]

The Reagan campaign coveted those evangelical voters, and campaign aides diligently tracked their sentiments. An internal memorandum in the Reagan camp called attention to a movement of perhaps seventy million evangelicals who were "mounting the political equivalent of a 20th century religious crusade to purge evil forces that they contend control the U.S. Government." The writer added that "its potential is enormous for the Reagan-Bush ticket if, and only if, the movement is handled properly." Another internal memorandum agreed that born-again Christians could provide crucial support, not only in the South. Another aide warned that the Carter campaign would contest Reagan for evangelical support. "This vote was critical to them in '76," he wrote, "and could well be again in '80."[22]

Another indicator suggested that the Reagan campaign might not be connecting with evangelicals. By September, the editors at *Christianity Today* began to have misgivings about the magazine's consistent cheerleading for Robertson, Falwell, and (by indirection at least) Reagan. An editorial asked a series of rhetorical questions, including, "Are all evangelicals necessarily politically conservative?" The magazine answered "no," citing the examples of Mark Hatfield, John B. Anderson, and Carter. "Too narrow a front in battling for a moral crusade, or for a truly biblical involvement in politics, could be disastrous," the editorial allowed. "It could lead to the election of a moron who holds the right view on abortion." The editorial demonstrates yet again that although political opposition to abortion was gaining traction among evangelicals, it was still not, even this late in the campaign, a make-or-break issue. Phyllis Schlafly disputed the assumption that evangelical voters would flock to the Reagan-Bush ticket because they had nowhere else to go; the real impediment to Reagan's election, she said, lay in evangelicals settling back into political apathy. "They do have a place to go," Schlafly declared, "the same place they have been for the rest of their lives: in their churches reading their Bibles."[23]

In the countdown to Election Day, however, the political dynamics began to change quickly as evangelical sentiments shifted unmistakably toward Reagan. Part of that movement was consistent with trends in the general population. Americans were weary of stagnant economic conditions, fearful of losing the nation's preeminent place in the world, and humiliated by the Iranian hostage drama, which played out nightly on the evening news. Carter seemed stymied by it all, and as the anniversary of the raid on the U.S. embassy approached, Americans were reminded of the intractable situation and Carter's apparent inability to solve it.

On top of those general complaints, evangelicals had been hearing from the Religious Right for more than a year that legalized abortion was a moral abomination, that homosexuality was a perversion, and that the Equal Rights Amendment represented a threat to the integrity of the family. Jimmy Carter, they learned, favored all of those terrible things. At the same time, Reagan promised (or seemed to promise) to make everything all right again, to vanquish secular humanism and restore traditional values.

Carter, meanwhile, suffered, both politically and personally, from the rhetorical lashes of the Religious Right. "My religious beliefs are very precious to me," he told a town-hall gathering in Memphis late in the campaign. "But until this year, I have never had anybody question the sincerity of my belief in God and my commitment of my life as a Christian believing in Jesus Christ as my savior." The president expressed confidence about his own relationship with God, reminded the audience of his long career as a Sunday-school teacher, and noted that he and Rosalynn read a chapter in the Bible every night. "I'm not in favor of a religious definition of an acceptable politician," he said, "and I'm not in favor of a political definition for Christian fellowship or for religious fellowship." Carter, in the face of political attacks that suggested otherwise, reiterated his support for a strong military defense, but, calling on the tradition of progressive evangelicalism, he also affirmed his conviction that "the best weapons are the ones that are never fired in combat, and the best soldier is the one that never has to shed his blood or give his life in battle." Despite his forceful rebuttal, the president was clearly stung by the criticism: "to have my opponent and those who support my opponent allege that I have a false belief or that I would twist my beliefs against the teachings, as I understand them, of the Bible is very, very disturbing to me."[24]

The president's foes were relentless. "I would never, as a preacher, stand up and pontificate on a candidate," Bob Jones III told a reporter for the *Greenville Piedmont*. "But when we live in a society that is increasingly un-Christian, my job as a preacher is to turn the light of the word of God on the work of Satan." Jones discerned the work of Satan in the actions of the Internal Revenue Service, the movement for gay rights, and the toleration of abortion. David D. Yearick, pastor of Hampton Park Baptist Church in Greenville, concurred, adding the Equal Rights Amendment to his list of concerns. "I find it hard to believe that a person can be religiously conservative and politically liberal, but there are some," he said, apparently oblivious to the history of his own tradition. "I wouldn't say you can't be both, but I'd find it hard myself to support the Democratic platform."[25]

By October, indicators from the grass roots tracked this movement on the part of conservative evangelicals from Carter to Reagan. "May I chronicle my disillusionment with Mr. Carter?" Billy G. Hurt wrote from Frankfort, Kentucky, on October 20. "At first I thought he was a good man of integrity with a new philosophy of responsible government," he said in his letter to Maddox. "Sir, I no longer believe that Mr. Carter is a good man." Other correspondents were more measured, even as they expressed reservations. "I would like to vote again for President Carter, but I'm finding it harder and harder to make this decision," Faye Spoth of Lubbock, Texas, wrote to the White House. "I firmly believe 'born again' voters elected him to this office or at least gave him the extra boost he needed," she added, but sentiment was shifting. "You might convey to Mr. Carter that the majority of my Christian friends are going to vote for Reagan. They are going from the democratic side to the Republicans." Floyd M. Shealy from Oklahoma City wrote that evangelical leaders "have already swung their followers to Ronald Reagan. This is not 'scare talk' nor negative thinking, but rather demonstrable fact." Shealy added: "You had their vote in 1976, but there has been a strong and concerted direction to the Republican candidate for the November election." Larry T. Floyd from Sycamore, Alaska, said that he was "not a member of morals majority [*sic*] but I do support what they stand for." He added: "I'm a Southern Baptist and my Bible tell me that homosexual is a sin, abortion is taking of Life and the man head of the house."[26]

Leaders of the Religious Right, meanwhile, kept pressing their crusade for traditional values. In the October 15, 1980, edition of his *Moral Majority Report,* just three weeks before the election, Falwell once again summarized his agenda: "We are opposed to abortion, pornography, the drug epidemic, the breakdown of the traditional family in America, the establishment of homosexuality as an accepted alternate life-style and other immoral cancers which are causing the U.S. to rot from within."[27]

By October, a month before the election, these relentless messages from leaders of the Religious Right were finally hitting their mark. Letters arriving at the White House in the final weeks of the campaign fairly throbbed with anger and indignation, even betrayal. "It doesn't do any good for a person to go to church, read the Bible, and pray every day if they don't live what they read in the Bible," Beth Pennington, who identified herself as a "Tupperware Manager" from Bow, Washington, wrote to Robert Maddox a month before the general election. "Pres. Carter & Mrs. Carter are for ERA, Gay Rights, Abortion (murder) and are against prayer in schools," she said. "I can assure you I will not vote for Pres. Carter this fall and I hope to influence a lot of other people to vote against him too." A correspondent from Akron, Ohio, Even Argante, weighed in with his views. "'Human rights' is Human Rot!" he wrote. "How can President Carter condone this godless farce?" Argante enclosed several clippings from Moral Majority with his letter. "Is he really in favor of ERA?" he asked about the president. "It can't be possible. He is a born again Christian?" Terry Miller from Dallas, Texas, was even more direct. "Start looking for a new job. The moral majority is going to put you and President Carter type of Christians out of a job," he wrote to Maddox, Carter's religious liaison. "Any staunch Christian would not support gays, would not support the ERA which contradicts God's plan for women and would support voluntary prayer in the school. You guys are real bummers. You don't even deserve to be called Baptists." Miller concluded with a promise: "We the moral majority are putting you guys out."[28]

By the final weekend of the campaign, everything was breaking in Reagan's direction. The Iranians had made another feint toward releasing the hostages just before Election Day, but those hopes were disappointed. (Years later, credible—albeit circumstantial—evidence surfaced that emissaries of the Reagan campaign, including George H. W. Bush, former director of the Central Intelligence Agency, and William Casey, who would become Reagan's CIA director, had secretly arranged with the Iranians to keep the hostages captive until after the election.) Carter's diary entries for the days immediately preceding the election mention surprisingly little about the campaign; it's clear that the president was preoccupied with securing freedom for the hostages. Election Day happened also to fall on the anniversary of the taking of the hostages at the American embassy in Teheran, so media coverage focused on both the election and the hostages—to Carter's detriment.[29]

On Monday, November 3, the day before the election, Carter wrote that his pollster, Patrick Caddell, "was getting some very disturbing poll results, showing a massive slippage as people realized the hostages were not coming home." The following day, voters chose Ronald Reagan over Jimmy Carter by a wide margin; the Carter-Mondale ticket won only 41 percent of the popular vote and carried only six states and the District of Columbia. Conservatives also exulted in the defeat of several liberal U.S. senators, including Birch Bayh of Indiana, John Culver of Iowa, George McGovern of South Dakota, and Frank Church of Idaho. Republicans had captured not only the presidency but also a majority in the Senate. "I promised you four years ago that I would never lie to you," Carter told tearful supporters at the Sheraton Washington Hotel. "So I can't stand here tonight and say it doesn't hurt."[30]

A preacher listening to the election returns down in Lynchburg, Virginia, fewer than two hundred miles southwest of Washington, was elated. "Can you believe it?" Jerry Falwell asked an associate. "I knew that we would have some impact on the national elections, but I had no idea that it would be this great." One analysis showed that Reagan received 56 percent of the evangelical vote, John B. Anderson pulled 4 percent, and Carter 40 percent, down nearly 10 percentage points from 1976. Although Carter received 83 percent support from African Americans, many of them evangelicals, the defection of white evangelicals sealed his loss. Falwell later quoted pollster Lou Harris, who found that Reagan would have lost the popular vote by one percentage point if not for the politicking of the Religious Right.[31]

If Jimmy Carter rode to the presidency on the current of probity, progressive evangelicalism, and his reputation as an avatar of the New South, a different confluence drove him from office. By any measure, his was a troubled presidency, beset by economic woes at home and overwhelmed by events abroad, especially the hostages in Teheran. Although Carter could have launched military strikes against Iran or even on the Soviets in Afghanistan, his preference for diplomacy over militarism and his deference to just-war principles constrained him. His decision to boycott the 1980 Olympic games in Moscow struck many Americans as a small and futile gesture, one that arguably punished the athletes themselves more than the Soviets.[32]

If Carter treaded carefully, however, Reagan swaggered, talking tough and in bellicose terms about what he would do as president. In contrast with Carter, Reagan's understanding of the world was uncomplicated and without discernible nuance. He resurrected the familiar categories of dualism. (Once in office, Reagan would memorably identify the Soviet Union as the "evil empire" in contrast to the United States, the "shining city on a hill.") Reagan's approach to domestic issues was similarly straightforward. Conservation was unnecessary, he promised to an electorate weary of Carter's fiscal and energy austerity; simply give oil companies free rein and we'll have plenty of energy—no more lines at gasoline pumps or thermostats turned down to sixty-five degrees. On social issues, Reagan promised a constitutional amendment to prohibit abortion and a return to traditional family values.[33]

Carter's defeat signaled the eclipse of progressive evangelicalism on the national stage. His renegotiation of the Panama Canal treaties, his pursuit of human rights, and even his diplomatic triumph in the Camp David accords were not enough to carry him to a second term. Carter's persistent efforts to limit the incidence of abortion were judged inadequate by an evangelical constituency newly attuned to the issue; his failure to support a constitutional amendment was deemed an unpardonable sin.

It is impossible, of course, to divine the motivations for an entire segment of the population. Perhaps, as they did in 1976, many white evangelicals were looking for an excuse to abandon their fellow evangelical and return to the more familiar precincts of the Republican Party. Carter's *Playboy* interview provided that pretext late in the 1976 campaign; the president's supposed tolerance for secular humanism and moral decay supplied the excuse four years later.

The oracles of the Religious Right amplified that message to voters, especially conservative evangelicals. "We must acknowledge an important role played by Jerry Falwell, Pat Robertson, James Robison, and other representatives of organizations representing politically conservative segments of evangelicalism," *Christianity Today* said after the election. These televangelists, the editorial continued, "functioned as responsible citizens seeking to further the cause of public morality in a pluralistic democracy." The editors failed to notice the repudiation of progressive evangelicalism, nor did they express remorse at the defeat of a fellow evangelical. The magazine simply counseled caution about inflated expectations for the new administration. "If evangelicals expect too much too soon, they may once again become disenchanted and withdraw; that would be a disastrous step backward."[34]

Backward from what? was never specified.

AFTER Jimmy Carter's loss, the postmortems began trickling in. The fact that the president had been forced to fend off a primary challenge from within his own party had certainly done nothing to enhance his chances in November. Edward Kennedy's decision to mount such a challenge in the first place suggested that Carter's support in the more liberal precincts of his own party was tenuous; Carter lost even the reliably Democratic state of Massachusetts, Kennedy's home state, in the general election. The international crises—the Soviets in Afghanistan and especially the hostages in Iran—sapped the president's energies personally and crippled him politically. Reflecting on his loss many years later, Carter said, "I wish I'd sent one more helicopter to Iran." If he had been able to free the hostages, he mused, "I would have won the election without much of a problem." Several decades later, Americans learned that Carter had authorized the risky evacuation of six Americans hiding in the private residences of the Canadian ambassador and an immigration official in Teheran, an operation dramatized in the 2012 motion picture *Argo.* Carter would have benefited politically from publicizing his bold action, but such publicity might have endangered the hostages remaining in Iran. The president remained silent. The domestic situation hardly looked brighter for the incumbent: a continuing energy crisis, persistent inflation, and stubbornly high interest rates.[35]

Carter himself believed that it was his willingness to confront difficult issues that eroded his popularity. "My political advisers and my wife were always saying, 'Don't get involved in that, wait until a second term. Don't address this issue because it's obviously and predictably unpopular,'" Carter recounted a decade later. "But it wasn't my nature. And I don't say I'm right. I didn't get re-elected." Thirty-three years later, Carter took the blame for his loss. "I failed to prepare adequately for reelection," he said. "I could have assuaged Kennedy's demands more than I did," especially Kennedy's scheme for health-care reform. Still, Carter bore no animus toward Kennedy, whose primary challenge crippled Carter's campaign and drove many liberals to John B. Anderson. Kennedy, Carter said, felt entitled to the presidency by virtue of his family pedigree, but he was "probably one of the best senators we ever had."[36]

Carter also suffered from the defection of evangelicals, many of whom had helped propel him to the presidency four years earlier. Tim LaHaye's analysis was succinct. Reagan won because of "our Heavenly Father," LaHaye declared, who "saw thousands of us working diligently to awaken his sleeping church to its political responsibilities."[37]

When did the president himself sense the erosion of support from fellow evangelicals? The 1979 conservative takeover of his own denomination, the Southern Baptist Convention, Carter said, signaled to him that the kind of progressive evangelicalism he espoused was no longer in favor among many evangelicals. Many progressive evangelicals themselves, a key element of Carter's vote in 1976, gravitated to Anderson or effectively sat out the 1980 election. *Sojourners*, for example, seemed more interested in the World Series than the election.[38]

By early 1981, however, some evangelicals were already suffering from buyer's remorse, worried about the new president's saber rattling, his proposals to elevate defense spending, his tax schemes benefiting the affluent, and his disregard for women's rights. "Ronald Reagan is now president of the United States," John F. Alexander of *The Other Side* wrote. "And that is bad news. It is especially bad news for poor people." Alexander, who had urged his readers to vote for Donald Duck, now worried that Reagan would send troops into El Salvador or Guatemala. "And then there's Israel, the environment, women's rights, control of government by big business," he wrote. Alexander conceded that evangelicals might have quibbled with Carter about abortion, "but I do not see how serious people can possibly oppose ERA or gay rights."[39]

Paul Weyrich had exploited precisely those issues in order to harvest evangelical votes. Without any question, the political and organizing skill of operatives like Weyrich, together with the television presence and media savvy of preachers like Jerry Falwell, combined to create a formidable grassroots movement. Weyrich's prescience about expanding abortion from a preponderantly "Catholic issue" into an evangelical preoccupation was nothing short of brilliant. His success in blaming Carter for the IRS action against Christian schools may also have been brilliant, but it was also mendacious because Carter bore no responsibility for that. After years of warnings, the Internal Revenue Service finally rescinded the tax exemption of Bob Jones University on January 19, 1976, because of its persistent racist policies. That date was a notable one for Jimmy Carter—but not because he was in any way responsible for the action against Bob Jones University; Carter won the Iowa precinct caucuses on January 19, 1976, his first major step toward capturing the Democratic presidential nomination. He took office as president a year and a day later. Weyrich and the Religious Right, however, persuaded many evangelicals that Carter—not Richard Nixon, who formulated the policy, or Gerald Ford, who was president when it was enforced—was somehow responsible for this unconscionable "assault" on Christian schools.

As a candidate in 1976, Carter had run as an evangelical, a Sunday-school teacher, and a man of evident piety and probity. Because of Ford's reluctance to broadcast his religious practices, Carter effectively had the religious vote to himself—at least until the *Playboy* interview peeled off some of that support—in an election year in which voters were eager to repudiate the moral lapses of the Nixon administration. As a consequence, Carter was never compelled to provide elaborate religious or theological justifications for his progressive evangelical views on war or the poor or women or the relationship of church and state.

By 1980, however, the religious terrain had shifted—and it had become considerably more crowded. Carter no longer had a presumptive claim to the evangelical vote, and he faced an array of Religious Right leaders who offered very different understandings of the faith and how it inflected their political views. Carter, unaccustomed to laying out his positions in a systematic way—and far too busy to do so as president—simply offered no countervailing arguments from the perspective of progressive evangelicalism, which informed his own approach to governing.

In that sense, at least, the 1980 campaign represented a missed opportunity. On the Religious Right's push for prayer in public schools, for instance, the president might have parried with the obvious rejoinder that prayer had never been outlawed in the schools. As Mark Hatfield, a fellow Baptist, often said, he prayed frequently and fervently in school, especially before and during exams. Carter, of all people, who claimed to pray as often as twenty-five

times a day, understood that the most efficacious prayers, in the best evangelical tradition, were spontaneous and heartfelt rather than rote and pre-
scribed. Besides, faith had flourished in the United States precisely because of
the First Amendment and the separation of church and state, precisely because the government had remained neutral on matters of religion. Legislat-
ing prayer in public schools would violate the "wall of separation" between
the "garden of the church" and the "wilderness of the world," the metaphors
advanced by Roger Williams, a fellow Baptist, in the seventeenth century.
Transgressing that wall, Carter might have added, ultimately endangered the
integrity of the faith by too close an association with the state.[40]

Robert Maddox believed that Carter, as president, took evangelical support for granted—What reason, after all, would they have for turning against
one of their own?—and by the time the Carter campaign apprehended the
gathering storm, it was too late. Maddox recalled that when he arrived at the
White House to help the president, evangelical leaders "had their minds
made up against him." Maddox also believed that Carter's failure to appoint
high-profile evangelicals to his administration hurt the president in the eyes
of evangelicals.[41]

In the course of an interview on Pat Robertson's *700 Club* television program during the 1976 campaign, Carter had assured Robertson of his willingness to make such appointments. Following that election, Robertson and
other evangelicals had compiled a list of nearly three dozen possible appoin-
tees, chartered a plane, and delivered the list to the president-elect in Plains.
The fate of that list remains a mystery; in the flurry of Carter's transition from
Plains to the White House, it apparently went astray. Perhaps it was mislaid,
or it was buried in a file folder of some staff member. Or, possibly, an aide un-
sympathetic to Robertson and suspicious of evangelicals dispatched it somehow. At any rate, Carter never acted on those appointments, and when
Maddox came to the White House and contacted Robertson for his reading
on the president, the matter came up immediately as a source of irritation.
Maddox asked for a copy of the list, but it was already too late in Carter's term
to act on the appointments—or to assuage the anger of evangelical leaders.[42]

By the 1980 election, Carter's apparent refusal to make such appointments
had become a festering wound. Tim LaHaye's assessment was unduly harsh, but
it reflected the sentiment of other conservative evangelical leaders: "we have
witnessed the presidency of a self-acknowledged, born-again leader who surrounded himself with amoral or immoral promoters during his campaign."[43]

In the course of his exit interview two months after Carter's defeat, Maddox suggested that if Carter had appointed someone like Harold Hughes to a cabinet post, the president would have helped himself enormously in the eyes of evangelicals. Hughes, a lay Methodist preacher from Ida Grove, Iowa, who had chosen not to seek reelection to the Senate in 1974, was a tireless advocate for progressive evangelicalism.[44]

Even the appointment of Hughes, however, would not have mollified leaders of the Religious Right. As a progressive evangelical, Hughes embodied a political iteration of evangelicalism far different from that articulated by Falwell or Robertson or Reagan; their understanding of evangelical politics emphasized free-market capitalism, paid scant attention to human rights or the plight of minorities, and asserted the importance of military might as resistance to communism. Hughes was a dove, not a hawk. He was an advocate for equal rights and understood that government had a role to play in the alleviation of poverty. As early as the spring of 1976, in fact, a group of conservative evangelicals, the precursors of the Religious Right, specifically identified Hughes and Mark Hatfield as examples of evangelicals they did not want in government because of their liberal politics.[45]

DESPITE his loss, the president used his remaining time in office to advance his agenda. In addition to pressing for the release of the hostages, he signed the Alaska National Interest Lands Conservation Act on December 2, 1980, which preserved a third of Alaska from commercial development and doubled the size of the nation's wildlife refuges and national parks. For too long, Carter argued, human beings had "despoiled God's earth." The president also signed bills to limit strip mining and to clean up toxic waste. Years later, Gaylord Nelson, U.S. senator from Wisconsin and one of the principal founders of Earth Day, would characterize Carter as "the greatest environmental president the country ever had."[46]

"I tried to shape the principles, morals, standards, and even laws of our country in a way that was beneficial to the people of this nation," Carter recalled many years later in summarizing his presidency. In the course of Carter's final cabinet meeting on December 3, the day after the president had signed the Alaska Lands Act, Carter invited each of his cabinet members to reflect on his or her service over the course of the Carter administration. It was, according to press accounts, a relaxed and good-natured meeting, punctuated by "many bursts of laughter." But it was bittersweet as well. Walter

Mondale went last. "We told the truth. We obeyed the law. We kept the peace," the vice president said. "And that ain't bad."[47]

What would a second Carter term have looked like? Carter himself speculated that, with the return of the hostages from Iran, he would have been free to forge ahead on energy independence and securing peace in the Middle East. Fiscal responsibility was important to Carter, and he took pride in the fact that (although his successor ignored it) he was able finally to propose a balanced federal budget before he left office. Human rights would have remained at the center of U.S. foreign policy in a second term. Carter may have lost the election, but he never repented of the principles that guided him in office. "I have no doubt that the ideas and beliefs that provided the foundation for everything I tried to accomplish as president," he wrote, "would have continued to guide me had I served another four years."[48]

Indeed, largely lost in the electoral landslide of 1980 was Carter's list of achievements. He extended diplomatic recognition to China, and his renegotiation of the Panama Canal treaties was essential not only to the sustenance of trade but to any hopes of a real and enduring relationship with Latin America. More important, it signaled to Third World nations that the Carter administration would be attentive to their concerns. Carter's shift in foreign affairs from the containment policies of the Cold War to an emphasis on human rights may have had limited immediate results, but it succeeded in freeing some political prisoners and prompting at least a few dictators to mend their ways. Carter's insistence on human rights also elevated the issue to prominence in discourse around the globe. At Camp David, Carter did more to advance peace in the Middle East than any president since the formation of the State of Israel in 1948, and his refusal to launch strikes in Iran or Afghanistan may have hurt him politically, but it was consistent with his commitment to military restraint and just-war principles.[49]

On domestic matters, Carter deregulated several sectors of the economy, including communications, energy, and transportation; the Paperwork Reduction Act of 1980 reduced paperwork requirements for private industry. Despite exorbitant interest rates, nearly eight million jobs were added to the economy during Carter's time in office; the unemployment rate remained high in part because large numbers of women and teenagers entered the work force in the late 1970s. In the course of the 1980 campaign, Reagan frequently invoked what he called the "misery index" of the Carter years, the sum total of inflation and unemployment. That index tallied a stubbornly high 14.5 percent during the Carter administration, but it was an improvement from 16.2

percent under Gerald Ford. (At the conclusion of Reagan's first term, the "misery index" stood at 14.5 percent, identical to that of Carter's presidency.) Carter appointed a record number of women and minorities and reorganized government in an effort to make it more efficient. The Civil Service Reform Act of 1978 was the first comprehensive reform of the civil service system in more than a century. Carter's "Crisis of Confidence" address in 1979 came to be ridiculed and maligned as the "malaise" speech, but if the United States had pursued the energy and conservation initiatives he proposed, the nation would be in a far different place. Many environmentalists praise Carter's legacy on conservation and the preservation of natural resources.[50]

Carter was certainly frustrated in other initiatives, including health-care reform, ratification of the Equal Rights Amendment, and a reduction in nuclear arms. But given the sour economy that prevailed throughout his time in office, his list of accomplishments is hardly negligible. Above all, whatever his shortcomings, Carter succeeded in restoring integrity to the White House following the moral debacle of the Nixon presidency. Even though Carter seldom lacked for critics, few of those critics claimed that Jimmy Carter lacked integrity.

Reflecting on his tenure as president, Carter said that his faith played a large role. "I prayed more during those four years than at any other time in my life, primarily for patience, courage and the wisdom to make good decisions," he wrote in 1996. "I also prayed for peace—for others and ourselves."[51]

NINE

STEPPING
STONE

On their ride from the White House to the Capitol for the swearing in of the new president on January 20, 1981, Jimmy Carter found his successor, Ronald Reagan, distracted and disconcerted by the banners heralding support for the Equal Rights Amendment along the route. Skies were cloudy on Inauguration Day. In a separate car, Rosalynn Carter and Nancy Reagan exchanged small talk on their way to the Capitol.[1]

The president (still president for a few more minutes) was exhausted. He had been working tirelessly to secure the release of the hostages, and now, on the 444th day of their captivity, the drama was finally coming to a close. At 6:05 Washington time that morning, the control tower in Teheran reported that Flight 133 (actually three planes) was on the tarmac. Carter phoned Reagan at 7:00 to brief him on the situation, but the president was informed that Reagan was asleep and should not be disturbed. At 7:55, the planes half a world away were ready for takeoff, but Iran delayed their departure; Carter and Reagan left for the inauguration before final word of the hostages' freedom arrived. In a final, cruel paradox, it was the new president, Ronald Reagan, who announced to the nation that the fifty-two American hostages in Iran had been freed—at 12:15, fifteen minutes after his swearing-in as Jimmy Carter's successor.[2]

As the Reagans celebrated the inauguration, the Mondales and the Carters rode in the same limousine to Andrews Air Force Base. When the ex-president approached the plane for his journey home to Georgia, he greeted the wife of the senior military officer among the hostages in Teheran.

"Mr. President, we thank you for what you've done," she said. "I hope some-day you'll have a chance to meet my husband." Carter recorded in his diary that as he formulated his response, "I broke down and began to cry."[3]

No one doubted for a moment that Jimmy and Rosalynn Carter would some-day leave Washington and return to Plains, but that journey came four years earlier than Carter had planned or wanted. If Carter himself was disappointed about his loss, Rosalynn was embittered. "I was mad," she recalled. "I was mad at everybody. I was mad with the press. I was mad with Ted Kennedy. I was mad with Ronald Reagan. I was mad with the press for not trying to straighten out facts to people."[4]

Jimmy Carter approached the loss with more equanimity. "Retirement is a turning point in life," he recalled philosophically, "either a downhill slope into inactivity and resentment, or a time filled with new enjoyment, learning, and adventure." The ex-president was fifty-six years old, the youngest man to leave the White House since William Howard Taft, and he refused to succumb to inactivity. He had far too much energy and passion.[5]

Jimmy and Rosalynn Carter would soon learn that their business back in Plains was in shambles from mismanagement, a million dollars in debt. As a response to Nixon-era corruptions, Carter had demanded that his staff place all of their assets into blind trusts so that they could not allow even the ap-pearance of self-interest to color their actions. The president adhered to those standards as well.[6]

The financial effects were devastating. Unlike many politicians on the national stage, Carter was not an independently wealthy man, so he could ill afford the collapse of his business interests. The Carters were hardly penni-less, but the Carter Warehouse had been their primary asset, and now the ex-president faced the task of rebuilding his portfolio. He sold what remained of the business, salvaging the Carters' home in Plains as well as two tracts of land that had been in the family for decades, one of them since 1833. Carter also signed a contract to write his presidential memoirs.[7]

The next task was planning for the Carter presidential library. In 1955, Congress had passed the Presidential Libraries Act, which encouraged presi-dents to donate the historical materials associated with their presidencies to the American people. Beginning with Herbert Hoover, every president has a library, which generally includes a museum that functions as a kind of tribute to his presidency. Although the libraries are maintained with public funds, each former president is responsible for raising the money to construct the library. Carter, however, wanted something more than a place to warehouse archival materials. He wanted a place where he could continue to pursue his interests and passions.

The idea for the Carter Center came in the middle of the night. "We can start an adjacent institution, something like Camp David, where people can come who are involved in a war," Jimmy told Rosalynn. "I can offer to serve as a mediator, in Atlanta or perhaps in their countries. We might also study and teach how to resolve or prevent conflict." The former president accepted an offer from James T. Laney, president of Emory University, to become a distinguished professor, a post that provided Carter considerable latitude in the courses he would teach and the opportunity to create an institute or center. The Carter Center would thereafter enjoy a close institutional relationship with Emory. The Jimmy Carter Presidential Library and the Carter Center were dedicated at a site midway between Emory and downtown Atlanta on October 1, 1986, Jimmy Carter's sixty-second birthday. Ronald Reagan spoke at the festivities. Reagan acknowledged his predecessor's religious commitments, noting that "when we dedicate this center, Mr. President, we dedicate an institution that testifies as does your life itself to the goodness of God and to the blessings he bestows upon those who do their best to walk with him."[8]

James Laney initially had reservations about Carter's plan, fearing that it was too grandiose. "Frankly, I was embarrassed for him," Laney recalled. "He was at the nadir of popularity." Laney, however, understood the potential for such an enterprise, and it was he who provided the best and most succinct characterization of the thirty-ninth president of the United States. Jimmy Carter, Laney remarked, was "the first president to use the White House as a stepping stone."[9]

FROM all of his years teaching Sunday school, Jimmy Carter knew as well as anyone that the crucifixion of Jesus on Good Friday is not the end of the Christian narrative of redemption. The story culminates in the triumph of the resurrection on Easter morning, when, according to the gospels, Jesus broke the bonds of death and emerged victoriously from the grave. For Carter, the Christian story held temporal as well as spiritual meaning. "Christ's death and resurrection proved to us that there's life after death," he told his Sunday-school class in Washington in 1978, "but it also proved to us that preoccupation with the present human life should not be ascendant in our consciousness." Although Carter may have seemed to others as a kind of Christ-like figure, especially during the 1976 campaign, he never made messianic claims for himself; indeed, as a good and faithful Baptist, he would have adjudged any such notion both preposterous and blasphemous. With that important caveat in place, however, it's difficult not to see a parallel between the gospel narratives and Carter's transformation from the ashes of political annihilation in 1980 to elder statesman, world-renowned humanitarian, and winner of the Nobel Peace Prize.

The Carter Center would be the former president's vehicle for rehabilitation, and Carter's activities were undeniably informed by his faith. He told an interviewer in 1988 that the life of Christ had always been his guide. "I don't see any disharmony in this life between evangelistic effort on the one hand and benevolent care of people who suffer or who are in need on the other," he said. "I think they are intimately tied together." Carter increasingly came to understand problems afflicting the world as spiritual challenges, noting that industrialized Western society had failed to adopt Christian principles of concern and sharing. Carter believed that people of privilege, and especially people of faith, bear a special responsibility for those less fortunate, for those who suffer and who are deprived. "That's where Jesus spent all his ministry," Carter said. "He was among those who suffered most, who were outcasts, who were deprived, who were hungry, who were charged with crimes they didn't commit." Piety alone wasn't sufficient, Carter said; followers of Jesus must live out their convictions with acts of charity.[10]

Carter's post-presidency would be marked by programmatic acts of charity. As Carter set about organizing the Carter Center, the contours of his plan came into focus. He wanted a place that would not duplicate the activities of other institutions, such as the United Nations, and he wanted its efforts to be nonpartisan. Most important, Carter wanted an "action agency," an institution devoted to change and amelioration rather than simply "theoretical or academic analysis."[11]

The Carter Center's initiatives have centered on two broadly defined areas: health and peace. In the decades following Carter's electoral defeat, he could point to some remarkable accomplishments. Working with small farmers in Africa, the Carter Center has helped to increase production to help feed people in places like Tanzania, Ghana, Benin, Sudan, Togo, and Zambia. Using education and simple, low-cost methods, the Carter Center's health initiatives cooperate with other organizations to fight trachoma, schistosomiasis, lymphatic filariasis, and malaria, most of which are known as "neglected tropical diseases"; other programs have targeted guinea worm and river blindness (onchocerciasis), extraordinary initiatives that have achieved near eradication of the diseases in regions where the Carter Center has focused its efforts. Carter identified access to health care, including mental health, as a fundamental human right, noting that forty thousand children die every day from preventable diseases.[12]

The second focus of the Carter Center, peace and conflict resolution, built on Carter's success as president in negotiating the Camp David accords. "We need to deal with other people with mutual respect," Carter told an audience at Messiah College in 1986, "and through that kind of approach there can be peaceful resolution of differences through the use of diplomacy and negotiation, not through the use of military power." The center conducts programs on democracy and human rights, especially in China and the Americas, and in 1986 Carter and Dominique de Menil, a philanthropist and patron of the arts, established the Carter-Menil Human Rights Prize. The Carter Center monitors situations around the world to see if mediation might bring resolution. It also monitors elections in an effort to ensure integrity, and Carter himself mediated various disputes in places like Guyana, Ethiopia, Korea, and Serbia. In Haiti in 1994, U.S. military planes were headed toward the island when Carter, together with Sam Nunn and Colin Powell, persuaded the military junta to abandon power. Carter had long advocated the restoration of diplomatic relations with Cuba; he considered the punitive embargo against Cuba both "ill-advised and counterproductive." Carter also believed that "the intense animosity toward Cuba has also distorted our diplomatic relations with other Latin American countries."[13]

Rosalynn and Jimmy Carter also extended their reach beyond the Carter Center. The Carters lent their name and their efforts to Habitat for Humanity International, which Jimmy Carter once described as "the most practical, tangible way I've ever seen to put Christian principles into action." Founded in 1976 by Millard and Linda Fuller, Habitat grew out of Koinonia Farm, the interracial Christian community outside of Americus, Georgia, just a few miles from Plains. The Fullers, together with Clarence Jordan, founder of Koinonia, came up with the idea of "partnership housing," under the terms of which people in need of housing would work alongside volunteers in constructing their homes. A revolving fund finances the purchase of these homes at no interest. "The homes are modest in size but comfortable, and the designs are compatible with surrounding architecture," Carter wrote. "The families must pay full price for their homes, but we follow the biblical admonition against charging interest to poor people."[14]

The Carters signed on with Habitat for Humanity in 1984 and headed the Jimmy Carter Work Project in New York City. The sight of a former president expertly wielding a hammer attracted media notice, and Habitat was able dramatically to expand its reach. "I don't know a better way to demonstrate in practical terms the teachings of Jesus than to work side by side with people to alleviate suffering and to give people shelter," Carter told World Vision, the evangelical relief organization. The Carters annually devoted a week to Habitat construction projects, alternating every year between the United States and foreign nations. Carter believed that adequate shelter provides a foundation for hope, noting that many of those who move into Habitat houses aspire to work their way out of poverty and provide better lives for their children. "Whereas before their kids hadn't dreamed of staying in school past the mandatory age," Carter said, "in many cases the families almost immediately start talking about having their kids graduate from college."[15]

Carter's formation of the Carter Center as an activist organization, rather than merely as a celebratory institution, and his involvement with Habitat for Humanity suggest that the lessons from Carter's childhood were not lost on him. The Carter farm in Archery, Georgia, was known among migrants during the Great Depression as a place where they would find a friendly smile and a morsel of food; they left scratches on the mailbox post to signal a hospitable household. Jimmy Carter understood his life's work in part as an opportunity to advance the principles of progressive evangelicalism; he took his parents' faith and acts of charity and transformed them into programs to provide housing and promote causes like peace and health.

As might be expected with politicians from two different political parties and two disparate ideological positions, Carter and Reagan kept one another at arm's length. Although Reagan, faithful to presidential protocol, had attended the dedication of the Carter Center and offered gracious words about his predecessor, the two men were never close—in contrast to Carter's warm relationship with his predecessor, Gerald R. Ford. Carter was miffed that the Reagans refused to invite Rosalynn and him to the White House for the unveiling of their official portraits. "We got no invitation to participate in the ceremonies," Carter complained to his Sunday-school class, surmising that Ronald and Nancy Reagan "just stood around and watched them hang" the portraits.[16]

The styles of the two men could not have been more different, one of them notorious for micromanagement and the other known for his hands-off approach to governing. Carter had invited Reagan to the White House during the transition and had prepared extensively for the meeting. He briefed the president-elect on sensitive matters, including the mechanisms for response to a nuclear attack. Reagan, according to Carter, evinced little interest, offered no comments, posed few questions, and—much to Carter's astonishment—took no notes. "I consider him to be an affable and decent man," Carter recorded in his diary. "His life seems to be governed by a few anecdotes and vignettes that he has memorized. He doesn't seem to listen when anybody talks to him."[17]

In the midst of constructing his post-presidency, Carter occasionally weighed in on his successor. He expressed disappointment that Reagan had dismantled Carter's policies, especially in foreign affairs, human rights, energy policy, and environmental issues. Some of Reagan's initiatives struck directly at the heart of Carter's legacy, and the former president was not pleased to see hard-won initiatives ignored or even negated. Shortly after taking office, for example, Reagan had appointed Ernest Lefever as his chief human rights official; Lefever was on record as saying that the United States "cannot export human rights." Carter characterized Reagan's secretary of the interior, James G. Watt, as someone who believed that wilderness was a parking lot with no yellow lines. "It was incredibly frustrating watching Reagan's people undermine so much of my agenda," Carter acknowledged.[18]

Shortly after taking office, Reagan had reversed Carter's energy directive that federal buildings be heated no more than sixty-five degrees in winter or cooled below seventy-eight degrees in summer. In 1986, Reagan ordered the removal of the solar panels that Jimmy Carter had installed at the White House to call attention to the nation's need for energy independence. Although Carter had finally been able to propose a balanced federal budget after years of deficits, Reagan, a devotee of "supply-side economics," pushed simultaneously for a reduction in taxes and increased spending for defense. Reagan also repaid the political support of the Religious Right by appointing C. Everett Koop, Francis Schaeffer's collaborator on *Whatever Happened to the Human Race?*, as surgeon general. Robert J. Billings, who had left Moral Majority to serve as religious liaison for the Reagan campaign, worked for the Department of Education in the Reagan administration, as did Gary L. Bauer, another evangelical. Watt, the secretary of the interior, was a member of the Assemblies of God and an advocate for the development of wilderness lands.[19]

Midway through Reagan's second term, Carter registered surprise at Reagan's enduring popularity, especially in the face of unprecedented deficits, trade imbalances, and the improprieties of several members of his administration. Carter expressed disappointment that Reagan had demonstrated no interest in pushing along the Camp David peace process, and he found the popular approbation for his successor more than a little puzzling. "He avoids responsibility, successfully, for anything that's unpleasant or unpopular or disappointing or embarrassing or a failure," Carter said. "It's never his fault. It's always the fault of his cabinet members, of Congress, his predecessor in the White House, or some foreigner." Still, Carter expressed admiration for his successor's political skills, acknowledging that Reagan was "just a better politician—than I am, or was."[20]

Carter was especially disappointed with what he considered his successor's lack of concern for human rights, which Carter saw as a uniquely American responsibility. The Reagan administration's neglect on this matter, Carter believed, was tragic, because silence in Washington leads to more abuses. "That's a silence that oppressors want to hear," Carter added. "It's a silence that those who are oppressed fear most."[21]

Although Carter seldom hesitated to criticize his successors, whether Republican or Democratic, he also sought to reconcile with his political adversaries. In 1996, he confessed that he bore a grudge against George Will, a conservative columnist in Washington. Before Carter's debate with Reagan in the 1980 campaign, someone in the White House had purloined the president's briefing book, which, in Carter's words, "described every question that I was going to ask or be asked and my answers to all the questions and my response to things that I thought Reagan might say." The briefing book ended up in the hands of Will, who used it to prepare Reagan for the debate. Carter confessed that he found it difficult to forgive Will, but he believed that his faith required that he do so. Carter purchased a copy of Will's book about baseball (albeit from the remaindered-book table), and after he had read it, sent Will a note of appreciation. "I've had this grudge against you ever since the debate with Reagan," Carter wrote, asking that the two of them be reconciled. Will graciously accepted the former president's olive branch, though he joked that he wished Carter had paid full price for the book.[22]

LEADERS of the Religious Right, who had helped Reagan defeat Carter, had every reason to believe that Reagan would reward them for their support, and the appointments of Koop, Watt, Bauer, and Billings arguably represented a greater return than evangelicals had secured from Carter for their support in 1976. But Reagan failed to deliver on many of the substantive promises he made to the Religious Right during the course of the 1980 campaign. Most notably, Reagan continued to lend his rhetorical support for a constitutional amendment outlawing abortion, but he never seriously pressed the matter. A decade after Reagan's election, Paul Weyrich would complain bitterly that Reagan officials had neglected the Religious Right agenda of social issues in favor of economic reforms, including increased defense spending and tax cuts weighted toward the affluent. According to Weyrich, leaders of the Religious Right were content with their access to the White House and did not want to say anything that would jeopardize that. Ed Dobson, one of Falwell's lieutenants at Moral Majority, conceded that Reagan "ultimately did nothing in terms of our long-term agendas."[23]

Reagan even wobbled on the issue that had been responsible for the emergence of the Religious Right, tax exemptions for racially discriminatory institutions. By late 1981, Reagan's first year in office, Bob Jones University's challenge to the federal government's revocation of its tax-exempt status was making its way to the U.S. Supreme Court. When the Internal Revenue Service first moved against the university because of its segregationist policies, the school had admitted a married black man as a part-time student, although he left the university after less than a month. Despite this gesture toward racial inclusion, the school retained its policies against interracial dating. "We have had what we feel are biblical convictions for keeping the races separate," Bob Jones III, the school's president, said at the time. "We have been able to maintain these convictions through the years by taking Orientals and Caucasians with the understanding that they may not date."[24]

As the case headed toward the Supreme Court, the university sought once again to frame the case as a test of religious liberty, enlisting many of its fundamentalist allies. *"Pray that God will intervene when the Supreme Court evaluates the case in October,"* the fundamentalist newspaper *Sword of the Lord* declared in italics. "It is not a question of Bob Jones University, although that institution certainly has our sympathy. It is a question of religious liberty!" Jones, meanwhile, continued to insist that there was no racial bias at his university, despite the fact that by 1982, as the *New York Times* reported, fewer than a dozen African Americans attended Bob Jones University, out of a student population in excess of 3,000. "You know very well that there is no discrimination at this school," Jones told his students. "There is absolute racial harmony at this school." The people who oppose the university's tax-exempt status simply hate God, Jones said. "That's what this is all about," he added. "They hate his church and his people."[25]

For its part, the Reagan administration flip-flopped spectacularly on the Bob Jones University case. On January 8, 1982, the Reagan administration declared that the treasury department and the IRS would abandon the policy of denying tax exemptions to schools that practiced racial segregation; at the same time, the administration asked the court to drop the case and vacate the previous rulings against Bob Jones University, thereby restoring its tax exemption. That announcement, however, met with a public outcry, which prompted the administration to reconsider. Four days later, Reagan called for legislation to outlaw tax exemptions for racially discriminatory organizations. "I believe the right thing to do on this issue is to enact legislation which will prohibit tax exemptions for organizations that discriminate on the basis of race," he said in announcing the abrupt reversal of administration policy.[26]

The Supreme Court, however, refused to drop the case. Because the Reagan administration had abandoned defense of the IRS and its policy of refusing tax exemptions to racially discriminatory institutions, the court, in an unusual move, appointed William T. Coleman, who had served as secretary of transportation during the Ford administration, to file an *amicus* brief in opposition to Bob Jones University's claim of tax exemption. The court heard the arguments on October 12, 1982, and on May 24, 1983, the Supreme Court rendered its decision in *Bob Jones University v. United States*. By an eight-to-one margin, the court found that racial discrimination in education violated "fundamental national public policy" and that "not all burdens on religion are unconstitutional." The Internal Revenue Service, the decision stipulated, acted well within its legal authority in rescinding the tax-exempt status of Bob Jones University because the school was both a religious institution and an educational institution. "The IRS policy thus was properly applied to Bob Jones University," the opinion concluded. The university had lost its bid to retain both its racially discriminatory policies and its tax exemption.[27]

Jerry Falwell characterized the ruling as a "blow against religious liberty." Bob Jones III ordered the flags on campus to fly at half-mast. "We're in a bad fix in America when eight evil old men and one vain and foolish woman can speak a verdict on American liberties," Jones told the students in a sermon. "Our nation from this day forward is no better than Russia insofar as expecting the blessings of God is concerned. You no longer live in a nation that is religiously free." Jones added: "I have pity for the heathens who sit on the Supreme Court, pity for their damned souls and their blighted minds."[28]

Jones's father and predecessor as university president publicly questioned Reagan's faith. "I think he's a good man, not an evil man," Bob Jones Jr. said of the president, "but I don't trust professional actors because you don't know when they're acting and when they're not." Reagan, however, eventually made amends to the Religious Right. On June 17, 1986, Reagan elevated William Rehnquist, the sole dissenter in the *Bob Jones* case, to chief justice of the U.S. Supreme Court and at the same time nominated Antonin Scalia as associate justice.[29]

If evangelical leaders were not pleased with the Reagan administration's reversal on the very issue that had galvanized them into a political movement, they maintained their silence and instead directed their anger at the Supreme Court. Despite Reagan having abandoned the leaders of the Religious Right on the Bob Jones matter, the Religious Right refused to abandon Reagan, in part because opposition to abortion had emerged by the early 1980s as the litmus issue for the movement, eclipsing the less popular stance of defending racial discrimination at places like Bob Jones University. The Religious Right, in fact, gained organizational strength during Reagan's presidency and began to exercise its electoral muscles; conservative activists ever more determinedly drew evangelicals into their ambit and, in the process, widened the distance between the progressive social ethic of nineteenth-century evangelicals and those of the late twentieth century.

With Reagan's reelection in 1984, the wish list many of the conservatives associated with the Religious Right became more expansive; they believed that Reagan, now assured of a second term, would finally attend to their concerns. "The kind of judges who have been on the bench until now have given us forced busing, abortion on demand, more protection for criminals than for their victims, free expression for pornographers but not for school children who want to pray," Paul Weyrich complained on Falwell's radio program *Listen America Report* in 1986. Weyrich also delivered a ringing endorsement of Chilean dictator Augusto Pinochet, responsible for the torture and death of thousands of Chileans, over Falwell's airwaves, and he warned darkly in September 1986 that, "If the Democrats win the Senate the very liberal Senator Clayborne Pell of Rhode Island would become chairman of the Foreign Relations committee which would make Communist leaders around the world rejoice."[30]

Weyrich's right-wing "orthodoxy" knew no limits, and Falwell was happy to oblige by providing access to his media empire. "Many professing Christians do not translate conservative theology into conservative politics,"

Weyrich lamented in another broadcast. "It would be far better, for example, to elect a non-believer who shares your family, national and economic values than to elect a professing believer who does not." He railed against "godless public schools" and against gun control, suggesting that listeners consult either the National Rifle Association or the Gun Owners of America for voting records.[31]

Weyrich also crusaded against women's rights and for the death penalty, positions clearly at odds with those of nineteenth-century evangelicals who sought to accord equal rights, including voting rights, to women and who introduced the notion of a "penitentiary," a place of rehabilitation. "States that have the death penalty such as Illinois should enforce it," Weyrich intoned. "And states that don't, ought to adopt it." Occasionally, Weyrich leveled his sights at Reagan himself, who, Weyrich came to believe, did not prosecute the Religious Right agenda as vigorously as he had promised. "We like to think of Ronald Reagan as the President of traditional values," Weyrich said. "Consider these facts: in Jimmy Carter's last three years as President, there were 66 federal obscenity prosecutions. In Ronald Reagan's six years, there have been a grand total of only 34." Charles E. Judd, former staff member at the Republican National Committee and head of Falwell's Liberty Federation, complained that "In President Reagan's two terms in office, his administration has failed to convince the Congress to pass a pro-life measure protecting the lives of the unborn, at least from federal funded abortions."[32]

Weyrich was not the only activist who sought to cash in on the political capital he had accrued from evangelical voters by way of the election of 1980. Falwell lent his media apparatus to such conservative stalwarts as Robert Dornan, Phil Gramm, Dick Armey, Connie Marshner, Jesse Helms, and Dee Jepsen, wife of the Republican senator from Iowa who had defeated Dick Clark in 1978.

Carter, for his part, took a dim view of the machinations of the Religious Right—but not because he quarreled with the involvement of evangelicals in politics. He dissented from the rightward drift of evangelicals because he deemed their politics—support for Reagan's tax policies favoring the affluent, for example, or opposition to women's rights—as inconsistent with the teachings of Jesus. Speaking at the height of the influence of the Religious Right, Carter lamented that Reagan's trickle-down economics and the "greed is good" ethic of the 1980s represented a departure from the New Testament, citing Jesus's declaration that it is easier for a camel to pass through the eye of a needle than for a rich person to enter heaven. "We each establish our own goals in life, and if you put the acquisition of money as your top priority in life, then I think that's where the danger comes," he said. "If the accumulation of riches is the only purpose in life, then that's avarice or greed, and inherently that is bad."[33]

CARTER's charitable and peacemaking activities in general and his work at the Carter Center in particular had gone a long way toward refurbishing his image. While few Americans hankered for his days as president, Carter's conduct as a former president had redeemed him in the eyes of many, and thus rehabilitated, Carter might have retreated finally to Plains rather than court controversy by injecting himself into international matters. On selected issues close to his heart, however, Carter chose to speak up.

Because of his Camp David initiatives and because of his Christian faith, Carter maintained a strong interest in the Middle East, frequently expressing his exasperation at the failure of his successors to follow through on the hard-won progress he made during his presidency. Carter's many visits to the region had persuaded him that the two-state solution—Israel and a Palestinian state—was the only way to ensure lasting peace. Several of his books addressed the situation in the Middle East, but none generated as much controversy as *Palestine: Peace Not Apartheid*, published in 2006. The use of *apartheid* in the title was incendiary in itself, a reference commonly associated with white South Africa's brutal segregationist regime that Carter had denounced as president, although Carter was careful to say that he was referring not to racial apartheid but to Israeli appropriation of Palestinian lands. The former president argued that Israeli policies toward the Palestinians, including the steady encroachment of Israeli settlements on the West Bank and the construction of a wall to separate the two peoples, were shortsighted and an impediment to peace in the Middle East. Israeli leaders believed mistakenly, Carter wrote, that a physical barrier would finally resolve the Palestinian problem. The wall, however, constructed by successive Israeli governments, was an affront to the Palestinians and an impediment to peace. It was built primarily on Palestinian land, and it intruded deep into the disputed territory of the West Bank.[34]

Carter described the construction of this wall, beginning with the use of bulldozers to plow through Palestinian communities. The wall itself consisted of concrete, razor wire, electrified fencing, two-meter-deep trenches, roads for patrol vehicles, electronic ground and fence sensors, thermal imaging and video cameras, and sniper towers—almost entirely on Palestinian land. The fortress approach, Carter warned, would never succeed. "Some Palestinians react by honoring suicide bombers as martyrs to be rewarded in heaven and consider the killing of Israelis as victories," he wrote. Israel invariably responds with retribution, which in turn stiffens the resolve of Palestinians' refusal to recognize the legitimacy of Israel. "The cycle of distrust and violence is sustained," Carter wrote, "and efforts for peace are frustrated."[35]

Many American Jews were outraged. Alan Dershowitz of Harvard asked, "what would motivate a decent man like Carter to write such an indecent book." Even *Christianity Today* piled on. "Though saintly to many, Carter has often been strangely naïve about world leaders," David Aikman wrote. He belittled Carter's confidence in the good intentions of Palestinian leaders. "Mr. President, fellow born-again Christian," Aikman concluded, "your role as an impartial 'man of peace' has never been more in question." Carter acknowledged several minor mistakes in the original edition of the book, which he corrected for the paperback edition, and he allowed that a couple of sentences in the book might have been poorly worded. But he stood by his argument that the Israeli government's unnecessary provocations, including the wall and the steady encroachment of Israeli settlements on the West Bank, rendered the possibility of a two-state solution more and more remote.[36]

A subsequent book, *We Can Have Peace in the Holy Land*, sought to quell the storm. Carter explained that although his working title for the previous book had been simply "Palestine Peace," he wanted a title that would be both descriptive and provocative. He confessed that he was unaware how freighted the term *apartheid* would be, even though it was widely used by the Israeli courts and government, and Nelson Mandela, the first black president of South Africa, had employed the same term to describe Israel's policy toward the Palestinians. The new book, however, reiterated many of the same arguments from the previous one, all leavened with Carter's trademark optimism: "Peace is possible."[37]

Many Jews refused to forgive the former president. When the *Cardozo Journal of Conflict Resolution*, a scholarly publication out of Yeshiva University's Benjamin N. Cardozo Law School, chose to honor Carter with its International Advocate for Peace award in 2013, a group calling itself the Coalition of Concerned Cardozo Alumni registered its dissent. "Jimmy Carter is anathema to the aspirations of the Jewish people and the survival of the State of Israel," the group wrote. "Yeshiva University and Cardozo should not give a platform to his slander."[38]

Carter's continuing activism for peace in the Middle East and, especially, his critical posture toward the Israeli government, illustrate both the power of his connections as president and his freedom, as an ex-president, to press his concerns without regard for the political consequences. A politician, especially one running for reelection, would be loath to cross a political entity like the pro-Israel lobby—or, for that matter, evangelicals who, since 1948, have been reflexively sympathetic to Israel. Whatever the specific merits of his criticism, Carter was able to strike a prophetic stance, one that called powerful interests and politicians to account.

Not infrequently, Carter also turned his criticism on his successors. In addition to his comments critical of Reagan, Carter late in 1990 sent a letter to members of the United Nations Security Council urging them to oppose George H. W. Bush's plans to dislodge Saddam Hussein forcibly from Kuwait. Carter publicly opposed the Clinton administration's plans to press the United Nations for sanctions against North Korea in 1994. Several years later, Carter rebuked Bill Clinton over the Monica Lewinsky scandal, when Clinton misrepresented his inappropriate relationship with a White House intern. Carter roundly criticized George W. Bush's invasion of Iraq, and he sought publicly to dissuade Barack Obama from sending troops to Syria in 2013, arguing instead for redoubled diplomatic efforts to resolve Syria's civil war.[39]

Not all of Carter's successors appreciated his comments or his interventions, and his frequent insistence on conducting a kind of freelance diplomacy—in North Korea or Haiti, for example—rankled presidents and diplomats. Still, at various times, presidents set aside their reservations and called on Carter to step into a messy situation and negotiate a peaceful end to a diplomatic stalemate. Carter would trade on his status as a former president, leverage his personal relationships to full advantage, and, more often than not, come away with an agreement in which the principals backed down from a potentially deadly confrontation.

Carter's unconventional approach worked with North Korea in 1993, when he persuaded Kim Il Sung to open his nuclear reactors to international inspectors. It worked in Haiti the following year, when Carter, together with Sam Nunn and Colin Powell, convinced Raoul Cédras, Haiti's military boss, to cede power only hours before a threatened military invasion by the United States. Carter also persuaded Daniel Ortega, leader of the Sandinistas and president of Nicaragua, to accede to election results in 1990 and leave office peacefully. Following Carter's successful resolution of the stalemate in Haiti, the *Los Angeles Times* praised the former president for his "two surpassing virtues: a preternatural patience and an unshakable faith in his fellow man."[40]

Carter, freed from the constraints of elective politics, operated as a kind of ambassador-at-large—even though his successors as president did not always appreciate his efforts because they often complicated, and at times contradicted, their own diplomatic initiatives. Carter, in turn, was especially critical of his successors for their failure to follow up on the Camp David accords, which he had so painstakingly brokered; he viewed their negligence almost as a personal affront. Carter's comments about the Israelis and the Palestinians may have been provocative, but he understood them as a good-faith effort to secure the peace that had ultimately eluded him as president, and he was willing to endure the opprobrium of interested parties in order to advance the process.

CARTER's jeremiads were not always greeted with enthusiasm, either in the arena of international politics or the arena of ecclesiastical politics. The brief resurgence of progressive evangelicalism had aided Carter in his quest for the White House, but his support among white evangelicals began to erode with the *Playboy* interview late in the 1976 campaign. The defection of white evangelicals continued during his presidency as leaders of the Religious Right ratcheted up their attacks. Eventually, the shifting sensibilities within evangelicalism not only forced Carter out of office but also out of his own denomination, the Southern Baptist Convention.

Although Carter tried to retain good ties with Southern Baptists during his presidency, that relationship had begun to unravel toward the end of his tenure in office. The conservative takeover of the Southern Baptist Convention in 1979, marked by the election of Adrian Rogers as president, had been a disappointment to Carter, especially as the denomination moved steadily to the right on social, political, and doctrinal issues. The stated catalyst for the takeover was the theological matter of biblical "inerrancy," the doctrine that the Bible was divinely inspired and entirely without error in the original manuscripts. The conservatives moved from there to other issues, seeking to enforce conformity. At home in Plains, when the deacons at Plains Baptist Church forced the resignation of Bruce Edwards as pastor in 1977 in response to a decision to allow African Americans into its worship services, his supporters formed a new congregation, Maranatha, on the edge of town. The Carters had attended both churches during their sojourns from Washington. "We'll try to stay neutral as long as possible between the churches," the president recorded in his White House diary. After they left the White House in 1981, however, Jimmy and Rosalynn Carter joined Maranatha Baptist Church, where they took their turn tidying up the property and mowing the church lawn.[41]

For decades, the relationship between Carter and the Southern Baptists had come to resemble a dysfunctional marriage, with frequent separations, threats of divorce, and periodic attempts at reconciliation. Carter was especially chagrined about matters related to the ministry of women. Although the Southern Baptist Convention, hewing to its tradition of congregational polity, had allowed individual congregations largely to determine their own affairs—including whom they would ordain—the new leaders of the Southern Baptist Convention sought to quash the ordination of women throughout the entire denomination. Such a centralized policy, however, countermanded traditional Baptist governance, so the transition to this new uniformity was long and, for many Southern Baptists, painful. It entailed the systematic appointment of theological and political conservatives to the boards of directors of Southern Baptist agencies, colleges, and seminaries. As conservatives attained majorities on these boards, they forced out "moderate" faculty and other personnel who were then replaced by reliable conservatives. Carter and many other Southern Baptists opposed these purges, but the unbroken string of conservatives elected to the presidency of the denomination ensured that the conservative takeover would ultimately succeed.[42]

Carter stood with those who protested the takeover, and he was especially chagrined by what he saw as the arrogation of power on behalf of the clergy, which violated not only Baptist principles but also the Reformation notion of the priesthood of believers. "Instead of pastors being servants of their congregations," Carter said in one of his Sunday-school classes, "some have become powerful demagogues, dominating the congregation and imposing their personal views and interpretations on everyone." In the late 1980s, the former president invited Southern Baptist leaders from both camps to the Carter Center in an attempt to mediate their differences. Those differences, however, proved insuperable, and when the Southern Baptist Convention passed a resolution at its 1987 meeting in St. Louis that limited women's role in the church, Carter began actively to distance himself from the conservative leadership of the denomination. Carter expressed solidarity with the Cooperative Baptist Fellowship, which sought to function as a moderate movement among Southern Baptists. But the leaders of the Southern Baptist Convention controlled the denomination's assets and institutional machinery; the Cooperative Fellowship, by contrast, was a start-up, unable to compete.[43]

In early 2008, Carter and William D. Underwood, president of Mercer University, organized a gathering of fifteen thousand Baptists in the Georgia World Congress Center in Atlanta. Jimmy Allen of the Southern Baptist Convention was there, as was William Shaw, president of the historically black National Baptist Convention. (Carter had insisted that the gathering be interracial.) "We convene with high hopes and expectations," Carter told the crowd, "with no criticisms of others or exclusion of any Christians now or in the future who want to join." Bill Clinton addressed the gathering, as did Al Gore and Charles Grassley, Republican senator from Iowa. Although Carter had personally invited the leaders of the Southern Baptist Convention, they elected not to attend; Frank Page, the denomination's president, suggested the meeting was a smokescreen for a leftist agenda. The attendees agreed on a "New Baptist Covenant," one that sought unity among Baptists but also paid heed to poverty, the environment, and global conflict.[44]

In an op-ed in the *Guardian* on July 11, 2009, Carter reflected on his long relationship with the Southern Baptist Convention. "I have been a practising Christian all my life and a deacon and Bible teacher for many years," he wrote. "My faith is a source of strength and comfort to me, as religious beliefs are to hundreds of millions of people around the world." Given the history of estrangement between himself and the Southern Baptist leadership, especially over the ministry of women, Carter's commentary broke no new ground, but it was also not without anguish. He acknowledged that his decision to sever ties with the Southern Baptist Convention had been painful and difficult, but he found the denomination's attitudes toward women unconscionable. Carter accused leaders of the Southern Baptist Convention of "quoting a few carefully selected Bible verses and claiming that Eve was created second to Adam and was responsible for original sin" to arrive at their decision to prohibit women from serving as pastors, deacons, or military chaplains. Carter found this attitude incompatible with his understanding of the Bible, which taught that everyone was equal in the eyes of God.[45]

The demand for subservience on the part of women, Carter continued, had implications well beyond rarefied discussions about doctrine. The former president lamented that women were relegated to secondary status in many religions, with profound social consequences. "This discrimination, unjustifiably attributed to a Higher Authority, has provided a reason or excuse for the deprivation of women's equal rights across the world for centuries," he wrote.

Male religious authorities the world over, Carter said, reinforce traditional practices and justify flagrant abuses of human rights, including education and employment inequality, arranged marriages, and, in extreme cases, sexual abuse, forced prostitution, and genital mutilation. "The truth is that male religious leaders have had—and still have—an option to interpret holy teachings either to exalt or subjugate women," Carter concluded. "They have, for their own selfish ends, overwhelmingly chosen the latter."[46]

Carter's declaration was utterly in keeping both with his own positions, theological and political, and with the venerable tradition of progressive evangelicalism. His stand, however, did nothing to endear him with the leadership of the Southern Baptist Convention; it signaled a parting of the ways, as the denomination—like the nation—veered toward the right. "It's a sad day for him," the president of the denomination said in response to one of Carter's earlier statements of alienation. "It's a sad day for us." Carter would remain active at Maranatha Baptist Church, which retained its affiliation with the Southern Baptist Convention. But he would never reconcile himself to the radically conservative direction of the denomination that had nurtured him for most of his life.[47]

AT four o'clock in the morning of October 11, 2002, the ringing telephone woke Jimmy and Rosalynn Carter at their home in Plains. The former president had grown accustomed to middle-of-the-night phone calls alerting him to some crisis or summoning him to mediate a festering dispute somewhere in the world. But this call was different, coming as it did from Oslo, Norway, informing Jimmy Carter that he was the recipient of the Nobel Peace Prize. At first, Carter recounted later that day, "I thought it was a joke." But it was no joke. "In a situation currently marked by threats of the use of power," the Nobel citation read, "Carter has stood by the principles that conflicts must as far as possible be resolved through mediation and international cooperation based on international law, respect for human rights and economic development."[48]

Many of Carter's supporters believed that the president should have been awarded the Peace Prize together with Menachem Begin and Anwar el-Sadat because of the Camp David accords, but according to the Nobel committee the paperwork for Carter's nomination that year arrived too late. Sadat and Begin shared the 1978 prize; Carter, who had orchestrated the agreement, had been excluded. Sadat, who enjoyed a close personal relationship with Carter, had initiated a campaign to recognize Carter with the Peace Prize.

He nominated the ex-president for his "genuine dedication to the cause of human rights," but Sadat's assassination in October 1981 deprived Carter not only of a friend but an advocate. In succeeding years, Carter had been nominated more than ten times for the Peace Prize, but the phone call on that October morning in 2002 caught him by surprise. "I didn't even know this was the day the prize was announced," the former president told reporters. "I usually follow these things, but this year I wasn't paying attention."[49]

News of the prize came as the administration of George W. Bush was maneuvering to invade Iraq in retaliation for the terrorist attacks of September 11, 2001. Carter had gone on record opposing the invasion, and the award was announced just hours after Congress had voted overwhelmingly to authorize military action against Iraq. In bestowing the Peace Prize to Carter, the Nobel committee was not only recognizing the former president's peacemaking initiatives, it was also making a statement about current U.S. policy; lest anyone miss the message, Gunnar Berge, chair of the Nobel committee, said that the prize "should be interpreted as a criticism of the line that the current administration has taken."[50]

Carter used the occasion to reiterate his commitment to human rights. "People everywhere share the same dream of a caring international community that prevents war and oppression," he said in a statement released by the Carter Center. "During the past two decades, as Rosalynn and I traveled around the world for the work of our center, my concept of human rights has grown to include not only the rights to live in peace, but also to adequate health care, shelter, food, and to economic opportunity." Carter added that, "This honor serves as an inspiration not only to us, but also to suffering people around the world, and I accept it on their behalf."[51]

George W. Bush called Carter with his congratulations, and Bill Clinton, with whom Carter sometimes had a chilly relationship, also applauded the former president. "I cannot think of anyone more qualified to receive this year's Nobel Peace Prize than President Jimmy Carter," Clinton said in a statement. "He continues to inspire people everywhere, young and old alike, through his vigorous quest for peace, justice and a better quality of life for all citizens of the world." Many saw the award as vindication for a beleaguered president who refused to skulk away in ignominy after his electoral loss in 1980. "The idealism that seemed naïve as president now seems admirable," an editorial in the *Knoxville News Sentinel* declared. "The award yesterday of the Nobel peace prize completes an unusual and moving recovery from political defeat and humiliation," Mark Lawson wrote in the London *Guardian*.

The lesson of Jimmy Carter, he said, was that, "for a man of dignity and goodness, political failure can be a beginning rather than an end."[52]

As the Bush administration was ramping up its rhetoric to justify a military invasion of Iraq, the Carters headed to Norway. In presenting the prize, in a ceremony at Oslo City Hall on December 10, 2002, Gunnar Berge, head of the selection committee, noted that the Nobel committee's failure to honor Carter earlier constituted "one of the real sins of omission in Peace Prize history." Carter, he said, lived by his religious principles, and he adhered to them even when it cost him political support. The committee finally chose to honor Carter "for his decades of untiring effort to find peaceful solutions to international conflicts, to advance democracy and human rights, and to promote economic and social development." Berge acknowledged that Carter would not be remembered as the nation's best president, but he was confident that Carter was its finest former president.[53]

"It is with a deep sense of gratitude that I accept this prize," Carter said. "I am not here as a public official, but as a citizen of a troubled world who finds hope in a growing consensus that the generally accepted goals of society are peace, freedom, human rights, environmental quality, the alleviation of suffering, and the rule of law." Carter decried the growing chasm between rich and poor around the world, and he quoted Julia Coleman, the beloved schoolteacher during his childhood back in Plains: "We must adjust to changing times and still hold to unchanging principles."[54]

For Carter, those unchanging principles centered around his Christian faith. "I worship Jesus Christ, whom we Christians consider to be the Prince of Peace," he said. Grounded in his own religious convictions, Carter sought to enlist the cooperation of other traditions. "I am convinced that Christians, Muslims, Buddhists, Hindus, Jews, and others can embrace each other in a common effort to alleviate human suffering and to espouse peace," he said. War may be necessary at times, Carter said, but it is invariably evil. "We will not learn how to live together in peace by killing each other's children."[55]

When the new Nobel laureate completed his speech, the king and queen of Norway rose to congratulate him, and the palace guard sounded their trumpets. Jessye Norman sang "He's Got the Whole World in His Hands," the same song that Leontyne Price had sung at the People's Prayer Service prior to Carter's inauguration as president in 1977. Before exiting the auditorium, Jimmy Carter handed the Nobel Peace Prize medal and diploma for which he had labored so long to Rosalynn, seated with their family in the first row. Rosalynn, his partner in life, in politics, and in the Carter Center, was the only person Carter had thanked by name.[56]

A time traveler from, say, the 1930s or even the 1830s who had dropped in on American society in the 1970s might be forgiven for believing that the world had turned upside down. The visitor from the 1930s would be astonished to see a relative political neophyte, Jimmy Carter, mounting a credible campaign for the presidency, all the while touting his credentials as a born-again Christian. And he might be even more surprised to learn that evangelicals themselves, who dithered about their engagement with politics in the middle decades of the twentieth century, were organizing into their own political movement in the late 1970s to oppose the very same president they had helped to elect in 1976.

The visitor from the 1830s would find the politics of this new political movement bewildering, even incomprehensible. The evangelicals of the late 1970s, the spiritual descendants of nineteenth- and early twentieth-century evangelicals, were propagating an agenda utterly at odds with progressive evangelicalism. Whereas earlier evangelicals had advocated for women's rights, including the right to vote, the Religious Right opposed the feminist movement and the proposed Equal Rights Amendment to the U.S. Constitution. Whereas antebellum evangelicals had pushed for the abolition of slavery, the Religious Right defended the racially discriminatory policies at places like Bob Jones University. Whereas nineteenth-century evangelicals had sought the rehabilitation of prisoners, the Religious Right pushed for capital punishment. Whereas evangelicals in the nineteenth century had been among the earliest supporters of public education as a seedbed of democracy and as a way to assist those on the lower rungs of society, the Religious Right sought to vitiate public education by supporting taxpayer vouchers for private and religious schools.[57]

The political casualty of this swing in evangelical sentiments was Jimmy Carter, himself a Southern Baptist and an evangelical. Political and social issues undeniably shift over the course of decades, not to mention centuries, but it is difficult to imagine that evangelicals like Charles Finney or Frances Willard would find much fault with Carter's policies or predilections. He renounced racism as governor of Georgia and advocated the rights of women. He renegotiated the Panama Canal treaty in a way that was less imperial and more just to the people of Latin America, and his Camp David accords advanced the cause of peace in the Middle East far beyond anything that his predecessors had accomplished. He authorized the use of military force only reluctantly, after extensive deliberation and with great consternation, and he took satisfaction that no soldier died in battle during his term in office.[58]

"In this present crisis, government is not the solution to our problem," Ronald Reagan famously declared in his first inaugural address, "government is the problem." That sentiment resonated with many voters, and, on the face of it, he had a point, one that might even solicit agreement from evangelicals of an earlier era who had organized into voluntary societies to combat social ills rather than look for the assistance of government. But the depredations of the Great Depression, when government stepped in to address overwhelming poverty and suffering, had altered that calculus, and religious organizations had never reassumed their ameliorating role in society, at least not in a systematic way. "Jesus proclaimed that his ministry was to 'bring good news to the poor, to proclaim freedom for the prisoners, recovery of sight for the blind, and to release the oppressed,'" Jimmy Carter wrote. Years earlier, however, Carter arrived at what he characterized as a reluctant conclusion: "In efforts to reach out to the poor, alleviate suffering, provide homes for the homeless, eliminate the stigma of poverty or racial discrimination, preserve peace, and rehabilitate prisoners, government office-holders and not church members were more likely to assume responsibility and be able to fulfill the benevolent missions."[59]

By the 1980 presidential election, however, politically conservative evangelicals had all but abandoned nineteenth-century notions of benevolence in favor of a politician who, whatever his other qualities, ridiculed welfare recipients, suggested that homelessness was a choice, advocated significant cuts in public education, and celebrated unfettered capitalism. In their eagerness to embrace a new political messiah, evangelicals cast aside one of their own, effectively terminating their long-standing affiliation with progressive evangelicalism.

But the march of history has a way of circling back upon itself. Carter's defeat in 1980 followed by Mark Hatfield's decision to retire from the Senate in 1997 left no white politician with national stature who advocated the principles of progressive evangelicalism. That doesn't mean, however, that the movement or the principles have died. "People who might be called progressive evangelicals," Bill Hybels of Willow Creek Community Church said in 2007, "are one stirring away from a real awakening." Jim Wallis of *Sojourners* insists that, well into the second decade of the twenty-first century, progressive evangelicalism is more robust than ever, with a new and younger generation carrying on the tradition with innovative strategies and unprecedented energy. Carter's success with the Carter Center initiatives was indeed impressive, and he had the foresight to set in place institutional mechanisms that would continue the work of the center long after his death.[60]

For a long time now, I have argued that religion functions best from the margins of society and not in the councils of power; once a religious group panders after political influence, it loses its prophetic voice. The Religious Right amply demonstrates that maxim, but I wonder if the life and career of Jimmy Carter doesn't illustrate it as well. As a politician and as president, Carter necessarily had to placate powerful interests and negotiate the demands of various constituencies. Given the diversity of adversaries arrayed against him, he succeeded remarkably well, but after leaving office he had the freedom to pursue his evangelically informed values—peace, human rights, care for "the least of these"—without the constraints of official responsibilities. Certainly, he traded on his fame and status as a former president—what former president has not done so?—but he used that status to pursue goals larger than mere self-aggrandizement or personal enrichment.[61]

IN 1985, reflecting on his career, Carter said, "I've had an underlying stability in my life derived from my community, family and religious beliefs." Such grounding, he suggested, allowed him to take risks that others might avoid. "One of the things that shaped my life was realizing that I have one life to live on this earth," he said, "and I ask God frequently not to let me waste it and to let my life be beneficial for my fellow human beings in His kingdom." What did Carter consider his legacy? In two hundred years, Carter said, he hoped his name would be associated with peace and human rights. "I feel at ease with history," Carter said later, expressing confidence that, once the dust had settled, historians would look more kindly on his time in office, especially the emphasis on human rights and his success in restoring integrity to the presidency.[62]

On matters of faith, the former president acknowledged the waxings and wanings common to most believers, but he expressed confidence that he had attained at least a measure of hard-won spiritual maturity. "I really honestly don't worry about the end of my life," Carter told an interviewer in 1996. "I've come a long way in my Christian faith—I've renounced God on occasion and been reconverted by my sister—that I hope that I'll continue to search and to seek answers and to grow as a Christian and as a human being."[63]

As he faced the inevitability of death, Carter looked once again, as he had done so often throughout his life, to Jesus. "Don't concentrate, he says, on the number of years we have left on earth. At best, life is short, and its duration is unpredictable," Carter wrote in *Sources of Strength*. Instead, a believer should focus on the most important questions, especially how to make life as meaningful as possible.[64]

By the time he wrote that, Jimmy Carter's life had taken him from Plains, Georgia, to the navy to the Georgia statehouse to the White House, back to Plains, many times around the world, and back again, finally, to Plains. Had Jimmy Carter lived a meaningful life? History, of course, would provide one forum for making that determination, but Carter was equally interested in a higher tribunal, and he faced the prospect of death with equanimity. "I feel that I have it well taken care of through my faith," he said.[65]

Jimmy Carter, after all, knew something about redemption.

EPILOGUE

Sunday Morning in Plains

Southwest Georgia is Baptist country. The back roads heading south out of Columbus are bracketed by red soil, scruffy pines, and clapboard buildings sporting names like Shiloh Marion Baptist Church, Zion Hill Baptist Church, Piney Grove Missionary Baptist Church, and Greater Good Hope Baptist Church. Love Jesus No Matter What, one roadside sign reads, and another: Only Jesus Saves. Outside of Preston, Georgia, still another sign implores, Take Jesus for Your Saviour, and the Preston Baptist Church has posted each of the Ten Commandments on a chain-link fence for the edification of travelers passing through town.

Just before crossing from Webster into Sumter County, signs on Georgia Highway 27 point toward Archery, the boyhood home of Jimmy Carter, and then the road eases into Plains, where it becomes Church Street. The business district, not much more than a block long, lies just beyond the railroad tracks, across the street from the former Seaboard Coast Line Railroad Depot that served as campaign headquarters for Carter's improbable run for the presidency in 1976 and now as a museum commemorating that campaign.[1]

Plains, Georgia, is no longer the hub of excitement that it was in the summer of 1976, when legions of journalists and thousands of tourists descended to learn more about the Democratic nominee for president. Then, Lillian Carter held court at the train station, and Billy Carter threw back a few beers and entertained visitors with quips like, "I've got a mother who joined the Peace Corps and went to India when she was 68. I've got a sister who races motorcycles and another sister who's a Holy Roller preacher. I've got a brother

185

who says he wants to be President of the United States." Then, pausing for dramatic effect, "I'm the only sane one in the family."[2]

Plains, with a population of only 766 souls, nevertheless has two Baptist churches, the large white clapboard Plains Baptist Church and the newer, brick building, Maranatha Baptist Church, on the north edge of town, just past the thirteen-foot sculpture of a smiling peanut, which *Time* magazine described as "the strangest monument ever to an American President." The Carter clan voted years ago to integrate Plains Baptist, but they were joined by only one other member. While Jimmy and Rosalynn Carter lived in Washington, a dissident group formed Maranatha Baptist Church shortly after Carter's inauguration. The Carters attended both churches during their visits to Plains, but when they moved home following the 1980 election, they cast their lot with racial inclusivity and joined Maranatha on January 25, 1981, the first Sunday after Carter left the White House.[3]

At Maranatha Baptist Church, a couple of squad cars sat at the foot of the driveway, and farther along a bomb-sniffing dog circled every vehicle before it was allowed to continue to the parking lot. By eight-thirty, ninety minutes before Sunday school, visitors began to queue up outside the front door. Inside, past the Secret Service agents waving security wands, Jan Williams, church member and retired schoolteacher—Amy Carter was one of her students—instructed visitors about protocol. On the weeks when Jimmy Carter teaches, she warned, photographs of the Sunday-school teacher are allowed only before the lesson begins. The thirty-ninth president of the United States wants no applause. "The applause you give him," she said, "is how you take the lesson and apply it to your life."[4]

When I first began seriously to consider writing a biography of Carter, his aides informed me that he generally talks with authors only when their projects are nearing completion—an understandable policy that shielded the former president from scholarly fishing expeditions. During my lunch with Carter in 2009, while I was a visiting professor at Emory, he welcomed my interest and instructed his aides to facilitate any request I had. Still, I sought to honor his general preference to weigh in at the end of the project—both to avoid troubling him and because I wanted no suspicion that this was in any way an authorized biography. By the time I headed to Plains, therefore, my research was finished and I had completed a draft of the entire manuscript. I was there to tie up a few loose ends. The aides had given me the option of meeting Carter in Atlanta, but I wanted to see him in Plains, specifically on one of the weekends he taught Sunday school—which is generally any Sunday when he is home and not traveling.

Jimmy Carter, notorious for punctuality, materialized precisely at ten o'clock, wearing a dark sport coat, a light-blue shirt, and a bolo tie. This was lesson number 613 he has given at Maranatha Baptist Church, Carter told us; he has the lessons numbered on his computer. (He's also notorious for quantification.) Having taught Sunday school since he was a midshipman at the U.S. Naval Academy, Carter clearly enjoys the classroom; even while president, he taught fourteen times at First Baptist Church in Washington.

Carter took the morning lesson from the New Testament book of Hebrews, the gist of which, he said, was "the Son of God explaining the character of God." Carter's take on the epistle was decidedly Protestant. "One of the things I have always been taught since I was a child was the priesthood of the believer," he said, a reference to Martin Luther's quarrel with the Roman Catholic Church, which had inserted a priestly caste between God and ordinary believers. Carter used this occasion once again to criticize the conservative takeover of the Southern Baptist Convention, one of the effects of which was an "exaltation" of the clergy, which he believed was contrary to the teachings of scripture. "As we approach the rest of our life," Carter said, "we can be reassured and have hope because we have a direct relationship with God Almighty."[5]

Carter, who tends to teach in syllogisms, was less interested in theological exposition than application. Our duty as believers, he said, is "to emulate, or copy, the life of our savior." Leaders who call themselves Christians, even political leaders, have an obligation to emulate Jesus, who was, Carter reminded us, the Prince of Peace.

The former president, who had looked every bit his eighty-eight years at the beginning of the lesson, seemed to gather energy as he warmed to his topic. He lamented that the United States has a reputation around the world as the most warlike nation on earth, and he noted that for most of the past seventy years we have been at war. "We have an obligation to promote peace," he insisted, "and justice." The United States has more people in prison than any nation on earth, he said, seven times the number when he left the White House in 1981. "I personally believe that Jesus Christ would be against the death penalty," Carter said, referring his auditors to the woman caught in adultery, the incident where Jesus invited any of the woman's accusers who were without sin to cast the first stone.[6]

Carter rarely signs autographs, but he and Rosalynn pose with visitors for photographs following the morning worship service, which begins at eleven. The "catch" for tourists is that if they want, as Jan Williams says, to "make a picture," they must stay for church. It's a clever ploy, and it's difficult to escape the impression that Carter's celebrity is keeping Maranatha afloat. Williams said that the church has 130 members, but only about thirty are active; most of those, she added, are older than she. "I don't know what's going to happen to us," she confessed. The financial report in the morning bulletin put the matter starkly. The weekly needs of the congregation were $1,375, and the receipts from the previous Sunday, not one of Carter's teaching Sundays, totaled only $697.

Williams had directed me to sit in the third row on what Episcopalians call the epistle, or right, side of the church. What I didn't know, until a couple of minutes before eleven, is that this was the Carters' pew. The president greeted me cordially, albeit in hushed tones, and Rosalynn and I exchanged pleasantries. Soon, with the help of a twelve-voice choir, we were all belting out such Baptist standards as "To God Be the Glory," "My Faith Has Found a Resting Place," and "Faith Is the Victory."

Jeffrey Summers, the pastor, a genial man barely a third the age of his most famous congregant, preached a sermon entitled "Finding Faith." Members of the choir by now had taken their places in the congregation. A Secret Service agent sat nearby, his restless eyes darting all around the sanctuary. "Faith is all around us," the preacher said, "we just have to embrace it." At five minutes before noon, the former president discreetly checked his watch, and as if on cue, Summers segued into the altar call. We sang "'Tis So Sweet to Trust in Jesus," the pastor stepped in front of the altar and beckoned, but no one was saved.

In the course of our interview in the pastor's study, after church and photographs on the side lawn, Carter declared himself "honored" to be numbered among such progressive evangelicals as Charles Grandison Finney and William Jennings Bryan. Mark Hatfield, he said, "was a kind of hero of mine." Carter characterized Hatfield as "a genuinely devout believer in Christ who sought to put Christ's teachings into practice." Carter also acknowledged that his own defeat in 1980 followed by Hatfield's retirement from the Senate in 1997 had left a void, at least among elected officials. Carter lamented the "new definition" of evangelicalism that had taken hold, one associated with "right-wing Christianity." He recalled hearing about Jerry Falwell "giving me a hard time" in 1976, but his was just a lonely voice at the time; Falwell and his asso-

ciates, however, "had remarkable success in four years in making that a driving force in American political history." When did the president have a sense
of the gathering storm as he prepared for reelection? Carter remembered that
his sister, Ruth Carter Stapleton, "told me that there was a stirring of animosity toward me because of some of the moderate positions I had taken on
human rights and so forth and that they thought I had betrayed their own
definition of Christianity. But I didn't really see it as a serious thing until the
altercation arose in the Southern Baptist Convention." After the conservative
takeover in 1979, he said, he began to recognize the ramifications of the evangelical shift away from progressive evangelicalism.

"I think the application of Christian faith to human beings is a crucial
part of faith," Carter said, and he expressed confidence that he had taken the
New Testament seriously throughout the course of his various careers, including his time as president. During Sunday school, Carter had told the
class that, by his own reckoning, the seventy-one years of his adult life could
be broken down to eleven years in the navy, seventeen as a farmer, twelve in
politics, and thirty-one as a professor and head of the Carter Center. The
Nobel Peace Prize laureate told me that he harbored no regrets, and that he
wanted to be remembered for peace and human rights. "Some people let
the past consume them," Carter had said during one of his Sunday-school
lessons nearly a decade earlier. But the former president has consistently
looked forward rather than backward.[7]

"The totality of my life has been enhanced," Carter said, by losing the
presidency in 1980. He scratched his chin thoughtfully and then flashed the
famous Jimmy Carter grin. He described the years since he left the White
House as the best of his life, but he acknowledged that "a lot of that is attributable to the fact that I was president—my knowledge of things and my access to leaders." His main regret about not serving a second term was not
being able to "consummate" the Camp David accords, "by giving the Palestinians their rights and by forming two nations," and he continued to regard
both of those steps as essential for peace. "I think I could have done that and
some other things if I'd been president." Still, he added, that he probably
would not have started the Carter Center had he remained in the White
House for a second term.

Jimmy Carter professed not to be worried about the judgment of history.
I remarked that he sounded gracious about his defeat in 1980, that his tone
betrayed no bitterness. "Well, there's nothing I can do about it," Carter replied with a smile. "You have to roll with the punches and make the best of

what I've got." Rosalynn, he said, was much more heartbroken and angry than he was. "I had to think of all the reasons that were positive to try to convince her not to be so despondent," he added. "And so I think that's why I was able to look at the bright side of things."

Carter takes justifiable pride in another career that he didn't list in Sunday school, that of author. He has written more than two dozen books, all but one (his campaign autobiography) since leaving Washington. Toward the end of our conversation, he insisted that I have a copy of his devotional book (adapted from his Sunday-school lessons), *Through the Year with Jimmy Carter: 366 Daily Meditations from the 39th President*.

"Why don't you come with me now?" he said at the conclusion of the interview. As instructed, I jumped into my rental car and followed the two-vehicle Secret Service convoy as it roared out of the church driveway and into town. The president had one brief stop to make, a meet-and-greet with supporters of Habitat for Humanity who were visiting Plains that weekend, and then on to the Carter home. Agents in the trailing Secret Service vehicle didn't want to admit me past the metal gates and into the compound—"Can I help you?" one asked pointedly—but Carter had already emerged from the other vehicle and waved me in.

Rosalynn and I resumed our conversation while Jimmy Carter disappeared into the house. She pointed with pride to the expanse of pink roses embroidered into a fence in front of their home, all from a single bush that her husband had given her for Mother's Day many years earlier. By now, in early June, the heat of a south Georgia summer had settled in, and the roses had begun to wilt. But they were still lovely.

"I couldn't find a new copy," Carter said as he handed me the book, so he had cadged Rosalynn's copy from the nightstand. "I figured I could get you another book," he said with a tentative smile as he glanced in her direction. "You're on page seventy." Rosalynn Carter's bookmark was still in my copy of *Through the Year with Jimmy Carter*—on page seventy, the meditation entitled "Patience in Love."

Both of the Carters apologized that previous commitments that afternoon precluded spending more time with me. They were off to another engagement. "Spend a little time here in Plains before you leave," Carter urged me as he waved goodbye.

As the caravan rumbled past the security gates toward Carter's next appointment, I headed out of town on Highway 61, also known as Old Plains

Highway, by way of Archery, which parallels the Seaboard Coast Line Railroad tracks that young Jimmy Carter walked as a boy in order to sell boiled peanuts in town for pocket money. All of Carter's life, it occurred to me, had been characterized by striving, an insatiable ambition to rise above his circumstances—as a country boy, as a navy midshipman, as a state politician, as president, and beyond as a respected world leader and humanitarian.

In the course of his Sunday-school lesson, Carter had referred to Martin Luther's notion of the priesthood of believers, that each of us is responsible directly to God and that the priestly caste or the arrogation of ministerial authority actually impeded that relationship. But Carter failed to note Luther's other central criticism of medieval Catholicism: works righteousness, the popular understanding that individuals could earn salvation by dint of good works. Protestants are equally susceptible, seeking to prove by their good works that they are among the elect. As I passed the hardscrabble farm in Archery, it was difficult to escape the impression that Carter was driven—almost obsessed—by a kind of works righteousness.

Carter always believed in the value of work. On the farm, hard work would sustain the family and bring profitability. At school, diligent study would lead to better opportunities. In Hyman Rickover's navy, hard work might win praise or even a promotion. On the campaign trail, working harder than your opponent—an hour earlier every morning or shaking more hands—would lead to victory. Once in office, long hours, the resolve to read every piece of legislation, and attention to the minutiae of negotiations would ensure success—and reelection.

Carter's term in the White House disrupted that calculus. He faced intractable obstacles as president—the nation's chronic energy dependence, soaring interest rates, an Islamic revolution in Iran, political opposition within his own party—that simply would not yield to hard work or longer hours. Carter's shattering electoral loss in 1980 represented not only the end of his political career but also a repudiation of the notion that if he just worked harder and longer, his efforts would be rewarded. How could the electorate not recognize that he was doing everything humanly possible—working as diligently as he could—to solve these problems?

After absorbing his defeat and returning to Plains, Carter reaffirmed his commitment to works righteousness as a way to redeem his loss. The Carter Center would be an activist institution, not merely a celebratory one. Habitat for Humanity was nothing if not an activist organization. This former president would not retire quietly into private life. There was work to be done—eradicating disease, monitoring elections, building houses, reprimanding dictators and obdurate politicians, teaching Sunday school, heading off military confrontations, ending hunger, making peace. If Carter could work hard enough, if (in religious terms) he could accumulate enough merit, he might be able to tilt the balance of history in his favor.

To a remarkable degree, Jimmy Carter's commitment to the ethic of works righteousness met with success. Although partisans continued to criticize, and even to ridicule, his presidency, historians now regard it more favorably, albeit with something less than unvarnished approbation. Carter's activities since leaving office earned him praise and even grudging admiration. The awarding of the Nobel Peace Prize in 2002 provided perhaps the ultimate validation of Carter's works righteousness.

At what point, however, does Carter earn a reprieve from his moral exertions? When can he relax and settle into a hard-won retirement? Certainly not on a Sunday in Plains—even after teaching Sunday school, attending church, posing with tourists, fielding questions from a biographer, and massaging Habitat for Humanity donors. As I was moseying down Highway 61 toward Archery, Carter was speeding off to the next event on a crowded calendar. The former president, pushing ninety years old, was still a restless man, consumed by a kind of frenetic benevolence. The striving continues. As Martin Luther recognized centuries earlier, those who subscribe to the ethic of works righteousness can never be certain they have accumulated enough merit. Jimmy Carter doesn't lack so much for passion as he does for respite.

The man whose improbable election in 1976 redeemed the nation from the sins of Watergate has finally earned his own redemption. Jimmy Carter himself, however, may be the last to know.

APPENDIX ONE

Life and Times of Jimmy Carter

1924   October 1: James Earl Carter Jr. is born in Plains, Georgia, to Bessie Lillian Gordy and James Earl Carter Sr.

1928   The Carters move to a farm in Archery, three miles from Plains.

1935   Summer: Jimmy Carter is born again and baptized at Plains Baptist Church.

1941   Jimmy Carter graduates from Plains High School; he enrolls at Georgia Southwestern College.

1942   Carter enrolls at Georgia Institute of Technology.

1943   June 30: Carter matriculates at the U.S. Naval Academy, Annapolis, Maryland.

1946   June 11: Carter, an ensign in the navy, graduates from Annapolis.
        July 7: Jimmy Carter and Rosalynn Smith are married in the Plains Methodist Church.

1947   July 3: John William "Jack" Carter is born to Jimmy and Rosalynn.

1950   April 12: James Earl "Chip" Carter III is born while the Carters are stationed in Hawai'i.

1952   August 18: Donnel Jeffrey "Jeff" Carter is born in New London, Connecticut.

1953   July 23: James Earl Carter Sr. dies of pancreatic cancer.

October: Jimmy Carter, over the vigorous objections of Rosalynn, resigns his navy commission to return to Plains.

1954　　May 17: In its *Brown v. Board of Education* decision, the U.S. Supreme Court rules that "separate but equal" is inherently unequal and mandates the desegregation of public schools.

1955　　December: Carter begins his service as a member of the Sumter County Board of Education.

1962　　March 26: The U.S. Supreme Court's *Baker v. Carr* decision invalidates voting procedures such as the county unit system of representation in Georgia, which had been used to forestall desegregation.
　　　　October 1: On Carter's thirty-eighth birthday, he files papers to run for the Georgia state senate.

1963　　January 14: After a contested election marred by corruption in Quitman County, Carter is sworn in as state senator.

1964　　July 2: Lyndon B. Johnson signs the Civil Rights Act.

1965　　March 21: On the same day that Martin Luther King Jr. led the march from Selma to Montgomery, Alabama, Jerry Falwell preaches the most famous sermon of his career, "Of Ministers and Marches," which explicitly condemns political activism on the part of religious leaders.

1966　　June 12: Carter announces his candidacy for governor of Georgia.
　　　　September 15: Carter finishes third in the Democratic primary, behind Ellis Arnall and Lester G. Maddox; the Georgia legislature eventually chooses Maddox as governor after no candidate wins a majority in the general election.

1967　　Following a conversation with his sister, Ruth Carter Stapleton, Carter reaffirms his faith; in Carter's words, the renewal was "a deeply profound religious experience that changed my life dramatically."
　　　　October 19: Amy Lynn Carter is born in Plains.

1968　　May: Carter does missionary work in Loch Haven, Pennsylvania, knocking on doors to tell others about Jesus.
　　　　November: Carter does evangelistic work in Springfield, Massachusetts, with Eloy Cruz, a Cuban-American pastor of a small church in Brooklyn.

1970　　April 3: Carter announces his candidacy for governor.
　　　　November 3: Carter wins election as governor over Hal Suit, Republican, with 59.3 percent of the vote.

1971   January 12: Carter is sworn in as the seventy-sixth governor of Georgia; in his inaugural address, he announces that "the time for racial discrimination is over."

        May 30: Carter appears on the cover of *Time* magazine as a representative of the new breed of so-called New South governors.

        June 30: In its *Green v. Connally* decision, the U.S. District Court for the District of Columbia upholds the Internal Revenue Service (IRS) in its decision to deny tax exemption to institutions that engage in racial discrimination.

1972   November 4: Hamilton Jordan presents Carter with his plans for Carter to capture the Democratic nomination and win the presidency in 1976.

1973   January 22: The U.S. Supreme Court's *Roe v. Wade* decision effectively strikes down laws limiting abortion before "viability," when the fetus can survive outside of the womb.

        November 25: Fifty-five evangelicals, meeting in Chicago, sign the Chicago Declaration of Evangelical Social Concern, a manifesto of progressive evangelicalism.

1974   May 4: Carter gives his address at Law Day at the University of Georgia, which captures the attention of Hunter S. Thompson, who declared it "a bastard of a speech."

        August 9: Richard Nixon, facing impeachment, resigns as president; Gerald R. Ford ascends to the presidency.

        December 12: Carter announces his candidacy for president at the National Press Club in Washington and, later that day, in Atlanta.

1976   January 19: Carter wins a plurality in the Iowa precinct caucuses, his first step toward the Democratic presidential nomination. The same day, after years of warnings, the IRS rescinds the tax exemption of Bob Jones University because of its racially discriminatory policies.

        March 9: Carter defeats George C. Wallace in the Florida Democratic primary.

        March 23: With 54 percent of the vote in the North Carolina primary, Carter wins a majority for the first time.

        July 15: Having chosen Walter Mondale, U.S. senator from Minnesota, as his running mate, Carter accepts the Democratic nomination for president at the Democratic National Convention in New York City.

        September 20: Carter's interview appears in *Playboy* magazine.

October 6: During the candidates' second debate, Ford insists that Eastern Europe was not under Soviet domination.

October 25: *Newsweek*'s cover declares 1976 the "Year of the Evangelical."

November 2: Carter is elected president with 50.1 percent of the popular vote and 297 electoral votes to Ford's 240.

1977   January 20: Carter is inaugurated the thirty-ninth president of the United States.

January 21: Carter pardons Vietnam-era draft resisters.

May 22: Carter's commencement address at the University of Notre Dame spells out a new direction in foreign policy, one shaped more by concern for human rights than by the polarities of the Cold War.

June 7: After a campaign led by Anita Bryant, voters in Dade County, Florida, rescind a law that prohibited discrimination against homosexuals.

June 30: Carter halts development and production of the B-1 bomber, angering conservatives.

July: Sandinistas come to power in Nicaragua.

September 7: The Torrijos-Carter treaties are signed; when ratified, they would transfer ownership of the Panama Canal to Panama in 1999.

September 21: Bert Lance resigns as head of the Office of Management and Budget.

1978   April 18: The second Panama Canal treaty is ratified by the U.S. Senate.

September 5: Camp David summit opens; over the ensuing thirteen days, Menachem Begin of Israel and Anwar el-Sadat of Egypt negotiate the framework for a peace agreement, with Carter as mediator.

November 7: Democrats lose a net three seats in the U.S. Senate; the defeat of Dick Clark in Iowa and Thomas McIntyre in New Hampshire, together with the Republican trifecta in Minnesota (both senators and a governor), persuade Paul Weyrich that abortion might work as a political issue among evangelicals.

1979   January–March: Francis A. Schaeffer and C. Everett Koop tour the country with their film series, *Whatever Happened to the Human Race?*, which decries abortion as a symptom of the nation's slide into "secular humanism."

January 1: The United States officially extends diplomatic recognition to the People's Republic of China, culminating a process begun during the Nixon administration.

March 26: Sadat and Begin sign a peace treaty at the White House, thereby ending a state of war between the two nations.

May: The *Atlantic* cover story is "The Passionless Presidency," by James Fallows, Carter's erstwhile speechwriter.

June 6: Moral Majority, Jerry Falwell's political organization, is incorporated.

June 12–14: Conservatives mount a takeover of the Southern Baptist Convention, Carter's own denomination, installing Adrian Rogers as president.

June 18: Carter and Leonid Brezhnev sign SALT II in Vienna.

July 15: Carter delivers his "Crisis of Confidence" speech from the Oval Office.

November 4: Iranian students breach the walls of the U.S. embassy in Teheran and take sixty-six Americans hostage (fourteen were soon released).

November 6: At Faneuil Hall in Boston, Edward M. Kennedy announces his intention to challenge Carter for the 1980 Democratic presidential nomination.

December 4: Carter announces his candidacy for a second term.

December 25: The Soviet Union invades Afghanistan in support of the communist government and its efforts to hold off a Muslim insurgency.

1980   January 3: In light of the Soviet invasion of Afghanistan, Carter asks the Senate to delay consideration of SALT II.

January 22: The day after addressing the National Religious Broadcasters, Carter meets with evangelical leaders, including Falwell, for breakfast at the White House.

January 23: Carter outlines the Carter Doctrine in his State of the Union address: Any Soviet action in the Middle East will be treated as a threat to U.S. security.

April 24: A daring rescue attempt of the hostages in Iran, authorized by Carter, is called off because of a damaged helicopter; in the course of retreat, one of the helicopters strikes a C-130 transport plane, killing eight soldiers.

April 29: An estimated 200,000 evangelicals take part in the Washington for Jesus rally on the Mall in Washington.

August 3: Ronald Reagan opens his fall campaign for president by calling for "states' rights" at the Neshoba County Fair in Philadelphia, Mississippi, site of the murder of three civil rights activists in 1964.

August 13: Following a bruising primary battle against Kennedy, Carter wins the Democratic presidential nomination on the first ballot at the Democratic National Convention in New York City.

August 22: At an event called the National Affairs Briefing in Dallas, Reagan tells thousands of politically conservative evangelicals, "I know this group can't endorse me, but I endorse you and what you are doing."

November 4: On the anniversary of the taking of American hostages in Iran, Carter loses his bid for reelection; Reagan captures the electoral votes of all but six states and the District of Columbia.

December 2: Carter signs the Alaska National Interest Lands Conservation Act, which doubles the size of the nation's wildlife refuges and national parks.

1981   January 20: Reagan is inaugurated as Carter's successor; a few minutes later, the American hostages in Teheran leave Iranian air space. The Carters return to Plains.

January 21: Carter flies to Germany to meet the freed hostages.

January 25: Jimmy and Rosalynn Carter join Maranatha Baptist Church in Plains.

1982   September: Carter begins teaching at Emory University.

1983   May 24: The U.S. Supreme Court rules 8–1 against Bob Jones University in *Bob Jones University v. United States*, thereby validating the principle that racial discrimination is grounds for revocation of tax-exempt status.

1984   September: The Carters participate in the Jimmy Carter Work Project for Habitat for Humanity in New York City, thereby providing publicity for the organization.

1986   June 17: Reagan nominates William Rehnquist, the sole dissenter in the *Bob Jones University* case, to become chief justice of the U.S. Supreme Court.

October 1: The Jimmy Carter Presidential Library and the Carter Center are dedicated in Atlanta.

1990   February: After observing the presidential elections in Nicaragua, Carter persuades Daniel Ortega to honor the outcome and leave office peacefully.

1994   September 5: Carter, together with Colin Powell and Sam Nunn, persuade Haiti's strongman Raoul Cédras to cede power and avert an imminent invasion by U.S. forces.

1998   December 10: On the fiftieth anniversary of the Universal Declaration of Human Rights, Carter receives the first United Nations Human Rights Prize.

1999   August 9: Rosalynn and Jimmy Carter are both awarded the Presidential Medal of Freedom by Bill Clinton.

2002   June: Carter, on a visit to Cuba, calls on the United States to end its trade embargo and on Fidel Castro to introduce democratic reforms.

       October 11: In an early-morning phone call from Oslo, Carter learns that he has been awarded the Nobel Peace Prize.

       December 10: Carter accepts the Peace Prize as George W. Bush prepares to invade Iraq.

2008   April 3: Carter, a "superdelegate" to the Democratic National Convention, hints that he is supporting Barack Obama, U.S. senator from Illinois, for the Democratic presidential nomination.

2013   April 10: Carter receives the International Advocate for Peace Award from the *Cardozo Journal of Conflict Resolution*, a publication of the Benjamin N. Cardozo School of Law at Yeshiva University.

APPENDIX TWO

"Crisis of Confidence,"
July 15, 1979

Widely known, and eventually reviled, as the "malaise" speech (even though the word malaise *appears nowhere in the address), Jimmy Carter's "Crisis of Confidence" speech was an attempt to revive his listless presidency. Returning from an energy summit in Tokyo, Carter was prepared to give yet another speech on energy, but both Jimmy and Rosalynn Carter disliked drafts that had been prepared by the White House staff. Carter called off the speech and instead invited a stream of visitors to Camp David to consult with him on the state of the country and on the state of his presidency. The president also visited with private citizens near Pittsburgh and Martinsburg, West Virginia.*

"Their criticisms of me were the most severe, questioning my ability to deal with the existing problems of the nation," Carter wrote in his presidential memoir. "They told me that I seemed bogged down in the details of administration, and that the public was disillusioned in having to face intractable problems like energy shortages and growing inflation after their expectations had been so elevated at the time of my election."[1]

Carter did not shrink from these criticisms; in fact, he quoted many of them in the beginning of the speech, which bewailed the widespread fixation on affluence at the expense of the common good and cautioned against "fragmentation and self-interest." Drawing on the long tradition of the American jeremiad, calling on people to repent of their sins and mend their ways, Carter warned about "the loss of unity of purpose for our nation" and summoned Americans to "the path of common

purpose and the restoration of American values." The second part of the
speech outlined specific proposals to push the nation toward energy
independence.

Initial public response to the speech was positive, and Carter's stand-
ing in the polls rose immediately thereafter. Pundits, however, quickly
derided it as Carter's "malaise" speech, and the Reagan-Bush ticket used
it against him—especially Carter's calls for restraint and self-sacrifice—
in the election campaign the following year. Carter, however, stood by the
speech and believed it was one of the best he ever gave.

Good evening. This is a special night for me. Exactly three years ago, on July 15, 1976, I accepted the nomination of my party to run for president of the United States. I promised you a president who is not isolated from the people, who feels your pain, and who shares your dreams and who draws his strength and his wisdom from you.

During the past three years I've spoken to you on many occasions about national concerns, the energy crisis, reorganizing the government, our nation's economy, and issues of war and especially peace. But over those years the subjects of the speeches, the talks, and the press conferences have become increasingly narrow, focused more and more on what the isolated world of Washington thinks is important. Gradually, you've heard more and more about what the government thinks or what the government should be doing and less and less about our nation's hopes, our dreams, and our vision of the future.

Ten days ago I had planned to speak to you again about a very important subject—energy. For the fifth time I would have described the urgency of the problem and laid out a series of legislative recommendations to the Congress. But as I was preparing to speak, I began to ask myself the same question that I now know has been troubling many of you. Why have we not been able to get together as a nation to resolve our serious energy problem?

It's clear that the true problems of our nation are much deeper—deeper than gasoline lines or energy shortages, deeper even than inflation or recession. And I realize more than ever that as president I need your help. So, I decided to reach out and listen to the voices of America.

I invited to Camp David people from almost every segment of our society—business and labor, teachers and preachers, governors, mayors, and private citizens. And then I left Camp David to listen to other Americans, men and women like you. It has been an extraordinary ten days, and I want to share with you what I've heard.

First of all, I got a lot of personal advice. Let me quote a few of the typical comments that I wrote down.

This from a southern governor: "Mr. President, you are not leading this nation—you're just managing the government."

"You don't see the people enough any more."

"Some of your cabinet members don't seem loyal. There is not enough discipline among your disciples."

"Don't talk to us about politics or the mechanics of government, but about an understanding of our common good."

"Mr. President, we're in trouble. Talk to us about blood and sweat and tears."

"If you lead, Mr. President, we will follow."

Many people talked about themselves and about the condition of our nation. This from a young woman in Pennsylvania: "I feel so far from government. I feel like ordinary people are excluded from political power."

And this from a young Chicano: "Some of us have suffered from recession all our lives."

"Some people have wasted energy, but others haven't had anything to waste."

And this from a religious leader: "No material shortage can touch the important things like God's love for us or our love for one another."

And I like this one particularly from a black woman who happens to be the mayor of a small Mississippi town: "The big-shots are not the only ones who are important. Remember, you can't sell anything on Wall Street unless someone digs it up somewhere else first."

This kind of summarized a lot of other statements: "Mr. President, we are confronted with a moral and a spiritual crisis."

Several of our discussions were on energy, and I have a notebook full of comments and advice. I'll read just a few.

"We can't go on consuming 40 percent more energy than we produce. When we import oil we are also importing inflation plus unemployment."

"We've got to use what we have. The Middle East has only 5 percent of the world's energy, but the United States has 24 percent."

And this is one of the most vivid statements: "Our neck is stretched over the fence and OPEC has a knife."

"There will be other cartels and other shortages. American wisdom and courage right now can set a path to follow in the future."

This was a good one: "Be bold, Mr. President. We may make mistakes, but we are ready to experiment."

And this one from a labor leader got to the heart of it: "The real issue is freedom. We must deal with the energy problem on a war footing."

And the last that I'll read: "When we enter the moral equivalent of war, Mr. President, don't issue us BB guns."

These ten days confirmed my belief in the decency and the strength and the wisdom of the American people, but it also bore out some of my long-standing concerns about our nation's underlying problems.

I know, of course, being president, that government actions and legislation can be very important. That's why I've worked hard to put my campaign promises into law—and I have to admit, with just mixed success. But after listening to the American people I have been reminded again that all the legislation in the world can't fix what's wrong with America. So, I want to speak to you first tonight about a subject even more serious than energy or inflation. I want to talk to you right now about a fundamental threat to American democracy.

I do not mean our political and civil liberties. They will endure. And I do not refer to the outward strength of America, a nation that is at peace tonight everywhere in the world, with unmatched economic power and military might.

The threat is nearly invisible in ordinary ways. It is a crisis of confidence. It is a crisis that strikes at the very heart and soul and spirit of our national will. We can see this crisis in the growing doubt about the meaning of our own lives and in the loss of a unity of purpose for our nation.

The erosion of our confidence in the future is threatening to destroy the social and the political fabric of America.

The confidence that we have always had as a people is not simply some romantic dream or a proverb in a dusty book that we read just on the Fourth of July. It is the idea which founded our nation and has guided our development as a people. Confidence in the future has supported everything else—public institutions and private enterprise, our own families, and the very Constitution of the United States. Confidence has defined our course and has served as a link between generations. We've always believed in something called progress. We've always had a faith that the days of our children would be better than our own.

Our people are losing that faith, not only in government itself but in the ability as citizens to serve as the ultimate rulers and shapers of our democracy. As a people we know our past and we are proud of it. Our progress has been part of the living history of America, even the world. We always believed that we were part of a great movement of humanity itself called democracy, involved in the search for freedom, and that belief has always strengthened us in our purpose. But just as we are losing our confidence in the future, we are also beginning to close the door on our past.

In a nation that was proud of hard work, strong families, close-knit communities, and our faith in God, too many of us now tend to worship self-indulgence and consumption. Human identity is no longer defined by what one does, but by what one owns. But we've discovered that owning things and consuming things does not satisfy our longing for meaning. We've learned that piling up material goods cannot fill the emptiness of lives which have no confidence or purpose.

The symptoms of this crisis of the American spirit are all around us. For the first time in the history of our country a majority of our people believe that the next five years will be worse than the past five years. Two-thirds of our people do not even vote. The productivity of American workers is actually dropping, and the willingness of Americans to save for the future has fallen below that of all other people in the Western world.

As you know, there is a growing disrespect for government and for churches and for schools, the news media, and other institutions. This is not a message of happiness or reassurance, but it is the truth and it is a warning.

These changes did not happen overnight. They've come upon us gradually over the last generation, years that were filled with shocks and tragedy.

We were sure that ours was a nation of the ballot, not the bullet, until the murders of John Kennedy and Robert Kennedy and Martin Luther King Jr. We were taught that our armies were always invincible and our causes were always just, only to suffer the agony of Vietnam. We respected the presidency as a place of honor until the shock of Watergate.

We remember when the phrase "sound as a dollar" was an expression of absolute dependability, until ten years of inflation began to shrink our dollar and our savings. We believed that our nation's resources were limitless until 1973, when we had to face a growing dependence on foreign oil.

These wounds are still very deep. They have never been healed.

Looking for a way out of this crisis, our people have turned to the federal government and found it isolated from the mainstream of our nation's life.

Washington, D.C., has become an island. The gap between our citizens and our government has never been so wide. The people are looking for honest answers, not easy answers; clear leadership, not false claims and evasiveness and politics as usual.

What you see too often in Washington and elsewhere around the country is a system of government that seems incapable of action. You see a Congress twisted and pulled in every direction by hundreds of well-financed and powerful special interests. You see every extreme position defended to the last vote, almost to the last breath by one unyielding group or another. You often see a balanced and a fair approach that demands sacrifice, a little sacrifice from everyone, abandoned like an orphan without support and without friends.

Often you see paralysis and stagnation and drift. You don't like it, and neither do I. What can we do?

First of all, we must face the truth, and then we can change our course. We simply must have faith in each other, faith in our ability to govern ourselves, and faith in the future of this nation. Restoring that faith and that confidence to America is now the most important task we face. It is a true challenge of this generation of Americans.

One of the visitors to Camp David last week put it this way: "We've got to stop crying and start sweating, stop talking and start walking, stop cursing and start praying. The strength we need will not come from the White House, but from every house in America."

We know the strength of America. We are strong. We can regain our unity. We can regain our confidence. We are the heirs of generations who survived threats much more powerful and awesome than those that challenge us now. Our fathers and mothers were strong men and women who shaped a new society during the Great Depression, who fought world wars, and who carved out a new charter of peace for the world.

We ourselves are the same Americans who just ten years ago put a man on the moon. We are the generation that dedicated our society to the pursuit of human rights and equality. And we are the generation that will win the war on the energy problem and in that process rebuild the unity and confidence of America.

We are at a turning point in our history. There are two paths to choose. One is a path I've warned about tonight, the path that leads to fragmentation and self-interest. Down that road lies a mistaken idea of freedom, the right to grasp for ourselves some advantage over others. That path would be one of constant conflict between narrow interests ending in chaos and immobility. It is a certain route to failure.

All the traditions of our past, all the lessons of our heritage, all the promises of our future point to another path, the path of common purpose and the restoration of American values. That path leads to true freedom for our nation and ourselves. We can take the first steps down that path as we begin to solve our energy problem.

Energy will be the immediate test of our ability to unite this nation, and it can also be the standard around which we rally. On the battlefield of energy we can win for our nation a new confidence, and we can seize control again of our common destiny.

In little more than two decades we've gone from a position of energy independence to one in which almost half the oil we use comes from foreign countries, at prices that are going through the roof. Our excessive dependence on OPEC has already taken a tremendous toll on our economy and our people. This is the direct cause of the long lines which have made millions of you spend aggravating hours waiting for gasoline. It's a cause of the increased inflation and unemployment that we now face. This intolerable dependence on foreign oil threatens our economic independence and the very security of our nation.

The energy crisis is real. It is worldwide. It is a clear and present danger to our nation. These are facts and we simply must face them.

What I have to say to you now about energy is simple and vitally important.

Point one: I am tonight setting a clear goal for the energy policy of the United States. Beginning this moment, this nation will never use more foreign oil than we did in 1977—never. From now on, every new addition to our demand for energy will be met from our own production and our own conservation. The generation-long growth in our dependence on foreign oil will be stopped dead in its tracks right now and then reversed as we move through the 1980s, for I am tonight setting the further goal of cutting our dependence on foreign oil by one-half by the end of the next decade—a saving of over $4\frac{1}{2}$ million barrels of imported oil per day.

Point two: To ensure that we meet these targets, I will use my presidential authority to set import quotas. I'm announcing tonight that for 1979 and 1980, I will forbid the entry into this country of one drop of foreign oil more than these goals allow. These quotas will ensure a reduction in imports even below the ambitious levels we set at the recent Tokyo summit.

Point three: To give us energy security, I am asking for the most massive peacetime commitment of funds and resources in our nation's history to develop America's own alternative sources of fuel—from coal, from oil shale, from plant products for gasohol, from unconventional gas, from the sun.

I propose the creation of an energy security corporation to lead this effort to replace 2½ million barrels of imported oil per day by 1990. The corporation will issue up to $5 billion in energy bonds, and I especially want them to be in small denominations so that average Americans can invest directly in America's energy security.

Just as a similar synthetic rubber corporation helped us win World War II, so will we mobilize American determination and ability to win the energy war. Moreover, I will soon submit legislation to Congress calling for the creation of this nation's first solar bank, which will help us achieve the crucial goal of 20 percent of our energy coming from solar power by the year 2000.

These efforts will cost money, a lot of money, and that is why Congress must enact the windfall profits tax without delay. It will be money well spent. Unlike the billions of dollars that we ship to foreign countries to pay for foreign oil, these funds will be paid by Americans to Americans. These funds will go to fight, not to increase, inflation and unemployment.

Point four: I'm asking Congress to mandate, to require as a matter of law, that our nation's utility companies cut their massive use of oil by 50 percent within the next decade and switch to other fuels, especially coal, our most abundant energy source.

Point five: To make absolutely certain that nothing stands in the way of achieving these goals, I will urge Congress to create an energy mobilization board which, like the War Production Board in World War II, will have the responsibility and authority to cut through the red tape, the delays, and the endless roadblocks to completing key energy projects.

We will protect our environment. But when this nation critically needs a refinery or a pipeline, we will build it.

Point six: I'm proposing a bold conservation program to involve every state, county, and city and every average American in our energy battle. This effort will permit you to build conservation into your homes and your lives at a cost you can afford.

I ask Congress to give me authority for mandatory conservation and for standby gasoline rationing. To further conserve energy, I'm proposing tonight an extra $10 billion over the next decade to strengthen our public transportation systems. And I'm asking you for your good and for your nation's security to take no unnecessary trips, to use carpools or public transportation whenever you can, to park your car one extra day per week, to obey the speed limit, and to set your thermostats to save fuel. Every act of energy conservation like this is more than just common sense—I tell you it is an act of patriotism.

Our nation must be fair to the poorest among us, so we will increase aid to needy Americans to cope with rising energy prices. We often think of conservation only in terms of sacrifice. In fact, it is the most painless and immediate way of rebuilding our nation's strength. Every gallon of oil each one of us saves is a new form of production. It gives us more freedom, more confidence, that much more control over our own lives.

So, the solution of our energy crisis can also help us to conquer the crisis of the spirit in our country. It can rekindle our sense of unity, our confidence in the future, and give our nation and all of us individually a new sense of purpose.

You know we can do it. We have the natural resources. We have more oil in our shale alone than several Saudi Arabias. We have more coal than any nation on Earth. We have the world's highest level of technology. We have the most skilled work force, with innovative genius, and I firmly believe that we have the national will to win this war.

I do not promise you that this struggle for freedom will be easy. I do not promise a quick way out of our nation's problems, when the truth is that the only way out is an all-out effort. What I do promise you is that I will lead our fight, and I will enforce fairness in our struggle, and I will ensure honesty. And above all, I will act.

We can manage the short-term shortages more effectively and we will, but there are no short-term solutions to our long-range problems. There is simply no way to avoid sacrifice.

Twelve hours from now I will speak again in Kansas City, to expand and to explain further our energy program. Just as the search for solutions to our energy shortages has now led us to a new awareness of our nation's deeper problems, so our willingness to work for those solutions in energy can strengthen us to attack those deeper problems.

I will continue to travel this country, to hear the people of America. You can help me to develop a national agenda for the 1980s. I will listen and I will act. We will act together. These were the promises I made three years ago, and I intend to keep them.

Little by little we can and we must rebuild our confidence. We can spend until we empty our treasuries, and we may summon all the wonders of science. But we can succeed only if we tap our greatest resources—America's people, America's values, and America's confidence.

I have seen the strength of America in the inexhaustible resources of our people. In the days to come, let us renew that strength in the struggle for an energy-secure nation.

In closing, let me say this: I will do my best, but I will not do it alone. Let your voice be heard. Whenever you have a chance, say something good about our country. With God's help and for the sake of our nation, it is time for us to join hands in America. Let us commit ourselves together to a rebirth of the American spirit. Working together with our common faith we cannot fail.

Thank you and good night.

ACKNOWLEDGMENTS

I'D like to thank, first of all, the staff members of the American Heritage Center at the University of Wyoming and the archivists at Bob Jones University and at Liberty University for their highly professional assistance during my visits. I'd especially like to acknowledge the help of Rachael Dreyer, assistant reference archivist at the American Heritage Center. My friend and colleague Christopher J. Anderson, Methodist librarian and coordinator of special collections at Drew University, was enormously helpful in directing me to materials relating to Methodism in the years prior to and during the Carter presidency, and he also gave the draft the benefit of his scrutiny. The Baker-Berry Library at Dartmouth is a wonderful resource, not least because the staff is unstintingly helpful. I'd specifically like to thank William Fontaine for his assistance and also Noah Bond, a student, for help in tracking down published sources in magazines. Andrew Balmer, my son, investigated an errant footnote for me while he was passing through Laramie, Wyoming, on tour with the theatrical production of *Dreamgirls*. Thank you, Son.

Dating back to my junior year of college, I have now conducted research in seven of the nation's presidential libraries, which, both singly and collectively, represent an extraordinary resource for understanding American history. Three presidential libraries were germane to this project: the Gerald R. Ford Library in Ann Arbor, Michigan, the Jimmy Carter Library in Atlanta, and the Ronald Reagan Library in Simi Valley, California. Staff members were invariably gracious and accommodating to my requests both before and during my visits. The Gerald R. Ford Foundation also provided me with a research grant, for which I am most grateful, and Barnard College awarded me a grant to defray some of my travel expenses. I thank Steven H. Hochman of the Carter Center for facilitating my contacts with President Carter and for suggesting several crucial changes to the manuscript, and I'm grateful to both President and Mrs. Carter for their gracious hospitality during my visit to Plains. I owe a special debt of gratitude to Jay Hakes, director of the Jimmy Carter Library and Museum, and his wife, Anita, not only for their friendship but also for inviting me to stay with them during one of my research forays at the Carter Library. Jay gave a draft of this manuscript a thorough reading and offered invaluable suggestions. His father, J. Edward Hakes, was academic dean at the small college I attended (as I tell my students these days) sometime back in the last century. As much as anyone I knew at the time, "Dean Hakes," as he was universally known, embodied the principles of progressive evangelicalism: opposition to reckless military engagement and concern for women, minorities, and the poor. Many of the qualities I so admired in the dean have passed down to the next generation.

During this book's gestation of more than a decade, I prevailed on many colleagues and friends for advice; their comments and suggestions helped shape this project more than they know. William vanden Heuvel, who served as deputy representative to the United Nations during the Carter administration, encouraged me several times in the early stages of this project and offered suggestions about the shape of the book. My scholarly interlocutors included Daniel Vaca, Terry Todd, Erika Dyson, Bruce Mullin, Rosemary R. Corbett, Harry S. Stout, Benji Rolsky, and Gary Laderman. Edward J. Blum did me the great honor of casting his critical gaze on the manuscript, as did E. Brooks Holifield, the venerable church historian recently retired from Emory University. John Wilson, avowedly no fan of Carter, read the manuscript, suggested several tweaks, and professed to come away with a new appreciation for the thirty-ninth president. Bill Leonard scrutinized the manuscript with particular attention to matters associated with the Baptist tradition. Robert A. Oden Jr. is both a good friend and a perceptive critic; I'm grateful for both. Douglas Frank's keen eye, trenchant criticism, and enduring friendship have guided me since I studied with him beneath the benign gaze and dry humor of Dean Hakes—which is to say back in the previous century. The members of the Columbia University Seminar on Religion in America provided me with an intellectual community for more than a decade; their comments on an early draft of the material on progressive evangelicalism were especially helpful. I also appreciate a grant from the Schoff

Fund at the University Seminars at Columbia University for assistance in publication. Members of the Religion Department at Dartmouth College helped me formulate my ideas in their Dickinson Visiting Scholar Seminar while I was a visiting professor, before they invited me to join them as a colleague in 2012. This book is immeasurably better for the scrutiny and the suggestions of these friends and colleagues, but any mistakes that remain belong to me alone.

My semester as the Alonzo L. McDonald Distinguished University Visiting Professor at Emory University in 2009 provided an occasion to meet both Alonzo McDonald and Jimmy Carter (the latter for the second time). I also presented earlier versions of some of this book in several public lectures at Emory and benefited greatly from the comments and suggestions of colleagues in both the Religion Department and Candler School of Theology.

Lara Heimert at Basic Books is an editor without peer. She diverted untold time and energy from her usual task of running the universe to provide me with the most thorough editing I've ever received; my gratitude knows no bounds. I'd also like to acknowledge the assistance of my agent, Jill Kneerim, and the consummate professionalism of John Donohue and his colleagues at Westchester Publishing Services. I'm grateful, finally, for the people willing to talk to me about their experience of the Carter presidency, especially Wesley Pippert, Robert Maddox, Elmer Rumminger, and Jim Wallis.

On the day I completed this manuscript, my wife, Catharine, commented cheerfully that she felt as though she'd been living with both Jimmy Carter and me for quite a while. I wonder if perhaps I should have tried to collect some rent from the former president.

Winter Solstice, 2013
Wilder, Vermont

NOTES

Preface: Jimmy Carter and Me

1. On the insularity of evangelical institutions, see the remarkable novel by Shirley Nelson, which offers a fictionalized portrait of Moody Bible Institute: Shirley Nelson, *The Last Year of the War* (New York: Harper & Row, 1978).

2. Patrick Allitt, *Religion in America Since 1945: A History* (New York: Columbia University Press, 2003), 154; Mark 16:15, New International Version (hereafter NIV). For "selective literalism," see Randall Balmer, *Thy Kingdom Come: How the Religious Right Distorts the Faith and Threatens America* (New York: Basic Books, 2006), chap. 1.

3. The "Great Commission" appears in Mark 16:15, NIV.

4. Jimmy Carter, *Sources of Strength: Meditations on Scripture for a Living Faith* (New York: Times Books, 1997), 4–6. Although I'm well aware of the technical distinctions between *evangelical* and *fundamentalist*, I will use the two terms more or less interchangeably. I will generally use the latter to refer to those more conservative and less pliable or open to compromise. Fundamentalism differs from evangelicalism not so much in doctrine but in temperament; it suggests a militancy that is generally missing from evangelicalism, or at least less overt. As Jerry Falwell himself said, "A fundamentalist is an evangelical who is mad about something." Jerry Falwell, *Strength for the Journey: An Autobiography* (New York: Simon & Schuster, 1987), 360. George Marsden, the premier historian of fundamentalism, has also used that formulation; I have been unable to determine who came up with it first. Marsden's book on the movement, however, is definitive: George M. Marsden, *Fundamentalism and American Culture: The Shaping of Twentieth-Century Evangelicalism, 1870–1925* (New York: Oxford University Press, 1980).

5. In such instances, it's appropriate to apply the duck test: If it walks like a duck, quacks like a duck, and so on. In the case of evangelicalism and the Southern Baptist

Convention, for example, it's a duck. It's most definitely a duck. Some years ago, when I was writing a feature article about Baylor University, for example, at a time when the Baptist school was trying to position itself within the broader stream of evangelicalism, everyone I interviewed during the course of my visit stumbled over the terms *evangelical* or *evangelicalism*. See Randall Balmer, "2012: A School Odyssey," *Christianity Today*, November 18, 2002, 62–69.

6. Matthew 25:35–36, 46, 40, NIV.

7. Charles G. Finney, *Sermons on Gospel Themes* (Oberlin, Ohio: E. J. Goodrich, 1876), 348, 356.

8. "Dying Confession of Joseph Hare, Remarks on the Penitentiary, &c," *Virginia Evangelical & Literary Magazine*, 1 (December 1818), 553; "Thoughts on the Importance and Improvement of Common Schools," *Christian Spectator*, n.s., 1 (February 1827), 85. On evangelicals and prison reform, see Jennifer Graber, *Furnace of Affliction: Prisons and Religion in Antebellum America* (Chapel Hill: University of North Carolina Press, 2011).

9. "On Mercy," *Piscataqua Evangelical Magazine*, 2 (September 1806), 181; "Liberty, No, LIV," *Herald of Gospel Liberty*, April 15, 1814, 585–586.

10. Finney, *Sermons on Gospel Themes*, 352, 354; "The Practice of Bearing Arms," *Western Christian Advocate*, March 13, 1835, 184; "New-York Peace Society," *Christian Spectator*, 1 (April 1819), 210.

11. On mid-twentieth-century attempts to politicize evangelicals, see two excellent studies: Darren Dochuck, *From Bible Belt to Sunbelt: Plain-Folk Religion, Grassroots Politics, and the Rise of Evangelical Conservatism* (New York: W. W. Norton, 2010); and Daniel Williams, *God's Own Party: The Making of the Christian Right* (New York: Oxford University Press, 2010).

12. I have written about Don Thompson and *A Thief in the Night* in Randall Balmer, *Mine Eyes Have Seen the Glory: A Journey into the Evangelical Subculture in America*, 4th ed. (New York: Oxford University Press, 2006), chap. 3. Some evangelicals make a distinction between the "second coming" and the "rapture"; premillennialists generally understand the two as synonymous, or at least coterminous.

13. Quoted in David R. Swartz, *Moral Minority: The Evangelical Left in an Age of Conservatism* (Philadelphia: University of Pennsylvania Press, 2012), 268. The following year, Nancy A. Hardesty, who taught in the English department at Trinity College, together with Letha Scanzoni, published a kind of manifesto of evangelical feminism: Letha Scanzoni and Nancy Hardesty, *All We're Meant to Be: A Biblical Approach to Women's Liberation* (Waco, Tex.: Word Books, 1974).

14. For "the least of these," see Matthew 25:45, New Revised Standard Version (hereafter NRSV).

15. Jimmy Carter, *Our Endangered Values: America's Moral Crisis* (New York: Simon & Schuster, 2005), 57; Jimmy Carter, "Prayer and the Civic Religion," *New York Times*, December 24, 1996, A11.

16. For a narrative of the energy crises of the 1970s, see Jay Hakes, *A Declaration of Energy Independence: How Freedom from Foreign Oil Can Improve National Security,*

Our Economy, and the Environment (Hoboken, N.J.: John Wiley & Sons, 2008), 24–70. On Carter's effectiveness in office, some scholars take a contrary view, arguing that he was indeed quite adept at politicking; see, for example, Scott A. Frisch and Sean Q. Kelly, *Jimmy Carter and the Water Wars* (Amherst, N.Y.: Cambria Press, 2008). The rumors of the president's keeping of the White House tennis court log were so pervasive that Carter felt obliged to deny the story in an interview midway through his presidency; see Bill Moyers, "Interview with the President, Nov. 13, 1978," in *Conversations with Carter*, ed. Don Richardson (Boulder, Colo.: Lynne Rienner, 1998), 163. A counterargument for micro-management, however, might be Carter's diary entry for July 18, 1977: "I discovered that Prime Minister Begin wants a full kosher meal in the White House Tuesday night, and I authorized it to be prepared." Jimmy Carter, *White House Diary* (New York: Farrar, Straus and Giroux, 2010), 71.

17. "For all those whose cares have been our concern, the work goes on, the cause endures," Kennedy declared in his valedictory at the convention, "the hope still lives, and the dream shall never die." Quoted in Jon Keller, "The Guy Behind the Guy," *Boston Magazine*, July 2004.

18. Jimmy Carter, *Through the Year with Jimmy Carter: 366 Daily Meditations from the 39th President* (Grand Rapids, Mich.: Zondervan, 2011), 199, 217.

19. See, for example, Samuel G. Freedman, "Help from Evangelicals (Without Evangelizing) Meets the Needs of an Oregon Public School," *New York Times*, August 9, 2013.

20. See Randy Sanders, "'The Sad Duty of Politics': Jimmy Carter and the Issue of Race in His 1970 Gubernatorial Campaign," *Georgia Historical Quarterly*, 76 (Fall 1992), 612–638.

21. Jimmy Carter, *Bible Study with Jimmy Carter: Leading a Worthy Life*, 4 CDs (New York: Simon & Schuster, 2007), disc 2, track 13.

22. I count *The Carpenter's Apprentice* as more of a compendium than a religious or spiritual biography: Dan Ariail and Cheryl Heckler-Feltz, *The Carpenter's Apprentice: The Spiritual Biography of Jimmy Carter* (Grand Rapids, Mich.: Zondervan, 1996).

Chapter One: The Household of Faith

1. Jimmy Carter, *Why Not the Best? The First Fifty Years* (Fayetteville: University of Arkansas Press, 1996), 28.

2. Jimmy Carter, *A Remarkable Mother* (New York: Simon & Schuster, 2008), 15–16, 19–20. The biblical reference to the Plains of Dura is Daniel 3.

3. Ibid., 23; E. Stanly Godbold Jr., *Jimmy and Rosalynn Carter: The Georgia Years, 1924–1974* (New York: Oxford University Press, 2010), 17.

4. Ibid., 9; Garry Wills, "The Plains Truth: An Inquiry into the Shaping of Jimmy Carter," *Atlantic Monthly*, June 1976, 49.

5. Jimmy Carter, *An Hour Before Daylight: Memories of a Rural Boyhood* (New York: Simon & Schuster, 2001), 15.

6. Ibid., 14–15, 70.

7. Quoted in ibid., 60.

8. Ibid., 75, 76; quoted in Godbold, *Jimmy and Rosalynn Carter*, 28.

9. Carter, *An Hour Before Daylight*, 219.

10. Peter G. Bourne, *Jimmy Carter: A Comprehensive Biography from Plains to Post-presidency* (New York: Scribner, 1997), 33–34, 38–39, 41. The slogan for Coleman's book club was "Readers Make Leaders." Carter's reading prowess caught the attention of reporters during the 1976 campaign; see Hugh Sidey, "A Man Among Old Friends," *Time*, September 6, 1976.

11. Carter, *Why Not the Best?*, 10; "*Living Faith*, Dec. 19, 1996," in *Conversations with Carter*, ed. Don Richardson (Boulder, Colo.: Lynne Rienner, 1998), 304.

12. Jimmy Carter, *Through the Year with Jimmy Carter: 366 Daily Meditations from the 39th President* (Grand Rapids, Mich.: Zondervan, 2011), 330.

13. Carter, *An Hour Before Daylight*, 221–222; Godbold, *Jimmy and Rosalynn Carter*, 15; quoted in David Kucharsky, "The Man from Plains," *Christianity Today*, November 19, 1976, 49; James Wooten, *Dasher: The Roots and the Rising of Jimmy Carter* (New York: Summit Books, 1978), 278; Jimmy Carter, interview with the author, Plains, Ga., June 2, 2013. The Baptist practice of scheduling revivals, also known as "homecoming" in some congregations, belies the claim on the part of some Southern Baptist leaders in recent years that Baptists are Calvinist (or Reformed) in theology. Calvinist theologians, such as Jonathan Edwards or even John Calvin himself, would recoil at the notion that a revival could be scheduled. Revivals, in Calvinist theology, represent a gracious visitation of the Holy Spirit, utterly unplanned and unscripted; in Edwards's words, they are "a surprising work of God."

14. Jimmy Carter, *Bible Study with Jimmy Carter: Measuring Our Success*, 5 CDs (New York: Simon & Schuster, 2007), disc 5, track 8.

15. Carter, *Why Not the Best?*, 34; Carter, *An Hour Before Daylight*, 230; Carter, interview with the author.

16. Godbold, *Jimmy and Rosalynn Carter*, 17; Carter, *Remarkable Mother*, 78, 81. On the reconstruction of southern memory, see Jonathan Sokol, *There Goes My Everything: White Southerners in the Age of Civil Rights, 1945–1975* (New York: Alfred A. Knopf, 2006).

17. Carter, *Remarkable Mother*, 41.

18. Carter, *Remarkable Mother*, 41; Jimmy Carter, *Bible Study: Measuring Our Success*, disc 1, track 10; Galatians 3:28 (New International Version); Jimmy Carter, *Bible Study with Jimmy Carter: Leading a Worthy Life*, 4 CDs (New York: Simon & Schuster, 2007), disc 2, track 10.

19. Quoted in Patrick Anderson, *Electing Jimmy Carter: The Campaign of 1976* (Baton Rouge: Louisiana State University Press, 1994), 10–11.

20. Bourne, *Jimmy Carter*, 44.

21. Quoted in Godbold, *Jimmy and Rosalynn Carter*, 54; quoted in Robert J. Schneller Jr., *Breaking the Color Barrier: The U.S. Naval Academy's First Midshipmen and the Struggle for Racial Equality* (New York: New York University Press, 2005), 217; Carter, *Bible Study: Measuring Our Success*, disc 5, track 8.

22. Quoted in Douglas Brinkley, *The Unfinished Presidency: Jimmy Carter's Journey Beyond the White House* (New York: Viking, 1998), 53; Godbold, *Jimmy and Rosalynn Carter*, 54; Carter, *Bible Study with Jimmy Carter: Measuring Our Success*, disc 1, track 8. On Carter's lifetime of teaching Sunday school, see Jimmy Carter, "Agape, Justice, and American Foreign Policy," *Reformed Journal*, April 1986, 15.

23. Jimmy Carter, *Turning Point: A Candidate, a State, and a Nation Come of Age* (New York: Times Books, 1992), 16.

24. Godbold, *Jimmy and Rosalynn Carter*, 57, 58, 60; Carter, *Bible Study with Jimmy Carter: Measuring Our Success*, disc 5, track 2.

25. Godbold, *Jimmy and Rosalynn Carter*, 61–62.

26. Carter, *Why Not the Best?*, 47–48.

27. Carter, *Turning Point*, 17–18; Godbold, *Jimmy and Rosalynn Carter*, 66. Godbold has this event occurring in Nassau rather than Jamaica.

28. Godbold, *Jimmy and Rosalynn Carter*, 67; Carter, *Why Not the Best?*, 57, 55; cf. Bill Moyers, "A Talk with Carter, May 16, 1976," in *Conversations with Carter*, ed. Don Richardson (Boulder, Colo.: Lynne Rienner, 1998), 10.

29. Carter, *Why Not the Best?*, 58; Godbold, *Jimmy and Rosalynn Carter*, 68.

30. Rosalynn Carter, *First Lady from Plains* (Boston: Houghton Mifflin, 1984), 35; Carter, *Why Not the Best?*, 58.

31. Carter, *Why Not the Best?*, 62; Godbold, *Jimmy and Rosalynn Carter*, 75.

32. Carter, *Turning Point*, 19; Carter, *Why Not the Best?*, 59; Rosalynn Carter, *First Lady from Plains*, 37.

33. Godbold, *Jimmy and Rosalynn Carter*, 70–71; Carter, *Why Not the Best?*, 58.

34. Godbold, *Jimmy and Rosalynn Carter*, 72–73.

35. Carter, *Turning Point*, 20; Godbold, *Jimmy and Rosalynn Carter*, 82–83. Godbold pegged the Carters' first-year profit at less than two hundred dollars.

36. Carter, interview with the author. In the course of my interview with Carter, he recounted in detail the fate of all six families who were considered racial moderates.

37. Carter, *Why Not the Best?*, 65; Carter, *Turning Point*, 42.

38. Quoted in Clayborne Carson, David J. Garrow, Bill Kovach, and Carol Polsgrove, eds., *Reporting Civil Rights: American Journalism, 1941–1963* (New York: Library of America, 2003), 272.

39. Carter, *Why Not the Best?*, 66.

40. Carter, *Turning Point*, 23.

Chapter Two: From Peanuts to Politics

1. Jimmy Carter, *Turning Point: A Candidate, a State, and a Nation Come of Age* (New York: Times Books, 1992), 45; Scott E. Buchanan, s.v. "County Unit System," *New Georgia Encyclopedia* (Athens: University of Georgia Press, 2005).

2. Carter, *Turning Point*, 48–49.

3. E. Stanly Godbold Jr., *Jimmy and Rosalynn Carter: The Georgia Years, 1924–1974* (New York: Oxford University Press, 2010), 89–90.

4. Carter, *Turning Point*, 21, 24–25; Godbold, *Jimmy and Rosalynn Carter*, 88. There is some dispute about the relationship of Carter to Koinonia. Clarence Jordan's widow, Florence, told a reporter in 1976: "I have to say I'm sorry, but I don't even know the man. I've never met him, and we've been living down the road for 34 years. People came here from all over the world, but he hasn't come seven miles." Another person associated with Koinonia, however, told of the intervention and the kindness of the Carters toward his family when their son was dying of leukemia. Robert Scheer, "Jimmy, We Hardly Know Y'all," *Playboy*, November 1976, 186.

5. Carter, *Turning Point*, 59.

6. Ibid., 48–49. Carter later marveled at his own callousness in not consulting Rosalynn about his prospective run for political office; he cited the incident as evidence of changed sensibilities surrounding husbands and wives, men and women—changes he welcomed. The fact that he didn't consult with Rosalynn about running for office, Carter told me in 2013, "is almost inconceivable to me now." Jimmy Carter, interview with the author, Plains, Ga., June 2, 2013.

7. Carter, *Turning Point*, 62.

8. Ibid., 63.

9. Ibid., 76, 88.

10. Godbold, *Jimmy and Rosalynn Carter*, 97.

11. Carter, *Turning Point*, 100.

12. Ibid.,129.

13. Godbold, *Jimmy and Rosalynn Carter*, 101.

14. Jimmy Carter, *Why Not the Best? The First Fifty Years* (Fayetteville: University of Arkansas Press, 1996), 87, 92.

15. Godbold, *Jimmy and Rosalynn Carter*, 131; Jimmy Carter, *Bible Study with Jimmy Carter: Leading a Worthy Life*, 4 CDs (New York: Simon & Schuster, 2007), disc 4, track 9.

16. Carter, *Why Not the Best?*, 94.

17. Rosalynn Carter, *First Lady from Plains* (Boston: Houghton Mifflin, 1984), 53.

18. Godbold, *Jimmy and Rosalynn Carter*, 107.

19. Carter, *Why Not the Best?*, 89; Godbold, *Jimmy and Rosalynn Carter*, 106–107, 108. In 2013, looking back on his stint in the Georgia senate, Carter recalled, "I went up with idealistic dreams I'd somehow preserve the public school system"; quoted in Bill Torpy, "The Class of '63," *Atlanta Journal and Constitution*, March 14, 2013. On the Baptist principles of liberty of conscience and separation of church and state, see Randall Balmer, *Blessed Assurance: A History of Evangelicalism in America* (Boston: Beacon Press, 1999), chap. 2; Randall Balmer, *Thy Kingdom Come: How the Religious Right Distorts the Faith and Threatens America* (New York: Basic Books, 2006), chap. 2.

20. Godbold, *Jimmy and Rosalynn Carter*, 106–107.

21. Ibid., 104; Lyndon B. Johnson: "Address Before a Joint Session of the Congress," November 27, 1963, online by Gerhard Peters and John T. Woolley, *The American Presi-*

dency Project, http://www.presidency.ucsb.edu/ws/?pid=25988 (accessed August 30, 2013).

22. Rosalynn Carter, *First Lady from Plains*, 57; Godbold, *Jimmy and Rosalynn Carter*, 110–111; quoted in Peter G. Bourne, *Jimmy Carter: A Comprehensive Biography from Plains to Postpresidency* (New York: Scribner, 1997), 152.

23. Quoted in Godbold, *Jimmy and Rosalynn Carter*, 117.

24. Carter, *Why Not the Best?*, 66–67.

25. Ibid., 67; Rosalynn Carter, *First Lady from Plains*, 56; quoted in Patrick Anderson, *Electing Jimmy Carter: The Campaign of 1976* (Baton Rouge: Louisiana State University Press, 1994), 13.

26. Carter, *Why Not the Best?*, 97, 98; quoted in Godbold, *Jimmy and Rosalynn Carter*, 115, 119; Rosalynn Carter, *First Lady from Plains*, 58–59.

27. Godbold, *Jimmy and Rosalynn Carter*, 117.

28. Richard Severo, "Lester Maddox, Whites-Only Restaurateur and Georgia Governor, Dies at 87," *New York Times*, June 25, 2003; Roy Reed, "Arnall Beaten by Segregationist in Georgia's Governor Primary," *New York Times*, September 29, 1966.

29. Reed, "Arnall Beaten by Segregationist," *New York Times*, September 29, 1966.

30. Jimmy Carter, *Bible Study with Jimmy Carter: Bringing Peace to a Changing World*, 4 CDs (New York: Simon & Schuster, 2007), disc 3, track 7; Jimmy Carter, *An Hour Before Daylight: Memories of a Rural Boyhood* (New York: Simon & Schuster, 2001), 264. Carter told me that he was "very disillusioned with God" (Carter, interview with the author).

31. Godbold, *Jimmy and Rosalynn Carter*, 126–127; quoted in Bruce Mazlish and Edwin Diamond, *Jimmy Carter: An Interpretive Biography* (New York: Simon & Schuster, 1979), 151.

32. Carter, *Why Not the Best?*, 98–99; quoted in Mazlish and Diamond, *Jimmy Carter*, 153.

33. Jimmy Carter, *A Remarkable Mother* (New York: Simon & Schuster, 2008), 29.

34. Quoted in Mazlish and Diamond, *Jimmy Carter*, 153–154; Jules Witcover, *Marathon: The Pursuit of the Presidency* (New York: Viking Press, 1977), 271; Carter, *An Hour Before Daylight*, 264; Carter, interview with the author.

35. Quoted in David Kucharsky, *The Man from Plains: The Mind and Spirit of Jimmy Carter* (London: Collins, 1977), 46.

36. "Interview with Ruth Carter Stapleton: The President's Evangelist Sister Talks About 'The Jimmy I Know,'" *U.S. News & World Report*, September 18, 1978, 24–26; quoted in Dan Ariail and Cheryl Heckler-Feltz, *The Carpenter's Apprentice: The Spiritual Biography of Jimmy Carter* (Grand Rapids, Mich.: Zondervan, 1996), 47. For a biographical sketch of Ruth Carter Stapleton, which includes an account of her encounter with her brother following the 1966 election, see Kenneth L. Woodward, "Sister Ruth," *Newsweek*, July 17, 1978, 58ff.

37. Ariail and Heckler-Feltz, *Carpenter's Apprentice*, 47. For an excellent analysis of Carter's religious coordinates, see E. Brooks Holifield, "The Three Strands of Jimmy

Carter's Religion," *New Republic*, June 5, 1976, 15–17. Holifield's essay appeared during the course of the 1976 presidential campaign.

38. Carter, *Why Not the Best?*, 100; quoted in Mazlish and Diamond, *Jimmy Carter*, 154.

39. Jimmy Carter, *Sources of Strength: Meditations on Scripture for a Living Faith* (New York: Times Books, 1997), 4; Jimmy Carter, "The Task of Evangelism," *Mennonite*, February 28, 1989, 75; Carter, *Bible Study: Leading a Worthy Life*, disc 3, track 14. I've taken Cruz's quotation from Carter's recounting of the experience in Jimmy Carter, *Sources of Strength: Meditations on Scripture for a Living Faith* (New York: Times Books, 1997), xvii.

40. Carter, *Bible Study: Leading a Worthy Life*, disc 3, track 14.

41. Carter, *Why Not the Best?*, 101.

42. Quoted in Dan T. Carter, *The Politics of Rage: George Wallace, the Origins of the New Conservatism, and the Transformation of American Politics* (New York: Simon & Schuster, 1995), 96.

43. Godbold, *Jimmy and Rosalynn Carter*, 135; Randy Sanders, "'The Sad Duty of Politics': Jimmy Carter and the Issue of Race in His 1970 Gubernatorial Campaign," *Georgia Historical Quarterly*, 76 (Fall 1992), 614–615; Nancy Gibbs and Michael Duffy, *The Preacher and the Presidents: Billy Graham in the White House* (New York: Center Street, 2007), 244.

44. Godbold, *Jimmy and Rosalynn Carter*, 138.

45. Sanders, "'Sad Duty of Politics,'" 616–617; Carter, *Why Not the Best?*, 102–103.

46. W. Van Loan, "Recommendations and Comments for the Jimmy Carter Campaign for Governor," February 12, 1970, Carter Family Papers, State Senate Papers, 1962–1967, Box 59, Jimmy Carter Library.

47. Sanders, "'Sad Duty of Politics,'" 618, 625, 622.

48. Ibid., 629, 627, 628.

49. Ibid., 631, 626; Christopher Allen Huff, s.v. "Roy V. Harris (1895–1985)," *New Georgia Encyclopedia* (Athens: University of Georgia Press, 2011).

50. Bruce Galphin, "Peanut Farmer Stuns Experts to Lead Ga. Governor's Race," *Washington Post*, September 11, 1970, A2; Sanders, "'Sad Duty of Politics,'" 630, 631, 633; quoted in Bill Torpy, "The Class of '63," *Atlanta Journal and Constitution*, March 14, 2013. See also Carl Sanders, interviewed by James F. Cook, August 5 and 12, 1986, P1986–06, Series A: Georgia Governors, Georgia Government Documentation Project, Special Collections and Archives, Georgia State University Library, Atlanta, 67–68.

51. Quoted in James Wooten, *Dasher: The Roots and the Rising of Jimmy Carter* (New York: Summit Books, 1978), 293.

52. Quoted in Marshall Frady, *Southerners: A Journalist's Odyssey* (New York: New American Library, 1980), 343; quoted in Wooten, *Dasher*, 293; Sanders, "'Sad Duty of Politics,'" 635–636, quoted on 628.

Chapter Three: New South Governor

1. Jimmy Carter, *Why Not the Best? The First Fifty Years* (Fayetteville: University of Arkansas Press, 1996), 106.

2. Quoted in James Wooten, *Dasher: The Roots and the Rising of Jimmy Carter* (New York: Summit Books, 1978), 295; E. Stanly Godbold Jr., *Jimmy and Rosalynn Carter: The Georgia Years, 1924–1974* (New York: Oxford University Press, 2010), 170.

3. Quoted in Wooten, *Dasher*, 299; quoted in Carter, *Why Not the Best?*, 106.

4. Jon Nordheimer, "New Governor of Georgia Urges End of Racial Bias," *New York Times*, January 13, 1971.

5. "New Day A'Coming in the South," *Time*, May 31, 1971.

6. "Playboy Interview: Jimmy Carter," *Playboy*, November 1976, 66; Carter, *Why Not the Best?*, 107.

7. Matthew 25:35–36; Carter, *Why Not the Best?*, 108; Godbold, *Jimmy and Rosalynn Carter*, 203, 209.

8. Howell Raines, "'One of Us': King Portrait Is a First at Capitol," *Atlanta Constitution*, February 18, 1974, A1, A14; quoted in Godbold, *Jimmy and Rosalynn Carter*, 209; Timothy Crimmins and Anne H. Farrisee, *Democracy Restored: A History of the Georgia State Capitol* (Athens: University of Georgia Press, 2007), 150–151.

9. Godbold, *Jimmy and Rosalynn Carter*, 175; Gary M. Fink, s.v. "Jimmy Carter (b. 1924)," *New Georgia Encyclopedia* (Athens: University of Georgia Press, 2008); quoted in Patrick Anderson, *Electing Jimmy Carter: The Campaign of 1976* (Baton Rouge: Louisiana State University Press, 1994), 93. On Carter's term as governor, especially his efforts to reorganize state government, see Gary M. Fink, *Prelude to the Presidency: The Political Character and Legislative Leadership Style of Governor Jimmy Carter* (Westport, Conn.: Greenwood Press, 1980).

10. Godbold, *Jimmy and Rosalynn Carter*, 178.

11. Ibid., 98.

12. Ibid., 123; E. R. Lanier, s.v. "Bert Lance (b. 1931)," *New Georgia Encyclopedia* (Athens: University of Georgia Press, 2004).

13. Edward A. Hatfield, s.v. "Hamilton Jordan (1944–2008)," *New Georgia Encyclopedia*, 2008.

14. Wooten, *Dasher*, 284–285.

15. Rosalynn Carter, *First Lady from Plains* (Boston: Houghton Mifflin, 1984), 107; Carter, *Why Not the Best?*, 137.

16. *Journal of the 1972 General Conference of the United Methodist Church*, vol. 1, ed. John L. Schreiber, 450.

17. Ibid.

18. Ibid.

19. Ibid., 451–452. See also David Kucharsky, *The Man from Plains: The Mind and Spirit of Jimmy Carter* (London: Collins, 1977), 42.

20. *Journal of the 1972 General Conference*, 452–453.

21. Ibid., 453.

22. Quoted in Kucharsky, *Man from Plains*, 67.

23. Billy Graham, *Just As I Am: The Autobiography of Billy Graham* (San Francisco: HarperSanFrancisco, 1997), 492.

24. Quoted in Kucharsky, *Man from Plains*, 68; quoted in Jules Witcover, *Marathon: The Pursuit of the Presidency, 1972–1976* (New York: Viking Press, 1977), 271.

25. Quoted in Godbold, *Jimmy and Rosalynn Carter*, 233.

26. Ibid., 235. In retrospect, given the troubles attending the Eagleton nomination, when his history of mental illness and shock treatments came to light, McGovern would have done well to choose Carter as his running mate.

27. Quoted in Hatfield, s.v. "Hamilton Jordan," *New Georgia Encyclopedia*; Douglas Brinkley, introduction to *Why Not the Best? The First Fifty Years*, by Jimmy Carter (Fayetteville: University of Arkansas Press, 1996), xi; "Memorandum," November 4, 1972, Hamilton Jordan to Jimmy Carter, Carter Center. "Chappaquiddick" refers to an incident that took place in the early morning hours of July 19, 1969, when the automobile Kennedy was driving veered off of a bridge and into a tidal channel on Chappaquiddick Island, Massachusetts. Kennedy's companion, Mary Jo Kopechne (not the senator's wife), drowned, despite Kennedy's apparent efforts to rescue her. Kennedy left the scene and did not report the incident to authorities until many hours later. He was convicted of causing injury and leaving the scene of an accident. He received a suspended jail sentence, but the incident, together with what was widely viewed as judicial leniency, badly damaged his reputation.

28. "Memorandum," November 4, 1972, Hamilton Jordan to Jimmy Carter, Carter Center.

29. Ibid.

30. Quoted in David R. Swartz, *Moral Minority: The Evangelical Left in an Age of Conservativism* (Philadelphia: University of Pennsylvania Press, 2012), 172.

31. This account of McGovern's visit to Wheaton is based on my own recollection. I was a first-year student at Trinity College in nearby Deerfield, Illinois, and I persuaded several of my classmates to accompany me to Edman Chapel that morning to hear McGovern. Although some accounts of McGovern's visit say that he was warmly received by the students that day, I can assure you that is not at all my recollection of the event, an event seared in my memory. For a contrary (secondary) narrative, see Swartz, *Moral Minority*, 176.

32. Quoted in Swartz, *Moral Minority*, 178.

33. Quoted in ibid., 178, 179; Jim Wallis, interview with the author, Washington, D.C., December 6, 2012. Names of the signatories appear in Swartz, *Moral Minority*, 268–269.

34. The text of the Chicago Declaration of Evangelical Social Concern, adopted November 25, 1973, is widely available on the web. It also appears as an appendix in Swartz, *Moral Minority*, 267–269.

35. Axel E. Schäfer, *Countercultural Conservatives: American Evangelicalism from the Postwar Revival to the New Christian Right* (Madison: University of Wisconsin Press, 2011), 83–86. On the Chicago gathering, see also David R. Swartz, "Identity Politics and the Fragmenting of the 1970s Evangelical Left," *Religion and American Culture: A Journal of Interpretation*, 21 (Winter 2011), 81–120. Swartz's focus is primarily the inability of the principals to hold together the coalition that produced the Chicago Declaration. Axel R. Schäfer reaches much the same conclusion: Schäfer, *Countercultural Conservatives*, 85–90.

36. Schäfer, *Countercultural Conservatives*, 78.

37. Swartz makes this point nicely in *Moral Minority*, 178. Some excellent recent scholarship has argued that evangelicals were indeed politically active in the middle decades of the twentieth century. See Darren Dochuck, *From Bible Belt to Sun Belt: Plain-Folk Religion, Grassroots Politics, and the Rise of Evangelical Conservatism* (New York: W. W. Norton, 2011) and Daniel K. Williams, *God's Own Party: The Making of the Christian Right* (New York: Oxford University Press, 2010). For a survey of evangelicals' nineteenth-century activism among urban-dwellers, see Norris A. Magnuson, *Salvation in the Slums: Evangelical Social Work, 1875–1920* (Metuchen, N.J.: Scarecrow Press, 1977).

38. See, for example, Mark O. Hatfield, "Finding the Energy to Continue: The Mandates of Stewardship," *Christianity Today*, February 8, 1980, 20–24; S. Thomas Niccolls, "Human Rights: A Concern of the Righteous," *Christianity Today*, May 25, 1979, 22–27; Ronald J. Sider, "Evangelism or Social Justice: Eliminating the Options," *Christianity Today*, October 8, 1976, 26–29; Frank E. Gaebelein, "Challenging Christians to the Simple Life," *Christianity Today*, September 21, 1979, 22–26; George Sweeting, "Our Response to the Poor: A Barometer of Belief," *Christianity Today*, September 5, 1980, 22–24. Liberal evangelicalism, however, clearly had its limits in the magazine. Although some of the articles addressed "edgy" matters, the editorial slant of the magazine continued to point to the right. A 1978 editorial about world hunger, for example, essentially placed the responsibility on Third World nations. "Rather than blame their poverty on others," the editorial concluded, "poor countries should take immediate and continuing steps to stabilize their populations" ("What Is to be Done about World Hunger?," editorial in *Christianity Today*, February 24, 1978, 20).

39. Quoted in Swartz, *Moral Minority*, 268.

40. Press release, "Address of Senator Edward M. Kennedy, Law Day Exercises, University of Georgia School of Law, Athens, Georgia, May 4, 1974," Office of Senator Edward M. Kennedy of Massachusetts.

41. Jimmy Carter, "A Message on Justice," Law Day Address at the University of Georgia, May 4, 1974, Carter Center.

42. Ibid.

43. Ibid.

44. Ibid.

45. Hunter S. Thompson, *Fear and Loathing at Rolling Stone: The Essential Writing of Hunter S. Thompson*, ed. Jann Wenner (New York: Simon & Schuster, 2011), 373, 378.

46. Quoted in Godbold, *Jimmy and Rosalynn Carter*, 264.

Chapter Four: He Came unto His Own

1. E. Stanly Godbold Jr., *Jimmy and Rosalynn Carter: The Georgia Years, 1924–1974* (New York: Oxford University Press, 2010), 241; the reference is to 1 Corinthians 14:8, King James Version (hereafter KJV).

2. Jimmy Carter, *Why Not the Best? The First Fifty Years* (Fayetteville: University of Arkansas Press, 1996), 123.

3. Jimmy Carter, "Address Announcing Candidacy for the Democratic Presidential Nomination at the National Press Club in Washington, D.C.," December 12, 1974, online by Gerhard Peters and John T. Woolley, *The American Presidency Project*, http://www.presidency.ucsb.edu/ws/?pid=77821.

4. Godbold, *Jimmy and Rosalynn Carter*, 271; David S. Broder, "Georgia Governor Declares '76 Bid," *Washington Post*, December 13, 1974, A1, A9; Andrew Young quoted in *American Experience: Jimmy Carter*, produced by Adriana Bosch, WGBH-Boston, 2002.

5. Thomas J. Fitzgerald, "Store that Made History Hears Time's Clock Ticking," *Bergen* (N.J.) *Record*, February 21, 1996, A7.

6. *American Experience: Jimmy Carter*; quoted in Marshall Frady, *Southerners: A Journalist's Odyssey* (New York: New American Library, 1980), 344. On another occasion, Carter told a relative, "I can will myself to sleep until ten-thirty and get my ass beat, or I can will myself to get up at six o'clock and become President of the United States" (ibid., 354) On Carter's abilities as a retail candidate, see Hamilton Jordan's comments at a conference on Jimmy Carter's presidency at Hofstra University: "Discussant: Hamilton Jordan," in *The Presidency and Domestic Policies of Jimmy Carter*, ed. Herbert D. Rosenbaum and Alexej Ugrinsky (Westport, Conn.: Greenwood Press, 1994), 163. Jordan called Jimmy and Rosalynn Carter "the two most effective campaigners that I have ever seen" (ibid.).

7. David Kucharsky, "The Man from Plains," *Christianity Today*, November 19, 1976, 71; memorandum, Tim Kraft to Hamilton Jordan, August 28, 1975, Jimmy Carter Library; Nancy Gibbs and Michael Duffy, *The Preacher and the Presidents: Billy Graham in the White House* (New York: Center Street, 2007), 245; Jules Witcover, *Marathon: The Pursuit of the Presidency, 1972–1976* (New York: Viking Press, 1977), 201; R. W. Apple Jr., "Carter Appears to Hold a Solid Lead as the Campaign's First Test Approaches," *New York Times*, October 27, 1975.

8. R. W. Apple Jr., "Carter Defeats Bayh by 2-to-1 in Iowa Vote; Many Uncommitted," *New York Times*, January 20, 1976, 1, 20.

9. Julian E. Zelizer, *Jimmy Carter* (New York: Times Books, 2010), 36; quoted in James Wooten, *Dasher: The Roots and the Rise of Jimmy Carter* (New York: Summit Books, 1978), 354; John Kifner, "Carter Campaigns in New Hampshire," *New York Times*, January 21, 1976.

10. Witcover, *Marathon*, 255; Warren Brown, "Carter's Special Appeal Among Blacks: Belief in Georgian Linked to His Charm, Embrace of Religion," *Washington Post*, June 20, 1976, 10. Among others, Marshall Frady sees Wallace as having paved the way for Carter's presidential bid; see Marshall Frady, *Southerners: A Journalist's Odyssey* (New York: New American Library, 1980), 337–338. Patrick Anderson, a campaign aide, wrote: "It was imperative that Carter defeat George Wallace in the Florida primary and thus demonstrate that he, not the Alabama segregationist, spoke for the South." Ander-

son, *Electing Jimmy Carter: The Campaign of 1976* (Baton Rouge: Louisiana State University Press, 1994), 6.

11. Gibbs and Duffy, *Preacher and the Presidents*, 241–242; Witcover, *Marathon*, 271.

12. Quoted in Randall Balmer, *God in the White House: How Faith Shaped the Presidency from John F. Kennedy to George W. Bush* (San Francisco: HarperOne, 2008), 180. Kennedy's entire speech before the Houston ministers is reprinted in ibid., appendix 1.

13. Kenneth A. Briggs, "Carter's Evangelism Putting Religion into Politics for First Time Since '60," *New York Times*, April 11, 1976; quoted in Kenneth E. Morris, "Religion and the Presidency of Jimmy Carter," in *Religion and the American Presidency: George Washington to George W. Bush with Commentary and Primary Sources*, ed. Gastón Espinosa (New York: Columbia University Press, 2009), 290. In a 1996 op-ed in the *New York Times*, Carter reflected on the Winston-Salem event: "From then until the end of the campaign, national reporters made a big deal of what seemed natural to me and my hosts, making clear to me that injecting religion into politics was a mistake" (Jimmy Carter, "Prayer and the Civil Religion," *New York Times*, December 24, 1996, A11).

14. Witcover, *Marathon*, 272–273; quoted in Anderson, *Electing Jimmy Carter*, 37.

15. News Release, United Methodist Communications, June 8, 1976.

16. Bill Moyers, "A Talk with Carter, May 16, 1976," in *Conversations with Carter*, ed. Don Richardson (Boulder, Colo.: Lynne Rienner, 1998), 9, 11, 14, 12, 13. On Carter's use of Niebuhr and his general posture about the relationship between religion and politics, see James S. Wolfe, "Exclusion, Fusion, or Dialogue: How Should Religion and Politics Relate?," *Journal of Church and State*, 89 (Winter 1980), 89–105.

17. E. Brooks Holifield, "The Three Strands of Jimmy Carter's Religion," *New Republic*, June 5, 1976, 15–17; e-mail correspondence with the author, March 28, 2013. Years later, after Carter left office and became a visiting professor at Emory, Carter and Holifield were on a panel together. Holifield asked Carter to sign the *New Republic* article, and Carter, according to Holifield, remarked that the campaign "had been pleased to see the article because of the misunderstandings and distrust of his religious views in certain sections of the country" (e-mail to the author, March 28, 2013).

18. Bob Allen, "Jimmy Carter Credits Jimmy Allen for Election," http://abpnews.com /archives/item/5369-jimmy-carter-credits-jimmy-allen-for-election#.URuXG6WMwZI (accessed February 13, 2013); Jimmy Carter, foreword to *Loving Beyond Your Theology: The Life and Ministry of Jimmy Raymond Allen*, by Larry L. McSwain (Macon, Ga.: Mercer University Press, 2010), 11.

19. Jimmy Carter, *Keeping Faith: Memoirs of a President* (New York: Bantam Books, 1982), 35, 37; Paul Kengor, *Wreath Layer or Policy Player: The Vice President's Role in Foreign Policy* (Lanham, Md.: Lexington Books, 2000), 85; Helen Dewar, "How Minnesotan Came to be Chosen," *Washington Post*, July 16, 1976, A1, A16; quoted in Douglas Brinkley, introduction to Carter, *Why Not the Best?*, xix. After the election, Mondale drafted a seven-page memorandum to Carter, outlining the vice president–elect's expansive vision of his responsibilities, including a role for his wife, Joan, with the national

Foundation on the Arts and the Humanities. Memorandum, Walter F. Mondale to Jimmy Carter, December 9, 1976, Walter F. Mondale Papers, Minnesota Historical Society.

20. Anderson, *Electing Jimmy Carter*, 171–175.

21. Quoted in Gibbs and Duffy, *Preacher and the Presidents*, 246. The biblical reference for the "Great Commission" is Mark 16:15 (KJV); "Battling for the Blocs," *Time*, September 13, 1976, 24–25.

22. Quoted in William Martin, *With God on Our Side: The Rise of the Religious Right in America* (New York: Broadway Books, 1996), 157; Billy James Hargis, "Jimmy Carter— Miracle Man or Super Politician," *Christian Crusade Weekly*, August 8, 1976. Bailey Smith would abandon Carter for Reagan four years later.

23. Albert J. Menendez, "Will Evangelicals Swing the Election?," *Christianity Today*, June 18, 1976, 32–33; Nicholas Wolterstorff, "Carter's Religion," *Reformed Journal*, September 1976, 4–5. Wolterstorff would later move from Calvin College to Yale Divinity School (1989).

24. R. W. Apple Jr., "A Quick Victory," *New York Times*, July 15, 1976.

25. Jimmy Carter, "Our Nation's Past and Future: Address Accepting the Presidential Nomination at the Democratic National Convention in New York City," July 15, 1976, online by Gerhard Peters and John T. Woolley, *The American Presidency Project*, http://www.presidency.ucsb.edu/ws/?pid=77821 (accessed November 1, 2013); "Poll Shows Carter Leads; Best Margin in 40 Years," *New York Times*, July 16, 1976.

26. "The Georgia Deacon's Day," *Time*, August 2, 1976.

27. Quoted in "Religion and the Presidency of Jimmy Carter," in *Religion and the American Presidency*, ed. Espinosa, 330.

28. Wes Michaelson, "The Piety and Ambition of Jimmy Carter," *Sojourners*, October 1976, 15, 17, 16.

29. "Election '76: Indifference Is No Virtue," editorial in *Christianity Today*, October 22, 1976, 37–38. On the ethical dimensions of the Nixon pardon as compared with Carter's pardon of draft evaders, see Raymond F. Bulman, "Love, Power, and the Justice of the U.S. Presidential Pardons," *Journal of Church and State*, 23 (Winter 1979), 23–38.

30. Quoted in Steven P. Miller, *Billy Graham and the Rise of the Republican South* (Philadelphia: University of Pennsylvania Press, 2009), 198, 196; quoted in Gibbs and Duffy, *Preacher and the Presidents*, 249.

31. Memo (Recommended Telephone Call), Richard S. Brannon to Gerald R. Ford, September 3, 1976, folder "Graham, Billy," Richard Cheney Files, 1974–77, Box 16, Gerald R. Ford Library; note, Gerald R. Ford to Richard Cheney [September 4, 1976], folder "Graham, Billy," Richard Cheney Files, 1974–77, Box 16, Gerald R. Ford Library; Letter, Billy Graham to Gerald R. Ford, September 10, 1976, White House Central Files, Name File, Gerald R. Ford Library.

32. Campaign Strategy for President Ford 1976 [notebook], Gerald R. Ford Library. The campaign also sought to court Hispanic voters, suggesting that the Ford children could help. "Does any of the Ford family speak Spanish?," the briefing book asked.

"Maybe Jack or Susan should learn. Does the Mexican ambassador to the United States have a daughter that Jack can date?" Ibid.

33. Jim Wallis, "The Election and Cheap Grace," *Sojourners*, October 1976, 4; David Kucharsky, "The Year of the Evangelical," *Christianity Today*, October 22, 1976, 12–13. There is nothing in Kucharsky's article to suggest he knew that *Newsweek* was about to make that designation, although George Gallup Jr. used the phrase several weeks earlier; see "Religion: Counting Souls," *Time*, October 4, 1976.

34. R. W. Apple Jr., "Muskie Is Victorious in Iowa Caucuses," *New York Times*, January 26, 1972, 16; Walter O. Spitzer and Carlyle L. Saylor, eds., *Birth Control and the Christian: A Protestant Symposium on the Control of Human Reproduction* (Wheaton, Ill.: Tyndale House, 1969), 414, xxv–xxvi, xxviii.

35. Carl F. H. Henry, "Abortion: An Evangelical View," in Matthew Avery Sutton, *Jerry Falwell and the Rise of the Religious Right: A Brief History with Documents* (Boston: Bedford/St. Martin's, 2013), 95; Harold Lindsell, *The World, the Flesh, and the Devil* (Minneapolis: World Wide Publications, 1973), 100, 101. The earliest outright evangelical condemnation of abortion I have been able to find is from the executive committee of the fundamentalist group American Council of Christian Churches, dated May 17, 1971: "Therefore, the Executive Committee of the American Council of Christian Churches, meeting in Valley Forge, Pa., May 17, 1971, goes on record as being unalterably opposed to 'abortion on demand' and pleads with our legislators to consider the serious consequences in endangering life and health by granting 'abortion on demand,' and that they further recognize their God-given responsibilities to protect the sanctity of human life and re-affirm the right to life for multitudes yet unborn." Press Release, May 17, 1971, Robert H. DuVall, president, American Council of Christian Churches, Valley Forge, Pennsylvania. This is Carl McIntire's ultrafundamentalist organization.

36. Quoted in Mark Tooley, *Methodism and Politics in the Twentieth Century* (Anderson, Ind.: Bristol House, 2012), 222, 224–225; *Annual of the Southern Baptist Convention, 1972* (Nashville, Tenn.: Executive Committee, Southern Baptist Convention, 1972), 72. On the reaffirmations of the 1971 resolution, see *Annual of the Southern Baptist Convention, 1974* (Nashville, Tenn.: Executive Committee, Southern Baptist Convention, 1974), 76. The 1976 resolution was more measured, calling on "Southern Baptists and all citizens of the nation to work to change those attitudes and conditions which encourage many people to turn to abortion as a means of birth control"; but it also affirmed "our conviction about the limited role of government in dealing with matters relating to abortion, and support the right of expectant mothers to the full range of medical services and personal counseling for the preservation of life and health." *Annual of the Southern Baptist Convention, 1976* (Nashville, Tenn.: Executive Committee, Southern Baptist Convention, 1976), 58.

37. Quoted in "What Price Abortion?," *Christianity Today*, March 2, 1973, 39 [565].

38. "Abortion and the Court," *Christianity Today*, February 16, 1973, 32 [502]; quoted in "What Price Abortion?," *Christianity Today*, March 2, 1973, 39 [565]; Floyd Robertson, *United Evangelical Action*, Summer 1973, 8–11 [quotes from 11].

39. Letter [handwritten], Jimmy Carter to Caroline Putnam [Springfield, Massachusetts], October 7, 1975, Carter Family Papers, 1976 Campaign Files, Box 31, Jimmy Carter Library.

40. Form letter, Pre-Presidential 1976 Presidential Campaign, Urban Affairs Desk—Tom Tatum, Subject Files, Box 280, File: Protestants [1], Jimmy Carter Library.

41. R. W. Apple Jr., "The Catholic in Politics: From Pariah to President," *New York Times*, September 12, 1976; memorandum, Birch Bayh to Jimmy Carter, September 16, 1976, Jimmy Carter Papers—Pre-Presidential, 1976 Presidential Campaign, Issues Office—Stuart Eizenstat, Box 1, Jimmy Carter Library.

42. "'Ford Has Been a Dormant President,' Sept. 13, 1976," in *Conversations with Carter*, ed. Richardson, 21, 27.

43. "Decision '76: What Stand on Abortion?," *Christianity Today*, September 24, 1976, 54. On Carter and the Catholic vote in 1976, see Andrew S. Moore, "'Jimmy Carter's 'Catholic Problem'—Not to Mention His Protestant One": The Democratic Coalition and the Struggle for Religious Liberty in the Late 1970s," *Journal of Church and State*, 53 (Spring 2011), 183–202.

44. Wooten, *Dasher*, 365; "Playboy Interview: Jimmy Carter," *Playboy*, November 1976, 64.

45. "Playboy Interview," 84.

46. Ibid., 66, 86.

47. Ibid., 84, 66, 69.

48. Ibid., 86.

49. Matthew 5:28 (New International Version); "Playboy Interview," 86. In a 1996 interview, Carter recounted a recent book-signing at a bookstore near Harvard University. A "beautiful young woman" walked by and, in a loud voice, said, "'Mr. President, if you still have lust in your heart, I'm available.'" Carter recalled that he "turned blood red. I was so embarrassed." "*Living Faith*, Dec. 19, 1996," in *Conversations with Carter*, ed. Richardson, 315.

50. Jimmy Carter, interview with Jim Lehrer, "Debating Our Destiny," PBS website, http://www.pbs.org/newshour/debatingourdestiny/1976.html (accessed January 1, 2013); "*Living Faith*, Dec. 19, 1996," in *Conversations with Carter*, ed. Richardson, 316.

51. Albert J. Menendez, *Religion at the Polls* (Philadelphia: Westminster Press, 1977), 184; quoted in Daniel K. Williams, *God's Own Party: The Making of the Christian Right* (New York: Oxford University Press, 2012), 126; Bill Inman, "Evangelist Jones Takes Slap at Betty Ford," *Greenville Piedmont*, October 19, 1976.

52. Kenneth A. Briggs, "Ford, in Appeal to Evangelists, Stresses His Religious Beliefs," *New York Times*, October 10, 1976; Myra MacPherson, "Evangelicals Seen Cooling on Carter," *Washington Post*, September 27, 1976, pp. A1, A3.

53. Anderson, *Electing Jimmy Carter*, 113.

54. Letter, Stephen Charles Mott, Gordon-Conwell Theological Seminary, to Mark Cole, October 20, 1976, Pre-Presidential 1976 Presidential Campaign, Urban Affairs

Desk—Tom Tatum, Subject Files, Box 280, File: Protestants [2], Jimmy Carter Library; "The Ridiculous Factor," editorial in *Omaha World-Herald*, September 22, 1976, 12.

55. On Carter's concession about the *Playboy* interview, see "Crusade for the White House: Skirmishes in a 'Holy War,'" *Christianity Today*, November 19, 1976, 48. Footage and interviews from Jim Lehrer, "Debating Our Destiny," PBS website, http://www.pbs .org/newshour/debatingourdestiny/1976.html (accessed January 1, 2013). A Gallup poll found that voters believed that Carter won the crucial second debate by 50 to 27 percent; John P. Robinson, "The Polls," in *The Great Debates: Carter vs. Ford, 1976*, ed. Sidney Kraus (Bloomington: Indiana University Press, 1979), 264. *Time* magazine later listed Ford's gaffe as one of "Top 10 Memorable Debate Moments."

56. Menendez, *Religion at the Polls*, 197–198. The election results in Georgia demonstrate that Carter's home state, where he had won the gubernatorial election rather narrowly, overwhelmingly supported their favorite son for president six years later; see Phinzy Spaulding, "Georgia and the Election of Jimmy Carter," *Georgia Historical Quarterly*, 61 (Spring 1977), 13–22. Carter later said that Ford's battle with Reagan in the Republican primaries gave Carter a more formidable lead in the polls than was really warranted and that the close general election, therefore, was not such a surprise; see "Interview with Jimmy Carter, Nov. 19, 1982," in *Conversations with Carter*, ed. Richardson, 224.

57. Letter, Pat Robertson and Louis Sheldon to President-elect Carter, December 1, 1976, "Office of Public Liaison, Bob Maddox, Religious Liaison," Box 5, Jimmy Carter Library.

58. "The Political Peak Is Also the Brink," editorial in *Christianity Today*, November 19, 1976, 33.

59. Stephen V. Monsma, "The Oval Office: Three Models for a Christian," *Christianity Today*, January 21, 1977, 28–29.

60. Ibid.

Chapter Five: Redeemer President

1. David E. Kucharsky, "Inauguration Day, 1977: Heralding a New Spirit," *Christianity Today*, February 4, 1977, 50.

2. Ibid.

3. "In Changing Times, Eternal Principles: President Carter's Inaugural Address," *New York Times*, January 21, 1977.

4. Ibid. For an analysis of Carter's rhetoric, including his inaugural address, see Dan F. Hahn, "The Rhetoric of Jimmy Carter, 1976–1980," *Presidential Studies Quarterly*, 14 (Spring 1984), 265–288.

5. Jimmy Carter, *White House Diary* (New York: Farrar, Straus and Giroux, 2010), 9–10.

6. I have developed this idea much more fully in *God in the White House: How Faith Shaped the Presidency from John F. Kennedy to George W. Bush* (San Francisco: Harper-One, 2008).

7. "'Ford Has Been a Dormant President,' Sept. 13, 1976," in *Conversations with Carter*, ed. Don Richardson (Boulder, Colo.: Lynne Rienner, 1998), 20; Steven H. Hochman et al., "Interview with Carter, Nov. 29, 1982," in ibid., 252; Billy Graham, *Just as I Am: The Autobiography of Billy Graham* (San Francisco: HarperSanFrancisco, 1997), 493; Jimmy Carter, *Through the Year with Jimmy Carter: 366 Daily Meditations from the 39th President* (Grand Rapids, Mich.: Zondervan, 2011), 340. Carter himself was well aware of Nixon's transgressions, and he wanted at all costs to avoid them. The first motion picture that the Carters watched in the White House was *All the President's Men*; Kevin Mattson, *"What the Heck Are You Up to, Mr. President?" Jimmy Carter, America's "Malaise," and the Speech that Should Have Changed the Country* (New York: Bloomsbury, 2009), 131.

8. Caspar Nannes, "New Teacher, Pupil at Sunday School," *Christianity Today*, April 1, 1977, 52.

9. Edward E. Plowman, "New Church Member in Town," *Christianity Today*, February 18, 1977, 54–55. For Carter's remarks at the Prayer Breakfast, see Kenneth E. Morris, "Religion and the Presidency of Jimmy Carter," in *Religion and the American Presidency: George Washington to George W. Bush with Commentary and Primary Sources*, ed. Gastón Espinosa (New York: Columbia University Press, 2009), 345–347.

10. Letter, Billy Graham to Rosalynn Carter, January 25, 1979, WHCF–Name File, Jimmy Carter Library; Malcolm Muggeridge, introduction to *The Man from Plains: The Mind and Spirit of Jimmy Carter*, by David Kucharsky (London: William Collins, 1977), [xi].

11. Bill Niekirk, "President Pardons Draft Evaders as First Official Act," *Chicago Tribune*, January 22, 1977, W1, 5; Patrick Anderson, *Electing Jimmy Carter: The Campaign of 1976* (Baton Rouge: Louisiana State University Press, 1994), 25.

12. Quoted in Kenneth E. Morris, *Jimmy Carter, American Moralist: The Life Story and Moral Legacy of Our Thirty-Ninth President* (Athens: University of Georgia Press, 1997), 242; John B. Anderson, "Faith, Virtue, and Honor Are Not Enough," *Christianity Today*, November 3, 1978, 18.

13. Memorandum, Stuart Eizenstat to Jimmy Carter, May 1, 1978, Jimmy Carter Library; George F. Will, "Is He Stonewall Jackson or Gen. McClellan?," *Los Angeles Times*, April 21, 1977, C7; Martin F. Nolan, "Bringing Credibility to Bear on Energy Issue," *Boston Globe*, April 19, 1977, 1, 12.

14. Quoted in Douglas Brinkley, "The Rising Stock of Jimmy Carter: The 'Hands on' Legacy of Our Thirty-ninth President," *Diplomatic History*, 20 (Fall 1996), 523; Jimmy Carter, "Human Rights: Dilemmas and Directions," *Transformation*, 1 (October 1984), 2–5.

15. David Schmitz and Vanessa Walker, "Jimmy Carter and the Foreign Policy of Human Rights: The Development of a Post–Cold War Foreign Policy," *Diplomatic History*, 28 (2004), 113–143.

16. "Text of President's Commencement Address at Notre Dame on Foreign Policy," *New York Times*, May 23, 1977, 12.

17. "A Conversation on Peacemaking with Jimmy Carter, June 7, 1991," in *Conversations with Carter*, ed. Richardson, 284.

18. Quoted in Wesley G. Pippert, "Moral Leadership Is Essential," *Christianity Today*, November 3, 1978, 19; Wesley G. Pippert, comp., *The Spiritual Journal of Jimmy Carter, In His Own Words* (New York: Macmillan, 1978), 29; Jimmy Carter, *Sources of Strength: Meditations on Scripture for a Living Faith* (New York: Times Books, 1997), 126; quoted in Gregory Domin and Jessica Lerir, "Jimmy Carter (1924–): Peanut Farmer Turned Human Rights Advocate," in *Twentieth-Century Shapers of Baptist Social Ethics*, ed. Larry L. McSwain (Macon, Ga.: Mercer University Press, 2008), 215.

19. Schmitz and Walker, "Jimmy Carter and the Foreign Policy of Human Rights," *Diplomatic History*, 28 (2004), 137, 141.

20. Ibid., 124, 135.

21. "Conversation on Peacemaking with Jimmy Carter," 284, 285.

22. Regarding Graham, see memorandum, TGS to President Carter, April 12, 1977, WHCF–Name File, Jimmy Carter Library; Richard Burt, "Reagan's Foreign Policy—From Someone Who Knows," *New York Times*, June 29, 1980, A5; "Happy Anniversary," editorial in *Wall Street Journal*, May 22, 1978, 22; Anderson, "Faith, Virtue, and Honor," *Christianity Today*, November 3, 1978, 18; Wes Michaelson, "Jimmy Carter, Jacques Ellul and Human Rights," *Sojourners*, June 1977, 4. On Carter's policy toward South Korea, see Jim Stentzel, "Praising Freedom, Blessing Dictatorship: President Carter's Message in South Korea," *Sojourners*, August 1979, 8–10.

23. "Interview with the President, Dec. 28, 1977," in *Conversations with Carter*, ed. Richardson, 148.

24. Frye Gaillard, *Prophet from Plains: Jimmy Carter and His Legacy* (Athens: University of Georgia Press, 2007), 14–17: Brinkley, "Rising Stock of Jimmy Carter," *Diplomatic History*, 20 (Fall 1996), 524.

25. "'I Look Forward to the Job,' Jan. 3, 1977," in *Conversations with Carter*, ed. Richardson, 68.

26. Quoted in Alan Riding, "Carter Banks Heavily on Panama as Panacea," *Toronto Globe and Mail*, June 20, 1978, 7; "Carter Signs Canal Treaties in Panama," *Toronto Globe and Mail*, June 17, 1978, 12.

27. Quoted in Craig Allen Smith, "Leadership, Orientation, and Rhetorical Vision: Jimmy Carter, the 'New Right,' and the Panama Canal," *Presidential Studies Quarterly*, 16 (Spring 1986), 323; Stephen R. Sywulka and William O. Taylor, "On the Panama Canal," editorial in *Christianity Today*, March 24, 1978, 35.

28. Mary McGrory, "Ronald Reagan Closes the Door," *Chicago Tribune*, September 14, 1977, B4. Carter was not without his defenders. One of them, John Wayne, movie actor and a staunch Republican, wrote angrily to Reagan and accused the politician of distortions. "Now I have taken your letter, and I'll show you point by goddam point in the treaty where you are misinforming people," Wayne wrote. "If you continue these erroneous remarks, someone will publicize your letter to prove that you are not as thorough in your reviewing of this treaty as you say or are damned obtuse when it comes to

reading the English language." "Reagan Angered John Wayne," *New York Times*, March 16, 1987, A15. See also Albert R. Hunt, "Reagan: 'A Man, a Plan, a Canal . . . ,'" *Wall Street Journal*, August 26, 1977, 8.

29. "Review & Outlook: The Panama Compromise," editorial in *Wall Street Journal*, February 3, 1978, 6; "Wading into the Canal Issue," editorial in *Los Angeles Times*, August 14, 1977, D4; "'Giving Away' the Canal," editorial in *Hartford Courant*, January 15, 1978, 2B; "The Panama Canal Pact: Editors' Reactions Vary Widely," *Chicago Tribune*, September 15, 1977, B2.

30. Hochman et al., "Interview with Carter, Nov. 29, 1982," 244; "Don Richardson, Oct. 17, 1997," in ibid., 335; Don Irwin, "Canal Pacts Are in Highest U.S. Interest—Carter," *Los Angeles Times*, February 2, 1978, A6; "Senate Ratifies Canal Treaty, 68–32: Carter Enjoys Biggest Victory," *Hartford Courant*, April 19, 1978, 1; quoted in Arthur Siddon, "Final Canal Treaty Ratified: 68 to 32 Vote Gives Up Seaway Senate Ratifies Final Canal Pact," *Chicago Tribune*, April 19, 1978, 1, 5.

31. "The Treaties at Last," editorial in *Christian Science Monitor*, April 20, 1978, 28: "The OAS After Panama," editorial in *Christian Science Monitor*, June 23, 1978, 24; Wallace Nutting, "Panama Canal Turnover Is a Magnanimous Gesture by a Great Nation," *Portland* (Me.) *Press Herald,* December 12, 1999, 1C; Maury Maverick, "Carter Did Good by Panama Canal Treaty," *San Antonio Express-News*, February 20, 2000, 3M.

32. On Hughes's initiative, see also Letter, Harold E. Hughes and Douglas E. Coe to President Carter, September 26, 1978, "Religious Matters," Box RM-1, WHCF–Subject File–General, Jimmy Carter Library. For further evidence of evangelicals praying for the Camp David negotiations, see Letter, Grady C. Cothen [president, Sunday School Board of the Southern Baptist Convention] to President Carter, September 13, 1978, "Religious Matters," Box RM-1, WHCF–Subject File–General, Jimmy Carter Library.

33. "Camp David: An Outpouring of Prayer," *Christianity Today*, October 6, 1978, 48; Letter, Pat Boone to President Carter, February 16, 1978, "Religious Matters," Box RM-1, WHCF–Subject File–General, Jimmy Carter Library. On Hughes's initiative, see also Letter, Harold E. Hughes and Douglas E. Coe to President Carter, September 26, 1978, "Religious Matters," Box RM-1, WHCF–Subject File–General, Jimmy Carter Library. For further evidence of evangelicals praying for the Camp David negotiations, see Letter, Grady C. Cothen [president, Sunday School Board of the Southern Baptist Convention] to President Carter, September 13, 1978, "Religious Matters," Box RM-1, WHCF–Subject File–General, Jimmy Carter Library.

34. "The Battle of the Advertisements," editorial in *Christianity Today*, March 24, 1978, 34–35; quoted in Caitlin Carenen, *The Fervent Embrace: Liberal Protestants, Evangelicals, and Israel* (New York: New York University Press, 2012), 161; quoted in Domin and Lerer, "Jimmy Carter (1924–)," 215–216.

35. Quoted in "Israeli-Egyptian Peace Treaty," editorial in *Christianity Today*, April 20, 1979, 8; quoted in Pippert, "Moral Leadership," *Christianity Today*, November 3, 1978, 21.

36. Telegram, Billy Graham to President Carter, March 26, 1979, WHCF–Name File, Jimmy Carter Library; "Israeli-Egyptian Peace Treaty," *Christianity Today*, April 20, 1979, 8.

37. "The Battle of the Advertisements," editorial in *Christianity Today*, March 24, 1978, 34–35; quoted in Caitlin Carenen, *The Fervent Embrace: Liberal Protestants, Evangelicals, and Israel* (New York: New York University Press, 2012), 161; "Text of President's Commencement Address," *New York Times*, May 23, 1977, 12; quoted in Domin and Lerer, "Jimmy Carter (1924–)," 215–216.

38. Nancy Gibbs and Michael Duffy, *The Preacher and the Presidents: Billy Graham in the White House* (New York: Center Street, 2007), 254–256.

39. Jimmy Carter, *Keeping Faith: Memoirs of a President* (New York: Bantam Books, 1982), 248.

40. Gigi Moses, "BJU to Finance Anti-Carter Drive," *Greenville Piedmont*, January 31, 1979. Another evangelical critic of Carter's recognition of China was Joseph Bayly; see "Grading Carter's Mid-Term," *Eternity*, March 1979, 59–60.

41. Brinkley, "Rising Stock of Jimmy Carter," *Diplomatic History*, 20 (Fall 1996), 523.

Chapter Six: Endangered Evangelical

1. Wesley G. Pippert, "Viewing the Family from the Oval Office," *Christianity Today*, September 9, 1977, 60–61.

2. Pippert, "Moral Leadership," *Christianity Today*, November 3, 1978, 17.

3. E. Stanly Godbold Jr., *Jimmy and Rosalynn Carter: The Georgia Years, 1924–1974* (New York: Oxford University Press, 2010), 212, 216; Andrew R. Flint and Joy Porter, "Jimmy Carter: The Re-emergence of Faith-Based Politics and the Abortion Rights Issue," *Presidential Studies Quarterly*, 35 (March 2005), 40, 41. See also Rosalynn Carter's account of her support for equal rights: Rosalynn Carter, *First Lady from Plains* (Boston: Houghton Mifflin, 1984), 101.

4. Jimmy Carter, *White House Diary* (New York: Farrar, Straus and Giroux, 2010), 253–254, 427–428; Rosalynn Carter, *First Lady from Plains*, 286. On Carter's commitment to women's rights and the ERA during the campaign, see Bill Peterson, "Carter Vows Fight for Women's Rights," *Washington Post*, October 2, 1976, A1, A3.

5. Democratic Party Platforms: "Democratic Party Platform of 1976," July 12, 1976, online by Gerhard Peters and John T. Woolley, *The American Presidency Project*, http://www.presidency.ucsb.edu/ws/?pid=29606 (accessed January 3, 2013); Republican Party Platforms: "Republican Party Platform of 1976," August 18, 1976, online by Gerhard Peters and John T. Woolley, *The American Presidency Project*, http://www.presidency.ucsb.edu/ws/?pid=25843 (accessed November 28, 2013). On the importance of access to abortion for feminists, see, for example, Rosalind Pollack Petchesky, "Antiabortion, Antifeminism, and the Rise of the New Right," *Feminist Studies*, 7 (Summer 1981), 206–246. Petchesky writes: "Abortion is not simply an aspect of social liberation; it is above all a condition of women's liberation" (210).

6. Quoted in Flint and Porter, "Jimmy Carter: Re-emergence of Faith-Based Politics," 38. In his diary, Carter noted a call from Califano while the president was at Camp David on July 16, 1977, "expressing his strong support of my expressed opinion that the federal government should not finance abortions." Carter, *White House Diary*, 70.

7. Quoted in David S. Broder, "Life Isn't Fair," *Nashua* (N.H.) *Telegraph*, July 25, 1977; Flint and Porter, "Jimmy Carter: Re-emergence of Faith-Based Politics," 39.

8. Memorandum, Margaret "Midge" Costanza to President Carter, July 13, 1977, Office of Public Liaison, Margaret "Midge" Costanza Papers, Box 1, Jimmy Carter Library. Costanza organized an informal caucus in the Executive Office Building of administration officials and others who were distressed by Carter's remarks. According to Evans and Novak, Carter was not amused and expressed his disapproval at the July 18, 1977, Cabinet meeting. Rowland Evans and Robert Novak, "Quashing an In-House Revolt on Abortion," *Washington Post*, July 30, 1977.

9. Rosalynn Carter, *First Lady from Plains*, 164; *Jimmy Carter, White House Diary*, 71.

10. Pippert, "Viewing the Family from the Oval Office," 61. On Bryant's campaign, Carter told me, "I didn't get involved in that." He added that about 5 percent of the population of Plains was gay, including one of his first cousins. "We don't even pay any attention to who's gay and who isn't," Carter told me. Jimmy Carter, interview with the author, Plains, Ga., June 2, 2013.

11. Anita Bryant, "When the Homosexuals Burn the Holy Bible in Public . . . How Can I Stand By Silently," in Matthew Avery Sutton, *Jerry Falwell and the Rise of the Religious Right: A Brief History with Documents* (Boston: Bedford/St. Martin's, 2013), 102–106.

12. "Taking the World's Temperature: An Interview with Billy Graham," *Christianity Today*, September 23, 1977, 16–19. A couple of years later, an editorial in *Christianity Today* applauded Bryant's courage; see "Taking a Costly Stand," editorial in *Christianity Today*, June 29, 1979, 11.

13. Jerry Falwell, sermon (transcript), "Why Some Christians Don't Serve God," 1 Corinthians 16:9, August 10, 1977, MW-101, Liberty University Archives; Jerry Falwell, *How You Can Help Clean Up America*, in Sutton, *Jerry Falwell and the Rise of the Religious Right*, 107, 109.

14. Carter, *White House Diary*, 127.

15. Ibid., 259; Letter, President Carter to Harold Hughes, October 31, 1979, "Religious Matters," Box RM-1, WHCF–Subject File–General, Jimmy Carter Library; Carter, interview with the author. On the Fellowship Foundation, also known as "The Family," see Jeff Sharlet, *The Family: The Secret Fundamentalism at the Heart of American Power* (New York: HarperCollins, 2008). Sharlet's book has many virtues, but the author's characterization of Harold Hughes as a fundamentalist borders on libel.

16. Letter, President Carter to Robert L. Maddox Jr. [prior to his appointment to the White House], October 3, 1978, "Religious Matters," Box RM-1, WHCF–Subject File–General, Jimmy Carter Library; Wesley G. Pippert, comp., *The Spiritual Journal of Jimmy Carter, In His Own Words* (New York: Macmillan, 1978), 12; Wesley G. Pippert, "Jimmy

Carter: 'Ways Other than Force,'" *Christian Life*, November 1980, 22–23. The verse is Psalms 19:14 (King James Version).

17. Douglas E. Kneeland, "Clark Defeat in Iowa Laid to Abortion Issue," *New York Times*, November 13, 1978; Daniel K. Williams, *God's Own Party: The Making of the Christian Right* (New York: Oxford University Press, 2010), 154; Dick Clark, interview with Bruce Morton, CBS News, November 13, 1978. See also Hedrick Smith, "A Pattern of Stability: With Incumbents Faring Well, Results Indicate that Fears of Voter Revolt Were Exaggerated," *New York Times*, November 8, 1978. Allegations later emerged that the white government of South Africa may have illegally contributed money toward Clark's defeat because of his strong stand against apartheid. Wendell Rawls Jr., "South African Role in Iowa Voting Charged," *New York Times*, March 22, 1979.

18. "Religion at the Polls: Strength and Conflict," *Christianity Today*, December 1, 1978, 40–41.

19. Letter, Georgia Glasman to Paul Weyrich, January 26, 1978, Box 3, Paul M. Weyrich Papers, American Heritage Center, University of Wyoming.

20. "The Moral Majority," undated paper, Box 19, Paul M. Weyrich Papers, American Heritage Center, University of Wyoming.

21. William Martin, *With God on Our Side: The Rise of the Religious Right in America* (New York: Broadway Books, 1996), 173. As early as February 1979, several months before the formation of an organization by that name, Howard Phillips was using the term "moral majority"; see Letter, Howard Phillips to Jerry Falwell, February 27, 1979, Evangelist Activism, Box 15, Paul M. Weyrich Papers, American Heritage Center, University of Wyoming. According to historian Robert Freedman, "The Supreme Court's banning of public school prayer (1962) and legalization of abortion (1973) outraged many evangelicals and fundamentalists. However, few decided to participate actively in politics as a result." He adds: "Weyrich believes that the Carter administration's policy toward Christian Schools was the turning point." Robert Freedman, "The Religious Right and the Carter Administration," *Historical Journal*, 48 (March 2005), 236. Michael Lienesch writes: "The Christian conservative lobbyists were originally concerned with protecting the Christian schools from Internal Revenue Service investigations over the issue of racial imbalance." Michael Leinesch, "Right-Wing Religion: Christian Conservatism as a Political Movement," *Political Science Quarterly*, 97 (Autumn 1982), 409. On the importance of schools to the nascent Religious Right, see also J. Charles Park, "Preachers, Politics, and Public Education: A Review of Right-Wing Pressures against Public Schooling in America," *Phi Delta Kappan*, 61 (May 1980), 608–612.

22. For the legal history surrounding tax exemptions to segregated schools that culminated in the Bob Jones case, see Olati Johnson, "The Story of *Bob Jones University v. United States*: Race, Religion, and Congress' Extraordinary Acquiescence," *Columbia Public Law & Legal Theory Working Papers*, Paper 9184 (2010).

23. For a superb review of the circumstances surrounding the *Green v. Kennedy* case, see Joseph Crespino, "Civil Rights and the Religious Right," in *Rightward Bound: Making America Conservative in the 1970s*, ed. Bruce J. Schulman and Julian

E. Zelizer (Cambridge, Mass.: Harvard University Press, 2008), 90–105. Crespino correctly identifies this case, together with *Green v. Connally*, as the catalyst for the Religious Right.

24. *Green v. Connally*, 330 F. Supp. 1150 (D. D.C.) aff'd sub nom; *Coit v. Green*, 404 U.S. 997 (1971).

25. "'Most Unusual': No Time for a Change," *Christianity Today*, December 17, 1971, 34.

26. Ibid. Bob Jones III insisted that "there was no connection between the enrollment of this one black student and the major threats facing the university."

27. Paul Weyrich, "The Pro-Family Movement," *Conservative Digest*, 6 (May–June 1980), 14.

28. Freedman, "Religious Right and the Carter Administration," *Historical Journal*, 48 (March 2005), 238–240; Wilfred F. Drake, "Tax Status of Private Segregated Schools: The New Revenue Procedure," *William and Mary Law Review*, 20 (1979), 463–512; quoted in Leslie Kalman, *Right Star Rising: A New Politics, 1974–1980* (New York: W. W. Norton, 2010), 273.

29. Quoted in Kalman, *Right Star Rising*, 273; Freedman, "Religious Right and the Carter Administration," 238, 240; Wilfred F. Drake, "Tax Status of Private Segregated Schools: The New Revenue Procedure," *William and Mary Law Review*, 20 (1979), 463–512; "Jimmy Carter's Betrayal of the Christian Voter," *Conservative Digest*, August 1979, 15; Michael Sean Winters, *God's Right Hand: How Jerry Falwell Made God a Republican and Baptized the American Right* (San Francisco: HarperOne, 2012), 110; Crespino, "Civil Rights and the Religious Right," 99–100. For a look inside the evangelical subculture, see Randall Balmer, *Mine Eyes Have Seen the Glory: A Journey into the Evangelical Subculture in America*, 4th ed. (New York: Oxford University Press, 2006). Although Carter appointed Kurtz as IRS commissioner, Kurtz did not consult Carter about the regulations. Jimmy Carter, "Internal Revenue Service Nomination of Jerome Kurtz to be Commissioner," March 21, 1977, online by Gerhard Peters and John T. Woolley, *The American Presidency Project*, www.presidency.ucsb.edu/ws/?pid7204 (accessed June 12, 2013); Carter, interview with the author. A 2006 article in the *New York Times* quoted Kurtz as adamantly opposed to modifying IRS policies because of political considerations; see David K. Johnston, "I.R.S. Going Slow Before Election," *New York Times*, October 27, 2006.

30. Freedman, "Religious Right and the Carter Administration," 240–241, 242; Duane Murray Oldfield, *The Right and the Righteous: The Christian Right Confronts the Republican Party* (Lanham, Md.: Rowman & Littlefield, 1996), 100.

31. Jerry Falwell, *Listen, America!* (Garden City, N.Y.: Doubleday, 1980), 220; quoted in Max Blumenthal, "Agent of Intolerance," *The Nation*, May 16, 2007; Dirk Smilie, *Falwell Inc.: Inside a Religious, Political, Educational, and Business Empire* (New York: St. Martin's Press, 2008), 73.

32. Quoted in *No Longer Exiles: The Religious New Right in American Politics*, ed. Michael Cromartie (Washington, D.C.: Ethics and Public Policy Center, 1993), 26.

33. Quoted in ibid., 52; Dan Gilgoff, "Exclusive: Grover Norquist Gives Religious Conservatives Tough Love," June 11, 2009, God & Country: On Faith, Politics, and Culture," www.usnews.com/blogs/god-and-country (accessed September 30, 2009).

34. Elmer L. Rumminger, telephone interview with the author, July 17, 2010.

35. Freedman, "Religious Right and the Carter Administration," 243.

36. Letter, Paul Weyrich to Daniel B. Hales, December 31, 1978, Box 3, Paul M. Weyrich Papers, American Heritage Center, University of Wyoming; Letter, Robert Billings "Bob," Christian School Action Inc., to Paul Weyrich, December 6, 1978, Box 3, Paul M. Weyrich Papers, American Heritage Center, University of Wyoming.

37. Letter, Paul Weyrich to Jerry Falwell, May 8, 1979, Paul M. Weyrich Papers, Box 3, American Heritage Center, University of Wyoming; Letter, Paul Weyrich to James Robison, May 11, 1979, Box 3, Paul M. Weyrich Papers, American Heritage Center, University of Wyoming.

38. Philip Yancey, "Schaeffer on Schaeffer, Part II," *Christianity Today*, April 6, 1979, 25.

39. Frank Schaeffer, *Crazy for God: How I Grew Up as One of the Elect, Helped Found the Religious Right, and Lived to Take All (Or Almost All) of It Back* (New York: Carroll & Graf, 2007), 283.

40. Francis A. Schaeffer and C. Everett Koop, *Whatever Happened to the Human Race?*, Program One: *Abortion of the Human Race*, DVD, directed by Frank Schaeffer (Grand Rapids, Mich.: Gospel Films Distribution, 1979).

41. Quoted in Jean Garton, "25th Anniversary of the Roe vs. Wade Case," "National Right to Life News" (newsletter), September 28, 1998; Frank Schaeffer, *Crazy for God*, 259, 293. The companion volume for the film series is Francis A. Schaeffer and C. Everett Koop, *Whatever Happened to the Human Race? Exposing Our Rapid Yet Subtle Loss of Human Rights* (Old Tappan, N.J.: Revell, 1979). The film series was produced by Billy Zeoli, Gerald Ford's religious adviser, financed in part by Richard DeVos of Amway, and directed by Schaeffer's son, Frank.

42. Letter, James Robison to Paul Weyrich, May 14, 1979, Evangelist Activism, Box 17, Paul M. Weyrich Papers, American Heritage Center, University of Wyoming.

43. Kara Rogge, " 'Freedom to Preach' Rally for Evangelist Packs Center," *Fort Worth Morning Star–Telegram*, June 6, 1979.

44. "Raising Millions of Dollars for Conservatives—The Way It's Done" [interview with Richard Viguerie], *U.S. News & World Report*, February 26, 1979, 54.

45. In one of the most bizarre secondary assessments of Carter's presidency, Kenneth E. Morris writes, "Whether the issue was funding for private Christian schools, abortion rights, alternative family forms, or the like, Carter never governed in a manner that suggested any impulse to inject his own faith directly into public policy." Carter's human rights initiative alone belies that statement, but, as is clear from Carter's writings, his faith also informed other policies, including the Middle East, his reluctance to respond with military force to the Iranian hostage situation, the environment, women's rights, and countless other issues. Even Carter's position on church-state separation

("funding for private Christian schools," which Morris mentions above) was informed by his Baptist convictions, a reflection of Roger Williams's concern that a conflation of church and state would ultimately be detrimental to the integrity of the faith. Morris, "Religion and the Presidency of Jimmy Carter," in *Religion and the American Presidency: George Washington to George W. Bush with Commentary and Primary Sources*, ed. Gastón Espinosa (New York: Columbia University Press, 2009), 326. Later in the same essay, Morris writes, "Carter was fairly indifferent to the prospect of converting others to Christianity," apparently willing to ignore the mission trips and Carter's careful accounting of the number of converts in the Billy Graham revival initiative in Americus, Georgia, which Carter chaired. Ibid., 328.

46. Robert D. Hershey Jr., "Bert Lance, Carter Adviser, Dies at 82," *New York Times*, August 15, 2013; E. R. Lanier, "Bert Lance (1931–2013)," in *New Georgia Encyclopedia* (Athens: University of Georgia Press, 2013).

47. "Lance: Going, Going . . . ," *Time*, September 19, 1977; *American Experience: Jimmy Carter*, produced by Adriana Bosch, WGBH-Boston, 2002; News Release, United Methodist Communications, September 16, 1977. The other incident that reflected badly on Carter was Billy Carter's relationship with Libya, which recruited the president's brother as a lobbyist in late 1978. Libya, however, received no return on its investment.

48. James Fallows, "The Passionless Presidency," *Atlantic*, May 1979.

49. Jimmy Carter, "The President's News Conference," April 30, 1979, online by Gerhard Peters and John T. Woolley, *The American Presidency Project*, http://www.presidency.ucsb.edu/ws/?pid=32254 (accessed December 4, 2013); Caryl Conner, "For a 'Passionless Presidency,' Feelings About Jim Fallows Run Pretty High at the White House," *People*, May 28, 1979.

50. Hendrik Hertzberg, "A Malaise Footnote (Bonus: Carter Cusses)," July 22, 2009, online at http://www.newyorker.com/online/blogs/hendrikhertzberg/2009/07/malaise-footnote-carter-cusses.html (accessed December 18, 2013).

51. Julian E. Zelizer, *Jimmy Carter* (New York: Times Books, 2010), 95; Helen Thomas, UPI dispatch, July 15, 1979. On the historical context for the speech as well as the reaction, see Kevin Mattson, *"What the Heck Are You Up to, Mr. President?" Jimmy Carter, America's "Malaise," and the Speech That Should Have Changed the Country* (New York: Bloomsbury, 2009). One of those in attendance at Camp David was Robert N. Bellah, the esteemed sociologist from the University of California, Berkeley. Bellah remembers arguing for an even stronger speech, a proposal that was supported (at least privately) by several of Carter's aides. Robert N. Bellah, interview with the author, Hanover, N.H., May 9, 2013.

52. "Steven H. Hochman et al., "Interview with Carter, Nov. 29, 1982," in *Conversations with Carter*, ed. Don Richardson (Boulder, Colo.: Lynne Rienner, 1998), 250, 251. Carter's "Crisis of Confidence" speech, July 15, 1979, can be found in Appendix Two of this book.

53. Randall Balmer, *God in the White House: How Faith Shaped the Presidency from John F. Kennedy to George W. Bush* (San Francisco: HarperOne, 2008), 206, 208.

54. "Winning Neither Confidence . . . ," editorial in *Chicago Tribune*, July 17, 1979, B2; Michael Novak, "Has the President Correctly Diagnosed Our National Malaise?," *Los Angeles Times*, July 22, 1979, F1; "The Real Jimmy Carter," editorial in the *Wall Street Journal*, July 17, 1977. 18. Richard Pious, while noting the groundbreaking character of the speech—the first presidential speech to be both "introspective and confessional"—also argued that Carter failed to reconcile the internal contradictions in his rhetoric. See Richard M. Pious, *Why Presidents Fail: White House Decision Making from Eisenhower to Bush II* (Lanham, Md.: Rowman & Littlefield, 2008), 103. Carter, for his part, stood by the "Crisis of Confidence" speech. In an interview on August 22, 1980, he declared that, aside from his Law Day speech at the University of Georgia, "that's the best speech I ever made." See Curtis Wilkie, "Carter Interview Excerpts, Aug. 22, 1980," in *Conversations with Carter*, ed. Richardson, 209. Several weeks later, at the groundbreaking for the William Cannon Chapel and Religious Center at Emory University, Carter repeated many of the same themes from his "Crisis of Confidence" speech: "We measure the real meaning of America in our intangible values—values which do not change: our care for each other, our commitment to freedom, our search for justice, our devotion to human rights and to world peace, and the patriotism and basic goodness of our people." "Text of Remarks of the President at Emory University," Office of the White House Press Secretary, August 30, 1979.

55. The relationship between Vance and Brzezinski was uneasy, even contentious, and some analysts of Carter's foreign policy believe that Carter himself never fully resolved the polarity between the views of these two advisers. See, for example, Kenneth W. Thompson, ed., *The Carter Presidency: Fourteen Intimate Perspectives of Jimmy Carter*, Portraits of American Presidents, vol. 8 (Lanham, Md.: University Press of America, 1990), 138, 206.

56. Carter, *White House Diary*, 208–210, 305–306; Kalman, *Right Star Rising*, 311–312; Jimmy Carter, *Keeping Faith: Memoirs of a President* (New York: Bantam Books, 1982), 86–87.

57. Carter, *White House Diary*, 305; Zelizer, *Jimmy Carter*, 99, 88.

58. *Annual of the Southern Baptist Convention, 1979* (Nashville, Tenn.: Executive Committee, Southern Baptist Convention, 1979), 57. On the religious and political agenda of those involved in the takeover, see Richard Marius, "The War Between the Baptists," *Esquire*, December 1981, 46–55. For scholarly treatments of the Southern Baptist takeover, see Bill J. Leonard, *God's Last and Only Hope: The Fragmentation of the Southern Baptist Convention* (Grand Rapids, Mich.: Wm. B. Eerdmans, 1990); Nancy Tatom Ammerman, *Baptist Battles: Social Change and Religious Conflict in the Southern Baptist Convention* (New Brunswick, N.J.: Rutgers University Press, 1990). As nearly as I can determine, Leonard's title is entirely innocent of irony.

59. Freedman, "Religious Right and the Carter Administration," 245; Winters, *God's Right Hand*, 113–120. Falwell's account of this gathering differs in a few details but is essentially the same. See Jerry Falwell, *Falwell: An Autobiography* (Lynchburg, Va.: Liberty House, 1997), 383.

60. Jerry Falwell, "How the 'I Love America Club' Was Born," "Clean Up America Hotline Report," n.d. [1979].

61. Quoted in Randall Balmer, *Grant Us Courage: Travels Along the Mainline of American Protestantism* (New York: Oxford University Press, 1996), 85.

62. Letter, Cal Thomas to Bob Maddox, July 24, 1979, "Office of Public Liaison, Bob Maddox, Religious Liaison," Box 1, Jimmy Carter Library. Thomas later became a conservative newspaper columnist for Tribune Media Services (1984) and a commentator on Fox News (1997). On his newspaper column, see Cal Thomas, transcript, *Moral Majority Report*, June 25, 1984, Liberty University Archives.

63. Thomas began work at Moral Majority in August 1980. E-mail correspondence with the author, January 21, 2013. As Billings, Moral Majority's executive director, declared, "The truth is, where the rubber hits the road, the Moral Majority is pro-Reagan." Quoted in Bill Keller, "Lobbying for Christ: Evangelical Conservatives Move from Pews to Polls, But Can They Sway Congress?," *Congressional Quarterly Weekly Report*, September 6, 1980, 2634. In *Blinded by Might*, Thomas makes no mention of his entreaty for a job in the Carter White House. He writes: "I learned later that Jimmy Carter was puzzled as to why I would go to work for Falwell. I'm not sure I could have answered the question if he had asked me, except to say something noble like 'I want to save America.'" Cal Thomas and Ed Dobson, *Blinded by Might: Can the Religious Right Save America?* (Grand Rapids, Mich.: Zondervan, 1999), 12–13.

Chapter Seven: *His Own Received Him Not*

1. Memorandum, Paul Laxalt to Chuck Tyson, September 12, 1980, folder "Political Ops—Voter Groups—Christians/Evangelicals" (1/4), Box 255, Reagan, Ronald: 1980 Campaign Papers, 1965–80, Edwin Meese Files, Ronald Reagan Library. See also Nancy Gibbs and Michael Duffy, *The Preacher and the Presidents: Billy Graham in the White House* (New York: Hachette Books, 2007), chap. 25. The definitive study of Graham's political machinations is Steven P. Miller, *Billy Graham and the Rise of the Republican South* (Philadelphia: University of Pennsylvania Press, 2009).

2. Letter, Billy Graham to Bob Maddox, September 23, 1980, "Office of Public Liaison, Bob Maddox, Religious Liaison," Box 4, Jimmy Carter Library.

3. Regarding Graham's letter to John F. Kennedy and the Montreux meeting eight days later, see Randall Balmer, *God in the White House: How Faith Shaped the Presidency from John F. Kennedy to George W. Bush* (San Francisco: HarperOne, 2008), 28–29. Graham's own account of the *Life* article appears in Billy Graham, *Just As I Am: The Autobiography of Billy Graham* (San Francisco: HarperOne, 1997), 392–393. In his autobiography, Graham says that he "wrote privately to both Kennedy and his running mate, Lyndon Baines Johnson, explaining why I was not going to vote for them"; he mentions nothing about his pledge not to raise the "religious issue." Ibid., 392.

4. Gibbs and Duffy, *Preacher and the Presidents*, 262; Letter, Billy Graham to President and Mrs. Carter, November 6, 1979, WHCF–Name File, Jimmy Carter Library. On

the relatively distant relationship between Carter and Graham, see Gibbs and Duffy, *Preacher and the Presidents*, chap. 24.

5. Gibbs and Duffy, *Preacher and the Presidents*, 260–261; Memorandum, Bob Maddox to President and Mrs. Carter, September 5, 1979, WHCF–Name File, Jimmy Carter Library.

6. Gibbs and Duffy, *Preacher and the Presidents*, 260–261; Letter, Adrian Rogers to Bob Maddox, August 23, 1979, "Office of Public Liaison, Bob Maddox, Religious Liaison," Box 1, Jimmy Carter Library. The following year, Graham somewhat disingenuously told the *National Layman's Digest*, "I admire Jerry Falwell as a tremendous preacher of the gospel—but I didn't join the Moral Majority because I do not agree in taking the pulpit into politics and identifying certain people for defeat." Billy Graham, quoted in *National Layman's Digest*, October 15, 1981.

7. Gibbs and Duffy, *Preacher and the Presidents*, 261; James Robison, "Remembering Reagan," June 8, 2004, http://archives.jamesrobison.net/columns/060804.htm (accessed January 7, 2014). There is some disagreement about who convened the meeting of evangelical leaders in Dallas. John G. Turner identifies Bill Bright as the organizer. See John G. Turner, *Bill Bright & Campus Crusade for Christ: The Renewal of Evangelicalism in Postwar America* (Chapel Hill: University of North Carolina Press, 2008), 189.

8. Robert Freedman, "The Religious Right and the Carter Administration," *Historical Journal*, 48 (March 2005), 249. According to some accounts, the leaders of the Religious Right also considered Philip M. Crane, U.S. representative from Illinois, Howard Baker, U.S. senator from Tennessee, and Jesse Helms, U.S. senator from North Carolina. See, for example, Memorandum, Anne Wexler and Bob Maddox to Phil Wise, October 22, 1979, "Religious Matters," Box RM-1, WHCF–Subject File–General, Jimmy Carter Library. Falwell also confirmed that Connally was under consideration. See Cal Thomas and Ed Dobson, *Blinded by Might: Can the Religious Right Save America?* (Grand Rapids, Mich.: Zondervan, 1999), 270. When Tim LaHaye caught wind that some conservatives were considering Connally, he objected vigorously. Writing to Weyrich about Connally, LaHaye said: "He is no born again Christian, is unelectable and has little or no conservative following in his home state." Note, Tim LaHaye to Paul Weyrich, March 2, 1980, Paul M. Weyrich Papers, Box 4, American Heritage Center, University of Wyoming.

9. Dudley Clendinen, "White House Says Minister Misquoted Carter Remarks," *New York Times*, August 8, 1980, A16; Andrew R. Flint and Joy Porter, "Jimmy Carter: The Re-emergence of Faith-Based Politics and the Abortion Rights Issue," *Presidential Studies Quarterly*, 35 (March 2005), 44–45; Michael Sean Winters, *God's Right Hand: How Jerry Falwell Made God a Republican and Baptized the American Right* (San Francisco: HarperOne, 2012), 145; Jim Castelli, "'Anecdote' Hurts Falwell Credibility," letter to the editor in *Washington Star*, August 23, 1980, B6; Jimmy Carter, interview with the author, Plains, Ga., June 2, 2013.

10. Robert Maddox exit interview, December 8, 1980, Jimmy Carter Library; Maddox, interview with the author, Bethesda, Md., December 6, 2012. For his part, Maddox pushed for the job. See Letter, Robert L. Maddox Jr. to President Carter, September 1,

1978, "Religious Matters," Box RM-1, WHCF–Subject File–General, Jimmy Carter Library.

11. Memorandum, Bob Maddox to President Carter, June 12, 1979, "Office of Public Liaison, Bob Maddox, Religious Liaison," Box 1, Jimmy Carter Library; Letter, Bob Maddox to Robert Anderson, July 26, 1979, "Office of Public Liaison, Bob Maddox, Religious Liaison," Box 1, Jimmy Carter Library; Maddox exit interview.

12. Jimmy Carter, *Our Endangered Values: America's Moral Crisis* (New York: Simon & Schuster, 2005), 40. Carter mistakenly attributed this remark to Adrian Rogers, not Smith; Carter apologized. Carter, interview with the author.

13. Memorandum, Bob Maddox to Jerry Rafshoon and Greg Schneiders, July 27, 1979, "Office of Public Liaison, Bob Maddox, Religious Liaison," Box 1, Jimmy Carter Library; Memorandum, Bob Maddox to Phil Wise and Anne Wexler, "Administratively Confidential," August 28, 1979, "Religious Matters," Box RM-1, WHCF–Subject File–General, Jimmy Carter Library. In an accompanying memorandum, Anne Wexler, Maddox's supervisor, agreed, writing: "These folks influence millions of people." Memorandum, Anne Wexler to Phil Wise, September 10, 1979, "Religious Matters," Box RM-1, WHCF–Subject File–General, Jimmy Carter Library.

14. Memorandum, Bob Maddox to Fran Voorde, November 16, 1979, "Religious Matters," Box RM-1, WHCF–Subject File–General, Jimmy Carter Library; Memorandum, Bob Maddox to President and Mrs. Carter, October 5, 1979, "Religious Matters," Box RM-1, WHCF–Subject File–General, Jimmy Carter Library; Ben A. Franklin, "200,000 March and Pray at Christian Rally in Capital," *New York Times*, April 30, 1980, A1, A20; quoted in Turner, *Bill Bright & Campus Crusade for Christ*, 196.

15. Letter, Bob Maddox to Jerry Falwell, September 4, 1979, "Office of Public Liaison, Bob Maddox, Religious Liaison," Box 1, Jimmy Carter Library. On Maddox's urgency in seeking a meeting, see also Memorandum, Anne Wexler and Bob Maddox to Phil Wise, October 22, 1979, "Religious Matters," Box RM-1, WHCF–Subject File–General, Jimmy Carter Library. On Maddox's efforts to placate Falwell, see also Memorandum, Bob Maddox to Jody Powell, July 20, 1979, "Office of Public Liaison, Bob Maddox, Religious Liaison," Box 1, Jimmy Carter Library.

16. Memorandum, Bob Maddox to Phil Wise and Anne Wexler, "Administratively Confidential," August 28, 1979, "Religious Matters," Box RM-1, WHCF–Subject File–General, Jimmy Carter Library; Letter, Ben Armstrong [National Religious Broadcasters] to Bob Maddox, September 18, 1979, "Office of Public Liaison, Bob Maddox, Religious Liaison," Box 2, Jimmy Carter Library.

17. Edward E. Plowman, "Carter's Presence Confirms Clout of Evangelical Broadcasters," *Christianity Today*, February 22, 1980, 48–49; quoted in Gary Scott Smith, *Faith and the Presidency: From George Washington to George W. Bush* (New York: Oxford University Press, 2006), 297.

18. Plowman, "Carter's Presence Confirms Clout of Evangelical Broadcasters," 48–49; "Evangelicals Share Their Concerns with President Jimmy Carter, January 21, 1980," in Matthew Avery Sutton, *Jerry Falwell and the Rise of the Religious Right: A Brief His-*

tory with Documents (Boston: Bedford/St. Martin's, 2013), 129–131; Maddox, interview with the author; Jimmy Carter, *White House Diary* (New York: Farrar, Straus and Giroux, 2010), 394. Ronald Flowers sees Carter in the tradition of strict separationist rather than accommodationist on matters of religion and politics, such as prayer in school or taxpayer support for religious education. See Ronald B. Flowers, "President Jimmy Carter, Evangelicalism, Church-State Relations, and Civil Religion," *Journal of Church and State*, 25 (Winter 1983), 113–132.

19. Quoted in Plowman, "Carter's Presence," *Christianity Today*, February 22, 1980, 48.

20. Maddox exit interview. Robert Dugan would emerge as an active behind-the-scenes force for the Religious Right; see Axel R. Schäfer, *Countercultural Conservatives: American Evangelicalism from the Postwar Revival to the New Christian Right* (Madison: University of Wisconsin Press, 2011), 137–145.

21. Maddox exit interview; George Vecsey, "Militant Television Preachers Try to Weld Fundamentalist Christians' Political Power," *New York Times*, January 21, 1980.

22. Russell Chandler, "Airwave Preachers Reach More at Once than Christ in Lifetime," *Los Angeles Times*, February 25, 1980, B3, B15; Deborah Huntington and Ruth Kaplan, "Whose Gold Is Behind the Altar? Corporate Ties to Evangelicals," *Contemporary Marxism*, 4 (Winter 1981/1982), 62–94.

23. Letter, Paul M. Weyrich to Pat Robertson, September 21, 1979, Weyrich Papers, Box 3, American Heritage Center, University of Wyoming; Huntington and Kaplan, "Whose Gold Is Behind the Altar?," 62–94. See also Barry Light, "Surge in Independent Campaign Spending," *Congressional Quarterly Weekly Report*, June 14, 1980, 1635–1639. On Bakker's loyalty to Carter, see Memorandum, Bob Maddox to Anne Wexler, August 20, 1980, "Office of Public Liaison, Bob Maddox, Religious Liaison," Box 3, Jimmy Carter Library.

24. Letter, Jack Hyles to Don Bergstrom, December 22, 1980, Papers of Gilbert Stenholm, "Moral Majority" file, Fundamentalism File, Bob Jones University Library; Letter, Bob Jones III to Robert J. Billings, November 20, 1979, Papers of Gilbert Stenholm, "Bob Jones University—Separation" file, Fundamentalism File, Bob Jones University Library; Letter, Bob Jones Jr. to Jack Van Impe, September 2, 1977, "Jones, Bob, 1911–1997—Correspondence" file, Fundamentalism File, Bob Jones University Library.

25. Falwell, "Ministers and Marches," in Sutton, *Jerry Falwell and the Rise of the Religious Right*, 59, 60.

26. Ibid.

27. Jerry Falwell, sermon, July 4, 1976, Liberty University Archives.

28. Jerry Falwell, "How the 'I Love America Club' Was Born," "Clean Up America Hotline Report," n.d. [1979].

29. Vecsey, "Militant Television Preachers," *New York Times*, January 21, 1980.

30. Steven H. Hochman et al., "Interview with Carter, Nov. 29, 1982," in *Conversations with Carter*, ed. Don Richardson (Boulder, Colo.: Lynne Rienner, 1998), 245. See also Erwin C. Hargrove, *Jimmy Carter as President: Leadership and the Politics of the Public Good* (Baton Rouge: Louisiana State University Press, 1988), 141.

31. News Release, United Methodist Communications, November 26, 1979; "The UMC's Message to President Carter," *United Methodist Reporter*, May 2, 1980, 2; Carter, *White House Diary*, 452.

32. Quoted in Wesley G. Pippert, "Jimmy Carter: My Personal Faith in God," *Christianity Today*, March 4, 1983, 6; Jimmy Carter, "Agape, Justice, and American Foreign Policy," *Reformed Journal*, April 1986, 18. For an excellent summary of Carter's handling of the Iranian hostage crisis, see Frye Gaillard, *Prophet from Plains: Jimmy Carter and His Legacy* (Athens: University of Georgia Press, 2007), chap. 4.

33. Quoted in J. Brooks Flippen, *Jimmy Carter, the Politics of Family, and the Rise of the Religious Right* (Athens: University of Georgia Press, 2011), 7; Jimmy Carter, "White House Conference on Families Statement Announcing the Conference," January 30, 1978, online by Gerhard Peters and John T. Woolley, *The American Presidency Project*, http://www.presidency.ucsb.edu/ws/?pid=29884 (accessed December 2, 2013).

34. Roger Wilkins, "U.S. Family Conference Delayed Amid Disputes and Resignations," *New York Times*, June 19, 1978, A1, B4.

35. Jim Guy Tucker, letter to the editor in *New York Times Magazine*, December 16, 1979; Maddox, interview with the author; "Evangelicals Share Their Concerns," in Sutton, *Jerry Falwell and the Rise of the Religious Right*, 130. On the Religious Right and the White House Conference on Families, see Seth Dowland, "'Family Values' and the Formation of a Christian Right Agenda," *Church History*, 78 (September 2009), 606–631.

36. "Focus on Family Begins," "Clean Up America Hotline Report," January 1980; "News Affecting the Family," "Clean Up America Hotline Report," March 1980; quoted in John Maust, "The White House Feud on the Family," *Christianity Today*, May 2, 1980, 47.

37. "Walk-out Dramatizes WHCF Stacked Deck," "Clean Up America Hotline Report," August 1980.

38. Ibid.; Betty Gray, "White House Conference on the Family," *Response*, October 1980, 10–13, 43; "Last Regional White House Conference on Families Ends," *Spartanburg* (S.C.) *Herald*, July 14, 1980, A3.

39. Flippen, *Jimmy Carter, the Politics of Family, and the Rise of the Religious Right*, 222.

40. Paul Weyrich, "The Pro-Family Movement," *Conservative Digest*, 6 (May–June 1980), 15; Undated Weyrich memorandum, The Religious Roundtable, Box 21, Paul M. Weyrich Papers, American Heritage Center, University of Wyoming.

41. Dowland, "'Family Values' and the Formation of a Christian Right Agenda," *Church History*, 78 (September 2009), 618; "Interview with Phyllis Schlafly on the Equal Rights Amendment," in Sutton, *Jerry Falwell and the Rise of the Religious Right*, 115, 117.

42. Letter, Curtis T. Porter [pastor, Amherst Baptist Church, Tonawanda, New York] to Bob Maddox, May 19, 1980, "Office of Public Liaison, Bob Maddox, Religious Liaison," Box 3, Jimmy Carter Library; Letter, Richard E. Wager [pastor, Emmanuel Baptist Church, Berwyn, Illinois] to Bob Maddox, May 2, 1980, "Office of Public Liaison, Bob Maddox, Religious Liaison," Box 3, Jimmy Carter Library; Letter, Carl W. Garrett [pas-

tor, First Baptist Church, Carthage, Missouri] to Bob Maddox, July 18, 1980, "Office of Public Liaison, Bob Maddox, Religious Liaison," Box 3, Jimmy Carter Library; Letter, Dallas E. Pulliam [Greenbelt, Maryland] to President Carter, August 19, 1980, "Office of Public Liaison, Bob Maddox, Religious Liaison," Box 3, Jimmy Carter Library; Elmer L. Rumminger, telephone interview with the author, July 17, 2010.

43. Telegram, Mr. and Mrs. Ralph C. Bearden [Plantation, Florida] to Ronald Reagan, July 14, 1980, folder "Correspondence Unit—[Anti-Abortion—July 1980] (1/2)," Box 825. Reagan, Ronald: 1980 Campaign Papers, 1965–80. Edwin Meese Files, Ronald Reagan Library; Mailgram, Patricia A. Fitzgerald [Covina, California] to Ronald Reagan, July 14, 1980, folder "Correspondence Unit—[Anti-Abortion—July 1980] (1/2)," Box 825. Reagan, Ronald: 1980 Campaign Papers, 1965–80. Edwin Meese Files, Ronald Reagan Library.

44. Maddox, interview with the author; Flint and Porter, "Jimmy Carter: Re-emergence of Faith-Based Politics," *Presidential Studies Quarterly*, 35 (March 2005), 42; Maddox exit interview. On evangelical discontent over Weddington, see "Jimmy Carter's Betrayal of the Christian Voter," *Conservative Digest*, August 1979, 15; Letter, Dale Francis [*Our Sunday Visitor*] to Walt Wurfel, September 14, 1978, "Religious Matters," Box RM-2, WHCF–Subject File–General, Jimmy Carter Library. On Carter's attempts to limit abortions, see Randy Frame, "Jimmy Carter Speaks His Mind," *Christianity Today*, March 21, 1986, 42.

45. Maddox, interview with the author; Letter James M. Dunn [director, Christian Life Commission, Baptist General Convention of Texas] to Bob Maddox, May 28, 1980, "Office of Public Liaison, Bob Maddox, Religious Liaison," Box 3, Jimmy Carter Library.

46. Memorandum, Phil Strickland to Robert Strauss and Hamilton Jordan, July 16, 1980, "Office of Public Liaison, Bob Maddox, Religious Liaison," Box 1, Jimmy Carter Library.

Chapter Eight: Election Year of the Evangelical

1. Remarks of Vice President Walter F. Mondale, North Christian Church Service, Chicago, March 16, 1980, "Office of Public Liaison, Bob Maddox, Religious Liaison," Box 1, Jimmy Carter Library.

2. Letter, R. Douglas Wead [Springfield, Missouri] to President Carter, August 14, 1980, "Office of Public Liaison, Bob Maddox, Religious Liaison," Box 3, Jimmy Carter Library; quoted in Bill Keller, "Lobbying for Christ: Evangelical Conservatives Move from Pews to Polls, But Can They Sway Congress?," *Congressional Quarterly Weekly Report*, September 6, 1980, 2630.

3. David R. Swartz, *Moral Minority: The Evangelical Left in an Age of Conservatism* (Philadelphia: University of Pennsylvania Press, 2012), 222–224.

4. Jim Wallis, "The 'Outsider' in the White House," *Sojourners*, January 1978, 6; John F. Alexander, "Welcome to the Election Circus," *The Other Side*, September 1980, 12–13.

5. J. Brooks Flippen, _Jimmy Carter, the Politics of Family, and the Rise of the Religious Right_ (Athens: University of Georgia Press, 2011), 11; "Onward Christian Soldiers," editorial in _Christianity Today_, May 23, 1980, 12.

6. Robert Maddox exit interview, December 8, 1980, Jimmy Carter Library.

7. Douglas E. Kneeland, "Reagan Campaigns at Mississippi Fair," _New York Times_, August 4, 1980. The choice of a southern venue by the campaign, as a means of resurrecting the so-called Southern Strategy, was no happenstance; see Memorandum, Bill Casey to Ronald Reagan, June 3, 1980, folder "Meese, Ed—Memos—June 1980 (1/2)," Box 124, Reagan, Ronald: 1980 Campaign Papers, 1965–80, Edwin Meese Files, Ronald Reagan Library. Carter himself understood the symbolism of Reagan's appearance; see "Kovach on Carter, Apr. 1990," in _Conversations with Carter_, ed. Don Richardson (Boulder, Colo.: Lynne Rienner, 1998), 278. One of the consequences of Reagan's appearance in Philadelphia, Mississippi, was an endorsement from the Invisible Knights of the Ku Klux Klan, an endorsement that Reagan eventually rejected. News Release, Reagan Bush Committee, August 22, 1980, folder "Ku Klux Klan," Box 132, Reagan, Ronald: 1980 Campaign Papers, 1965–80, Edwin Meese Files, Ronald Reagan Library. The controversy, however, lingered. On September 3, 1980, the Ku Klux Klan sent a telegram of support to Reagan: "WE WOULD LIKE TO REAFFIRM OUR SUPPORT OF YOUR STAND ON THE ISSUES OF ANTI WHITE DISCRIMINATION AND EMPLOYMENT, FORCED BUSSING [sic] FOR SCHOOL INTEGRATION, AND HIGH TAXES FOR MINORITY ORIENTED WELFARE. IF YOU CONTINUE YOUR POSITION ON THESE ISSUES, WE FEEL YOU WILL RECEIVE THE SUPPORT OF OUR MEMBERSHIP AS WELL AS THE MAJORITY OF ALL AMERICANS." Mailgram, Don Black [Grand Wizard, Knights of the Ku Klux Klan, Tuscumbia, Alabama], September 3, 1980, folder "Ku Klux Klan," Box 132, Reagan, Ronald: 1980 Campaign Papers, 1965–80, Edwin Meese Files, Ronald Reagan Library.

8. Memorandum, Bill Casey to Ronald Reagan, June 3, 1980, folder "Meese, Ed—Memos—June 1980 (1/2)," Box 124, Reagan, Ronald: 1980 Campaign Papers, 1965–80, Edwin Meese Files, Ronald Reagan Library.

9. Andrew Young, "Chilling Words in Nashoba County," _Washington Post_, August 11, 1980, A19.

10. Martin Schram, "Reagan Beats a Retreat on Klan Remark," _Washington Post_, September 3, 1980, A3, A6; Donald N. Rothberg, "Carter Raps Reagan for Klan Remark," Associated Press, September 9, 1980; Notes [no author], n.d., folder "Meese Files—Subject File—Ku Klux Klan (2/2)," Box 132, Reagan, Ronald: 1980 Campaign Papers, 1965–80, Edwin Meese Files, Ronald Reagan Library.

11. "Born Again at the Ballot Box," _Time_, April 14, 1980, 94.

12. Jerry Falwell, "Organizing the Moral Majority," in Matthew Avery Sutton, _Jerry Falwell and the Rise of the Religious Right: A Brief History with Documents_ (Boston: Bedford/St. Martin's, 2013), 123–124.

13. Tim LaHaye, _The Battle for the Mind_ (Old Tappan, N.J.: Fleming H. Revell, 1980), 194–195.

14. Ibid., 225; John Herbers, "Ultraconservative Evangelicals a Surging New Force in Politics," *New York Times*, August 17, 1980, 1, 52. Stewart was indeed defeated in the 1980 Democratic primary. Although the *Times* article attributed Stewart's 23 percent rating to Christian Voice, the *Encyclopedia of Alabama* says it was the Moral Majority that assigned that rating. See s.v. "Donald Stewart," *Encyclopedia of Alabama*, http://www.encyclopediaofalabama.org/face/Article.jsp?id=h-2971 (accessed January 25, 2013).

15. Letter [mass mailing], National Affairs Briefing, June 27, 1980, copy in "Office of Public Liaison, Bob Maddox, Religious Liaison," Box 3, Jimmy Carter Library. See also Letter, National Affairs Briefing host committee, to Dr. Mike Clingenpeel, June 27, 1980; Letter, James Robison to Ronald Reagan, June 3, 1980, folder "Voter Groups—Evangelical/ Born Again," Box 309, Reagan, Ronald: 1980 Campaign Papers, 1965–80, Edwin Meese Files, Ronald Reagan Library.

16. James M. Dunn, Notes on National Affairs Briefing, Dallas, Texas, August 23, 1980, Office of Public Liaison, Bob Maddox, Religious Liaison, Box 106, Jimmy Carter Library. Carter responded to Dunn with his thanks. Letter, President Carter to James Dunn, with attached report from Dallas, September 9, 1980, "Office of Public Liaison, Bob Maddox, Religious Liaison," Box 4, Jimmy Carter Library.

17. Howell Raines, "Reagan Backs Evangelicals in Their Political Activities," *New York Times*, August 23, 1980; News Release, "Address by the Honorable Ronald Reagan, the Roundtable National Affairs Briefing, Dallas, Texas," Reagan Bush Committee, August 22, 1980; quoted in Duane Murray Oldfield, *The Right and the Righteous: The Christian Right Confronts the Republican Party* (Lanham, Md.: Rowman & Littlefield, 1996), 117. The text of Reagan's remarks also appears in News Release [text of Reagan's address to the Roundtable, National Affairs Briefing, Dallas, Texas], August 22, 1980, folder "Tour Files—Dallas, Texas—8/21–22/1980," Box 144, Reagan, Ronald: 1980 Campaign Papers, 1965–80, Edwin Meese Files, Ronald Reagan Library.

18. Memorandum, Bill Gribbin to Ed Meese and Bill Gavin, n.d., folder "Speech Files—Drafts & Backup Documents—Religious Roundtable, Dallas, 8/1980 (1/3)," Box 437, Reagan, Ronald: 1980 Campaign Papers, 1965–80, Edwin Meese Files, Ronald Reagan Library. Gribbin's memorandum also identifies Isaac Backus.

19. "Reagan Edgy with Evangelicals," August 25, 1980, Editorials—Curmudgeon Column, 1980, Box 17, Paul M. Weyrich Papers, American Heritage Center, University of Wyoming.

20. "The Gallup Poll: Evangelical Views on Issues Are Similar to Others," *Washington Post*, September 8, 1980; Chain letter [targeted to "Church Voter Groups"], Ronald Reagan to George Zarris, September 18, 1980, folder "Political Ops—Voter Groups— Christians/Evangelicals (2/4), Box 255. Reagan, Ronald: 1980 Campaign Papers, 1965–80, Edwin Meese Files, Ronald Reagan Library.

21. "Gallup Poll"; Memorandum, Alex Ray to Drew Lewis, undated, folder "Voter Groups—Christians (2/2), Box 307. Reagan, Ronald: 1980 Campaign Papers, 1965–80, Edwin Meese Files, Ronald Reagan Library.

22. Memorandum, Eddie Mahe Jr. to Dick Wirthlin, September 10, 1980, folder "Political Ops—Voter Groups—Christians/Evangelicals" (1/4), Box 255. Reagan, Ronald: 1980 Campaign Papers, 1965–80, Edwin Meese Files, Ronald Reagan Library; Memorandum from William C. Chasey, "Reagan-Bush Committee Christian Voter Program," folder "Political Ops—Voter Groups—Christians/Evangelicals" (1/4), Box 255. Reagan, Ronald: 1980 Campaign Papers. 1965–80, Edwin Meese Files, Ronald Reagan Library; Memorandum, Max Hugel to Bill Timmons and Stan Anderson, September 11, 1980, folder "Political Ops—Voter Groups—Christians/Evangelicals" (1/4), Box 255. Reagan, Ronald: 1980 Campaign Papers, 1965–80, Edwin Meese Files, Ronald Reagan Library.

23. "Getting God's Kingdom into Politics," editorial in *Christianity Today*, September 19, 1980, 10–11; quoted in Laura Kalman, *Right Star Rising: A New Politics, 1974–1980* (New York: W. W. Norton, 2010), 347. Carl F. H. Henry, the magazine's former editor, opined that "Many evangelicals are intellectually unprepared for energetic social engagements." Carl F. H. Henry, "Evangelicals Jump on the Political Bandwagon," *Christianity Today*, October 24, 1980, 22.

24. Quoted in Kenneth E. Morris, "Religion and the Presidency of Jimmy Carter," in *Religion and the American Presidency: George Washington to George W. Bush with Commentary and Primary Sources*, ed. Gastón Espinosa (New York: Columbia University Press, 2009), 351–352.

25. Michael Ginsburg and Lyn Nabors Riddle, "Fundamentalists Exercise Political Muscles," *Greenville Piedmont*, November 3, 1980.

26. Billy G. Hurt [Frankfort, Kentucky] to Bob Maddox, October 20, 1980, "Office of Public Liaison, Bob Maddox, Religious Liaison," Box 5, Jimmy Carter Library; Letter, Faye Spoth [Lubbock, Texas] to Bob Maddox, July 14, 1980, "Office of Public Liaison, Bob Maddox, Religious Liaison," Box 3, Jimmy Carter Library; Letter, Floyd M. Shealy [Oklahoma City, Oklahoma] to President Carter, August 14, 1980, "Office of Public Liaison, Bob Maddox, Religious Liaison," Box 3, Jimmy Carter Library; Letter, Larry T. Floyd [Sycamore, Alaska] to Bob Maddox, September 15, 1980, "Office of Public Liaison, Bob Maddox, Religious Liaison," Box 4, Jimmy Carter Library.

27. Jerry Falwell, "Moral Majority Opposes 'Christian Republic,'" *Moral Majority Report*, October 15, 1980, 4.

28. Letter, Beth Pennington ["Tupperware Manager," Bow, Washington] to Bob Maddox, October 1, 1980, "Office of Public Liaison, Bob Maddox, Religious Liaison," Box 4, Jimmy Carter Library; Letter, Even Argante [Akron, Ohio] to Bob Maddox, September 2, 1980, "Office of Public Liaison, Bob Maddox, Religious Liaison," Box 3, Jimmy Carter Library; Letter (handwritten), Terry Miller [Dallas, Texas] to Bob Maddox, August 22, 1980, "Office of Public Liaison, Bob Maddox, Religious Liaison," Box 3, Jimmy Carter Library.

29. On the possibility that the Reagan campaign negotiated secretly with Iran to keep the hostages captive until the election, see Gary Sick, *October Surprise: America's Hostages in Iran and the Election of Ronald Reagan* (New York: Times Books, 1991). Sick,

a retired navy captain, served on the National Council Security staffs under Ford, Carter, and Reagan.

30. Jimmy Carter, *White House Diary* (New York: Farrar, Straus and Giroux, 2010), 479; quoted in Douglas Brinkley, *The Unfinished Presidency: Jimmy Carter's Journey Beyond the White House* (New York: Viking, 1998), 1.

31. Quoted in Cal Thomas and Ed Dobson, *Blinded by Might: Can the Religious Right Save America?* (Grand Rapids, Mich.: Zondervan, 1999), 16; Oldfield, *Right and the Righteous*, 118; Jerry Falwell, *Strength for the Journey: An Autobiography* (New York: Simon & Schuster, 1987), 365. Another survey pegged Carter's support among African Americans at 93 percent; Melissa V. Harris-Lacewell, "African Americans, Religion, and the American Presidency," in *Religion, Race, and the American Presidency*, ed. Gastón Espinosa (Lanham, Md.: Rowman & Littlefield, 2008), 216.

32. On the 1980 Olympic boycott, see Nicholas Evan Sarantakes, *Dropping the Torch: Jimmy Carter, the Olympic Boycott, and the Cold War* (Cambridge: Cambridge University Press, 2011). Sarantakes argues that Carter failed to understand the Olympic movement and that the boycott actually exacerbated Cold War tensions.

33. Paul Kengor, "Reagan's 'Evil Empire' Turns 30," *American Spectator*, March 8, 2013; for the "shining city on a hill," see Randall Balmer, *God in the White House: How Faith Shaped the Presidency from John F. Kennedy to George W. Bush* (San Francisco: HarperOne, 2008), appendix 5. The phrase "city on a hill" comes from John Winthrop's sermon to fellow Puritans in 1630; I've never been able to determine where Reagan derived the modifier "shining."

34. "Just Because Reagan Has Won . . . ," editorial in *Christianity Today*, December 12, 1980, 14–15.

35. " 'One More Helicopter . . . ,' May 12, 1986, in *Conversations with Carter*, ed. Richardson, 273. On Carter's authorization of the "Argo" action, see Carter, *White House Diary*, 395. On the ideological significance of the Carter-Kennedy matchup, see Timothy Randolph Stanley, " 'Sailing Against the Wind': A Reappraisal of Edward Kennedy's Campaign for the 1980 Democratic Nomination," *American Quarterly*, 43 (August 2009), 231–253. Stanley concludes that "Carter's inability to appeal to his liberal constituency was as important to understanding the final result as the defection of 'Reagan Democrats.' " Ibid., 251.

36. "Kovach on Carter, Apr. 1990," in *Conversations with Carter*, ed. Richardson, 279; Jimmy Carter, interview with the author, Plains, Ga., June 2, 2013.

37. Quoted in Gary Scott Smith, *Faith and the Presidency: From George Washington to George W. Bush* (New York: Oxford University Press, 2006), 319.

38. Carter, interview with the author.

39. John F. Alexander, "Did We Blow It?," *The Other Side*, February 1981, 10–15.

40. For a fuller explication of this classic Baptist argument, see Randall Balmer, *Thy Kingdom Come: How the Religious Right Distorts the Faith and Threatens America* (New York: Basic Books, 2006), chap. 2.

41. Maddox exit interview.

42. Maddox asked the televangelist for a copy in late 1980, and Robertson obliged. See Letter, Pat Robertson to Bob Maddox, September 5, 1980, "Office of Public Liaison, Bob Maddox, Religious Liaison," Box 5, Jimmy Carter Library.

43. Maddox exit interview; LaHaye, *Battle for the Mind*, 232.

44. Maddox exit interview. On Hughes, see Harold E. Hughes, *Man from Ida Grove: A Senator's Personal Story* (Waco, Tex.: Word Books, 1979).

45. Jim Wallis and Wes Michaelson, "The Plan to Save America," *Sojourners*, April 1976, 4–12.

46. Smith, *Faith and the Presidency*, 312; quoted in Walter Rodgers, "Stop Picking on Jimmy Carter," *Christian Science Monitor*, January 5, 2009, 9.

47. Jimmy Carter, "Agape, Justice, and American Foreign Policy," *Reformed Journal*, April 1986, 16; Brinkley, *Unfinished Presidency*, 28.

48. Carter, *White House Diary*, 530.

49. On the importance of the Panama Canal treaties, see Cyrus Vance's comments in Kenneth W. Thompson, ed., *The Carter Presidency: Fourteen Intimate Perspectives of Jimmy Carter* (Lanham, Md.: University Press of America, 1990), 137; on Carter's success in placing human rights on the national and international agenda, see Mary E. Stuckey, *Jimmy Carter, Human Rights, and the National Agenda* (College Station: Texas A&M University Press, 2008).

50. Herbert E. Abrams, "Jimmy Carter," in Frank Friedel and Hugh S. Sidey, *The Presidents of the United States of America*, 15th ed. (Washington, D.C.: White House Historical Association, 1999), 83; Stuart E. Eizenstat, "President Carter, the Democratic Party, and the Making of Domestic Policy," in *The Presidency and Domestic Policies of Jimmy Carter*, ed. Herbert D. Rosenbaum and Alexej Ugrinsky (Westport, Conn.: Greenwood Press, 1994), 15; Ann Mari May, "Economic Myth and Economic Reality: A Reexamination of the Carter Years," in ibid., 649.

51. Carter, "Prayer and the Civic Religion," *New York Times*, December 24, 1996, A11.

Chapter Nine: Stepping Stone

1. Jimmy Carter, *White House Diary* (New York: Farrar, Straus and Giroux, 2010), 513; Rosalynn Carter, *First Lady from Plains* (Boston: Houghton Mifflin, 1984), 351.

2. Carter, *White House Diary*, 512; Peter G. Bourne, *Jimmy Carter: A Comprehensive Biography from Plains to Postpresidency* (New York: Scribner, 1997), 473.

3. Carter, *White House Diary*, 514.

4. Quoted in Ginger Lundy, "Rosalynn Carter Was Bitter about 1980 Election," *Spartanburg* (S.C.) *Herald-Journal*, November 22, 1984, C12. In her autobiography, Rosalynn Carter writes, "I don't like to lose." Rosalynn Carter, *First Lady from Plains*, 357.

5. Jimmy Carter, *Through the Year with Jimmy Carter: 366 Daily Meditations from the 39th President* (Grand Rapids, Mich.: Zondervan, 2011), 324.

6. Jimmy Carter, *Beyond the White House: Waging Peace, Fighting Disease, Building Hope* (New York: Simon & Schuster, 2007), 1–3.

7. Ibid., 3.

8. Ibid., 4; transcript of *American Experience: Jimmy Carter*, PBS documentary, http://www.pbs.org/wgbh/americanexperience/features/transcript/carter-transcript/?flavour=mobile (accessed February 8, 2013).

9. Ibid.; transcript of interview of James T. Laney by David Reuther, March 26, 2004, Association for Diplomatic Studies and Training, Foreign Affairs Oral History Project.

10. "Working for a Healthy World: An Interview with Jimmy Carter," *Second Opinion*, March 1988, 57; "Jimmy Carter: A Passion for Human Rights," *The Other Side*, March 1985, 12, 15.

11. Carter, *Beyond the White House*, 7; for the "Basic Principles" guiding the Carter Center, see ibid., 7–8. For an overview of the history and mission of the Carter Center, see Steven H. Hochman, s.v. "Carter Center," *Encyclopedia of Human Rights*, ed. David P. Forsythe (New York: Oxford University Press, 2009).

12. "Working for a Healthy World," *Second Opinion*, March 1988, 50–51.

13. Jimmy Carter, "Agape, Justice, and American Foreign Policy," *Reformed Journal*, April 1986, 18; "A Conversation on Peacemaking with Jimmy Carter, June 7, 1991," in *Conversations with Carter*, ed. Don Richardson (Boulder, Colo.: Lynne Rienner, 1998), 291; Carter, *Beyond the White House*, 74.

14. "Jimmy Carter: A Passion for Human Rights," 13; Carter, *Beyond the White House*, 257.

15. "Conversation with Jimmy Carter," *World Vision*, August/September 1986, 15; "Working for a Healthy World," *Second Opinion*, March 1988, 54. On Carter's advocacy for Habitat, see Philip Yancey, "Jimmy Carter in Two Worlds," *Christianity Today*, October 3, 1986, 64.

16. Douglas Brinkley, *The Unfinished Presidency: Jimmy Carter's Journey Beyond the White House* (New York: Viking, 1998), 58.

17. Jimmy Carter, *Keeping Faith: Memoirs of a President* (New York: Bantam Books, 1982), 577–578; Carter, *White House Diary*, 513.

18. "'One More Helicopter . . . ,' May 12, 1986," in *Conversations with Carter*, ed. Richardson, 273; Brinkley, *Unfinished Presidency*, 60, 57; Joshua Muravchik, *The Uncertain Crusade: Jimmy Carter and the Dilemmas of Human Rights Policy* (Lanham, Md.: Hamilton Press, 1986), xvii.

19. Jay Hakes, *A Declaration of Energy Independence: How Freedom from Foreign Oil Can Improve National Security, Our Economy, and the Environment* (Hoboken, N.J.: John Wiley & Sons, 2008), 73; "Robert J. Billings: Moral Majority Co-founder Blended Religion, Politics," *Pittsburgh Post-Gazette*, June 1, 1995.

20. "'One More Helicopter . . . ,'" 273.

21. "Jimmy Carter: A Passion for Human Rights," 14.

22. "*Living Faith*, Dec. 19, 1996," in *Conversations with Carter*, ed. Don Richardson (Boulder, Colo.: Lynne Rienner, 1998), 322.

23. Michael Cromartie, ed., *No Longer Exiles: The Religious New Right in American Politics* (Washington, D.C.: Ethics and Public Policy Center, 1993), 54; "Interview: Ed

Dobson," *God in America,* October 15, 2009, http://www.pbs.org/godinamerica/inter views/ed-dobson.html (accessed December 8, 2013).

24. "'Most Unusual': No Time for a Change," *Christianity Today,* December 17, 1971, 34.

25. Robert L. Sumner, "The IRS and Religious Liberty," *Sword of the Lord,* September 11, 1981; Gregory Jaynes, "Unbending Bob Jones U. Is Again Focus of Furor," *New York Times,* January 15, 1982; Lyn Nabors Riddle, "Bob Jones Students Urged to Write Their Congressmen," *Greenville* (S.C.) *Piedmont,* January 15, 1982; "School's Critics 'Hate God,' Bob Jones III Says at Rally," *Greenville* (S.C.) *News,* March 2, 1982.

26. Howell Raines, "President Shifts View on Tax Rule in Race Bias Cases," *New York Times,* January 13, 1982, A1, A12.

27. *Bob Jones University v. United States* (No. 81-3) No. 81-1, 644 F.2d 879, and No. 81-3, 639 F.2d 147, affirmed.

28. Phil Gailey, "Bob Jones, in Sermon, Assails Supreme Court," *New York Times,* May 25, 1983, A23; "Supreme Court Denies Tax Breaks to Bob Jones University," *Fundamentalist Journal,* July–August 1983, 58; Aaron Epstein, "U.S. vs. Bob Jones: Bias Dooms Tax Break," *Miami Herald,* May 25, 1983.

29. "Bob Jones Jr. Says He Doubts Reagan's Faith," *Greenville* (S.C.) *Piedmont,* August 30, 1983. William Rehnquist, curiously enough, shares the same birthday as Jimmy Carter: October 1, 1924.

30. Paul Weyrich, transcript, *Listen America Report,* June 17, 1986, MOR 3-1, Folder 2, Liberty University Archives; Paul Weyrich, transcript, *Listen America Report,* June 24, 1986, MOR 3-1, Folder 2, Liberty University Archives; Paul Weyrich, transcript, *Listen America Report,* September 2, 1986, MOR 3-1, Folder 2, Liberty University Archives.

31. Paul Weyrich, transcript, *Listen America Report,* September 9, 1986, MOR 3-1, Folder 2, Liberty University Archives; Paul Weyrich, transcript, *Listen America Report,* July 21, 1987, MOR 3-1, Folder 2, Liberty University Archives.

32. Paul Weyrich, transcript, *Listen America Report,* May 5, 1987, MOR 3-1, Folder 2, Liberty University Archives; Paul Weyrich, transcript, *Listen America Report,* July 29, 1986, MOR 3-1, Folder 2, Liberty University Archives; Charlie Judd, transcript, *Listen America Report,* August 19, 1987, MOR 3-1, Folder 2, Liberty University Archives. Francis Wayland, for example, nineteenth-century Baptist leader, was one of the presidents of the Boston Prison Discipline Society.

33. "Legitimate Pride, Apr. 1985," in *Conversations with Carter,* ed. Richardson, 267, 269. The biblical references to a camel passing through the eye of a needle are Matthew 19:24, Mark 10:25, and Luke 18:25.

34. Jimmy Carter, *Palestine Peace Not Apartheid,* paperback ed. (New York: Simon & Schuster, 2007), 189, 190.

35. Ibid., 192, 206.

36. David Aikman, "Throwing Rocks at Israel," *Christianity Today,* April 2007, 82.

37. Jimmy Carter, *We Can Have Peace in the Holy Land: A Plan That Will Work* (New York: Simon & Schuster, 2009), xxii, xv.

38. Ariel Kaminer, "Law School Group Incites Fury with Choice to Honor Carter," *New York Times*, April 10, 2013, A21. Carter accepted the award on April 10, 2013.

39. See Nancy Gibbs and Michael Duffy, *The Presidents Club: Inside the World's Most Exclusive Fraternity* (New York: Simon & Schuster, 2012), passim, esp. 404–408, 450.

40. Gibbs and Duffy, *Presidents Club*, 438–447, 402–404; John M. Broder, "Patience and Faith Pay Off for Carter," *Los Angeles Times*, September 19, 1994.

41. Carter, *White House Diary*, 79.

42. For a chronology of these events, see Walter B. Shurden, ed., *The Struggle for the Soul of the SBC: Moderate Responses to the Fundamentalist Movement* (Macon, Ga.: Mercer University Press, 1993), xix–xviii. Regarding women in ministry in the Southern Baptist Convention, see Libby Bellinger, "More Hidden than Revealed: The History of Southern Baptist Women in Ministry," in ibid., 129–149. Nomenclature is one of the battlegrounds: "conservatives" call their opponents "liberals," and "moderates" refer to their adversaries as "fundamentalists." I have sought to strike a neutral tone, referring to the factions by their less incendiary monikers: "conservatives" and "moderates."

43. Carter, *Through the Year with Jimmy Carter*, 343; Larry L. McSwain, *Loving Beyond Your Theology: The Life and Ministry of Jimmy Raymond Allen* (Macon, Ga.: Mercer University Press, 2010), 225.

44. McSwain, *Loving Beyond Your Theology*, 24; Christopher Quinn, "Diverse Baptists Meet to Think Cooperatively," *Atlanta Journal-Constitution*, January 31, 2008, D3; Christopher Quinn, "Baptists Hope Unity Turns into Projects; Southern Branch Still Absent," *Atlanta Journal-Constitution*, February 3, 2008, C3; Bill Leonard, e-mail correspondence with the author, May 27, 2013. See also, Richard Fausset, "For Jimmy Carter, a More Personal Mission," *Los Angeles Times*, February 1, 2008.

45. Jimmy Carter, "The Words of God Do Not Justify Cruelty to Women," *Guardian*, July 11, 2009.

46. Ibid.

47. Somini Sengupta, "Carter Sadly Turns Back on National Baptist Body," *New York Times*, October 21, 2000.

48. Jeffrey Gettleman, "Nobel Peace Prize Awarded to Carter, with Jab at Bush," *New York Times*, October 12, 2002, A1.

49. Brinkley, *Unfinished Presidency*, 27; Gettleman, "Nobel Peace Prize Awarded to Carter," *New York Times*, October 12, 2002, A1.

50. Gettleman, "Nobel Peace Prize Awarded to Carter," A1; Mark Matthews, "Jimmy Carter Wins Nobel Peace Prize for 'Untiring Efforts,'" *Baltimore Sun*, October 12, 2002, 1A.

51. David M. Shribman, "Carter Awarded Peace Prize, Humanitarian Work Praised: Nobel Official Criticizes Bush," *Boston Globe*, October 12, 2002, A1; Matthews, "Jimmy Carter Wins Nobel Peace Prize," 1A.

52. Quoted in Ken Ellingwood, "Former President Carter Wins Nobel Peace Prize," *Los Angeles Times*, October 12, 2002, A1; "An Award for Peace: We Congratulate Former President Jimmy Carter for Well-Deserved Nobel Prize," editorial in *Knoxville*

News Sentinel, October 14, 2002, B4; Mark Lawson, "A Role Model for Ruined Politicians: Jimmy Carter's Peace Prize Is the Final Stage in His Redemption," *Guardian*, October 12, 2002, 1.22.

53. "The Nobel Peace Prize 2002—Presentation Speech," Nobelprize.org, Nobel Media AB 2013, http://www.nobelprize.org/nobel_prizes/peace/laureates/2002/presentation-speech.html (accessed December 31, 2013).

54. Jimmy Carter, "Nobel Lecture, Oslo, December 10, 2002," *International Journal of Humanities and Peace*, 19, 1 (2003), 8–10.

55. Ibid.

56. Moni Basu and Don Melvin, "Carter Accepts Peace Prize; Carters Get Royal Treatment," *Atlanta Journal-Constitution*, December 11, 2002, A12.

57. On the importance of public education throughout American history, see Randall Balmer, *Thy Kingdom Come: How the Religious Right Distorts the Faith and Threatens America* (New York: Basic Books, 2006), chap. 3.

58. "Don Richardson, Oct. 17, 1997," in *Conversations with Carter*, ed. Richardson, 336.

59. Ronald Reagan: "Inaugural Address," January 20, 1981, online by Gerhard Peters and John T. Woolley, *The American Presidency Project*, http://www.presidency.ucsb.edu/ws/?pid=43130.(accessed December 19, 2013); Jimmy Carter, *Our Endangered Values: America's Moral Crisis* (Simon & Schuster, 2005), 57. See also Jimmy Carter, "Prayer and the Civic Religion," *New York Times*, December 24, 1996, A11.

60. Jim Wallis, interview with the author, Washington, D.C., December 6, 2012; David Kirkpatrick, "The Evangelical Crackup," *New York Times*, October 28, 2007.

61. Douglas Brinkley offers a compelling argument that Carter's relentless drive since leaving office is an expression of his desire to finish the work he was not able to accomplish as president. See Brinkley, *Unfinished Presidency*. For a corroborating view of the incompatibility of religion (specifically the Baptist tradition) with power politics, see Lee Canipe, "Can a Baptist Be President? Jimmy Carter and the Possibility that John Smythe May Have Been Right After All," *Journal of Church and State*, 50 (Spring 2008), 277–297.

62. "Legitimate Pride," in *Conversations with Carter*, ed. Richardson, 268; " 'One More Helicopter . . . ,' May 12, 1986," in ibid., 273.

63. "*Living Faith*, Dec. 19, 1996," 320.

64. Jimmy Carter, *Sources of Strength: Meditations on Scripture for a Living Faith* (New York: Times Books, 1997), 204.

65. "*Living Faith*, Dec. 19, 1996," 320.

Epilogue: Sunday Morning in Plains

1. The Seaboard Air Line Railroad merged with the Atlantic Coast Line Railroad in 1967 to become the Seaboard Coast Line Railroad.

2. Quoted in David Treadwell, "Billy Carter Is Dead of Cancer at 51: Ex-President's Brother Capitalized on Country-Boy Image," *Los Angeles Times*, September 26, 1988.

3. Nate Rawlings, "Jimmy Carter Peanut Statue, Plains, Ga.," *Time*, July 28, 2010; Douglas Brinkley, *The Unfinished Presidency: Jimmy Carter's Journey Beyond the White House* (New York: Viking, 1998), 52–53. The population figure is from the 2010 census: see James E. Bagwell, s.v. "Plains," *New Georgia Encyclopedia* (Athens: University of Georgia Press, 2011).

4. This visit to Plains (my second), the Sunday-school class, and my interview with Carter took place on June 2, 2013.

5. Hebrews is, by almost any measure, an odd text; a recent book by Garry Wills cast doubt on its merits, especially the reference to the Melchizedek priesthood, which appears only twice elsewhere in the scriptures, both in recondite passages in the Hebrew Bible. See Garry Wills, *Why Priests? A Failed Tradition* (New York: Viking, 2013); cf. Randall Balmer, "Apostolic Transgression," review of *Why Priests? A Failed Tradition*, by Garry Wills, *New York Times Book Review*, February 17, 2013, 11.

6. This passage is John 8:1–11.

7. Jimmy Carter, *Through the Year with Jimmy Carter: 366 Daily Meditations from the 39th President* (Grand Rapids, Mich.: Zondervan, 2011), 355.

Appendix Two: *"Crisis of Confidence," July 15, 1979*

1. Jimmy Carter, *Keeping Faith: Memoirs of a President* (New York: Bantam Books, 1982), 117.

ABOUT THE AUTHOR

RANDALL BALMER is chair of the Religion Department and Mandel Family Professor in the Arts and Sciences at Dartmouth College. Before coming to Dartmouth in 2012, he was Professor of American Religious History for twenty-seven years at Columbia University, after earning his Ph.D. from Princeton University in 1985. In addition, he has been a visiting professor at various places, including Princeton, Yale, Drew, Emory, and Northwestern universities and in the Columbia University Graduate School of Journalism. An Episcopal priest since 2006, he was adjunct professor of church history at Union Theological Seminary for seventeen years, and from 2004 to 2008, he was visiting professor at Yale Divinity School.

The author of more than a dozen books, Mr. Balmer has published widely in both scholarly journals and in the popular press. His commentaries have appeared in newspapers around the nation, including the *Des Moines Register*, the *Philadelphia Inquirer*, the *Dallas Morning News*, the *Los Angeles Times*, the *St. Louis Post-Dispatch*, the *Nation*, the *Omaha World-Herald*, the *Anchorage Daily News*, *New York Newsday*, the *Hartford Courant*, and the *New York Times*, among others. He has lectured in such places as the Chautauqua Institution, the Commonwealth Club of California, and, under the auspices of the U.S. Department of State, in Austria and Lebanon. He has written and hosted three documentaries for PBS; for one of those productions, a three-part adaptation of his book *Mine Eyes Have Seen the Glory*, Mr. Balmer was nominated for an Emmy.

He lives in Vermont with his wife, Catharine Randall, who is also a professor, an author, and an Episcopal priest.

INDEX